W9-ANV-941

MODES OF REPRESENTATION
IN SPANISH CINEMA

Hispanic Issues

HISPANIC ISSUES
VOLUME 16

MODES OF REPRESENTATION
IN SPANISH CINEMA

JENARO TALENS AND SANTOS ZUNZUNEGUI
◆
EDITORS

FOREWORD BY TOM CONLEY

UNIVERSITY OF MINNESOTA PRESS
MINNEAPOLIS   LONDON

Chapter 12, "Homosexuality, Regionalism, and Mass Culture: Eloy de la Iglesia's Cinema of Transition," copyright Paul Julian Smith 1992. Reprinted from *Laws of Desire: Questions of Homosexuality in Spanish Writing and Film, 1960–1990* by Paul Julian Smith (1992) by permission of Oxford University Press.

The editors of this volume gratefully acknowledge assistance from the Program for Cultural Cooperation between Spain's Ministry of Culture and United States Universities; and the College of Liberal Arts and the Department of Spanish and Portuguese at the University of Minnesota.

Published by the University of Minnesota Press
111 Third Avenue South, Suite 290, Minneapolis, MN 55401-2520
http://www.upress.umn.edu

Printed in the United States of America on acid-free paper

Library of Congress Cataloging-in-Publication Data

Modes of representation in Spanish cinema / Jenaro Talens and Santos
   Zunzunegui, editors ; foreword by Tom Conley.
      p.   cm. — (Hispanic issues, v. 16)
   Includes bibliographical references and index.
   ISBN 0-8166-2974-9 (alk. paper). — ISBN 0-8166-2975-7 (pbk. :
alk. paper)
    1. Motion pictures—Spain.   I. Talens, Jenaro, 1946–
II. Zunzunegui Díez, Santos.   III. Series.
PN1993.5.S7M58   1998
791.43'0946—dc21   98-5971

The University of Minnesota is an equal-opportunity educator and employer.

10 09 08 07 06 05 04 03 02 01 00 99 98   10 9 8 7 6 5 4 3 2 1

Hispanic Issues

Contents

V. *Representations: Reshaping the Margins*

◆ Foreword

A Land Bred on Movies

In memory of Christian Metz

Tom Conley

A viewer of Luis Buñuel's *Tierra sin pan* (*Unpromised Land, Land without Bread, Pays sans pain, Las Hurdes*) might be led to believe that Spain was a land without bread. Because the camera is there, in southwestern Spain, the spectacle of the montage shows that cinema has finally come to the aid of the Republic. Buñuel's film does not prove that the nation never lacked a movie camera. To the contrary, since the end of the nineteenth century Spain has remained a nation nourished on celluloid. The essays written for this volume are assembled to reflect the wealth, diversity, and, especially, the singularities of Spanish cinema. No national history of the seventh art quite follows the career of the Hispanic experience of cinema. The medium comes to Barcelona early and is developed with precocious talent that rivals Porter, Lumière, and Méliès. A strong silent tradition spreads roots in Catalonia before Madrid. Once established, a *tradition de qualité* commands Spanish cinema up to the advent of the Civil War. Not only does there appear a vanguard in the work of Buñuel, the most dominant Iberian *auteur*, but so does — also through the labors of the same director — a great narrative style that rivals Hollywood, French poetic realism, and Italian cinema under the reign of fascism.

But in its development from the 1890s up to the early years of the Depression, when international cinema thrived as it never had before, an encounter between history and ideology utterly changes Spanish film. A unique body of work, laced with local themes, styles, and obsessions, dominates peninsular film before Franco takes power. The reader of this volume will quickly discover that the reign of Franco did anything but extinguish creativity or aesthetic experiment. It may have intensified specific kinds of cinematic expression from the fall of the Republic up to the generalísimo's death in 1975. The era of repression and censorship may have conferred on the film a national signature, based on a variety of signs that grow into complex networks of abstraction and realism, which is no less remarkable than what French viewers witnessed with the advent of the *nouvelle vague* from 1955 to the early 1970s. A parallel growth in aesthetic, political, and cinematic labor in both France and Spain needs to be emphasized, but not, as the rhetoric of an introduction generally requires, merely to redeem a tradition of film ostensibly curbed by the controlling hand of a fascist dictator who long outlived Hitler and Mussolini.

Gilles Deleuze (1983: 284–87) has argued that the years following the end of the Second World War saw shifts in cinematic consciousness coming at different speeds, with different effects, and by virtue of many historical and geographical causes. Italian neorealism, what he defines as the beginning of a disjunctive cinema whose politics are visible in its new relation to time (at the cost of a classical articulation of narrative based on continuities felt through the camera's affinities for movement), literally *took place* as it did because the country had lived through the birth, growth, and debacle of fascism.[1] Italy had been an active observer of the total disruption that war precipitated within its borders, but only after it had established a great ideological mechanism that rivaled Hollywood and the French film industry during the entre-deux-guerres (Hay 1987: 97–98). No wonder, Deleuze remarks, that Roberto Rossellini was able to create a revolutionary style in *Rome, Open City, Paisan,* and *Germany, Year Zero* because of the immediacy of the relations of film, history, myth, and politics to the site where the films take place: his war trilogy brings us to see in a paratactic style — unconnected "image-facts" (Bazin 1970 2: 30) that compose a loose narration that the spectator pieces together—the story of a nation that lives in a universal dialectic of coextensive destruction and reconstruction. The films afford a view of that dialectic in a condition of collapse because of the proximity of the past to the present being shown. The spectator sees only the thinnest and most tenuous line of demarcation between the violence of the German occupation and the dilemmas of reconstruction that situate each of the three films in its specific moment. France, however, never experienced the same tribulations. There was a timelag between the war and the perception that the French *tradition de qualité* was a bogus construct that in fact isolated spectators from the conflicts of its historical consciousness of the years 1940–1946. In 1954, when François Truffaut launched his polemical and precocious tract "A Certain Tendency of French Cinema" (in Nichols 1976 1: 224–37) to call an end to pretensions about "quality," he was effectuating in criticism and aesthetics of cinematic reception what Rossellini and Vittorio de Sicca had fomented almost a decade earlier in filmmaking. Postwar French cinema, then, was unable to take positions in any adequate way with respect to its ghoulish relation to the Second World War. The war was both present and absent in its confines. France had been "in" the violence and yet held pro-Nazi sympathies. At the risk of appealing to personification, we might say that its conscience needed a decade to translate into healthy oedipal terms a dilemma that has since, in the post–New Wave years, become both a storehouse of ideology and a litmus test of national identity. The wave of "retro" films that set out to psychoanalyze France's relation to the war avow a deficit in the country's relation to a failed response on the part of film to the demands of history.

Missing from Deleuze's sketch is a third parallel with Spanish film. If Italian cinema drew a line of rupture between a classical and a modern epistemology in the 1940s, and if France required a hiatus of ten years to begin to work through its own sordid relation with its past, whither Spain? A Frenchman might be best prepared to answer: "Never were we so free than under the German occupation," wrote Jean-Paul Sartre in "The Republic of Silence," an essay appearing in the *Lettres françaises* on the day following the liberation of Paris in 1944.[2] Will readers of this volume of essays be led to surmise that "never was Spanish film so free than under the yoke of Franco"? We can answer yes if we recall that the narcotic effects of his regime began *before* the occupation of France and that their imprint was firm two decades *after* the impact of New Wave cinemas in France and Italy. Moreover, Spain did not experience the circulation of international cinematic commerce as had France, a country that had been bombarded and invaded after the Second World War by thousands of American commodities as diverse as housewares, soldiers, and college students. A second beachhead was crossed when Waring blenders, Frigidaires, Sweet Briar coeds, GIs, and a conglomerate of film noir, Jerry Lewis, June Allyson, and Dana Andrews "liberated" Paris in the early 1950s. We need only recall the pathos inscribed in the words of the deeply regretted Christian Metz, born too late to take part in the Resistance and too early to use film as an overt proponent of social change, who confessed that his entire childhood was written by cinema imported to Paris.[3] Or else ourselves, now graying professors of letters and cinema, born during the war, who sought in new film aesthetic politics that would dismantle the Hollywood models that had formed our oedipal ties to our kin: unless French critics could tell us otherwise, American film was pure crap. These American films and their French critics — of whom Metz was the greatest leader of a second generation after Bazin and his enfants terribles at *Cahiers du cinéma,* then published in both French and American editions — allowed us to engage in a healthy analytical conflict with Hollywood through necessarily perverse detours into *auteur* theory, linguistics, and formalism. French and American viewers realized that Hollywood's response to the circulation of creative and critical energies was belated. A moment of exchange came to an end when Arthur Penn, Sidney Pollack, and other directors of the 1970s served up a *nouvelle vague récupérée.* It was a chic, streamlined political aesthetics that resembled a Ford Fairlane (a pity, however, that it wasn't driven into the ocean the way Belmondo and Karina wasted a Ford Galaxy convertible in *Pierrot le Jou* of 1965). None of the repression or violence that had inspired neo-realism or new wave cinemas inaugurated by Resnais and Godard was visible in films such as *Bonnie and Clyde* or *The Graduate.*

This is why Spain helps us test the validity of Deleuze's hypothetical parabola of history. From the 1930s to the 1970s Spanish cinema did not circulate as did that of France and the United

States. It had a *tradition de qualité*, but it also developed a panoply of styles that responded to its own "traditions" — what Freud calls our "blurred memories" of a past that we invent to fashion the apparel of an identity — in geographical and economic spheres. Certain post–World War II directors, such as Fernando Fernán Gómez and Luis García Berlanga, had detected a "certain tendency of Spanish cinema" within the inherited style of Hollywood and Spanish narrative films. Further, there emerged during the same postwar years, as if they were sprouting out of the mulch of French film journals, new reviews of cinema — *Nuestro cine, La Mirada, Contracampo* (see Zunzunegui in this volume, n. 14) — that took different perspectives on international cinema, film theory, and the relation of cinema to the unknown: Spanish film in dialogue with its international origins.

One of the principal ends of this volume is to construct that perspective and demonstrate the vitality of a protracted historical moment and its effects today.[4] Two approaches are apparent by the way they are braided together. First, this collection offers a comprehensive review of the Spanish past that includes many of its films that have remained unseen in the United States or have been passed over in most film histories.[5] Second, the contributions use critical modes that test the limits of semiotics, psychoanalysis, and new historicisms in different cultural contexts. Emerging from the material and the approaches that the authors have taken to analyze it are new relations to the *conditions of visibility* of Spanish film. Why did it remain invisible to American eyes? What was it that made it ineffable? Something akin to Michel de Certeau's category of the *pensable* — "what makes something thinkable" (1982: 123), or that which makes an object emerge into view as an *intelligible* form — is at stake. Americans are able to see film *after* Franco, but no history — except perhaps what was written by the Communist Georges Sadoul (1968) — of its past is readily discernible to an American public. A psychoanalysis of historical visibility is implied in the essays, because it does not suffice to argue merely that early Spanish film was not "innovative," had no founding "auteurs," or that its service to the Republic or to Franco made its ideology "predictable" or "unpalatable." More commanding systems of repression or *recusación* (see

Requena in this volume) appear to be at work in the fortunes of the visibility of Spanish film.

The dynamic revision at work in these essays hinges to a great extent on the question of the duration of Franco's influence on national production. To be sure, like Griffith, Hitler, Mussolini, Lang, Goebbels, and Eisenstein, the generalísimo saw early on that film could be the most effective ideological agency of any given state apparatus.[6] Franco wrote the scenario of *Raza*, a founding film that maps out the regime's imagination of its relation of family, history, and destiny. Many of the contributions locate their analysis with respect either to this film or to Franco's influence on the medium. Jesús González-Requena takes up the national production of films in the heyday of his era while appealing to a Lacanian model of repression and perversion to show that signs of denial, inversions of oedipal conflicts, and movements between denial and repudiation favor statewide adoption of melodramas (family romances) over American war films or action movies when matters of state are at issue. In a reading that uses Gilles Deleuze to follow a line of demarcation between dream and history to study Víctor Erice's *El espíritu de la colmena* (1973) (*The Spirit of the Beehive*), Santos Zunzunegui shows how a number of interfilmic allusions invite the viewer to behold the Franco regime as a strangely protected narcosis. The film, set "somewhere in La Mancha in the 1940s," begins with a long shot that displays an itinerant movie truck emerging on the horizon, like a knight-errant riding from one town to the next in search of romantic adventures, bringing to a hamlet a showing of James Whale's *Frankenstein* (1932). The citation of Whale's film in a utopian setting (rural Spain outside of the world at war) at the moment the regime is about to disappear (1972) brings forth an uncanny set of relations. Is Erice, suggests Zunzunegui, denoting twentieth-century Iberian history as the era of the monster whose name carries an almost graphic rhyme with the generalísimo? *Franco/Frankenstein*? *Dr. Francostein*? A regime accessible to a child of today only through the filter of an intensely self-referential monadic film of infinitely tiny spaces? In both Requena's and Zunzunegui's essays on the years 1932–1973 we see pass before our eyes the ghosts that continually return to haunt the Spanish subject.

These two essays confirm what Antonio Monegal sums up about a good deal of filmmaking over the past four decades. In attempts to "escape the control of the censors during Franco's dictatorship, Spanish cinema developed a remarkable tendency to disguise its political message by means of a highly codified symbolic discourse." Both state-sponsored film and its opponents saw allegory as an adequate mode of expression. For Franco, the motif of enemy brothers could be staged to oppose a credulous Christian boy to his ill-behaved communist *hermano*. Both sides appealed to "private experience" to express the collective effect of the Civil War and its aftermath. Most of the Spanish contributors to this volume suggest that foreign intertexts of Hitchcock (*Rebecca*), Whale (*Frankenstein*), Hawks (*Ball of Fire*), and Renoir (*The Rules of the Game*) are crucial for the poetics that move between personal and historical registers. A heightened sense of perspective thus orients the film that is said to be local and even insular in its form.

Given the fact that censorship seems to inspire a productive or creative approach to cinema on the part of an institution and its strategists or the auteur and his or her tactical schemes, the reader of this volume will probably note how, after 1978, Spanish cinema immediately shifts over to the psychoanalytical arena. Americans have paid quite a bit of attention to director Pedro Almodóvar, who projects scenarios of perversion, note Kathleen L. Vernon and Lesley Heins-Walker, to reshape political allegories of repression into films that seek a mark that will buy into "modern female subjectivity" insofar as the director equates the family romance with the overbearing "maternal" aura of Francoist icons. The experience of the fetishist provokes Bigas Lunas, argues Ann Marie Stock, to attempt to "dispense with a past" through pastiche. That same mode, claims Oscar Pereira in a historical study of nostalgia and the ideology of memory, allows José Luis Garci to revalorize fascism shortly after Franco's death. Teresa Vilarós makes explicit the affinities of Freudian dynamics and the writing of Spanish history in Manuel Gutiérrez Aragón's *El corazón del bosque* (*The Force of the Forest*). The Spain that the filmmaker inherits is deforested, a tabula rasa that had been *el espíritu de una raza*, that is an *erasure* bringing forth "uncanny ghosts, memories, and nostalgia."

In these essays the reader will inevitably notice how Spanish cinema's recent explosion into violence, perversion, fetishism, and pastiche cannot be explained away by what Almodóvar reductively calls "its post-Franco 'mentality.'" As Kinder, Torreiro, and Vernon seem to suggest, the director's words may be ideologically suspect: they essentialize a complex body of events as the personality of a nation at a time when the concept of nationhood no longer exists, except insofar as they, perhaps like Almodóvar himself, purvey idealized images of a new time and space to a common market ready to buy Spanish fashion dolls draped in black mantillas and waving painted fans. Hence also the feeling that post-1980 Hispanic film is bred on theory, nourished on film analysis. The generations of viewers, trained in intellectual countermovements of the 1960s, reach back to precepts of New Criticism, subjectivity, stylistics, and cultural analysis so that the spectator will be encouraged to gain agency enough to displace the ideology of a good deal of post-Franco cinema. The latter disappears when the former gains ascendancy. For this reason, the "transitions" of Spanish film have to do with an expanding historical awareness that is not merely owned by directors. It is found in the very imprint of the interpretive essays that take up the classical years of film both before and during the regime of censorship.

We witness how the viewer—and this means *anyone*—is enabled to work through the classical canon with a political efficacy that matches that of filmmakers. In this sense the essays on *La verbena de la paloma* (Gubern), Juan de Orduña (Llinás), and Berlanga (Beckwith) are decisive. Each looks back to the classical canon in order to detect how its principles are crafted; how an ideal public is formed; how, in effect, its own absence of reference (except to cinema) functions in relation to its promotion or rejection of clichés. In these essays we see how film history gains a political force through interpretation following lines that cut back to the early Truffaut and to Godard. For Godard, studying, viewing, and making cinema are tantamount to philosophical writing that opens aporias in the network of commercial production.[7] Like the cinema of Saura and Erice, these essays work within the heritage of Franco without ever claiming that they can transcend or escape from it. Stressing the articulations that are used to construct the "Spanish tradition," the essays bring to American readers a sense of the past that informs many of the more recognizable titles that have become visible in anglophone countries over the past two decades (Hopewell 1990; D'Lugo 1991).

The hypotheses are telling. Talens and Zunzunegui, quoting Pérez Perucha's work, show how the commercial system of the Lumière Brothers was brought to Spain. Films made by the French brothers' industry were used to advertise their firm. When the Lumières shot "Workers Leaving a Factory," their employees are seen *endimanchés,* in their Sunday clothing, and not wearing overalls or work shoes. In 1897 Fructuoso Gelabert shoots two documentaries, *Salida de los trabajadores de la España industrial* and *Salida del público de la iglesia parroquial de Sants,* that inaugurate a serial approach to production. The filmmaker could fabricate clichés of Catalán and Castilian customs that might eventually figure in a catalog of things Spanish: church processions, parades (even in the rain), bullfights, flamenco dancing, and so on, that would be shown anywhere in the world, from Siberia to Salamanca. The seeds of a national and narrative cinema are soon planted in documentary footage. A tradition of dialogue and fiction is begun within the new genre of documentary tourism. Just as Lumière and Méliès stand as the mythic origins of "realism" and "fantasy" in the earliest years of cinema, so too are Gelabert and Chomón in Iberia. Chomón's *Electric Hotel* resembles *A Trip to the Moon* and *The Man with a Rubber Head.* As an eventual employee of the Pathé firm (in 1905), Chomón produced such accomplished special effects that in 1926 Abel Gance sought his talents while he was making *Napoleón.*

When Antonio Cuesta produces *El ciego de la aldea* in 1907, a tradition of realism becomes firmly anchored in the ideology that equates truth with what it portrays as the timeless rhythms of rural ways of life. The Valencian director mixes urban and pastoral scenes in a full narrative treatment, taken from popular literature, articulated along the double axis of film. His *Benítez quiere ser torero* (1909) launches comedy that anticipates René Clair. Thus begins a creation that later finds its most gifted—and ideologically charged—exponent in Florián Rey, whose *La aldea maldita* (1929) crowns the end of Spanish silent cinema. The film became so influential that it was produced in three versions: a silent film, a silent version with an added sound track (1930), and a synchronized talkie (1942). The theme of country life, so dear to fascism in the years just following the shift from silent to sound cinema — and from which Erice draws so much in his *El espíritu de la colmena* — is cemented to an "Institutional Mode of Representation" which produces myths about "the Spanish earth" across ancient and modern history. It is not surprising that Luis Buñuels who, after the censorship of *Land without Bread*, was working at the Warner Brothers' offices in Madrid as a dubbing supervisor, found himself marshaled to establish an efficient, profitable operation under the name of *Filmófono* enterprises. When success allowed him to hire José Luis Sáenz de Heredia — shortly thereafter the director of Franco's *Raza* — we see a first tie that binds the beginnings and growth of Spanish cinema to the regime that would dominate Spain over the next thirty years.

A classical phase had been in place for a long time. The model for institutional cinema in the 1930s was shaped by CIFESA (Compañía Industrial Film Español Sociedad Anónima) productions. Román Gubern and Francisco Llinás demonstrate how technical means furthered the cause of ideology. In *La verbena de la paloma* (The carnival of the dove) the director Benito Perojo countered the "rural, conservative, clerically contaminated" film of Florián Rey with a peculiarly Spanish type of screwball comedy. Drawing on comic operetta of dialogues and songs (especially by Calderón de la Barca) that played in ten different theaters in Madrid and included 1,500 different works performed between 1800 and 1900, Perojo revolutionized the tradition by transferring it to the medium of the talkie. Dating to 1894 (at Madrid's Apollo Theater), the libretto of *La verbena de la paloma* was adapted to cinema in the wake of models proposed in recent films by Lloyd Bacon, Busby Berkeley, William Keighly, Frank Borzage, and even Fred Astaire and Ginger Rogers. Innovation takes place both in the "hieroglyphic understatement" at the basis of the medium and in the art of montage. Román Gubern shows how a background of popular, urban theater is used to produce a new consciousness — witty, sparkling, ironic — at the threshold of the Civil War. It may be that the *zarzuela* tells us more about the underpinnings of social conflict than the documentary tradition that soon (as Jenaro Talens argues in his study of referential effects in war films) became a battleground of clearly marked ideological forces.[8]

Francisco Llinás studies CIFESA productions after the conclusion of the Civil War. In "Redundancy and Passion: Juan de Orduña and CIFESA," he shows that the director crystallizes much of the comic material of the 1930s and 1940s, linked to Italian cinema and the screwball comedy (and especially the variant on *Snow White and the Seven Dwarfs*, Howard Hawks's *Ball of Fire*). But Orduña goes further: instead of masking the point of view of the spectator, or of taking advantage of the weakened deixis of the medium in order to mobilize a play of spectatorial positions (Metz 1991), he locates the spectator's point of view. The latter is associated with "God and history" in such a way that the implicitly subversive mobility of the Hollywood model of the late 1930s (Browne 1975: 207–8) serves the dominant order. Without naming the impact of Franco on popular cinema, Llinás demonstrates how an ironclad ideology is imposed on the spectator by minimal shifts in the articulation of styles of editing issuing from Hollywood.

It may be that what these Spanish historians and interpreters of cinema show about the medium indicates how an Iberian new wave is born at the height of the collusions of Franco and North America. A classical *tradition de qualité* is evident at CIFESA productions; Buñuel's work, censored in Spain, is now executed quickly and on low budgets in Mexico; the *costumbrista, zarzuela cuartelera,* and rural films have defined major themes; Heredia's *Raza* has been imposed as a national epic and as filmic truth. It remains for gifted Spanish directors to work within these constraints and to produce films that run against the grain of Florián Rey, Heredia, and Orduña. Two of the most seminal cineasts of the postwar years have accomplished this: Fernando Fernán Gómez and Luis García Berlanga. Analyzing the profilmic and intertextual webbing of Berlanga's *Novio a la vista,* Stacy N. Beckwith determines how the director turns an innocuous comedy of the 1950s into an extensive meditation on the way the medium opens rifts in the representation of the fabric of consumer society. Berlanga uses understatement and absence — no doubt learned from Perojo — to problematize spectatorial positions; a montage of writing and images to yield other meanings within what seems patent or obvious; themes from other films — such as binoculars in Renoir's

Rules of the Game (1939) — to foster "analytical projection" that brings perspective to generational and ideological conflicts; icons removed from their identifying function or tendency to circulate fixed images in matters of race, class, and gender. The reader is reminded of the subversive potential that characterizes Hitchcock, Lang, and Lewis of the 1950s. By taking stock situations (the conspiracy at the crux of *North by Northwest*), using postcard decors (the pasteboard vistas of *Rancho Notorious*), and predictable lunacy (the double identity of *The Nutty Professor*), they call into question the economic infrastructure on which major cinema is based.[9]

For the same reason Ann Marie Stock's study of Bigas Lunas's work says much about the fortunes of the medium between the epoch of a proto-Iberian new wave and international cinema of today. The director uses a fast-paced montage, roughly the same proportion as a televised spot, to insert an "ideological commentary" within the fabric of a classical narrative. Like Raoul Walsh (*Gentleman Jim*) and Preston Sturges (*Sullivan's Travels*), Bigas Lunas inserts into the easy flow of narrative an intense and powerful reflection on social and familial conflicts. The director uses a classical mode of transition to make a patent dilemma imponderable and resolutely undecidable. Gubern proceeds to ask why the technique has since disappeared: Is it because ellipsis might be less conclusive and thus not as "difficult" to view now as it was then? Because today the collage appears too obvious or smacking of earlier styles in "film history"? Because we have been brainwashed by beer spots on NFL broadcasts? Gubern hints that the destructive potential is too great for use in contemporary film. Mark Crispin Miller (1990: 206) would subscribe to this view. After seeing hundreds of films of the past decade, he notes a disappearance of the fade and lap dissolve (and, he implies, collage) that places renewed emphasis on the straight cut: the gray area of doubt or indecision in these transitional areas of classical film might represent an irruption of the unconscious (where opposing positions are conflated and minuscule explosions of energy result), a part of the psyche that ideology wishes to eradicate because the collage wastes time that would otherwise be used for the investment of clearly identified brand names. Within the classical moment of Spanish cinema of the 1950s, 1960s, and 1970s we witness creative and caustic countermovements that signal an epistemological shift not unlike what Deleuze has located in French, Italian, and American traditions in the postwar years.

Elements of this kind may indeed be what a good deal of post-Franco film retrieves and thematizes. Yet we also find in these and other contributions to this volume of Hispanic Issues the vitality of a deeply embedded history of film and ideology that since 1975 has ventured in many different directions. For the first time American readers can avail themselves of the history of a "land with a movie camera" to determine how and where the origins of Spanish cinema have developed, how they innovate, how they negotiate a dominant event in twentieth-century history, and how they are rearticulated in a common market of international cinema, in a free-for-all of flexible capital investment. The contributors suggest that a parabola is evident: at its beginnings, Spanish cinema is born into aesthetic and commercial domains in the same moment. It becomes an institutional model at a date synchronous with other national cinemas, and it develops along lines that are comparable, if more modest in scope, to French, American, and Italian paradigms. The Civil War marks the cinema so indelibly that even today the aftershocks of a new wave have not yet subsided, even if, for more than forty years, analogous movements in Italy and France have been history. The wealth of cinema that may paradoxically owe to the repercussions of repression is visible in an inner innovation, *en sourdine*, that takes place among certain directors in the 1950s and 1960s, prior to or concurrent with the experiments of Truffaut, Resnais, Godard, and Antonioni, that entirely change the medium. The effects of this era continue well into the 1980s when they take the form of obsessive traits and scenarios of perversion not only intended to *épater le bourgeois*, to shock the middle class, but also to mobilize a psychoanalysis of a history that is quickly receding from view and from the register of spectators' memory. Contemporary directors sense that there are economic reasons why history is being quashed. Under the impact of global and flexible capitalism, they intuit, the counterproductive potential of the Spanish past has to be eradicated; only then, with internationalization of the entertainment industry, can Iberia "keep pace" in a competitive market. In that market the memory of Franco, the Civil War, or the work of earlier directors might pose threats to strategists of consumption.

In any event, Spain has remained a land bred on film. If we recall the sanctimonious voice of the English voice-*off* of *Land without Bread*, the film tells us that the staff of life has come only "very recently" to the remote Hurdes region in the Southwest. Bread is suggested to resemble alphabetization and schooling. If Buñuel displays the model of perversion that recent film has tried to revive since the demise of Franco, we might wonder if the director was also implying that a *Tierra sin pan* is also a land bereft of the perspectivism, the *panoramic* force of the cinematic medium that he is manipulating. If so, then Buñuel was arrogating the image of the apparatus, as had Griffith before him, for the sake of becoming an immortal personification of Spanish cinema. To become the foremost director of his country, Buñuel had to represent Spain as a land lacking not only bread but also a movie camera. Sovereign, unique, a myth of the vanguard and of the establishment, Buñuel could thus produce in himself the image of the cause and finality of "Spanish cinema." That his work remains the greatest single expression of Iberian film is not to be called into question. That he emerges from a rich and complex arena of history and experiment is a fact less known. It is hoped that readers of these essays will discover in the breadth of Spanish cinema new vistas, new objects of perspective, and new shapes of intelligibility.

Notes

1. Deleuze's history of cinema bears an uncanny resemblance to the history of national "styles" of medieval architecture. Italy, for example, never abandoned its classical past in the Middle Ages because it was surrounded by a continuous and strong tradition; it stubbornly rejected the French model of the flying buttress in the history of the building of Milan cathedral (Ackerman 1990). Spain held to local and geographical expression by turning influence from the Île-de-France into filigree creations (the Alhambra), by keeping Romanesque forms allowing cathedrals to resist the entry of heat and light (Cuenca) or, if it did yield to the Gothic, it was in deference to different colors and schemes of lighting (León), or late and in secular terms (San Juan de los Reyes). Deleuze's vision of the rebirth of cinema catches sight of stone, the architectural medium par excellence, in its most Nietzschean sense of a matter undergoing transvaluation. "In the city being demolished or reconstructed [Italian] neorealism causes given zones to proliferate, an urban cancer, a undifferentiated flesh, vague terrains, that are opposed to the delimited spaces of the earlier realism" (286). Spanish cinema likewise resists

and reformulates influence from without on a land of its own that is dry, dusty, whitewashed, but speckled with Moorish filigree and laden with ponderous Romanesque spaces of pilgrimage, suffering, and sunshine. A *different* model emerges, one that cannot easily be held up to Italy, Hollywood, Russia, or France.

2. The text still sparkles: "Jamais nous n'avons été plus libres que sous l'occupation allemande. Nous avions perdu tous nos droits et d'abord celui de parler; on nous insulatiat en face chaque jour et il fallait nous taire; on nous déportait en masse, comme travailleurs, comme Juifs, comme prisonniers politiques; partout sur les murs, dans les journaux, sur l'écran, nous retrouvions cet immonde et fade visage que nos oppresseurs voulaient nous donner de nous-mêmes: à cause de cela nous étions libres" (Never were we so free than under the German occupation. We had lost all our rights and first of all that of speech; we were insulted to our face every day, and we had to remain silent; we were deported en masse, as laborers, as Jews, as political prisoners; everywhere on walls, in newspapers, on the movie screen, we saw over and over again this eerie and tasteless face that our oppressors wanted to project upon us of ourselves: for that reason we are free. In *Situations, III* [Paris: Gallimard, 1949], 11). The cinematic mechanism of strategic projection of identity and of the repressive apparatus of censorship is evident. It strongly contrasts with the repressive agency of Franco that invested an illusion of power and choice into popular channels, as Llinás demonstrates here in Chapter 5.

3. "I too had been among those who, in the 1970s, used to speak of transparent cinema. It was hardly by chance, in an article entitled 'History/Discourse: A Note on Two Voyeurisms,' a very personal and, in some places, a lyrical piece that launched a political critique of Hollywood film at the same time that it stood as an amorous personification of this same kind of film on which I had been weaned since adolescence (I was born in 1931)" (1991: 178).

4. Recent publications available in the United States include Hopewell, D'Lugo, and Kinder, and generally deal with cinema *after* Franco. Here, no doubt because of the Iberian origin of many of the essays, emphasis is placed on the pervasive effects that the regime left on both filmmakers and spectators who have lived through the shift. Like Christian Metz in his great contributions to film theory that lasted from the 1960s until recently, many of the contributors to this volume—Company-Ramón, González-Requena, Gubern, Llinás, Talens, Torreiro, Zunzunegui—have "introjected" the era of repression in order to use its aftereffects for creative and critical ends.

5. Ephraim Katz (1979) has long entries for France, Italy, the Soviet Union, and the United States in his comprehensive *The Film Encyclopedia,* but no entry for Spain. Gerald Mast's (1971) *A Short History of the Movies* says nothing about Spain, nor does Arthur Knight (1957) in *The Liveliest Art: A Panoramic History of the Movies.* It appears that only the assiduous Georges Sadoul, a good Communist, had vision enough to include Spain—even if summarily—in the human adventure of film.

6. See, for example, the influence that Noël Burch brings to many of the essays in his *Light to Those Shadows* (1990), a work that locates the initial use of film as an "Institutional Model of Representation." Its Spanish translation as *El tragaluz del infinito* (Madrid: Cátedra, Signo e imagen Series, 1987), prior to an English version (1990), is noteworthy.

7. Again following de Certeau, we can say that analysis of classical film, like reading and storytelling, is a subversive activity if it does not fit into strategic diagrams. See L'invention du quotidien (1990), 118–35.

8. Gubern's analysis might remind American readers of Andrew Bergman's We're in the Money: Depression America and Its Films (1972), in which escapism, like regionalism or rural cinema, reaches back to desperate utopias, to the pastoral romance, or to "tradition" in moments of economic crisis.

9. In fact, Berlanga's El verdugo (1957) may rank as one of the most violent and utterly subversive films. One need not wonder why the film is virtually unknown in North America.

Works Cited

Bazin, André. What Is Cinema? Translated by Hugh Gray. Vol. 2. Berkeley: University of California Press, 1970.

Berman, Andrew. We're in the Money: Depression America and Its Films. New York: Harper Colophon, 1972.

Browne, Nick. "Rhétorique du texte spéculaire." Communications 23 (1975): 202–11.

Certeau, Michel de. L'écriture de l'histoire. Paris: Gallimard, 1982.

———. L'invention du quotidien. Paris: Gallimard/Folio, 1990.

Deleuze, Gilles. Cinéma 1: l'image-mouvement. Paris: Seuil, 1983.

D'Lugo, Marvin. The Films of Carlos Saura: The Practice of Seeing. Princeton, N. J.: Princeton University Press, 1991.

Hay, James. Popular Film Culture in Fascist Italy. Bloomington: Indiana University Press, 1987.

Hopewell, John. Out of the Past: Spanish Cinema after Franco. London: British Film Institute, 1986.

Katz, Ephraim. The Film Encyclopedia. New York: Perigree Books, 1979.

Knight, Arthur. The Liveliest Art: A Panoramic History of the Movies. New York: Mentor Books, 1957.

Mast, Gerald. A Short History of the Movies. New York: Pegasus, 1971.

Metz, Christian. L'énonciation impersonnelle ou le site du film. Paris: Meridiens/Klincksieck, 1991.

Miller, Mark Crispin. "End of Story." In Seeing Through Movies, edited by Mark Crispin Miller, New York: Pantheon Books, 1990. 186–246.

Nichols, Bill, ed., Movies and Methods. Vol. 1. Berkeley: University of California Press, 1976.

Sadoul, Georges. Histoire du cinéma mondial: Des origines à nos jours. Paris; Flammarion, 1949/1968.

History as Narration

Rethinking Film History from Spanish Cinema

Jenaro Talens and Santos Zunzunegui

En fait, l'histoire du cinéma, si on voulait la faire, ce serait comme un territoire complètement inconnu, qui est enfoui on ne sait pas où.

Jean-Luc Godard

Man muß die Quelle des Irrtums aufdecken, sonst nütz uns das Hören der Wahrheit nichts ... Einen von der Wahrheit zu überzeugen, genügt es nicht, die Wahrheit zu konstatieren, sondern man muß den Weg von Irrtum zur Wahrheit finden.

Ludwig Wittgenstein

Prolegomena

One evening, toward the end of the eighties, one of us was seated in a theater in Minneapolis, while the audience was waiting for a late-night showing of the cult movie *The Rocky Horror Picture Show.* John Waters appeared on the screen to ask the audience not to smoke, even if he obviously did. When he was compelled to explain why he did not follow the same norms, Waters stated with irony that it is difficult not to smoke when one is dealing with "these boring, intellectual, European movies." In effect, it is common currency to admit that for most people interested in film, the terms *cinema* and *American cinema* are synonymous. From this point of view, film history is usually nothing but the history of cinema according to what American cinema has decided a film should be. Even if, within that view, there is always a place reserved for the "otherness" (ethnic cinema, women's cinema, national cinemas, and so on), it is interesting to emphasize that the adjective is always used to define the exception rather than the rule. From time to time, Cinemax, the cable channel, programs a series called "Avant-Garde Films." Yet, it is safe to say that most of them are not "avant-gardist" at all, but are simply unusual or incomprehensible. Moreover, all of them used to be either European or related to the so-called *rest of the world's* cultures.

It would be easy to blame American audiences for permitting that misunderstanding, but this is not the point. European or Asian audiences do the same (even if they are usually unaware of that circumstance) and nobody cares. When we try to explain how people in Lebanon could follow the adventures and misadventures of J. R. in *Dallas,* as if Texas were around the corner, while their country was being destroyed by civil war, or how peasants in southern Spain could see as quite normal the soft comedies of Rock Hudson and Doris Day or the unsubtle plots of *Starsky and Hutch,* we are not dealing with local everyday life's experiences anymore, but with global, programmed, expanded, and institutionalized ways of perception.

Since cinema is not primarily art (despite the fact that some films could be seen as such) but business, the control of the distribution and showing of the so-called movies is an important part of the problem. The global power in the hands of U.S./multinational film companies makes alternative modes of representation difficult, since release is problematic in a market that privileges U.S. products. Let us recall how one of the turning points in the GATT talks, on the part of the European Community, was to leave out of the agreements everything related to culture. In effect, almost 75 percent of the movies that Europeans are supposed to watch in theaters or on TV are primarily made for American audiences. The existence of some legal restraints (for instance, the obligation to compensate the control of the supply, forcing the release, let us say, of one European film for every ten U.S. films) does not really work. To legally fool the law, a major studio has only to coproduce with a European country. In this respect, a movie such as *Superman,* a U.S./British production, is for all practical purposes, a European, that is to say, a Spanish film. On the contrary, most of the films produced totally in Europe can only be seen in small venues such as art theaters and university film societies. The practice of subtitling rather than dubbing foreign films, as a general rule, can be presented as a way to respect the work of art's integrity, but its goal, in fact, is to protect national products, that in English are more easily consumed.

In this kind of context, audiences like to watch what they are used to watching and it is easy to forget that Spanish or Lebanese or Palestinian films are not merely analyzable in the same terms as U.S. movies, since they are not necessarily based on a similar conception of what a film is supposed to do and how a set or a performance has to be dealt with. They come from different cultural traditions and constitute totally different cultural artifacts. The examples of French, Swedish, Italian, or German cinema do not escape this approach, even if in their case movies can be recuperated as something belonging to a previously accepted high cultural status of the respective countries. It is not by chance that the closer a movie gets to the expectations of U.S. audiences, the more it is considered a good film. José-Luis Garci's, Fernando Trueba's (both of them winners of an Academy Award), and, above all, Pedro Almodóvar's work can be quoted as paradigmatic examples.

It has been said that history is always written by the winners. If this is so regarding the general history of humankind, we can expand such an assertion to any discourse whose goal should be to narrate the becoming and development of all human activity through time. Film history is no exception.

When film history is instituted as a discipline, that institutionalization is not related to the desire of accounting for what happened in the realm of movies; it is a way to construct such a realm in a mode that could lead to the constitution of an uncritical glance over the world.[1] In short, film history is institutionalized, not in order to recover a past, but to help create and justify a present.

Thus the choice of a corpus upon which to work, the establishment of criteria that either include or exclude works and authors to be coherent, and the periodization/taxonomization of the material was not based on an external truth, i.e., one that could be proved, but on the will to produce a manageable referent. Obviously, one can only speak from a theoretical, political, and ideological position. The important thing in this case is that this set of norms was established as something objective and scientific.

Criteria were articulated around three basic ideas: (1) the value of tradition as a model; (2) the notion of nationality; and (3) the assumption that history has a central, individualized subject.

The first idea originated (a) the acceptance of the normative character of what Noël Burch has defined as Institutional Mode of Representation. This one can be transgressed, inverted, or ironized, but never discussed as such; and (b) the search for an essentiality that is consubstantial to filmic discourse. In short, the goal is to elaborate some explicative principles that could erase from filmic practice the very traces of its historicity.

The second idea would initiate the conception of film history as an artistic correlative of a national community's political history, while from the third there derives the tendency to periodize and deal with film practice taking as a reference the notion of "authorship" — the author as the private owner of meaning. The latest displacement from "authorship" toward "movements," "genres," and so on will not have meant any epistemological change at all, since the name of the author — usually, the director — is still nowadays, not just a way to name a typology of discourse but a signature, one that refers an object, a film, to a personal *Weltanschauung*. In so doing, we can continue to analyze film history by focusing on its main characters — its subjects — instead of examining the gear that makes it work out.

For our purpose, what is important in this historical process is that it shows itself as having come to light naturally, erasing any of the historical and ideological implications that made possible the rise of such a methodology.

To accept the way film history works out in scholarly disciplines means something that goes beyond the mere analysis of films and authors; it means accepting the canon whose very existence omits as unnecessary the question of what to study, from what critical perspective to do it, and for what purposes.

Evidently, this institutionalization has produced not only a canon but a critical habit to accept it as natural. Such a habit is hard to question, especially among scholars. In view of the expanded curricula in film studies, as university programs have generated ways for professional specialization, it would be difficult to dissolve concepts such as "art film" or "avant-garde cinema" (what do these labels really mean?) when there are so many academic positions created specifically to teach them, and when the livelihoods of so many people depend upon them.

The canon is more than an instrument used to catalog and classify history: it is, first and foremost, a way to deal with and rewrite it. As a discipline, film history describes the obviousness of some metamorphoses, but it reveals neither the webs of power within which these metamorphoses take place nor the extrafilmic motivations that exist behind them.

Writing History/Writing Film History

According to the well-known *Thomas theorem,* if people define certain situations as "real," such situations become "real" in their consequences.[2] Therefore, there is no doubt that speaking of something has the nonnegligible effect of making it exist automatically. Moreover, it also has the effect of endowing it with some relevance, mainly in the field of that complex area of social life that we call "culture." If we adopt such a point of view we should accept the existence of what institutional practice has defined as film history.

There are many signs that seem to allow us to summon its presence without the shadow of a doubt: there are texts that are ascribed to such a denomination; there are authors who claim to practice it; there are national and international symposia and conferences that debate it; associations are organized using it as a pretext; and, finally, there are academic curricula that intend to give an account of it. Accordingly, film history seems to be a discipline beyond any suspicion, guaranteed by that dispersion of signs that prove, first, its existence and, second, the sound grounds of its epistemological position. Yet, today more than ever it is necessary to reflect upon the very grounds that seem to hold the edifice of the historiographic discipline.

Any etymology of the word *history* places us before an identical field of conceptual references: testimony, inquiry, knowledge, and so on, since the Greek word *histōr* meant *the witness.* Thus, history would be (1) a *testimony* about those facts or people that one tries to retain in the memory of humanity forever; (2) an *inquiry* in order to fix appropriately such facts or people; and (3) a *knowledge* that stems from the two former actions and seeks to establish unequivocally the chain of causes and effects — where to link the human actions that are worth preserving for the education of future generations.

However, to speak of a testimony, an inquiry, and a knowledge presupposes a distinction that is established between the object of knowledge, on the one hand, and the method used in order to produce that knowledge on the other, that is, between what we could define as "all the facts that occurred in the past" and the "narration of those facts." In the first case there is an explicit reference to the past, although, contrary to what it may seem, the reference to the past of history does not come from any clear evidence. Let us remember a well-known fact: for the founding fathers of historical reflection, all work that wanted to be included within such a method of approaching reality appeared to be directly related to the observation of the events of which one tried to give an account.

In Hegel's words, Greeks did not conceive of any other history than the immediate one. Herodotus, for instance, affirmed his condition of witness of the narrated facts ("I have seen it") or, at least, of hearer of stories about those events that escaped his direct perception (Hartog 1980).

As for Thucydides (*The Peloponnesian War*, book I chap. 1), when he has to deal with the way history works, he states the following:

> In this history I have made use of set speeches some of which were delivered just before and others during the war. I have found it difficult to remember the precise words used in the speeches which I listened to myself and my various informants have experienced the same difficulty; so my method has been, while keeping as closely as possible to the general sense of the words that were actually used, to make the speakers say what, in my opinion, was called for by each situation.
>
> And with regard to my factual reporting of the events of the war I have made it a principle not to write down the first story that came my way, and not even to be guided by my own general impressions; either I was present myself at the events which I have described or else I heard of them from eye-witnesses whose reports I have checked with as much thoroughness as possible. Not that even so the truth was easy to discover: different eye-witnesses give different accounts of the same events, speaking out of partiality for one side or the other or else from imperfect

memories. And it may well be that my history will seem less easy to read because of the absence in it of a romantic element. It will be enough for me, however, if these words of mine are judged useful by those who want to understand clearly the events which happened in the past and which (human nature being what it is) will, at some time or other and in much the same ways, be repeated in the future. My work is not a piece of writing designed to meet the taste of an immediate public, but was done to last for ever. (24–25)

Thus, as early as the fifth century B.C. history was connected with several ideas that we would summarize as follows.

(1) Direct perception privileges sight as a method of knowledge. Hartog (1982: 23–24) who speaks of *autopsy* to describe this position, later proposes a possibility of rewriting history (1986: 55):

There is a history of visuality, or in a wider sense, of the visible and of the invisible; of their organization and partition, a history that changes from one epoch to another; a history made of multiple components: scientific, artistic, religious, but also political, economic, and social; and also a history of truth. Within this general history, one chapter could be devoted to an archaeology of the historian's glance, one that would highlight, from the eye and the place it occupies, the different regimes of historicity that have prevailed from antiquity to the present: Thucydides' *autopsy*, the medieval *auctoritas*, the ocular discovery of the world during the Renaissance, the synoptic and almost divine vision of Bossuet, the synoptic and philosophical vision of Voltaire, the realism, or better, the realisms of the nineteenth century; a history where the visible is neither given nor discovered, but constructed; the inclusion of the observer within his or her own observation . . . who would show how, once there where the visible and the invisible crisscross, historians could have looked like masters of truth, to become schoolteachers, or functionaries of forgetfulness.[3]

(2) History is understood in terms of immediateness. As Arthur Danto has reminded us, certain facts are directly observed in order to be able to write their history someday afterward.

(3) The description of the events must be guided by the criterion of accuracy. The historian becomes a faithful notary public

of some facts whose existence and meaning are presupposed to be guaranteed.

(4) It is pursued to produce a useful history. But useful in what sense? Danto (1985: 20) indicated that, at first, usefulness was related to the notion of truth, although it was about a usefulness that went beyond the limits of history as such in order to orient itself toward the future ("perhaps what will be again similar and alike").

In this manner, a science of the historical was established around what we might call *perceptive paradigm*.

A substantial change of viewpoint definitely takes place in the sixteenth and seventeenth centuries,[4] when history as science will begin to deal with the conception of the past as past, with the knowledge of the mediate itself. Thus here emerged a new paradigm that centered on making the invisible visible.

With the aim of embracing all possible positions, K. Pomian (1984) suggests that we distinguish among several types of history: (a) contemporary history, which would deal with the field of the visible for both authors and readers; (b) History of the near past, which would give an account of visible events for its authors but not for its readers; (c) History of the far past,[5] which is characterized as the realm of the invisible. Such a realm arises, though partially, through the traces that the happenings of the past have left behind them, embodied in monuments[6] and documents whose appropriate study will shed light on their invisibility.

In this last case, the debate on the accuracy of historical narration, formerly based on the eyewitness, is displaced toward a discussion about the validity of the techniques and the methods of research that are at stake.

All the histories that have been named so far share the same point of identity: they are positivistic histories. Although they are said to be based on direct observation or claim that the exhumation of documents is the only possible way of reviving the past, they contemplate that past as fixed, as made up by events that are independent of the description that could be made of the events themselves. Hence the insistence on the definition of the historian's task as "seeing clearly," "bringing to light," or, to put it in L. von Ranke's renowned words, "showing things just as they happened."[7]

At this point we would do well to explore more closely the recent reflections that have taken place in historiography in regard to this problem.

Against Positivist History

It can be affirmed that the traditional notion of history that has prevailed in many academic fields has come under attack from many angles. The "event" and its predetermined existence have long been at the center of a series of reflections that, beyond their apparent disparity, share a common confrontation with the central paradigm of positivist historiography. Let us examine the most important ones.

Macrolevel and Microlevel

Already in the founding texts of Herodotus and Thucydides a reference is made to the event, i.e., to the facts and their truth, as the privileged place to construct history as a way of knowledge. It is precisely the notion of event that reaches a crisis point as a consequence of the nouvelle histoire, on the one hand, and of microhistory, on the other.

For the historiography connected with the teachings of Marc Bloch and the Annales school, history should be not so much the recounting of a series of facts — let us remember the well-known statement by Fernand Braudel, *"les événements sont poussière"* — as the recognition that events can only give rise to a "Histoire événementielle," overflowed time and time again by the majestic display of a "plurality of lengths" of which the history of events would be only the lower level made of "sound and fury" (Braudel 1968, 1976, 1977).

Next to that "history of events," it is absolutely necessary to underscore the existence of another history, almost geological, which deals with the slow cycles of time and weather, one that covers decades or centuries; such a history would give an account of the relations of people with the medium in which they locate themselves. There is also a "long-life" history/a history of the "longue durée," that allows one to tackle social history, the history of mentalities, and the history of political institutions. It is, in short, about a proposal to set aside both the individuals and the events in order to determine, beyond the superficial descriptions, that profound level in which the development of history is shaped.

Whatever status one wanted to give to that temporal stratification, it is clear that the displacement from an interest in the particular facts to the study of the large demographic, economic or cultural cycles, supposes a reformulation of the historical problems by allowing the rise of what Paul Ricoeur has called the "eclipse of the event." Within this approach, history is shaped like a construction that, on the "long-life" level, does not fail to be related to the structural designs that show the invariants of a model on the fringe of the flux of time. This assault on the "event," which is full of consequences for a history of a positivist nature, has been completed by the recent revaluation of the (apparently) insignificant event.

In a well-known text ("Spie. Radici di un paradigma indiziario," in Ginzburg 1986: 184) Carlo Ginzburg has proposed an epistemological model that can be considered, at the same time, "venatorio, divinatorio, indiziario o semeiotico" (venatic, divinatory, conjectural, or semiotic, 117), and that emerges in human sciences between the eighteenth and nineteenth centuries.[8] By studying "involuntary symptoms," "minuscule singularities," and "apparently negligible details" it is possible to construct, following the model of Gabriele Morelli, Sigmund Freud, and Sherlock Holmes, a historical discourse that deals with those levels left aside by both the traditional "histoire événementielle" and the most ambitious "history of mentalities." Further, Ginsburg advances the hypothesis that it is in the singularity of the *indiziario* analysis that the very possibility of reaching the level of totality stands:

> The existence of a deeply rooted relationship that explains superficial phenomena is confirmed the very moment it is stated that direct knowledge of such connection is not possible. Though reality may seem to be opaque, there are privileged zones—signs, clues—which allow us to penetrate it. (123)[9]

Such is the conceptual basis of the microhistorical proposal, which, by taking into consideration the little "cases" or the utilization of documents considered marginal, is intended to reconstruct fragments of some happenings that are very often buried under official ideologies. From this analytic perspective, the positivist belief in the events is undermined by the proposed conceptual inversion, for which the fact in itself is less important than the vital labor of tracking, researching, putting in relation and establishing inferential hypotheses that allow us to explain a "case." Here, the "event" is overflowed "underneath," and, at the same time there appears a new consideration of the role of the "document" as "testimony" of some facts.

Reconsidering the Role of a Document

Within the framework of positivist thought the document and files were being considered, in Michel Foucault's words (1969), in the following way:

> These problems may be summed up in a word: the questioning of the *document*. Of course, it is obvious enough that ever since a discipline such as history has existed, documents have been used, questioned, and had given rise to questions; scholars have asked not only what these documents meant, but also whether they were telling the truth, and by what right they could claim to be doing so, whether they were sincere or deliberately misleading, well informed or ignorant, authentic or tampered with. But each of these questions, and all this critical concern, pointed to one and the same end: the reconstitution, on the basis of what the documents say, and sometimes merely hint at, of the past from which they emanate and which is now disappeared far behind them; the document was always treated as the language of a voice since reduced to silence, its fragile, but possibly decipherable trace. (6)[10]

However, Foucault himself underlines the appearance of an alteration in regard to the consideration of the document to which we continue to attend nowadays. From the valuation of the document as guarantee of the correct reconstitution of the past we have started to think that:

> History has altered its position in relation to the document: it has taken as its primary task, not the interpretation of the document, nor the attempt to decide whether it is

telling the truth or what is its expressive value, but to work on it from within and to develop it: history now organizes the document, divides it up, distributes it, orders it, arranges it in levels, establishes series, distinguishes between what is relevant and what is not, discovers elements, defines unities, describes relations. The document, then, is no longer for history an inert material through which it tries to reconstitute what men have done or said, the events of which only the trace remains; history is now trying to define within the documentary material itself unities, totalities, series, relations. (6–7)[11]

Drawing the evident conclusions, Foucault can assert that while history once turned monuments into documents, now, on the contrary, the documents themselves are becoming monuments. New history ceases to be the old establishment of univocal bonds among facts or events and begins to be a complex constitution of series and relations that can juxtapose or overlap, thus giving rise to the central idea of discontinuity:

For history in its classical form, the discontinuous was both the given and the unthinkable: the raw material of history, which presented itself in the form of dispersed events — decisions, accidents, initiatives, discoveries; the material, which, through analysis, had to be arranged ... it is the result of his description (and not something that must be eliminated by means of his analysis) ... it is the concept that the historian's work never ceases to specify ... it assumes a specific form and function according to the field and the level to which it is assigned. (8–9)[12]

The idea is that the event is not something waiting to be rescued from the bottom of the files in which its traces lie, but the irresolute, changing result of the formation's system of historical statements through which either the concepts of history or history's own facts are formed.

Foucault ties these ideas to the eclipse of the history he calls global, a history that is doomed to be replaced by a general history: not the attempt to reconstruct the "overall form of a civilization" (the equivalent of Nietzsche's *Antiquary History*) but rather the edification of a description that, instead of articulating "all phenomena around a unique center: beginning, signification, spirit, vision of the world, overall form . . . , would display, on the contrary, the space of a dispersion."

From the Sectorial to the Global

It is precisely here that things begin to get complicated, when it comes to film history, which must clarify its relation with what we shall call, so to speak, general history, before starting to produce its intended effects of knowledge. From our perspective this relation has not been interrogated with enough intensity by all those who, in one way or another, intend their work to be situated in direct relation to the problems arising in writing history and, more specifically, sectorial history.

We will do well to remember that there are two ways of understanding the statute of sectorial histories. The first denies them, in a radical way, any kind of autonomy, whether explicitly rejecting their possible epistemological independence or emphasizing their character of simple regionalized expressions of a global history, some of whose appendixes they would constitute. The second, while recognizing their existence as special histories, reminds us of the not so innocent implications that this conceptual position supposes. Maurice Mandelbaum has stressed that if general histories deal with entities — societies, towns, nations — of continuous existence, then the aim of special histories is what one calls *aspects left out of culture*: arts, religion, technology, and so on.[13] Those aspects are "pertinent facts" only because of the historian's own decision to select them from among the concurrence of activities that shape human life, to focalize them, and relate them among themselves, thus turning them into transitional objects.

Since their first constitution, these histories have the indelible mark of the operative choices of the historian or, what is the same, no matter the validity we want to give to the claims for objectivity on the part of global history, we shall have to be still more restrictive and cautious whenever we enter the field of the particular.

There is no need to insist on the fact that a film history moves directly into this field of problems. What would be, then, its possible relevance? It might be said that the constitution of any sectorial history is subjected to the following question: to speak of a film history—and also of painting, photography, and so on—is this not perhaps to privilege a technological medium in order to separate the study of an institutional discourse from the framework in which it could make sense, a history of visual representation? If the visual cannot be easily separated from the nonvisual, it is even less permissible to isolate, under the pretext of a technological variation (no matter how important it is), the distinct stages of the development of the universe of the visible. Such stages can only be understood when analyzed as a whole.

Historical reasons explain the privilege acquired by the discipline called film history in the syllabi and course descriptions at different universities. Less explicable is the nonexistence in these same syllabi of a "History of Visual Representation" or a "History of Vision" with which film history could begin a fruitful dialogue. Therefore, between a "History of Mass Media" and "film history" there are at least two conceptual gaps that need to be covered at some point: one refers to the relation between cinema and other visual arts, that is, the so-called history of representation; the other refers to the implicit existence of a "history of vision," understood as a general global framework.

Recently there have appeared some stimulating proposals which insert their reflections in the center of a history of vision or, more specifically, of a history of the scopic regimes. Martin Jay (in Foster 1988: 3–23), developing a suggestion of Christian Metz, tries to describe the "scopic regimes of Modernity." The oculocentrism of modern Western civilization is broken into three main visual subcultures: (a) the hegemonic model, inherited from Renaissance perspective and from Cartesian rationality; (b) the model manifested in the seventeenth-century Dutch painting, understood as an art of description rather than of narration, and subdued by the ideas of the fragmentation and topography—whose philosophical counterpart would be Bacon's thought; and finally, (c) Baroque scenography, with its insistence on opacity, the "tactile" character of the visual discourse and the intention of "presenting the unpresentable," directly comparable to the loss of unicity and center, the original ideas of Leibniz's monadism.

Jay is conscious, however, of the difficulties encountered in attempting to distinguish the first two models in a thorough way, since both are articulated by a complementary logic that relates them to the appearance of bourgeois thought and the expansion of the capitalist market. We propose to recognize two large-scale scopic regimes that might be compared to the great distinction proposed by Wölfflin (1985) between Renaissance and Baroque art. Such a distinction would foster within the first element of the contradiction a subclass to which seventeenth-century Dutch painting could be ascribed.

The positions of Jonathan Crary (1988a, 1988b) also seem to be very stimulating, as he tries to rewrite the history of Western vision by articulating it around the discontinuity created by the insertion of the problem of body, which allows him to recognize (1) a vision that is based on the construction provided by the obscure camera—characterized by a "metaphysics of interiority" of Cartesian origin—and (2) another vision that hinges on the giving up of that paradigm, at the beginning of the nineteenth century, through the irreducible recognition of the subjectivity of the observer and the corporal anchorage of such subjectivity.

Rosalind Krauss (1988, 1989) has tried to fix the parameters that shape modern vision. These parameters would be (a) the specific autonomy of opticality and (b) the establishment of an intensified and abstract opticality that ends in what will be "the formal premises of modernist opticality, the dematerialization of the visual field and the peculiar timelessness of the moment of its perception." These in turn lead to the laying of a perception that, at the same time that the retinal experience is situated as central datum of a cognitive nature, is postulated to have an intemporal character.

With all of these new approaches yet to be discussed and evaluated, it is evident that, from numerous angles, we are attending to a profound restatement of the way to understand the arts of vision. It is in this sense that one has to assume Jacques Aumont's (1989) proposal when he calls upon us to "assess the place occupied by cinema, next to painting and, with it, in a history of representation, that is, in a history of the visible" (estimer la place que le cinéma occupe, à côté de la peinture et avec elle, dans une histoire de la réprésentation, donc dans une histoire du visible).

From History to Morphology

A common trend in academic scholarship has been to confront history and historical analysis by considering the study of structures: the realm of diachrony against that of synchrony, process against system, the dynamic as opposed to the static.

In these pages we shall not find what Foucault called a "structuralization of history" since as Foucault himself recalls, for a long time, historians located, described and analyzed structures without ever having wondered if they had let go of the living, fragile, or shaken "history."

However, in a text written in 1985 and later used as preface to his *Storia notturna: Una decifrazione del sabba* (1989b: 14–15), the Italian historian Carlo Ginzburg gave an account of the dilemma that arose from his research in progress on the *sábbat*, which he did not know if he was carrying out successfully. Confronted with the fact that myths and works of art are the fruit of specific sociocultural contexts and have a notorious formal dimension, Ginzburg was obliged to combine the historical method with morphological analyses, which can be used "like a probe, in order to measure the location of a stratum inaccessible to the habitual instruments of the historical knowledge." Once he had carried out his research successfully, Ginzburg (1989) could explain more clearly the true dimensions of his work:

> Only in the advanced stages of my research did I find the theoretical justification for what I had been doing for years, when I was feeling my way. It is contained in some dense remarks of Wittgenstein on the margin of Frazer's *Golden Bough*: "An historical explanation, an explanation as an hypothesis of the development, is only *one* kind of summary of the data—of their synopsis. We can equally well see the data in their relations to another and make a summary of them in a general picture without putting it in the form of an hypothesis regarding the temporal development... This perspicuous presentation[14] (*übersichtlichen Darstellung*)— Wittgenstein stated—makes possible that understanding

which consists just in the fact that we *see the connections.* Hence the importance of finding *intermediate links.*"

But was an ahistorical exposition of the obtained results sufficient? Wittgenstein's answer was clear: the perspicuous representation was not only an alternative way of presenting data but was implicitly superior to the historical representation because a) it was less arbitrary and b) it was free of non demonstrated evolutionary hypothesis. Wittgenstein observed that "[a]s one might illustrate the internal relation of a circle to an ellipse, by gradually transforming an ellipse into a circle; but not in order to assert that a given ellipse in fact, historically, came from a circle (hypothesis of development) but only to sharpen our eye for a formal connection."

This example seemed to me *too* demonstrative. Instead of dealing with circles and ellipses (entities by definition taken out of time) I had to deal with men and women... Human history is not developed in the world of ideas, but in the sublunar world in which individuals are irreversibly born, suffer or produce suffering, and die.

Thus it seemed to me that the morphological investigation could not substitute (for intellectual as well as moral reasons) the historical reconstruction.... Wittgenstein's thesis had to be inverted: in the realm of history (not in that of geometry, obviously) the formal connection can be considered an evolutionary hypothesis, or better a genetic one, formulated in a different way. Through comparison, one had to attempt to translate in historical terms the distribution of data, presented until that moment on the basis of their internal, formal affinities. Morphology, thus, though achronical, would be the one to establish diachrony according to Propp's example.[15]

The aim of this long quotation is to show how, in modern historical research, systematic considerations relate directly to those of processes. Ginzburg himself does not cease relating his work to that of Claude Lévi-Strauss, although he keeps his distance from the latter in regard to the subordinate role he gave to historiography in relation to anthropological approach.

But it is important to take into account that morphological analyses, far from being situated on the fringe of the historic domain, provide unexpected viewpoints that can be exploited (in the very precise territory of film history) in establishing bridges among works, periods, and authors, significant bonds that the mere evolutionary explanations are not able to advance.

The Discourse of History

Although the set of arguments presented above supposes, at least from our point of view, a serious attack on the positions of positivist history, the decisive battle over this issue is initiated under the guidance of British analytic philosopher Arthur C. Danto (1965, 1985, 1989).

The basic idea advanced by Danto is simple and full of implications such as the following: "there is no history without narrator." In order to make this assertion clear, it is advisable to go through, at least superficially, the index of Danto's basic work, his *Analytical Philosophy of History* (later included in *Narration and Knowledge*).

As Danto writes, the nodal point of the positivist conception of history is none other than the presupposition that "the past is fixed," or that events exist independently of the description one makes of them. If this were so, an event would be subject to the possible full description registered by what Danto (1985: 143–81) calls an *Ideal Chronicler* contemporary of such an event. However, the production of the so-called narrative sentences would be forbidden to this Ideal Chronicler. A narrative sentence is one that, referring to two events separated in time, describes the first of them. Or, in other words, it describes event A referring to a future event B that could not have been known when A occurred. For instance: "John Ford, author of *The Searchers,* was born in 1985." It is evident that even this Ideal Chronicler would not be able to note down, as a relevant fact, the birth of a person whose importance has yet to be developed *in the future.*

"In the future": This is precisely the key expression. If we examine it closely, we can discover several implications and consequences (following Ricoeur 1987: 246–55).

Implications: Since an event is significant in light of other posterior events, its own possibility of being considered the cause of another can take place *after* that new event. Thus, a history of the present time does not exist; the historical description is nothing but a "retroactive readjustment of the past" (White).

Consequences: It is possible to alter the description of one or several events in terms of what we can know of posterior facts. If this is so, any definitive description of a past event cannot be articulated. The past is not fixed since the future is open.

History and the Construction of the Plot

Assuming the former positions, it is possible to build a narrativist theory of history that adopts, as a basic starting point, that the very writing of history is not something exterior to history itself; on the contrary, it is the basic element of its configuration.

Elsewhere—and within a voluntarily polemic framework—Zunzunegui wrote the following:

> The problem is to build a story; to produce, conscientiously, a historical discourse. This implies a rethinking of the statute of history, beyond the crisis of traditional models, in order to recognize the final meaning of all historiographical operation: to create a narration that organizes the past. The sine qua non of this task is to abandon all pretensions of objectivity that are sustained in the supposed adherence of the analysis to the object analyzed. According to the ancient axioms, such pretensions should guarantee the reconstruction of the reality of things. On the contrary, it seems vital to assume that the mere existence of a subject—the analyst—conditions the objectivity of the analysis. It is the very movement of the historian that creates the object of analysis when he or she highlights some facts that are automatically elevated to the category of *events*. In other words, facts only exist in relation to a hypothetical point of view that gives them an order. From this position—which reviews history not as an operation to cast light on a past but as a construction of such a past—history can be understood as an act that makes possible a plot—in Paul Ricoeur's Aristotelian sense of the term—that configures a meaning and imposes it upon the endless succession of events.
>
> Thus, history would be a *retroactive readjustment of the past* (White). That is why it is fair to say that history is never rewritten: one can only write *another history* (Ricoeur).[16]

Within this framework we can say, with Hayden White (1973, 1978, 1987), Dana Polan (1984), and Michel de Certeau (1988), that history and fiction are typological variants of narrative discourses (see also Lozano 1987), or to use Paul Veyne's words (1984), the summary of a plot, which supposes that when we speak of film history we speak, basically, of a narration, of a story:

> Everything begins with a shop window of a legend that arrays "curiosities" in an order in which they *must be read*. The legend provides the imaginary dimension that we need so that the elsewhere can reiterate the very here and now. A received meaning is imposed, in a tautological organization expressive only of the present time. When we received this text, an operation has already been performed: it has eliminated otherness and its dangers in order to retain only those fragments of the past which are locked into the puzzle of a present time, integrated into the stories that an entire society tells during evenings at the fireside. (1984: 287)

For A Typology of Film Histories

Is it possible to carry out a systematization that gives an account of the panorama of film histories written throughout the century? We think so, as long as the criteria of classification are clarified. In a first approach — in which we shall exploit a great many of the general reflections accomplished until now — we shall propose to articulate this field into three groups: *mirroring* or "Stendhalian" histories, "cartographic" histories, and "diagrammatic" or "natural" histories.

Of Mirroring History

How have traditional film histories, those on which we have been brought up, been written so far? If we review the most important ones, it will be easy for us to arrive at a series of common characteristics:

(a) There are histories that have been written from their burning proximity to the facts they *relate* (we see before our very eyes how the last witnesses disappear from the originary stage); they even try to continue to be stuck to the nearest past. From this viewpoint, it is about narrations that would satisfy the Greeks, i.e., the founders of the historiographic discipline, to whom, as we indicated above, history's specificity resided in the fact that the historian himself was a direct witness of the events of which he gave account. Today, on the contrary, there arises the question of the absence of the object as a condition of history (or, more precisely, the absence of the raw material on which that object is built).

(b) They display a decisive bias toward what we shall call the accumulative character of history. Their focus is, time and time again, on "the decisive moments," on "the first times," on the authors who with their works found certain practices considered "new" or on the works that staked out an aesthetic development that paradoxically, by virtue of being aesthetic, would fail to be such a development, since in this area, there were no comparative criteria of goodness.

It is about a historical writing dominated by the guiding criteria of chronology and linearity. It is the world of the texts of Georges Sadoul (1946–1975, 1972) and Jean Mitry (1966–1980), if we refer to the great globalizing histories, or of Juan Antonio Cabero (1949) and Fernando Méndez-Leite (1965). They are texts that are written on the fringes of theoretical reflection, as if the field of the facts (films, authors) were on one side, and the empirical field of ideas on the other. It is the unfolding of diachrony against the statism of a theory that would deal only with ideal objects.

(c) As histories, their aims are globalizing. They tend to explain everything with the unique movement of an omniscient rationality that knows no fissures and that covers the set of objects within its field of activity.

(d) We find in those histories a surreptitious elevation of the concrete to the general. On the one hand, the particularity of the "great works" is vindicated; on the other hand, several operations are perpetrated, some of them as significant as that one which — though hardly justified theoretically — confirmed the existence of the so-called national cinemas. By elevating to general features what in many cases were "stylistic particularities" of certain important filmmakers, it proceeded to create categories as confusing as those that allow us to speak of "French cinema," "Swedish cinema," "Italian cinema," and others, on the basis of criteria as fragile as the aesthetic ones.

These would be, in short, "monumental" histories, in which certain works reside in a definite Olympus, producing a Pantheon that would welcome the Fathers of cinema. If we take into account that the conditions of work of the period in which they were written were not suitable for the accuracy, and that access to the films was more often than not difficult,[17] it is not surprising that mistakes would multiply and that commonplaces would be perpetuated until they become dogmas. The confusion between "film history" and "history of movies," placed the social, political, economic and cultural dimensions in the lowest stage of the cinematographic phenomenon.

(e) All these histories have been constructed in the flagrant absence of something that has been a central element of other sectorial histories such as, for instance, art history. It is possible to find in art history a whole series of methodologies of analysis that, in their approach to the object, understand the flow of art discourse quite independently of individual works. We cannot find anything similar within the field of the filmic reflection, where the history is permanently contaminated by value judgments — cinephilia is an attitude that has no counterpart in the universe of the other so-called artistic practices; and what really matters is that these value judgments try to hide their true nature under the presupposition of their perfect adjusting to the "very being" of things.

(f) Besides conceiving of the story they narrate as an individual adventure, in what refers to their methods of production, these film histories have also been expounded, on many occasions, as real personal adventures where the particular tastes and drives shape the personal implication of the historian, decisive subject of the project.

(g) In all cases we are dealing with histories of a positivist-based nature that presuppose the existence of the facts they describe prior to that same description and that conceive of the film historian's task as one of bringing out the facts "as they really happened." For this reason we propose to call these histories *mirroring* or Stendhalian since in them, as in Henri Beyle's conception of the novel, history is thought to be like a mirror that goes for a walk along the way.

Of Cartographic History

If in the histories belonging to the group that we have criticized above the will of *totality* is one of their identifiable features, in cartographic history this dimension is explicitly refused. It should not be surprising that it is a kind of historiography practiced by nonhistorians. Furthermore, in the case we present here, it is about somebody whose concern does not really have to do with problems of a historicist disposition but with a theoretician in whose theory a particular position toward history is revealed. We are referring to André Bazin.

As is well known, Bazin builds his ontology of cinema around the identification of two theoretical parameters: the sequence shot and deep focus. Bazin proceeds to rethink, retroactively, the evolution of filmic language, precisely, from the implications that, in a given moment, the emergence of the development of cinematography, in its technical-aesthetic aspects, brings to the foreground. Thus we are with an operation of a cartographic nature, in which by means of the discovery of certain aspects and moments (neorealism, for instance) a global and oriented vision of the historical panorama can be obtained. Therefore, it is not a matter of proceeding to a diachronic and exhaustive description of a vast field (that of cinema). Rather, through the discovery and identification of a series of problems, historically dated, a guide obtains from which the past can be conceptually reorganized.

The first film theoreticians studied an ideal, abstract object, in which they tried to assure its possibilities of reaching appropriate levels of aesthetic nobility (Canudo, Delluc). Their goal was the same legitimating movement that soon after was to give rise to the first attempts at keeping memory of cinematographer. Coordinated and circular movements: a history is written because it is decided, previously, that cinema is an art; it is an art because it is worthy of memory.

For his part, Bazin, when dealing with how things have been done, locates himself in the perspective of how they will have to be done in order to arrive at a movie that in the end would mingle with life. It is a model of analysis that permanently oscillates between how things have to be done (the normative) and how

things have been done (history). Bazin's work is deeply teleologi-
cal and, as such, mobilizes a hidden causality, idealist, oriented history, in which works are inscribed in a predetermined diachrony.
From this point of view, Bazin's work participates in the same
characteristics that organize and make sense of biblical narrations: from beginning to end cinema goes through a way of sal-
vation. Bazinian film history spreads like a transcendental adventure in which an ontological "must be" is expressed.

Elements for a Diagrammatic History. Jean-Luc Godard's "True" History

Next to the two models cited above, there is a third one that cannot be reduced to a unique example. This fact places us before
the same flotation of the concept, before the vagueness of its limits, before the complex character of its configuration.

In 1978, Jean-Luc Godard traveled to Montreal invited by Serge
Losique, director of the Conservatoire d'art Cinématographique,
for what he himself (Godard 1980) has called "a type of copro-
duction which would be a sort of screenplay of an eventual series
of films titled Introduction to a true History of cinema and television, true in the sense that it would be made of images and
sounds rather than of illustrated texts."[18] Godard thought of "producing . . . experiences of vision: to show films, to place small fragments, some beside others."[19]

The program was structured into ten sessions, in which a film
by Godard was juxtaposed with several historical films chosen
by him.

Later, the transcription of the presentation as well as the commentary of each set of films shown were published in book form
with the title Introduction à une véritable histoire du cinéma. Obviously Godard was not intent on pointing out those works that
had, supposedly, influenced his own film to which each intervention was referring. On the contrary, the guiding idea was to use
Godard's own work to illuminate the past retrospectively.[20] Godard himself has expressed this idea clearly:

> To each trip I provided a bit of my own story, and thus I
> once again immersed myself in the rhythm of two of my
> movies at the end of each month, but the bath water

revealed to me something different from what my memory had registered; and that comes from the fact that the movie fragments of the history of cinema shown in the morning were those that *in that particular moment* had for me some relation to what I had made. (our italics)[21]

For this reason it is not difficult to understand the two meanings that, as Godard pointed out, we can attribute to the notion of "true film history." First, a "true film history" would be an audiovisual history of cinema in opposition to the traditional histories that were "printed on paper." Such audiovisual history was to some extent realized in the *Histoire(s) du Cinema,* carried out by Godard for French television (Channel Plus). Second, a "true film history" would cast light on the past, attending to the establishment of a relational logic that is not mediated by the traditional notion of causality. Rather than searching for a film's dependence on previous models, the models themselves are recast from the perspective of the present, thus reversing the sense in which one habitually speaks of influences.

Godard's proposal did not run its course. As he points out in the volume which we are now dealing with:

> Before producing a history of cinema, one would have to produce the vision of films, and producing the vision of films does not consist — if before I had doubts, I am now persuaded of this — simply in seeing them and soon after speaking of them; it consists perhaps in knowing how to see. One would perhaps show... the story of the vision that the cinema that shows things has developed, and the history of the blindness that it has begotten.[22]

It is important to retain the idea that emphasizes the existence of a dark side of film history. The blindness produced by the very development of cinematography tends to highlight the provisional character of vision, which is always liable to be subjected to new evaluations and to as yet unknown reformulations of the historical landscape.

Godard puts into play a "variable eye" (to use the beautiful expression minted by Jacques Aumont), which, in its oscillation, focalizes on different, individualized aspects of the multiform body that constitutes cinema's past. This variable eye is a reflection of the drives of the present time, which through the establishment of perishable criteria, privileged the importance of narration:

> The history of cinema must not be told only in a chronological way, but more, perhaps, in a little . . . archaeological, or biological fashion. To try to show how movements have taken place, the same as in painting, one could relate its history, how, for example, perspective was created, when oil painting was invented, etc. . . . And there must be geological strata, shiftings of cultural lands, and what is needed to make that work are means of vision and means of analysis. . . . And I have realized, upon coming here, that a kind of research had been planned: I myself had certain topics, such as what has been crucial in cinema, what is called — though people do not know what it is — montage. One must conceal this aspect of montage, because there is something quite important about it: *it means connecting things and making certain that people see things.* (our italics).[23]

In fact, the true film history proposed by Godard is a direct inheritor of the Wittgensteinian tradition. Let us recall that, according to the Viennese philosopher, "to resolve the aesthetic questions, we need indeed certain confrontations — we need to regroup certain cases" (Wittgenstein 1966: 29).

History as Logic of Relations

An echo of Godard's ideas is heard in one of the most influential texts of modern cinematographic literature. We are referring, in short, to the diptych subtitled *Studies on Cinema* published between 1983 and 1985 by the French philosopher Gilles Deleuze.

In the first volume, entitled *L'image-mouvement* (Deleuze 1983) it is categorically maintained that the pages eyed by the reader are not a film history; that what is offered is nothing but "a taxonomy, an essay of classification of images and signs."

Should we take Deleuze's assertion literally? No doubt we should, if we think in terms of traditional historiography. From this angle, one can even claim that while the author seems to adopt a historicist position — the text's strategy decides, even if partially, the conventional chronology of the evolution of cinematography—the gaps are so flagrant that the sentence that opens his work supposes, first of all, a *captatio benevolentiae.*

In fact, to understand Deleuze's work in this manner is to miss the most revolutionary part of it. It seems to us that one of the elements that helps unify these texts into a singular work is precisely their way of understanding film history as a diagrammatic history.

A few years after the publication of *L'image-mouvement,* Deleuze himself (1990: 67 and 71) clarified his position by asserting that his book was

> a history of cinema, in a certain way, but a "natural
> history." One must classify the types of images and the
> corresponding signs as one classifies animals. . . .
> Nevertheless this history of images does not seem to me to
> be evolutionary. I believe that all images combine
> differently the same elements, the same signs. But not
> every combination is possible at any moment: for an
> element to be developed the existence of certain conditions
> is necessary, otherwise that element remains atrophied or
> secondary. Thus there are development levels, each of
> them as perfect as it could be, rather than descendants or
> filiations. It is in this sense that one can speak of "natural
> history" rather than of historical history.[24]

One can see then that we are faced with a transcendental displacement in the way of conceiving history, which no longer presents itself as the realm of a positivist history or of the "oriented" history of Bazin but as a much more rigorous "history of the possible." The logic of the development of forms is no longer represented as a causal continuity but as the articulation of the opposition virtual/present, which is capable of expressing a logic of the morphogenesis that is not at all chronological.

We believe that the tradition in which Deleuze's nonhistoricist work is inscribed brings him closer to authors such as Henri Focillon or Heinrich Wölfflin (to cite two outstanding thinkers on art history) than to the historians of cinematographic tradition. To these authors the life of forms cannot have an explanation based solely on the parameters of linearity and continuity.

Omar Calabrese (1987: 38) has perfectly characterized this way of approaching the problem of history:

The historicity of the objects is restricted to an "appearing-in-history," both in terms of surface manifestation (variable within and between epochs) and of the effect produced by morphological dynamics. It is no longer a question of comparing, even formally, a series of distinct moments of historically determined facts. On the contrary, we must verify the various historical manifestations of morphologies belonging to the same structural plane. History is seen as the place in which difference, rather than continuity, is manifested. An empirical (rather than deductive) analysis of history allows us to rediscover general working models for cultural facts. (21–22)[25]

Reconsiderations

It is now time to try a synthesis of the displacement that the writing of film history has suffered lately. We have already indicated that a mistake of traditional histories was to confuse film history with the history of films (or of authors), leaving aside the complex and versatile character of the cinematographic phenomenon. Such a phenomenon cannot be understood without considering economic and sociological factors, as well as linguistic and cultural ones.

Today it is hard to conceive of any fruitful approach to cinematography without modifying the position of one's analysis or without accomplishing a displacement toward a conception of film history whose final horizon is no longer the materialization of a supposed objective truth. As Sergio Sevilla (1993: 1) has written:

The crisis of scientism — which in its most general aspects can be presented as a loss of trust in science as the model that determines what has the status of the real — has produced a change of theoretical perspective. The new one is characterized by two general features: a suspension (*epoché*) of the problem of truth, or the validity of theory; this does not always mean a denial of the problem of truth (*Schepsis*), but a provisional suspension of the closed perspective that forces us to accept or reject a proposition, a theory, or a point of view, that makes us take into account the plurality of theories that actually exist.[26]

This displacement has other notable manifestations. Let us enumerate them:[27]

(1) From a history of "totalizing" claims we are moving toward a fragmentary history. In the most recent historiographic efforts one detects an increasing refusal of the possibility of a global History.[28] The multiplication of analyses of particular films, of the so-called national films ("autonomic" films in Spain would be a clear example), is virtually a restatement of the historical approach — not as an analysis of major, shaping movements, but of the little seisms around which multiple microhistories are joined.[29] At the same time, the increasing insertion of texts into their contexts eliminates the unilateral idea of causality. Similarly, the idea of totality seems to be left aside, replaced by the ideas of plurality, fragmentation, and absence of center. Films are no longer related to their inscription in a causal chain but are fruits of condensations, confrontations, breakings, and slidings that come from innumerable poles of reference.[30]

Therefore, one should strive to go beyond the mere "event," paying attention to significant details as well as to those aspects that are apparently insignificant, in a pincer operation that grasps the history that seems to slip through the fingers of the analyst.

(2) In a parallel direction, history is no longer viewed as a field in which all elements can be reduced to a basic homogeneity. On the contrary, one tends to think that the discontinuity among facts, the irreducible singularity of certain events must be taken into account. In other words, history presents itself as the realm of heterogeneity.

(3) In a broad overall movement we tend to substitute a self-founded history (voluntarily an autonomous science endowed with its own criteria of legitimation) for a heterofounded history (which does not refuse to confront general epistemological questions). There are two hypotheses that underlie this movement of transfer: the first is that it is necessary to be situated outside the cinematographic field to explain the cinematographic phenomenon; the second, a logical corollary of the first, is that historical facts cannot be reduced to an explanation only in historical terms.

Sergei M. Eisenstein's way of conceiving film history offers a perfect paradigm of this way of understanding things. For Eisenstein, to reflect on cinema was to move continuously outside of the object. This movement takes place in two different directions: toward other arts and toward a past that placed the cinematographer within the framework of "long duration," the only one capable of making sense of cinema as an avatar of the history of representation. There is, therefore, a radical refusal of the specificity of the sectorial project, a resolute bet on the insertion of cinema into an extended context in which one can hear echoes of all arts, in all cultures.

(4) The reference to Eisenstein and Deleuze moves us from a history committed by historians to one that is carried out by scholars from the most varied fields. The question, therefore, is whether or not the historian exists. Or whether, perhaps, his position is that of the analyst who is situated at the crossroads of several disciplines. We think that the answer to the first question must be affirmative, provided that we bear in mind that the historian must get rid of the extreme positivism that has been characterizing his or her work, especially in the area of cinema; and provided that we know that, as every constructor of plots, he or she keeps an arsenal of tools that were once reserved to the cultivators of fiction. Those tools give the historian the power to shape a historical narration that accounts for the complexity, multiplicity, and disparity of rhythms that constitute the unconnected set of cinematographic facts. The historian is doomed to make sense of such facts, inscribing them in a plot that allows for an explanation of their flux. Such an explanation will no longer be afraid of being replaced by others, as long as it recognizes its singular and provisional character.

(5) It also seems evident that technological changes make possible the emergence of a multimedia film history that substitutes (or complements) the histories "printed on paper." There is no doubt that, for the moment, the most stimulating case is Godard's *Histoire(s) du cinéma*. Is it a coincidence that this history presents itself with all the attributes of the modern "diagrammatic" conception in which one looks at — to use Walter Benjamin's beautiful expression — "taking possession of a memory"? In these admirable videos, Godard faces the past, not with the aim of making an inventory of it or rewriting it, but as a way of constructing an authentic virtual memory by means of which the cinematographer transforms its "false movement" into a renewed wish of images and sounds.

(6) We also witness the substitution of the diachronic models that are characteristic of "historicist history" for the intemporal "states of things" of "structural history." Leaving aside the causal explanation, we enter the realm of the morphological comparison advanced by Wittgenstein. Such comparison reveals an obvious insertion of synchrony into diachrony, which, proceeding from the crossing of textual analysis with history, becomes hermeneutically productive. The new conditions of reception of film texts, supported by the VCR and videodisk, make possible a detailed reading of cinematographic works. From now on, film history cannot leave aside its confrontation with the meaning of individual films.

(7) Finally, all these oppositions can be extended to another one: that which presents as opposite terms documental history, in which facts preexist the description that one can make of them, and conjectural history, in which the object of study is constructed through research.

It is precisely the latter type of history that openly shows its criteria of relevance, that functions through hypotheses, and that is able to be aware of the "rhetorical" dimension of its presentation of data, which can articulate a project conscious of the decline of the validity of the great metanarratives at the end of the millennium.

What are we talking about, then, when we talk about film history, if not about a narration, about the articulated disposition of plot, characters, and events (or quasi plot, quasi characters, and quasi events, according to Ricoeur's accuracy); about the establishment of an order and of a meaning? Such an order and such a meaning are no longer hidden, as in the old histories, in order to convey the ideological message in a more effective way. Rather, they are openly situated at the beginning of the analysis as verifiable hypotheses. Therefore, the starting questions will be the ones that determine the analysis. Can it be otherwise? This way of understanding things assumes that, since history is a construction, its statute cannot merge with that of the "hard" sciences. But it is about a recognition without which history would not be possible, except by mistaking it for a quasi-religious discourse.

From this vindication of history as narration we immediately infer that this attitude seems to erase every claim about the ve-

racity of historical narration. Let us say that even though we agree
to accept as a mark of historical discourse its aim of being considered truthful, this goal can only be reached through the production of a discursive effect: that of making it to seem true. Only
in this way the adherence of the potential receiver of the narration will be guaranteed, as that receiver is mobilized by believing it to be true. But that is not all, since the fiduciary contract
arising from the historical narration implicitly promises its reader
the necessary existence in a utopian past of the events, a past of
which he is in charge. Without wanting to raise here the problem
posed by the "existence" of the elements taken into account by a
history of long duration against events, we shall point out that
the position of "believing it to be true" stems from a purely discursive effect to which the facts are not at all strange.

In that context the considerations developed by Noël Burch
(1979), Youssef Ishaghpour (1986, 1995), and Silvestra Mariniello
(1989, 1992) are very attractive and useful. When addressing the
analysis of form and meaning in Japanese cinema, Burch states
that "the phenomenon which virtually all specialists of Japanese
cinema, Occidental and Eastern, regard as the 'lag' between Japan
and the West prior to 1920 and even 1930, was actually the manifestation of a fundamental incompatibility between the West's
developing 'codes of illusionism' and Japanese indifference to 'illusionism' in the Western sense" (66). Burch explains this incompatibility by referring to the different cultural background that
formed the audience's popular taste:

> The tastes of plebeian Western audiences had . . . been
> formed by vaudeville, circus, magic lanterns and other
> popular arts, but these were viewed by the dominant
> bourgeois taste as archaic forms, suitable at best for
> children and their nannies, for they were in complete
> contradiction with the fully developed "illusionism" of the
> dominant theatre of the period. (67–68)

Japanese audiences, on the contrary, had been formed in the
tradition of kabuki and the doll theater, which "despite [the] tendency towards bourgeois realism . . . remained essentially *presen-
tational* . . . rejecting representationalism, [and evolving] a type of
performance which further bore *the inscription of its own production*" (69 and 71).

On his part, and speaking of the discursive triad that serves as the basis for the transition of medieval culture to modernity (Elizabethan tragedy, the Spanish picaresque novel, and Italian opera), Ishaghpour inscribes the origins of the sociological success of "cinema" in the decline of the opera rather than in the development of the naturalistic popular narrative of the nineteenth century. Although he does not deal with the epistemological question of historiography, his reflections point out stricto sensu a very suggestive research, above all in what refers to the causes that turn the Hollywood mode of representation into the hegemonic (institutional) one for Western audiences. Finally, Mariniello, while analyzing the way in which Lev Kuleshov's work has been inscribed in canonical film histories under the label of a technical experimentor as well as inventor of the so-called Kuleshov effect, points out the reduction that has been accomplished on the very notion of cinema that his work foregrounds. People have thus come to ignore that his work as filmmaker centered mainly on a relentless analysis of the dialectical relationship between the cinematic medium and the process of discursive production, rather than on the production of filmic objects. Moreover, a specific moment within the open process of investigation is turned into a constructive principle; by isolating it from the overall project, it is classified merely as an abstract technical device. The result of this twofold operation is the reintroduction of what Kuleshov always fought against: the distinction between form and content, a dichotomy that never succeeded as such in his work. For Kuleshov, Mariniello argues, the space of filmic discourse cannot be reduced to the production of a filmic object; it constitutes instead a mobile continuum, produced within the dialectical interaction between cinema and reality on the one hand, and between film and reading appropriation on the part of the spectator, on the other. What matters is not the finished and edited film, but the social process of meaning production within which the film's presence is inscribed (see also Talens 1993). Thus, by including the dialectic interchange between technical procedures and ways of reception, Burch, Ishaghpour, and Mariniello open a space that allows us to rethink both the historically produced and developed cinematic apparatus and the history of cinema as such. In cultural traditions such as that of Spain, where the expectations of popular audiences were rooted in *zarzuela*, in blindmen's narrations (*romances de ciego*), in the *esperpento* and the *sainete*, rather than in the high-cultural bourgeois models, the history of cinema has to be thought in different terms. This is precisely the case of the present volume, which is inscribed within the reassuring genre called "history," a genre in which is expressed the idea of Lyotard when he maintained that "if this world is declared historical, then it means that we intend to treat it in a narrative way."

Screening the Margins: Rethinking Film History from Spanish Cinema

Let us tell the story of how a land with a movie camera could not find a place in the main plot, perhaps because its characters were, in fact, neither secondary nor strangers but inhabitants of a very different tale that was never told. The reference to Vertov can be seen as metaphorical, but it is not gratuitous. While American cinema had rooted its development in nineteenth-century bourgeois narrative toward the consolidation of what Noël Burch has called the institutional mode of representation, many other filmmakers were working, with or without a strong industry supporting them, in a different way and with different expectations. What made the latter different was the different conception of what cinema was supposed to be.

The common term "film" (cinema or cinematography) includes two concepts that, however much they are conflated nowadays, are quite different when studied in a historical perspective. The term in question refers first to the production of images in movement destined to be consumed by a sizable public of paying spectators; second, to a body of technical procedures—a properly patented invention—allowing that production to take place: the latter is the apparatus of the French industrialists, the Lumière brothers.

From this last point of view, cinema—or more precisely, the moving images socially consumed by means of their reproduction through the Lumières' apparatus—was introduced in Spain, in Madrid, on May 15, 1896, by a confident delegate from the Lumières, Eugène Promio. As we know, the Lumières were a reputable and powerful firm of camera and photographic plate manufacturers. They used their commercial prestige as much as their line to distribute to the world not only the invention they called the "cinematograph," but also the films they offered as public demonstrations of the excellence of their apparatus. The obvious intention was to sell the largest number of machines as well as copies of their films.

It is not surprising, therefore, that the Lumière brothers were building a catalogued assortment of geographical views—in addition to embryonic microfictions—appropriate to the many countries which their representatives were visiting. According to their catalog, they endowed their invention with the allure of a recreational-cultural utility that went beyond its strictly scientific curiosity. Their potential spectators would enjoy not only such exotic and unknown panoramas in every new viewing; they would also experience the exciting novelty of self-recognition through shots filmed in their own social and local surroundings.

This is the origin of the first films shot in Spain.[31] Promio emblematically filmed urban places of the capital: the Puerta del Sol, the Puerta de Toledo, the Palacio Real. Some accredited topics for the use of romantic travelers such as bullfighters arriving at the Plaza de Toros were included. These materials were incorporated into the Lumière catalog and could be enjoyed as much by Spaniards in Spain as, for example, by Russians in St. Petersburg.

But, as Julio Pérez-Perucha has stated, if cinema is understood according to the first definition we gave earlier the people of Madrid had in fact discovered the reproduction of moving images four days before Promio's show, in a circus, and through a technical system different from that of the Lumières. This is not surprising: cinema exhibits in its genesis a multipaternity. In terms of the properly patented and better-known systems that enjoyed greater diffusion, four, at least, deserve credit: the "Bioscope" by the German Skladanovski (commercially produced in 1895); the Lumières' Cinematograph (December 28, 1895); the Englishman Robert W. Powell's procedure, consecutively called the Bioscope, Animatograph, and Theatrograph (mid-March 1896), and Thomas Edison's Vitascope (April 23, 1896). The latter entailed some modifications of Armat and Henkins's Phantascope, presented in mid-September 1895.

Thus, someone arrived in Spain just days before the Lumière brothers' representative. His name was Erwin Rousby, and, under the label Animatograph (a denomination that corresponds to Robert W. Powell's patent) he commercially introduced cinema in Madrid on May 11, 1895. The spectacle took place in a circus, next to other attractions, and not in an old and exclusive aristocratic salon. The political and cultural significance of this event is obvious, especially in light of the widely accepted myth of the Lumières as founding fathers. What is interesting for us is whether or not the story would be the same had it been narrated from the point of view of reception rather than that of production. The answer is clearly no. For Spanish cinema is narrated (historicized) on the basis of its proximity or lack thereof to some rules belonging to mainstream film history. Spanish movies are good, bad, or a mixture of both, depending on the extent to which they fit into the structural, technical, and narrative patterns that are consensually accepted as models. If the narration is conceived on any other basis, we would be dealing with social and cultural practices (modes of representation/modes of reception) rather than with foreclosed individual objects (films). Thus, technique has to be defined in relation to its function within a particular cultural tradition.

Spanish audiences in early cinema were rooted neither in a tradition of narrativity or music hall (such as U.S. cinema), nor in opera (such as Italian cinema) or painting (such as German cinema), but in that of the popular *sainete* and the *zarzuela*. Thus, it seems to us that the process of constitution of its particular mode of representation has to be dealt with in a different way. What Spanish audiences were expected to accept was related to a social imaginary for which performance, set, and subjects did not necessarily need to move toward either "naturalization" or high cultural status.

Nevertheless, what we are proposing in this volume is not a history of Spanish cinema but a sample of how that history could be dealt with. The choice of articles that look for the close analysis of film texts instead of looking for partial or general surveys is not arbitrary. Most of the existing histories of Spanish cinema tend toward sociological approaches, economic descriptions of the Spanish film industry, and so on. Often the films themselves, as cultural artifacts, are missing, either because of the critical point of view adopted by the authors or simply due to the lack of space. Our goal is not to connect Spanish cinema with the general history of world cinema, but to assert that defining a Spanish classical film, as most do, in terms of *españolada* (a typical Spanish show) is a way of avoiding the problem of analyzing how the modes of representation work in Spanish cinema. Thus, for example, concepts such as Actor's Studio technique regarding performance, transparent editing, naturalistic sets or strict narrative patterns mean little when we deal with a cultural tradition such as Spain's. This is why we cannot even imagine Spanish supporting actors and actresses such as José Isbert, Manolo Morán, Guadalupe Muñoz-Sampedro or Julia Caba-Alba working in a U.S. movie. They are neither better nor worse than Thomas Gomez, Joe Brown, Thelma Ritter, or Agnes Morehead. They simply belong to another typology of performers and deal with another typology of audiences and expectations. Even bad actors and/or bad performances have been used as such in order to transgress hegemonic modes of representation, as we can see, for example, in most of Buñuel's films. Sometimes — Buñuel can be quoted again as a paradigm — narrative breaks, apparent lacks of rhythm, "raccords" that do not work, and so on, are inscribed in Spanish films not as mistakes but as decisions. In this sense, Spanish cinema can help us to rethink film history as such, not to convert differences into variables or deviances of established rules, but to include them as differences. Film history will be either multifaceted and multicultural, or it will not be.

The book is divided into five parts. Each of them focuses on a particular period, from the beginning of sound to the Socialist decade. The idea is to map the historical development of the Spanish mode of representation through films that, in one way or another, inscribe and sample difference.

In this sense, we did not necessarily deal with Spanish movies that are well known for U.S. audiences simply because they are well known. We selected those movies that were useful to explain why Spanish cinema is not analyzable if we use as reference the modes of representation of mainstream cinema.

The fifth and last section, "Representations," tries to offer a closing survey, from the independence and radicality of Pere Portabella's *Informe general* to reflections on Hollywood's omnipresent counterpart. Paraphrasing Glauber Rocha (quoted by Kathleen Vernon in the final essay) we could say that if, "when one talks of cinema, it is implicit that one talks of American cinema, every discussion of cinema made outside Hollywood must confront Hollywood."

Notes

Two portions of this chapter appeared, in previous forms, respectively, as *Rethinking Film History: History as Narration* (Valencia: Episteme, *Eutopías/Working Papers*, vol. 100 [1995]), and "Towards a 'True' History of Cinema" (*boundary 2*, vol. 24, no. 1 [Spring 1997]), while the project of this book was in its last stages of preparation. We are indebted to Nicholas Spadaccini—who, as an uncredited coeditor, assumed the final revision of the entire volume—for his suggestions when translating the quotations from Deleuze, Godard, Hartog, Sevilla, and Zunzunegui as well as for his friendly help in the process of cleansing these pages of inconsistencies and awkward expressions.

1. In his book *The Celluloid Mistress*, Rodney Ackland, speaking about his work with Alfred Hitchcock, says the following: " 'Surely,' I said to Hitch, 'we'll have to explain somehow why she's dumb, or the audience won't stand for it.' 'They stand for anything,' said Hitch, 'as long as you don't give them time to think.' "

2. In A. Schutz, *El problema de la realidad social*. Buenos Aires: Amorrortu, 1974: 340.

3. Il y a une histoire de la vision, ou, d'une façon plus large encore, du visible et de l'invisible, de leur organisation et de leur partage, changeant d'une époque à l'autre; histoire aux multiples composants, scientifique, artistique, religieuse, mais aussi politique, économique, sociale; histoire de la verité, aussi. A l'interieur de cette histoire générale, un chapitre pourrait être consacré à une archéologie du regard historien, qui répererait, à partir de l'oeil et de sa place, les divers régimes d'historicité qui de l'Antiquité à nos jours ont prévalu: l'*autopsie* Thucydidéenne, l'*auctoritas* médievale, la découverte oculaire du monde à partir de la Renaissance, la vision synoptique et quasi divine d'un Bossuet, la vision synoptique et philosophique d'un Voltaire, le ou plutôt les réalismes du XIX siècle; une histoire où le visible n'est ni donné ni découvert mais construit; l'inclusion de l'observateur dans son observation . . . ; qui montrerait comment portés là où visible et invisible s'entrecroisent, les historiens ont pu apparaître comme des maîtres de vérité, devenir des maîtres d'école, ou des fonctionnaires de l'oubli.

(Except when otherwise indicated in Works Cited, all the English translations of the quotations are our own.)

4. In the Middle Ages knowledge through direct perception was substituted for trust in ecclesiastical *auctoritas* (see Lozano 1987: 38–35).

5. Film history is slipping away, before our very eyes, from the status of contemporary to that of near past.

6. Nietzsche distinguished between a *monumental history* that paid attention to the study of the natural and archaeological medium and was inclined toward

the establishments of parallels among different civilizations; an antiquarian history, complementary of the former, that would try to reconstruct the prevailing forms in a given period; and, finally, a critical history that would question the past from an ethical perspective. A brilliant application of the latter typology to the world of film history can be found in Gilles Deleuze, 1983.

7. Cited in Lozano 1987: 80.

8. The text appeared for the first time in A. Gargani (a curi di), *Crisi della ragione*, Turin: Gargani, 1979: 59–106.

9. L'esistenza di una connessione profonda che spiega i fenomeni superficiali viene ribadita nel momento stesso in cui si afferma che una conoscenza diretta di tale connessione non è possibile. Se la realtà è opaca esistono zone privilegiate — spie, indizi — che consentono di decifrarla (191).

10. Ces problèmes, on peut les résumer d'un mot: la mise en question du *document*. Pas de malentendu: il est bien évident que depuis qu'une discipline comme l'histoire existe, on s'est servi de documents, on les a interrogés, on s'est interrogé sur eux; on leur a demandé non seulement ce qu'ils voulaient dire, mais s'ils disaient bien la vérité, et à quel titre ils pouvaient le prétendre, s'ils étaient sincères ou falsificateurs, bien informés ou ignorants, authentiques ou altérés. Mais chacune de ces questions et toute cette grande inquiétude critique pointaient vers une même fin: reconstituer, à partir de ce que disent ces documents — et parfois à demi mot — le passé dont ils émanent et qui s'est évanoui maintenant loin derrière eux; le document était toujours traité comme le langage d'une voix maintenant réduite au silence, — sa trace fragile, mais par chance déchiffrable (13–14).

11. ... l'histoire a changé sa position à l'égard du document: elle se donne pour tâche première, non point de l'interpréter, non point de déterminer s'il dit vrai et quel est sa valeur expressive, mais de le travailler de l'intérieur et de l'élaborer: elle l'organise, le découpe, le distribue, l'ordonne, le répartit en niveaux, établit des séries, distingue ce qui est pertinent de ce qui ne l'est pas, repère des éléments, définit des unités, décrit des relations. Le document n'est donc plus pour l'histoire cette matière inerte à travers laquelle elle essaie de reconstituer ce que les hommes ont fait ou dit, ce qui est passé et dont seul le sillage demeure: elle cherche à définir dans le tissu documentaire lui-même des unités, des ensembles, des séries, des rapports (14).

12. Pour l'histoire dans sa forme classique, le discontinu était à la fois le donné et l'impensable: ce qui s'offrait sous l'espèce des événements dispersés — décisions, accidents, initiatives, découvertes; et ce qui devait être, par l'analyse, contourné, réduit, effacé pour qu'apparaisse la continuité des événements. La discontinuité, c'était ce stigmate de l'éparpillement temporel que l'historien avait à charge de supprimer de l'histoire. Elle est devenue maintenant un des éléments fondamentaux de l'analyse historique. Elle y apparaît sous un triple rôle. Elle constitue d'abord une opération délibérée de l'historien (et non plus ce qu'il reçoit malgré lui du matériau qu'il a à traiter) ... Elle est aussi le résultat de sa description (et non plus ce qui doit s'éliminer sous l'effet de son analyse) ... Elle est enfin le concept que le travail ne cesse de spécifier ... elle prend une forme et une fonction spécifiques selon le domaine et le niveau où on l'assigne ... (16–17).

13. Cited in Ricoeur 1987: 322–323.

14. These ideas of Wittgenstein also can be found in his *Investigaciones filosóficas* (1988) paragraph 122. The term "perspicuous presentation" used by Ginzburg— even if the Italian changes "presentation" into "rappresentazione"—comes from the English translation by A. C. Miles (Wittgenstein 1979). The curator of the edition, Rush Rhees, includes a sentence between parentheses to explain its meaning: "a way of setting out the whole field together by making easy the passage from one part of it to another." He also adds a footnote: "Introduced in translation, not in Wittgenstein text. His word is 'übersichlich.' He uses this constantly in writing of logical notation and of mathematical proof, and it is clear what he means. So we ought to have an English word. We have put 'perspicuous' here, but no-one uses this in English either. Perhaps a reader with more flexible writs will hit on something." The Spanish translators of *Investigaciones filosóficas* (Wittgenstein 1988), Alfonso García Suarez and Ulises Moulines, translate *übersichtlichen Darstellung* as "representación sinóptica" [synoptic representation], which, at least in Spanish, makes more sense than "perspicuous."

15. Solo a ricerca avanzata ho trovato la giustificazione teorica di quanto stavo facendo da anni, a tentoni. Essa è contenuta in alcune densissime riflessioni di Wittgenstein in margine al *Ramo d'oro* di Frazer: "la spiegazione storica, la spiegazione come ipotesi di sviluppo è solo *un* modo di raccogliere i dati - la loro sinossi. E ugualmente possibilie vedere i dati nella loro relazione reciproca e riassumerli in una immagine generale che non abbia la forma di un sviluppo cronologico". Queste "rappresentazione perspicua (*übersichtlichen Darstellung*)" osservava Wittgenstein, "media la comprensione, che consiste per l'appunto nel "vedere le connessioni." Di qui l'importanza del trovare *anelli intermedi*" ....

Ma un'esposizione pressoché astorica dei resultati raggiunti era sufficiente? La risposta de Wittgenstein era chiara: la "rappresentazione perspicua" era un modo di presentazione dei dati non solo alternativo ma, implicitamente, superiore alla presentazione storica perché a) meno arbitrario e b) inmune da indimostrate ipotesi evolutive. "Una relazione interna tra cerchio ed ellisse", osservava, viene illustrata "trasformando gradualmente l'ellisse in un cerchio, *ma non per affermare che una ellisse è scaturita effettivamente, storicamente da un cerchio* (ipotesi evolutiva) bensí solo per rendere il nostro occhio sensibile a una connessione formale".

Quest'esempio mi pareva *troppo* probante. Anziché con cerchi ed ellissi (enti per definizione sottratti a un ambito temporale) avevo a che fare con uomini e donne...La storia umana non si svolge nel mondo delle idee, ma nel mondo sublunare in cui gli individui irreversibilmente nascono, infliggono sofferenza o la subiscono, muoiono.

Mi pareva dunque che l'indagine morfologica non potesse (per motivi al tempo stesso intellettuali e morali) sostituire a la ricostruzione storica....La tesi di Wittgenstein doveva quindi essere rovesciata: nell'ambito della storia (non in quello della geometria, ovviamente) la connessione formale può essere considerata un'ipotesi evolutiva, o meglio genetica, formulata in maniera diversa. Attraverso la comparazione, bisognava cercare di tradurre in termini storici la distribuzione dei dati, presentati fino ad allora sulla base di affinità interne, formali. Sarebbe stata la morfologia, dunque, benché acronica, a fondare, sull'esempio di Propp, la diacronia.

(Quotations by Wittgenstein included in Ginzburg's text come from Wittgenstein 1979: 8e-9e.)

16. Construir una historia, he aquí el problema: producir, conscientemente, un discurso histórico. Ello implica repensar el estatuto de la historia, más allá de la crisis del modelo tradicional, para reconocer el sentido final de toda operación historiográfica: *crear un relato que organice el pasado*. En esta tarea es *conditio sine qua non* desprenderse de las pretensiones de objetividad que se sustentan en la supuesta adherencia del análisis al objeto analizado; dichas pretensiones, según los antiguos axiomas, serían capaces de garantizar la reconstrucción de la realidad de las cosas. Parece vital, por el contrario, reconocer que la mera existencia de un *sujeto*—un analista—condiciona la objetividad del análisis. Es el movimiento mismo del historiador el que crea el objeto de análisis al hacer pertinentes unos hechos que, automáticamente, son elevados a la categoría de acontecimientos. O dicho de otra manera, los hechos no existen sino en función de un hipotético "punto de vista" que los ordena. Desde este planteamiento—que reconoce la historia, no como la operación a través de la que se saca a la luz un pasado preexistente, sino como una construcción—puede entendérsela como el acto de otorgar un *trama*—en el sentido aristotélico en el que Paul Ricoeur utiliza el término—que configure un sentido y lo imponga a la sucesión interminable de acontecimientos.

La historia, pues, sería un *reajuste retroactivo del pasado* (White). Por eso es lícito decir que la historia nunca se reescribe: sólo es posible escribir *otra* historia (Ricoeur) [Zunzunegui 1989: 21–22].

17. The appearance of video, and the consequent access to films in videocassette, have allowed for a substitution of the visual memory of the historian for the direct viewing of film texts; moreover, these texts are transformed in various ways—cutting of the framing, or reconversion in the case of credits, change or loss of original color, pieces of spurious music added on soundtrack, and so on—so that at times their usefulness is quite precarious. *Videomania,* however, has discovered the extent to which scenes of films or supposed technical discoveries used as historiographic plot, existed only as deceptive excrescences of the memories of the historian. This situation is beginning to change as recordings with original formats and soundtrack are becoming available in videocassette or laser disc. Although they will never be able to reproduce the same effects of the big screen, they will increase the *textual* knowledge that every film history must assume.

18. "un genre de co-production qui serait une sorte de scénario d'une eventuelle série de films intitulée: *introduction à une véritable histoire du cinéma et de la télévision,* véritable en ce sens qu'elle serait faite d'images et des sons et non de textes même illustrés" (9).

19. faire... experiences de vision: projeter des films, mettre des petits morceaux les uns à côté des autres (134).

20. As Jean Louis Leutrat has written (1994: 18), when Godard said, "we are the first to know that Griffith exists," he meant that they were the first critics/filmmakers with historical consciousness.

21. à chaque voyage j'apportais un peu de mon histoire et j'y replongeais au rythme de deux de mes films par fin de mois, mais l'eau du bain me révélait souvent autre chose que ce que ma mémoire avait enregistré, et cela venait de ce que l'on projetait le matin des morceaux de films de l'histoire du cinéma qui *à l'époque* avaient pour moi un rapport avec ce que j'avais fait (9).

22. Avant de produire une histoire du cinéma, il faudrait produire la vision des films, et produire la vision des films ne consiste pas -je m'en doutais un peu, mais maintenant j'en suis persuadé- ne consiste pas simplement à les voir et puis ensuite à en parler; ça consiste peut-être à savoir voir. Il faudrait peut-être montrer... l'histoire de la vision que le cinéma que montre les choses a développée, et l'histoire de l'aveuglement qu'il a engendré (133).

23. [r]aconter l'histoire du cinéma pas seulement d'une manière chronologique mais plutôt un peu archéologique ou biologique. Essayer de montrer comment se sont faits des mouvements, de même qu'en peinture on pourrait raconter l'histoire, comment s'est créée la perspective, par exemple, à quelle date a été inventée la peinture à l'huile, etc.... Et il doit avoir des couches géologiques, des glissements de terrains culturels, et pour faire ça effectivement, il faut des moyens de vision et des moyens d'analyse... Je mesuis aperçu en venant ici qu'on avait prévu de faire une espèce de recherche, moi j'avais quelques thèmes comme ce qu'il y a eu de principal dans le cinéma, qui s'appelle—mais les gens ne savent ce que c'est—le *montage*. Cet aspect du montage, il faut le cacher car c'est quelque chose d'assez fort, c'est *mettre en rapport les choses et faire que les gens voient les choses* (19–20).

24. une histoire du cinéma, d'une certaine manière, mais une "histoire naturelle." Il s'agit de classer les types d'images et les signes correspondants comme on classe les animaux.... Toutefois cette histoire des images ne me semble pas évolutive. Je crois que toutes les images combinent différemment les mêmes elements, les mêmes signes. Mais n'importe quelle combinaison n'est pas possible à n'importe quel moment: pour qu'un élément soit developpé, il faut certaines conditions, sinon il reste atrophié, ou secondaire. Il y a donc des niveauxde développement, chacun aussi parfait qu'il peut l'être, plutôt que de descendances ou des filiations. C'est en ce sens qu'il faut parler d'histoire naturelle plutôt que d'histoire historique.

25. La storicità degli oggetti viene limitata ad un "apparire-nella-storia", sia come manifestazione di superficie (variabile in ogni tempo, così come in uno stesso tempo), sia come effeto di dinamiche morfologiche. Non si tratterà più di confrontare, sia pure formalmente, momenti diversi e isolati di fatti storicamente determinati, bensì di verificare *la diversa manifestazione storica di morfologie appartenenti al medesimo piano strutturale*. La storia viene vista come il luogo di manifestazione di differenze, e non di continuità, la cui analisi empirica (e non deduttiva) permette di ritrovare modelli di funzionamento generale di fatti culturali.

26. La crisis del cientifismo, que en sus aspectos más generales puede presentarse como una pérdida en la confianza de que la ciencia sea el modelo que determine lo que ha de valer como real, ha conducido de hecho a un cambio de perspectiva teórica. La nueva perspectiva se caracteriza por dos rasgos muy generales: una suspensión (*epoché*) del problema de la verdad o la validez de la teoría; lo que no siempre significa una negación del problema de la verdad (*Schepsis*), sino una provisional suspensión de la perspectiva cerrada que crea la obligación de aceptar o rechazar una proposición, una teoría o un punto de vista, para abrir nuestro panorama a la consideración de la pluralidad de teorías realmente existente.

27. For our purposes we use a great many of the oppositions individualized by Francesco Casseti in the text that served as an outline to the *VIII Convegno In-*

ternazionale di Studi sul Cinema e gli Audiovisivi that took place in Urbino (Italy) in July 1989, under the title *La storia del cinema come discorso sul cinema.*

28. An evident danger is to attach too much importance to concrete periods or aspects, not because of their function or in order to privilege in such a history the so-called "origins of cinema," but because of the status that these problems had prior to 1908: there was an absence of "authors" *stricto sensu,* works were brief, the constitution of cinematographic language was more evident due to its own simplicity, and so on. Jean Louis Leutrat (1994b) already referred to it in regard to the *History of the American Cinema* (The University of California Press, 1994. At the present time only the first five volumes have been published). In effect, the first—and excellent—volume (Charles Musser, *The Emergence of Cinema: The American Screen to 1907*) has more than six hundred pages, whereas some of the later volumes (Eileen Bowser, *The Transformation of Cinema, 1907–1915,* or Richard Koszarski, *An Evening's Entertainment*) hardly exceed three hundred pages.

29. As Paul Veyne (1995: 217) has stated, "les idées générales ne sont ni vraies, ni fausses, ni justes, ni injustes, mais creuses" (general ideas are neither true nor false, nor just, nor injust, but hollow).

30. Let us quote Paul Veyne again: "l'histoire, comme la météorologie, qui se trompe un jour sur deux, est imprévisible. Les mathématiciens, qui ont beaucoup étudié le hasard, ont prouvé ceci: une variation infime dans le conditions de formation d'un orage sur la Californie (mettons qu'un oiseau ait traversé l'orage et un peu agité les molécules avec ses ailes) fiche tout en l'air. Il est donc impossible de savoir s'il pleuvra sur Los Angeles. Dans d'autres secteurs de la réalité, comme dans la cinétique des gaz ou l'explosion d'une bombe atomique, le résultat est toujours le même. Ce n'est pas de l'irrationalisme, ce n'est pas de l'indéterminisme. C'est seulement l'histoire des avalanches ou du nez de Cléopâtre. Voilà: histoire et météorologie, même combat" (1995: 152–153) [history like meteorology, which errs every other day, is unpredictable. Mathematicians, who have assiduously studied chance have proven as much. A minuscule change in the condition of storm formation over California (let us say that a bird has crossed the storm and has stirred the molecules with its wings) undergoes everything. It is therefore impossible to know if it will rain in Los Angeles. In other realms of reality, as in the kinetics of gas or the explosion of an atomic bomb, the result is always the same. It is not irrationalism, it is not indeterminism. It is only the history of avalanches or of the nose of Cleopatra. There it is: history and meteorology, the same struggle].

31. See Julio Pérez-Perucha, in Román Gubern *et al.* (1995, Part 1).

Works Cited

Ackland, Rodney, and Elspeth Grant. *The Celluloid Mistress; or, The Custard Pie of Dr. Caligari.* London: A. Wingate, 1954.

Aumont, Jacques. *L'oeil interminable.* Paris: Librairie Séguier, 1989.

Braudel, Fernand. *La historia y las ciencias sociales.* Madrid: Alianza Editorial, 1968.

———. *El Mediterráneo y el mundo mediterráneo en la época de Felipe II.* 2 vols. 2nd ed. Mexico: Fondo de Cultura Económica, 1976.

———. *Ecrits sur l'histoire.* Paris: Flammarion, 1977.

Burch, Noël. *To the Distant Observer.* Revised and edited by Annette Michelson. London: Scolar Press, 1979.

————. (1983). *Itinerarios*. Bilbao: Festival Internacional de Cine Documental.

————. *El tragaluz del infinito*. Madrid: Cátedra, 1987. (*Life to Those Shadows*. Trans. and ed. Ben Brewster. Berkeley: University of California Press, 1990).

Cabero, Juan Antonio. *Historia de la cinematografía española (1896–1949)*. Madrid: Gráficas cinematográficas, 1949.

Calabrese, Omar. *L'età neobaroca*. Bari: Laterza, 1987.

————. *Neo-Baroque. A Sign of the Times*. Trans. Charles Lambert. With a foreword by Umberto Eco. Princeton, N.J.: Princeton University Press, 1992.

Crary, Jonathan. "Techniques of the observer," *October* 45 (1988a): 3–35.

————. "Modernizing Vision," in *Vision and Visuality*. Ed. H. Foster, 29–44. Seattle: Bay Press, 1988b.

Danto, Arthur C. *Analytical Philosophy of History*. Cambridge: Cambridge University Press, 1965.

————. *Narration and Knowledge* (including the integral text of *Analytical Philosophy of History*). New York: Columbia University Press, 1985.

————. *Connections to the World: The Basic Concepts of Philosophy*. New York: Harper and Row, 1989.

de Certeau, Michel. *The Writing of History*. Trans. Tom Conley. New York: Columbia University Press, 1988.

Deleuze, Gilles. *L'image-mouvement*. Paris: Minuit, 1983.

————. *Pourparlers*. Paris: Minuit, 1990.

Foster, Hal, ed. *Vision and Visuality*. Seattle: Bay Press, 1988.

Foucault, Michel. *L'archéologie du savoir*. Paris: Gallimard, 1969.

————. *The Archaeology of Knowledge & The Discourse on Language*. Trans. A. M. Sheridan Smith. New York: Harper Torchbooks, 1972.

Ginzburg, Carlo. *Miti, emblemi, spie. Morfologis e storia*. Turin: Einaudi, 1986.

————. *Clues, Myths, and the Historical Method*. Trans. John and Anne C. Tedeschi. Baltimore: Johns Hopkins University Press, 1989a.

————. *Storia notturna: Una decifrazione del sabba*. Turin: Einaudi, 1989b.

Godard, Jean-Luc. *Introduction à une veritable histoire du cinéma*. Paris: Albatros, 1980.

Gubern, Román, et al. *Historia del cine español*. Madrid: Cátedra, 1995.

Hartog, François. *Le miroir d'Hérodote*. Paris: Gallimard, 1980.

————. "L'oeil de Thucydide et l'histoire 'véritable'," in *Poétique* 49, 1982.

————. "L'oeil de l'historien et la voix de l'histoire," *Communications* 43: 55–69, 1986.

Ishaghpour, Youssef. *Cinéma contemporain: De ce côté du miroir*. Paris: Dénoël, 1986.

————. *Opéra et théâtre dans le cinéma d'aujourd'hui*. Paris: La Différence, 1995.

Jay, Martin. "Scopic Regimes of Modernity," in *Vision and Visuality*. Ed. H. Foster. 3–23. 1988.

Krauss, Rosalind. "The Im/pulse to See," in *Vision and Visuality*. Ed. H. Foster. 51–75. 1988.

————. "L'impulse de voir," *Cahiers du Musée National d'Art Moderne* 29: 35–48, 1989.

Leutrat, Jean-Louis. *Le cinéma en perspective: Une histoire*. Paris: Nathan, 1992.

————. "Histoire(s) du Cinéma ou comment devenir maître d'un souvenir," *Cinéthique* 5: 28–39, 1994a.

————. *Cinéma et histoire*. Valencia: Episteme, *Eutopías/Documents de travail*, vol. 72, 1994b.

Lozano, Jorge. *El discurso histórico*. Madrid: Alianza Editorial, 1987.

Lyotard, Jean-François. *La posmodernité (expliquée aux enfants)*. Paris: Galilée, 1986.

Mariniello, Silvestra. *Kuleshov*. Florence: Il Castoro, 1989.

———. *El cine y el fin del arte*. Trans. Anna Giordano and Poncio Almodóvar. Madrid: Cátedra, 1992.

Méndez-Leite, Fernando. *Historia del cine español*. 2 vols. Madrid: Rialp, 1965.

Mitry, Jean. *Histoire génerale du ciném*a. Vols. 1, 2, 3. Paris: Éditions Universitaires; Vols. 4 and 5. Paris: Jean-Pierre Delarge, 1967–1980.

Polan, Dana. "La poétique de l'histoire. *Metahistory* de Hayden White," *Iris* 2, 2 (1984): 31–40.

Pomian, Krzysztof. *L'ordre du temps*. Paris: Gallimard, 1984.

Ricoeur, Paul. *Time and Narrative*. Trans. Kathleen McLaughlin and David Pellauer. Chicago: University of Chicago Press, 1984.

Sadoul, Georges. *Histoire du cinéma des origines à nos jours*. 9th ed. Paris: Flammarion, 1972.

———. *Histoire générale du cinéma*. 6 vols. Paris: Denoël, 1946–1975.

Schutz, A. *El problema de la realidad social*. Buenos Aires: Amorrortu, 1974.

Sevilla, Sergio. *El imaginario y el discurso histórico*. Valencia: Episteme. *Eutopías/ Documentos de trabajo*, vol. 23, 1993.

Talens, Jenaro. *The Branded Eye: Buñuel's* Un chien andalon. Trans. Giulia Colaizzi. Minneapolis: University of Minnesota Press, 1993.

Thucydides. *The Peloponnesian War*. Translated with an introduction by Rex Warner. London: Cassell & Company Ltd. (The Belle Sauvage Library), 1962.

Veyne, Paul. *Writing History. Essay on Epistemology*. Trans. Mina Moore-Rinvolucri. Middletown, Conn.: Wesleyan University Press, 1984.

———. *Le quotidien et l'intéressant. Entretiens avec Catherine Darbo-Peschanski*. Paris: Les Belles Lettres, 1995.

White, Hayden. *Metahistory: The Historical Imagination in Nineteenth-Century Europe*. Baltimore: Johns Hopkins University Press, 1973.

———. *Tropics of Discourse: Essays in Cultural Criticism*. Baltimore: Johns Hopkins University Press, 1978.

———. *The Content of the Form: Narrative Discourse and Historical Representation*. Baltimore: Johns Hopkins University Press, 1987.

Wittgenstein, Ludwig. *Lectures and Conversations on Aesthetics, Psychology and Religious Belief*. Edited by Ciryl Barret. Oxford: Blackwell, 1966.

———. *Bemerkungen über Frazers Golden Bough/Remarks on Frazer's Golden Bough*. Edited by Rush Rhees. English translation by A. C. Miles, revised by Rush Rhees. Atlantic Highlands, N.J.: Humanities Press, 1979.

———. *Investigaciones filosóficas*. Barcelona: UNAM/Crítica, 1988.

Zunzunegui, Santos. "De qué hablamos cuando hablamos de historia (del cine)," in *Metodologías de la historia del cine*. Ed. J. Romaguera and J. Bonifacio, 17–23. Gijón: Festival Internacional de Cine de Gijón/Fundación Municipal de Cultura de Gijón, 1989.

Part I
Sampling the Difference:
The Thirties

◆ Chapter 1

Benito Perojo's *La verbena de la Paloma*

Román Gubern

(translated by Nicholas Spadaccini and Jenaro Talens)

In 1935, while working for CIFESA Productions, Benito Perojo directed *La verbena de la Paloma,* an adaptation of a very popular operetta that many considered his best film. Following his career in silent films produced for French studios and his early "sound" Spanish comedies of modernist and international style, Perojo might have selected this text as an answer to a recurring criticism that viciously accused him of being a cosmopolitan and culturally unpatriotic cineast. In fact, situated at the antipodes of the rural, conservative, and clerically contaminated type film that was cultivated by Florián Rey, the urbane, uninhibited, and hedonistic comedies of Perojo provoked the ire of the most traditional sectors of criticism. Thus, *La verbena de la Paloma,* with its Madrilenian traditionalism, offered him an opportunity to present a new public image of himself and placate his enemies. The professional encounter between Perojo and CIFESA in 1935 gave rise to a turning point in his career as CIFESA Productions had demonstrated its predilection for "nationalist" themes.

This option was not loathsome to the artistic personality of Perojo who, in an interview with Manuel del Arco in 1966, responded to a question regarding his own cinematographic understanding: "starting with the idea that regional is universal, that the problem posed be universal and that the spirit, climate, and mentality be Spanish."[1] Based on this premise it is not surprising that Perojo, whose interest in musical film was already well established, would decide to adapt an operetta; as explained by his friend and collaborator Enrique Llovet, Perojo was convinced that the operetta was an expression of living popular culture, representative of the public and capable of reaching it, even when the librettos were bad or the music of average quality.

As is well known, the operetta constitutes a genuine lyrical theatre (or Spanish comic opera) that combines singing and recitation. When this mixed genre (of dialogues and songs) consisted of three acts, it was called "major operetta." In this form it was cultivated by Calderón de la Barca in the second half of the seventeenth century. The operetta's golden age was between 1851 and 1895, and was associated with the desire to face the powerful Italian challenge with a national opera. The "minor operetta" asserted itself during the last third of the nineteenth century, thanks to the commercial formula known as "theater by the hour" in which four independent one-act works, each lasting one hour, were performed consecutively, each with a separate admission and affordable price (the syntax of the programming was similar to the heterogeneous accumulation of primitive film sessions). At the heart of this formula, which was in effect between 1865 and 1910, there flourished a work of both speech and song which contrasted in magnitude with the major operetta of three or four acts. Although the minor genre received bad press, since it was considered to be a subproduct or degradation of major operetta, its existence was consolidated by massive public acceptance. In 1890 there were ten theaters in Madrid that cultivated the minor genre: Eslava, Zarzuela, Novedades, Cómicos, Recoletos, Felipe, Romea, Maravillas, Eldorado and Apolo (which would come to be known as "the cathedral of the operetta").

Gaining global recognition, it has been estimated that some 1,500 works of this genre premiered in Madrid between 1800 and 1900. Among them is *La verbena de la Paloma*, which premiered at the Apolo Theater on February 17, 1894, with the libretto written by Ricardo de la Vega and the music composed by Tomás Bretón. The libretto consisted of an exaltation of the youthful love of a printer named Julián and a dressmaker from Madrid named Susana. The printer is jealous because Susana and her sister Casta go out on a summer night on the occasion of the Carnival of the Dove (the fifteenth of August), with the lecherous rich old pharmacist don Hilarión. In the end the two men confront each other, Julián reconciles with Susana, and don Hilarión is humiliated. The plot takes place over the course of a single day.

This libretto, at first rejected by the musician Ruperto Chapí, was later entrusted to Tomás Bretón, who wrote the musical score very quickly and felt uncertain about its acceptance and good fortune (Chapí would later attempt to console his frustration with *La revoltosa*). *La verbena de la Paloma* consists of a single act which takes place in the popular milieu of Madrid and contains five musical numbers, the first of which is made up of four pieces, the fifth of three, and the fourth of two. Therefore the score consists of eleven numbers with two preludes and a brief finale during the curtain's descent.

Perojo had been born the same year in which *La verbena de la Paloma* premiered, but his early departure from the peninsula to pursue his studies in Hastings probably prevented his becoming familiar with the lyric genre. However, between 1900 and 1936, due to the fashion of Viennese operetta,[2] it enjoyed a revival, which was actually the swan song of that archaic genre just before the emergence of the gramophone and film. On the eve of the production of Perojo's film the operetta was still thriving. María Victoria Jiménez de Parga had kept records of twenty-one operettas, both premieres and revivals, which achieved great success in Madrid in 1934 and were performed in the seven theatres dedicated to the lyric genre.[3] The absence of *La verbena de la Paloma* from the list of works performed would serve as an incentive for the cinematographic project that had already been formulated in the press at the beginning of 1935. It must also be taken into account that in Madrid around 1932 Perojo had attended a revival of the *chotis*, a rhythm of Austrian origin naturalized as the emblematic dance of a traditional and popular Madrid, a fashionable element which must be considered when one enumerates the factors that influenced CIFESA's undertaking of the venture.

On the other hand, the colorful bustling atmosphere of the carnival, which had imbued Ernesto Giménez Caballero's *Esencia de verbena* (1930) with a certain vanguardist tendency, had already appeared in Spanish cinema before Perojo. In *La condesa María* (1927) he offered a sequence of the Madrilenian carnival, with shawls from Manila, merry-go-rounds, dances, and a sequence that features the reunion between Luis and Rosario after a lovers' quarrel. And in *Rumbo al Cairo* (1935), as Quique and Jaime disembark from the yacht, they are welcomed by a beneficent carnival in the midst of which the protagonists are introduced to one another.

Perojo's familiarity with collective musical spaces must be seen within the context of the apogee of musical film during the early years of sound movies from Hollywood, Berlin, and Paris. Whether or not Perojo was influenced by Germany (Geza von Bolvary), France (René Clair) or the United States has been sufficiently discussed. In 1935, the year in which *La verbena de la Paloma* was produced, Hollywood laid heavy stakes on the genre, with films like *Wonder Bar, Broadway Gondolier* and *In Caliente* by Lloyd Bacon, *Golddiggers* (1935) by Busby Berkeley, *Go Into Your Dreams* by Busby Berkeley and Archie Mayo, *Stars Over Broadway* by William Keighly, *Shipmates Forever* by Frank Borzage, *The Broadway Melody* (1936) by Roy Del Ruth, *We're in the Money* by Ray Enright, *Carnival* and *Hooray for Love* by Walter Lang, *Follow the Fleet* and *Top Hat* by Mark Sandrich with Fred Astaire and Ginger Rogers, *Strike Me Pink* and *The Big Broadcast* (1936) by Norman Taurog, *Two for Tonight* by Frank Tuttle, and *Rose Marie* and *Naughty Marietta* by W. S. Van Dyke.

The announcement of Perojo's project began to circulate in the cinematographic press in February of 1935. In answer to various insinuations expressed about the theatricality of his project, Perojo declared: "I am not going to make a movie in one act and three scenes. Moreover, I am not going to photograph *La verbena de la Paloma* as the audience sees it on stage. My intention is to get an absolutely and eminently cinematographic work. To detheatricalize the subject and to insert musical numbers is a film technique; for embellishing the apparel without disfiguring the style there are illustrators and costume designers; for faithfully reproducing the milieu there are writers versed in the customs of the day."[4] Faithful to his declarations regarding the division of artistic labor, Perojo requested the services of writer Pedro de Répide, then the official chronicler of the city of Madrid, who had been librarian to Isabel II in Paris and was the intimate friend of Manuel Azaña. Benito Perojo, who had studied in Paris with Russian set designers of the stature of Pierre Schildknecht and Lazare Meerson, demanded that the staging be handled with absolute meticulousness. Accordingly, the budget rose to 940,000 pesetas (a fortune at the time) of which 200,000 went for sets, while salaries rose to 80,000. The critic Florentino Hernández Girbal, who visited the CEA studios during filming, remembers how an entire street from the period of old Madrid was constructed in the open air and pulled by a mule-drawn cart for 500 or 600 meters. It was an unprecedented scenographic effort in Spanish film that evoked memories of Lazare Meerson's reconstructions of popular Parisian quarters for the films of René Clair.

Perojo's adaptation was dominated by great formal inventiveness. The film has an almost ideogrammatic explosion, with four close-ups which, with unsurpassable hieroglyphic understatement, situate the chronology and motive for the action that evolves over the course of a single day. The first close-up is an inscription indicating the year 1893. The second is the page of a calendar indicating Tuesday the fifteenth. The third is a close-up of the image of the Virgin of Paloma. And the fourth and final close-up is of a clock tower reading seven o'clock. This might be compared to a minimal unit of montage, peculiar to the classical Soviet school, which Perojo had admired in Paris. Thus he structures the montage with information that goes from the general to the particular (year, day, virgin, hour), inserting into the numeric sequence an emblematic religious image that anchors the ritualistic meaning of the sequence. Spanish film had never before shown such an ability in its use of the hieroglyphic logic of pure montage.

With *La verbena de la Paloma*, Perojo created an adaptation that was both faithful and unfaithful to the scenic text. It was very faithful in its plot and in the radical quaintness of Madrid, but its primary narrative structure was enriched with purely filmic resources. The film's eight musical blocks do not faithfully follow the order of the scenic text. Its continuity, on the other hand, is improved by effective ellipses and adept transitions in which Perojo uses a panoramic sweep fourteen times and fine lace curtains six times. But Perojo also skillfully handles the montage determined by the association of ideas, allusions or figurative motifs. He moves from Julián's print shop to Susana's dress shop, or from the revolving wheel of the printing press to the revolving wheel of the sewing machine (a visual motif already skillfully used in *La condesa María*); or from Don Hilarión's top hat to the hats on the coat rack at the police station. On other occasions there is a transition to a scene showing the person alluded to, thereby reinforcing narrative fluidity. Such is the case with the introduction of Aunt Antonia at the beginning and later Don Hilarión. But the iconographic associations are sometimes more distant or subtle. Don Hilarión's alleged night of carnival pleasure opens with a close-up of his top hat, a garment emblematic of luxury and recreation. But after his flight—or defeat—motivated by Julián's bursting onto the merry-go-round and dispelling the celebratory mood, Perojo, punctuating the narrative segment of the apothecary's frustrating carnival evening, abandons Don Hilarión with another close-up of his top hat, this time overturned. On other occasions the association is almost subliminal, as occurs in some of the well conceived and constructed movements of the camera. Thus, the ascending sweep of Julián's gaze from the street to Susana's balcony later has its inverse corollary in the panoramic shot descending from the balcony to the street to discover Julián with Doña Rita when the latter has detected her beloved's presence in the apartment.

Nor could the operetta, because of its scenic nature, connect parallel actions, such as those that tie Perojo to Julián and Susana, or to Don Hilarión and the sisters, who unify the action with solidity and fluidity. Filmed on great urban sets worthy of Lazare Meerson, Perojo also marks the action with his numerous camera movements. His dynamizing volition is evident in the invention of the intense duo's streetcar journey (which proved possible to execute on stage), when Julián recriminates Susana for not having gone to the carnival with him. But this richness of movement actually serves as an element of meritorious laconic style. The contrast between social classes offered by the montage (Susana's humble apartment contrasted with the sisters dancing together, followed by a palace dance in Technicolor) is a true rarity in Spanish film of the period. And the scene of the nuptial couple in the photographer's studio and a good part of the scene in the pawnshop are resolved without dialogue, with an expressivity inherited from the best of silent film. A unique concession to Baroque and formal styles stands out on two occasions, in the use of gigantic shadows (the horse-drawn carriage that passes by the apothecary, and the ferris wheel's shadow on a facade), a sensationalism belonging to the German school of lighting in which the cameraman Fred Mandel had been trained. Yet some background compositions for the carnival, in which the merry-go-rounds constitute an important leitmotif, are not as sensational since they are consistent with the dynamism of the film. It is almost certain that Perojo had seen Jean Epstein's *Coeur fidele* (1923) in Paris, with its popular carnival and renowned merry-go-round scene which impressed the critics of the period.[5] In composing certain carnival shots, Perojo juxtaposes the circular movement of the vertical ferris wheel with the horizontal rotation of the merry-go-round. These shots of structurally dynamized composition appear when Perojo begins his visual description of the carnival, as well as at the end of the film. And it would not be an overstatement to associate them with Eisenstein's theory of the conflict of forms described by the Soviet director in a theoretical text dated 1929.

La verbena de la Paloma masterfully combines descriptive, traditional and musical elements in its regionalist inclination. The descriptive display of the film takes place during summer twilight, with a visual journey over housetops with their attics and lofts, a journey that evokes René Clair's earlier description of a popular Paris, accomplished with a jolt of the crane in his *Quatorze juillet* (1932), a far less dynamic and agile film than Perojo's, although both have in common the unitary framework of a celebrative urban day's journey. And one of the best displays of musical staging comes from the brilliant iconic splitting of Julián at work printing, with another image superimposed in a close-up shot as he sings of his heartache. What is shown, then, is the co-existence of his dual condition as love-struck proletarian, on the one hand, quietly dedicated to his printing tasks, and the other expressing his grief in a song. Then, in the same scene, a superimposed image of Susana will sing to Julián the worker, while the image of Julián the singer fades away with the appearance of this feminine element, thereby unifying the subject of passion. Although Perojo's version is based on the literary-theatrical-musical substratum of Madrilenian traditionalism which had been formalized in the operetta genre, it seems to us that it is affected by the double cinematographic influence of René Clair's urban populism and the mobility and rhythm of the American musicals of the period. And so, the transcription of an outdated scenic text was successfully executed with modern cinematographic writing.

Not since *Esencia de verbena* by Giménez Caballero had Spanish film launched such an exalted proclamation in favor of Madrid, despite the abundance of stereotypes and traditionalism. Perhaps such exalted proclamation was due, on the one hand, to an uninhibited musical treatment or to the intellectual distance of the cosmopolitan Perojo regarding the operetta genre, which was treated on this occasion, as Fanés observes, "a la americana" (American-style),[6] using all the formal resources of Hollywood musicals. On the other hand, Madrilenian populism offered a charming democratic touch when including the plebeian love between a printer and a dressmaker, a love hindered by an apothecary who, being richer and older, will therefore be the loser because of his economic power and his devirilization. In this sense, the psychological schematization was associated with the interclass ethos of the genre, in a work in which Julián, at first with joy, celebrates his boss's wedding in a scene where they treat each other as equals at the breakfast table. This precapitalist solidarity was characteristic of the endogamous social universe of a Madrid neighborhood in 1894 operettas.

Félix Fanés, upon examining the insertion and congruence of this film within the production policy of CIFESA, has called to our attention the typical centrality of the love story, even if it was "less classy and more racy" than what was usual for this production company. And as a eulogy he adds that "the honor theme does not appear at all, and jealousy — which is indeed present — is a less pathological sentiment."[7] On this point, while comparing the themes of jealousy and sexual honor as they appear in Florián Rey's films, Perojo's lucidity is evident. Manuel Rotellar, supporting this assessment, also rates the sister-protagonists as "two rotting females."[8] Thus, despite the ideological conservatism of CIFESA, the liberal wind of republicanism filtered into the uninhibited treatment with which Perojo fashioned his representation of the endogamous and archaic universe of a popular Madrilenian district at the end of the nineteenth century.

It should not surprise us that *La verbena de la Paloma* became one of the major commercial successes during the brief history of Republican cinema, and one of the favorite films of its director, who, in 1963, would produce a remake, this time directed without any wit by José Luis Saénz de Heredia.

Notes

1. "Mano a mano" with Manuel del Arco, *La Vanguardia,* Jan. 18, 1966.
2. Espín Templado, María del Pilar. "La zarzuela: esquema de un género español," in *La zarzuela de cerca,* ed. and with an introduction by Andrés Amorós, Madrid: Espasa Calpe, 1987: 33–34.
3. Jiménez de Parga Cabrera, María Victoria. "La zarzuela en Madrid en 1934," in *La zarzuela de cerca,* 209–211, 215.
4. *La verbena de la Paloma. Unas palabras de Benito Perojo. Noticiario Cifesa* 11, December 1935.
5. Leprohon, Pierre. *Jean Epstein.* Paris: Seghers, 1964: 35.
6. Fanés, Félix. *El cas Cifesa: vint anys de cinema espanyol (1932–1951).* Valencia: Filmoteca de la Generalitat Valenciana, 1989: 77.
7. Ibid., 78.
8. Rotellar, Manuel. *Cine español de la República.* San Sebastián: XXV International Film Festival, 1977: 142.

Works Cited

Espín Templado, María del Pilar. "La zarzuela: esquema de un género español." In Andrés Amorós, ed. *La zarzuela de cerca.* Madrid: Espasa Calpe, 1987: 33–34.

Fanès, Félix. *El cas Cifesa: vint anys de cinema espanyol (1932–1951).* Valencia: Filmoteca de la Generalitat Valenciana, 1989.

Jiménez de Parga Cabrera, María Victoria. "La zarzuela en Madrid en 1934." In Andrés Amorós, ed. *La zarzuela de cerca.* Madrid: Espasa Calpe, 1987: 209–215.

Leprohon, Pierre. *Jean Epstein.* Paris: Seghers, 1964.

Perojo, Benito. With Manuel del Arco. "Mano a mano," *La Vanguardia,* Jan. 18, 1966.

———. "La verbena de la Paloma. Unas palabras de Benito Perojo." *Noticiario Cifesa* 11 (Dec. 1935).

Rotellar, Manuel. *Cine español de la República.* San Sebastián: XXV International Film Festival, 1977.

◆   Chapter 2

The Referential Effect:
Writing the Image of the War

Jenaro Talens

Although the filmed memory of the Spanish Civil War would seem to be a desert, few events have attracted more attention of filmmakers from all over the world than the absurd tragedy that turned Spain, during three long years, into a strategic laboratory to stop the spread of communism in Europe. This circumstance makes the analysis of the films related to this event particularly important, not only for historical reasons—which would suffice to justify this undertaking—but also because of its capacity to offer texts to scholars working in the history and evolution of cinematographic discourse.

The First World War had already attracted a large number of filmmakers interested in using the new medium, given the character of immediacy and realism that the image could bring to the traditional media of written and radio journalism, to report about the events that were taking place in Europe. However, it is with the Spanish Civil War, after the invention of sound film, that these possibilities could best be exploited. For the first time in the history of cinema, people from all over the world, those with their cameras over their shoulders at the scene of the war, and others physically far from it, decided at the same time to invest their energy in dealing systematically with the topic of the Spanish Civil War. Their intention was either informative (elaborating newsreels) or overtly industrial (making movies for regular commercial movie theaters).

From today's point of view, this material shows to what extent both possibilities were not absolute alternatives but complementary to each other, to the extent that they made explicit the arbitrariness of the opposition between documentary film and fiction film. This allows us to integrate both practices not so much as different discourses but as different modalities to operate from within a single discourse.

The inventors of cinema were legion, although the honors and glory have been attributed almost exclusively to the Lumière brothers. Among those inventors, some were outside the show business industry, and interested above all in documenting phenomena. So, the experiences of Pierre Jules Cesar Janssen and his "photographic gun" to catch with the camera the planet Venus moving across the sun. So again, Earweard Muybridge's "magic lantern" which created the illusion of horses in full run. Although in these cases it would not be possible to speak of cinema strictly intended, they laid the foundations for its rise, with a very well defined finality and direction: to reproduce the image of a reality in movement. The first reels by the Lumière brothers did not hide such an obvious constructive principle. In fact, they were the first—although without planning it, without using it as an explicit compositive procedure—to inscribe in the materiality of the screen the invisible presence of an external eye which, occupying a space *off*, would supplant our gaze, selecting what to watch and from where. Consider the famous shot of the photographers tipping their hats and looking right into the camera in *Congrès de photographie à Neuville-sur-Saône* (1895). The functionality given to the new invention by Edison and his nickelodeon displaced the articulating point from a mechanical operation—to reproduce the image—to a signifying effect—to present the image as reality. Not only would it originate what Noël Burch has called "Institutional Mode of Representation" (IMR)[1], but it also established the basis for the birth of a possibly more dangerous categorial dichotomy in an almost imperceptible way: that between the so-called fiction film and the documentary film. In fact, the erasure of the enunciation that begins with Edison and, through Porter, reaches its definitive consecration with Griffith's technique of editing, cannot be assimilated to the European model that arose with Lumière-Meliès. In this model the procedural explicitation, its mise-en-scène, sets up inside the discourse itself a metadiscursive glance, capable of discerning in the object what constitutes it as such: to be not a fact, but an interpretation.[2]

From the epistemological perspective underlying the Porter-Griffith model one could speak of fictionality versus non-fictionality, not starting from the mechanisms of composition, but from pure and simple referentiality. It is not by chance that the concept of documentary — and its implicit characterization as direct discourse, supposedly without mise-en-scène — originated in the twenties from within the IMR. This dichotomy explains how one could make a distinction between *Broken Blossoms* (Griffith, 1922) and *Nanuk of the North* (Flaherty, 1922). However, in the Soviet Union, for example, the difference between *Potemkin* (Eisenstein, 1925) or *The Mother* (Pudovkin, 1926), on one side, and *The Man with the Movie Camera* (Dziga Vertov, 1930) or *The Extraordinary Adventures of Mr. West in the Land of the Bolsheviks* (Lev Kuleshov, 1924), on the other, could be described in terms that are not related to the aforementioned binomial. It is significant, therefore, that Eric Barnow's monograph about this topic should be titled *Documentary: A History of the Non-fiction Film*.[3] Thus, documentary is considered synonymous with "non-fictional," focusing on content rather than on discursive articulation.

The problem posed by this displacement is not new. Pierre Bourdieu had already hypothesized about the existing relationship between the rise of the capitalistic mode of production in bourgeois society and the institutionalization of fiction in art. In effect, if the decodification of the basic discursive elements depended on the decodification of its artistic use, the artistic practice would become the feud of a privileged minority — the only one to have enough knowledge to impose and control the codes — which would reproduce on this ground its class domination.[4]

The contemporary intent to break with this state of things led, however, to an ambiguous issue: the "realistic" incidency would only be possible through the elimination of fictionality. This principle, having arisen from a certain reduction of the much more complex naturalism of Zola,[5] granted the distinction between a true (= documentary) and a false (= fictional) state of naturality. It validates one hypothesized discursive transparency. Cinema has not been an exception. However, there is no film without montage, whether this is intended in terms of editing or of mise-en-scène, that is, montage within the shot.[6] Montage implies intervention and manipulation of the material being used for the purpose of further elaborating it. A newsreel is considered true if it is credible. The truth, consequently, is the result of an effect produced on the spectator by means of a rhetorically constructive process, through which the articulation of images and sounds acquires a status of verisimilitude. In its denial of the hypothesized discursive transparency, this process seems to put into question the existence of the "documentary" itself.

To affirm, however, that every discourse is fictional, because it is structured as narration in order to be convincing of something by means of a story—whether or not this story is true on the referential level—resolves nothing. The differences between the so-called "documentary film" and a fiction film are evident. Therefore, it becomes necessary to analyze the location of these differences. This place, which is not so much a prior and external presupposition as it is a discursive product, leads us inevitably to speak not of the referent (with autonomous existence outside discourse) but of a referential (produced) effect when we look for an element of analytic validation.

This perspective has the advantage of transforming the old opposition between different referential realities into the opposition between forms of producing different perceptions through different effects. So it can be understood how it is possible to make a documentary with materials that are referentially fictional. In the same way it is possible to make a fiction film with materials that are referentially truthful. In both cases, the sense of the text does not depend on these materials, but on the operation that will articulate the whole.

The most immediate consequence of this transformation is that we are led to the unavoidable necessity of applying textual analysis to filmic mechanisms, instead of dealing with the topics at the level of the plot or with their historical sociological horizons. This does not deny the importance of the study of the topics, or of those horizons. On the contrary, it makes the approach to them more productive and scientific. It is the specific articulation of the structure which produces both topics and horizons.

If we assume these theoretical presuppositions when dealing with the large number of movies made during—or about—the Spanish Civil War, the first thing we discover is the extent to which the war, the apparently main topic of the films, is just a pretext to speak of something else, namely, that which structures and gives them sense. The opposite also applies: most of the comedies made on the Francoist rebel side that present themselves as just entertainment are closely related to the war.[7] Let's look at some examples.

Spanish Earth, directed by Joris Ivens and produced with American funds, is usually considered one of the most historically faithful "documentaries." The film was made, however, not so much to inform the American government and public opinion, showing the horrors of the war, but in order to convince them to take sides in favor of the Spanish Republic against the military rebellion initiated by General Franco. This support was hoped for in spite of the existence of The American Embargo Act of 1936, which continued the Neutrality Act of 1935, on the basis of which Congress decided in favor of a politics of non-intervention.

This point of departure explains why Ivens necessarily had to use some aspects of the discursive model of the classic American cinema, in some of its basic aesthetic presuppositions, at the time when he formalized his work. If one wants to be understood, one has to speak in a comprehensible language, adequate to the horizon of the audience's expectations. In effect, the film chooses a simple but significant fictional plot in order to function as a vehicle for its documentary discourse: Juan, a soldier in the Republican army, returns for a short period of time to his little village, far from the war front. This minimal anecdote allows Ivens to show the everyday life of people who live close to the horrors of war, who work in the fields with energy and trust, and who believe in the possibility of a better future, in spite of bombs and destruction.

The symbolic value attributed to the land works favorably on spectators whose collective unconscious granted the land a fundamental status as historical mythical element of its own constitution as a country. It would not be possible, otherwise, to understand the sort of American para-history, via Hollywood, that is the Western. In it, the usual quarrels between ranchers and farmers are resolved usually in favor of the latter. Thus, to work in the fields and live off their fruits becomes a foundational category. Consider how one of the biggest popular literary best sellers of these years, *Gone with the Wind* by Margaret Mitchell—converted in 1939 to a successful film by Victor Fleming *et al.*—established Tara as a central point of its mythology. On the other side, Juan's presence in *Spanish Earth* as axis-character underlines the need to individualize a collective history, inscribing in its development a single protagonist, a kind of anti-hero—that is to say, a hero—who is able to symbolize it.

What, as document, tried to be the testimony of a conflict explicable in political terms, had to be disguised as a story with a plot and a main character, thus displacing its emphasis to the level of the fiction film. It makes no difference that in this case the hero was the symbol of a collectivity. As Marx had theorized, the problem of history is not to know who its subject is—whether individual or collective—but what is the motor that moves it.

The film, shot in 1937, offered an optimistic image of the war's development insofar as a victory for the Republicans seemed feasible. It is unlikely that this perspective could have been held in 1938. Ivens's intelligent maneuvering did not reach its goal for reasons that are sufficiently well-known and documented. However, this should not make us forget that *Spanish Earth* was de facto a film subliminally articulated around certain concepts and around a system of values that were alien to Spanish audiences, since such values belonged to the American cultural tradition. One might say that this was probably the only way that Ivens could do his job without being accused of bolshevism and political propaganda—although eventually both he and his film were. Ivens made reference to a system of values that were at stake in Spain at that particular moment. Those very values are usually assumed by the American audiences as their own. Thus, because of *Spanish Earth*'s ideological strategy of shaping American public opinion for the Republican side, the film is not really about the Spanish Civil War but about ethical and political issues belonging to an American social imaginary. Spectators were subliminally urged to take the position that the Republicans were to be helped not because they were right or wrong but because they were a sort of specular image of their own.

The same thing can be said about *Spanija*, a film edited in the (then) U.S.S.R. by Esther Shub at the time of the Second World War, partly with materials taken from archives, partly with material shot by Roman Karmen. The film, shown in the U.S.S.R. during Stalin's rule, articulates its discourse around the different positions that Anarchists, Trotskyists and Communists took in regard to the Spanish Civil War. It curiously and abruptly concludes its narration with the International Brigades' departure from the port of Barcelona in 1938, leaving out the final part of the war. As soon as those who were for Soviet audiences the main characters of the film disappear from the screen, the war disappears with them.

As in the previous example, *Spanija* takes the Spanish war as a pretext to speak of a different problematic, in this case the conflict within the Third and Fourth International Brigades, with its scales tipped in favor of the former. It is evident that the difference in the audience for whom the film was made and the different filmic tradition in which it inserts itself as textual dispositive — Esther Shub had worked as editor in Dziga Vertov films — determine the distinctiveness of its structure in relation to Ivens's film. But this does not change our general argument. The fact that there are no individualized protagonists articulating the story being narrated, unlike the Hollywood mode of representation, does not imply that there are no protagonists, as subjects of history in the film. Instead of human beings, there are specific political options. More than a film about the Spanish Civil War, *Spanija* is a film about the official reasons Stalinism is brandished to justify its condemnation of Trotskyism at the international level.

In this sense, *Sierra de Teruel* (André Malraux and Max Aub, 1937),[8] *The Good Fight* (USA, 1984) and *Espíritu de una raza* (José Luis Sáenz de Heredia, 1940) are, perhaps, three of the films that make explicit the pretextual character of the Spanish Civil War as a topic at the level of the plot.

The first one, based on a fragment from the novel *L'Espoir* by André Malraux, articulates itself around a small anecdote. In its first part, a group of aviators of the International Brigades had to bomb a landing field of the rebel army. After the bombing, one of the planes is shot down by enemy fire and crashes on a mountain of the Teruel Sierra. The second part of the film narrates the recovering of the bodies by members of the Republican militia. The final, impressive sequence of the descent of the wounded soldiers down the steep paths of the Sierra, and their entering the village, is perhaps the best example of how to dissolve the notion of protagonist-subject—individual or collective—into a popular and materialistic point of view, that is to say, of how to displace the point of discursive articulation from utterance to enunciation. This is probably the only case in which a film about the Spanish Civil War stages the real motivations of the war as such, in spite of the fictional character of the screenplay. Through the displacement that operates in the story by dissolving a centered individual narrative into the social situation which frames and contextualizes it, the discursive film scope is displaced to a political terrain from which to offer a correct ideological view of what was actually at stake in that armed conflict. However, when the film was edited, at the end of the Second World War, a prologue was added—supposedly with Malraux's explicit acquiescence—a fact that changes completely the meaning of the whole film. Someone, facing the camera, speaks through a radiophonic microphone praising the action of the protagonists of the film, relating them to French resistors fighting against Hitler and the Vichy government. This unusual prologue turns *Sierra de Teruel*, in its final version, into a film about resistance in which the Spanish Civil War is just a metaphorical background.

The Good Fight, made by the survivors of the Lincoln Brigade during Nixon's presidency, mixes archive images of the Spanish Civil War with present-day interviews of the participants. Although most of the film is devoted to showing scenes from the Civil War, it is obvious that, as the title itself indicates, the film deals less with the war than with the ideological reasons that justified the participation of several thousands of Americans on the side of the legal government in Spain. In effect, the film ends with the images of a brigadists' protest rally in front of the White House in the seventies. More than a film about the Civil War, *The Good Fight* narrates the survival of a left-wing tradition in the United States.[9]

The third of the aforementioned films is, from this perspective, of particular interest, despite its openly fascist and manipulatory

character. The filmic complexity that Sáenz de Heredia incorporates in a quite simple and Manichaean screenplay written by
General Franco — who appears in the credits under the pseudonym Jaime de Andrade — makes *Espíritu de una raza* an appropriate text for the analysis of the strictly formalistic mechanisms that
cinema can use to stage the mystification of history.

The emblematic character that the film claims to have is made
explicit not only by the text that appears in transparency at the
end of the credits[10] but fundamentally by the still photographs
that open and close the film, and by the image of a bucolic landscape at dawn, materially arising from the former images at the
beginning of the film. The still photographs reproduce paintings
of Spaniards discovering the New World in 1492 and paintings
of ships of the Spanish Imperial Navy. As a result of the interconnected position of both images through the editing, it seems
that the idea of quietness, idyll and bucolic feeling is related to
the world of Imperial "grandeur," symbolized by the paintings of
discoverers and ships. The landscape has also its symmetrical
counterpart at the end of the movie in the image of the waving
Francoist banner. Between these two interrelated pairs of emblems — Imperial world = bucolic and quiet country = Francoist
banner — the film develops its story: the story of the reconquest
of a glorious past supposedly threatened by new ideas about popular power and democracy.

If we set aside the explicit Freudian connotations that the plot
offers to analyze the "family story" of the screenwriter,[11] what is
important in the film as such is the way in which the Civil War is
used as pretext to constitute a defining metaphor of Spanish history in general terms, a history that is seen, from this perspective, as the story of a family in continuous disagreement. In this
story the ongoing quarrel between the two brothers can be kept
under control only by the mediation of the mother who holds in
her loving arms both the good and the rebel son.

The family anecdote with which the film begins is connected
to the topic of the Civil War by means of two series of dissolves
and collages while a voice in *off* speaks about the "communist
and atheistic storm" which "threatening the family would eventually upset the nation as a whole."[12] The first series of collage-
dissolves ends with the wedding of the main characters' sister

taken in a long shot inside the church. A lateral movement from right to left on the screen shows the mother, the bride and the bridegroom in a kind of mystical rapture and the best man (identified in the next sequence as a leftist Republican) bored and mentally absent. The camera jumps to a medium lateral shot of the brothers: José and the little one, dressed as soldiers, follow the events in the same kind of mystical rapture as the bride, the mother and the bridegroom. Pedro, the Republican, dressed in a tuxedo, fans himself nonchalantly with his top hat and shows the same gesture of boredom as the best man. When, a few shots later, the best man goes to Pedro and asks him if it is difficult to live in this kind of family, Pedro answers: "Not much; the brothers, one in Cádiz, the other serving in Africa or in the provinces, rarely happen to be in Madrid at the same time. As far as my mother is concerned, the problem disappears. You know already that mothers are a bit of a moderating power."[13]

The second series of collage-dissolves brings us to the beginning of the military rebellion. Coinciding with the blurred image of the mother receiving the extreme unction, the voice in *off* relates the family anecdote to the history of Spain.[14] The death of the mother, emblematizing here the wider and more general notion of Spain, is what symbolically originates, at the textual level, the Civil War.

All that follows, up to the final sequence of the arrival of the Francoist troops to Barcelona, after the Republican defeat, seems to speak — in a mystificatory but explicit way — of the topic of the Civil War. The final sequence, however, again displaces the meaning to a more general and emblematic level, with the use, in a technically brilliant way, of a procedure which, in poetic literary terms, has been defined as "disseminative-recollective.[15] Thus, the film mixes in collage: (a) the image of the sculpture of Don Quixote and Sancho in the Plaza de España in Madrid; (b) the image of the official portrait of Franco superimposed as transparency to the image of the troops entering Barcelona; (c) the image of José riding and leading his legionaries; (d) the image of Pedro — taken from below and with a kind of light reminiscent of the light in Murillo's Virgins — who is betraying the Republicans and regretting his "sordid and materialistic" (sic) sins; (e) the image of the father dying in the Cuban war; and (f) a series of other characters disseminated throughout the central part of the film: the doctor who helped José after he had been shot, the old indiano returning from Cuba to participate in the war alongside the rebels, the boy escaped from Madrid, the prior shot by the "milicianos," and the image of the younger brother dead on a beach near Barcelona.

The evident association that the collage establishes among all these facts is underlined by the voice in *off*, repeating the father's words to his son José at the beginning of the film[16] as the now adult José is riding in the winner's parade. The textual work by Sáenz de Heredia thus displaces the topic of the Civil War from its central position, transforming it into a metaphorical example of another more general and falsifying discourse about the history of Spain. History is presented in terms of a continuous struggle between good and evil, Abel and Cain. This perspective would indicate what has been defined as a "Crusade model." *Espíritu de una raza*, then, does not speak about the Civil War but about the system of values that could justify, in the forties, the construction of a fascist post-war Spain.[17]

What has been said up to now might seem to be somewhat obvious. In fact, since no one speaks in a void, it makes little sense to talk of documentary objectivity—it does not have even the slightest chance to exist. However, the examples that we have summarily analyzed above allow us to pose a problem which is not so obvious: the one that refers us back to discursive forms for the production of a referential image of the world. In other words, how to distinguish a correct inscription of history—in this case, the Spanish Civil War, but we could extend it to other cases—in a film without focusing on topics or on the political social significance of the filmmakers. In effect, if we accept as problematic the notion of the Sartrian compromise in the Arts, we will have to conclude that the one who speaks in a film is neither a person nor a topic but a structure, that is to say, an enunciative point of view, constructed through specific textual operations. Sáenz de Heredia, one of Buñuel's outstanding disciples and very knowledgeable about the techniques of Soviet montage, manipulates the meaning of the procedures as they were formalized in the original texts. He could do that because even though there are no innocent procedures, the meaning is not located in the procedures as such but in the concrete function they assume in relation to the global articulation of the filmic text in which they are inserted and operate.

The film shows, then, how much historical analysis depends on textual analysis. As someone wrote, history is made by people but written by masters. Dissolving the notion of documentary and of the fictional in a common discursive-narrative universe, History could be reconstructed, in both cases, not so much as transparent presence or absence, respectively, but as absent presence, that is, as *sense effect*.[18]

Notes

1. See Noël Burch, *El tragaluz del infinito*. Madrid: Cátedra, 1987. (Translated from the French by Francisco Llinás). The original French version is not yet available. [An English slightly different version has appeared lately as *Life to Those Shadows* (Berkeley: Univ. of California Press, 1990].

2. See Vicente Sánchez-Biosca, *Del otro lado, la metáfora. Modelos de representación en el cine de Weimar*. Valencia-Minneapolis: Hiperión, 1985; See also Jenaro Talens, *El ojo tachado*. Madrid: Cátedra, 1986 [English version as *The Branded Eye*. Trans. Giulia Colaizzi. Minneapolis: The Univ. of Minnesota Press, 1993, and Jesús González-Requena, *La metáfora del espejo. El cine de Douglas Sirk*. Valencia-Madrid: Hiperión, 1986.

3. New York: Oxford Univ. Press, 1974.

4. Pierre Bordieu, "Elements d'une théorie sociologique de la perception artistique," *Révue Internationale des sciences sociales*, vol. xx, pp. 640–664.

5. See Juan-Miguel Company-Ramón, *La realidad como sospecha*. Valencia-Minneapolis: Hiperión, 1986.

6. See Vicente Sánchez-Biosca, op. cit.

7. This is what happens with most of the films made in the Francoist zone during the period 1936–39, as *La canción de Aixa* or *Carmen de Triana*, both by Florián Rey, or *Suspiros de España* or *El barbero de Sevilla* by Benito Perojo. This kind of pseudo-populist films developed a model, already established before the beginning of the war with movies as *Morena Clara* (Florián Rey, 1935) or *La verbena de la paloma* (Benito Perojo, 1935). After the end of the war, and during the forties, this model would coexist with the more explicit "Crusade model." In effect a big part of the so-called evasive comedies of the period are incomprehensible if not related to the omnipresent absence of the war.

8. The film is also known under the title *L'Espoir*, curiously "humanized" and/or "individualized" in the English version, *Man's Hope*. Even though it is usually known as authored by Malraux, the film was actually co-authored by the Spanish screenplayer Max Aub whose ideological influence in the final results has to be thus recognized. See Juan-Miguel Company & Vicente Sánchez-Biosca's

interesting analysis of the film in *Guerra y franquismo en el cine*, Monographic issue of *Revista de Occidente*, no. 53, October, 1985.

9. After having finished this paper, I read an article written by Noel Bucker, Mary Dore, David Paskin and Sam Sills as a response to Robert Rosenstone's "History. Memory. Documentary: A Critique of *The Good Fight*" [Cineaste, XVBII, 2, pp. 18–21]. When they answer Rosenstone's attacks ["Following (t)his advice would be well worth the risk, he argues, 'of losing an audience conditioned by Hollywood esthetics, an audience which, in general, prefers nostalgia to history and emotion to thought' "] the authors explicitly accept to have worked for the American audience: "Of course, those conditioned by Hollywood esthetics, namely the American public, are exactly the audience we aimed for (...) At screenings around the country, non leftist viewers have expressed consternation with its portrayal of radicals. 'Are you saying' we are often asked, 'we were on the wrong side, and *communists* were on the right side?'. One film can never revise a person's political orientation, but if it challenges the honest mind, it just might break through America's collective amnesia."

10. "La historia que vais a presenciar no es un producto de la imaginación. Es historia pura, veraz y casi universal, que puede vivir cualquier pueblo que no se resigne a perecer en las catástrofes que el comunismo provoca."

11. This topic has been studied en several occasions by Román Gubern. See among others, his article in the monographic issue of *Revista de Occidente* quoted in footnote 7. Aside from the little interest that this aspect has in relation to the subject we are dealing with here, there is another reason to leave it apart: this kind of approach usually allows to mix the screenplay by Franco and the film by Sáenz de Heredia. Doing so, it is possible to forget the explicit productivity of the work of filmmaking. In fact the big work in terms of ideological manipulation belongs to the filmmaker, not to the screenplayer. It is his technique in narrating and in editing which gives a certain subliminal credibility to the extremely simple argumentations of the former.

12. The bucolic beginning of the film, after this mentioned intertitle, is closely the same that opens *Blockade* (1938). It is interesting to underline how the same mechanism of using one topic to speak, indirectly, of other kind of problems — see Tom Conley's presentation quoted at the end of this article — would inspire another film produced by the same apparently liberal producer of *Blockade*, Walter Wanger. This new movie, made at the time of the cold war, is *The Invasion of the Body Snatchers* (Don Siegel, 1955). In it, the science fiction plot is only a pretext to develop subliminally a discourse about the danger of the infiltration of communism in American society; just the some kind of reasoning that used to be the basis of the Senator McCarthy's argumentations. This is because the plot can be located in the past or in the future, but the filmic enunciation works always in the present tense.

13. "—En esta casa debe serle difícil la convivencia."

"—No crea que mucho; los hermanos, el uno en Cádiz, el otro destinado en Africa o en provincias, rara vez coincidimos en Madrid. Respecto a mi madre, el problema se anula. Ya sabe que las madres son un poco el poder moderador."

14. "En los años que siguieron, el vendaval político arrastraba irremisiblemente a la nación hacia el abismo comunista. Como si el reto de los dos her-

manos tuviese un signo profético y fatal, *así iba a dividirse la familia española.*" (My italics).

15. This terms was used by D. Alonso and C. Bousoño in *Seis calas en la expresión literaria española.* Madrid: Gredos, 1951.

16. "—Papá, ¿qué son los almogávares?"

"—Eras guerreros elegidos, los más representativos de la raza española; firmes en la pelea; ágiles y decididos en el maniobrar; su valor no tenía línites y daban muestras de él en todo momento."

"—¿Cómo no hay ahora almogávares?"

"—Cuando llega la ocasión, no faltan; sólo se perdió tan bonito nombre, pero almogávar será siempre el soldado elegido, el voluntario para las empresas arriesgadas y difíciles, las fuerzas de choque o asalto."

17. When this book was already finished, and in the process of copyediting, I had an opportunity to see a new and very different copy of Sáenz de Heredia's film. In mid December 1995, on the occasion of the 1st Congress of the Spanish Association of Film Historians (*Asociación española de historiadores de cine*), held at the Universidad Autónoma of Barcelona, a restored copy of *Raza* was shown. Such a copy, discovered only months before in Berlin, had a different title was (*Raza* instead of *Espíritu de una raza*), a totally different soundtrack, as well as a partially different story. While the new copy was dated on 1941—the year that film was officially shot and released—we went to discover that *Espíritu de una raza* was a 1951 re-editing of the original film, with no participation, neither of the director nor the actors, whose voices were dubbed. In *Raza* (1941, when Hitler's Germany and Stalin's USSR were still allies) the bad guys are called "antifascists," or "pro-americans," and priests and other members of the Catholic Church appear doing the fascist salute, with open hand down, and right arm erected. Ten years later, the political situation had changed. The cold war had already started, and consequently, to be "pro-american" was no longer a bad thing, and thus "anti-fascists" became "communists," a word never uttered in the 1941 version. All sequences regarding the old attitude against the US were cut, and the fascist cardinals and bishops dissolved into thin air, in the editing room. The new 1951 version substituted the original one in the archives, and that's all.

In line with the thesis that I am maintaining in this essay, it is obvious that neither the 1941 copy nor its 1951 remaking were dealing with the Spanish Civil War as such, but with its ideological justification, respectively, a) for Spanish audiences coming from the disasters of the war, as calculated self-assuring propaganda, or b) for the new generations to come, which would be educated since then in the idea of friendship towards the US.

18. See Hayden White, *Tropics of Discourse* (Johns Hopkins Univ. Press, 1978), especially the chapter "Historical Text as Literary Artifact" (1974), and the monograph by Jorge Lozano, *El discurso de la Historia.* Madrid: Alianza, 1987.

Works Cited

Alonso, D. and C. Bousoño. *Seis calas en la expresión literaria española.* Madrid: Gredos, 1951.

Bordieu, Pierre. "Elements d'une théorie sociologique de la perception artistique," Revue Internationale des sciences sociales, vol. xx: 640–64.

Bucker, Noel, Mary Dore, David Paskin and Sam Sills. Response to Robert Rosenstone's "History. Memory. Documentary: A Critique of *The Good Fight.*" *Cineaste* 17.2: 18–21.

Burch, Noël. *El tragaluz del infinito.* Madrid: Cátedra, 1987. (*Life to Those Shadows.* Trans. Ben Brewster. Berkeley: Univ. of California Press, 1990.)

Company-Ramón, Juan-Miguel. *La realidad como sospecha.* Valencia-Minneapolis: Hiperión, 1986.

Company-Ramón, Juan-Miguel, and Vicente Sánchez-Biosca, "Sierra de Teruel," in *Guerra y franquismo en el cine,* monographic issue of *Revista de Occidente* 53 (Oct. 1985): 7–19.

Conley, Tom. "*Blockade* sin embargo," in *The Spanish Civil War and the Visual Arts.* Ed. Kathleen M. Vernon (Ithaca: Cornell Studies in International Affairs, Western Societies Papers [no. 24], 1991): 25–36.

González-Requena, Jesús. *La metáfora del espejo. El cine de Douglas Sirk.* Valencia-Minneapolis: Hiperión, 1986.

Lozano, Jorge. *El discurso de la Historia.* Madrid: Alianza, 1987.

Sánchez-Biosca, Vicente. *Del otro lado, la metáfora. Modelos de representación en el cine de Weimar.* Valencia-Minneapolis: Hiperión, 1985.

Talens, Jenaro. *El ojo tachado.* Madrid: Cátedra, 1986.

White, Hayden. *The Tropics of Discourse.* Baltimore: Johns Hopkins Univ. Press, 1978.

◆ Chapter 3

The Brigadier's Crusade[1]:
Florián Rey's *Carmen, la de Triana*

Juan-Miguel Company-Ramón

(translated by Monica Allen and Gwendolyn Barnes-Karol)

Within the complex frame of the relationships between Franco's Civil War government in Burgos and the future Axis powers of World War II, Germany and Italy, it appears clearly demonstrable that German and Italian cinematographic studios provided Franco's rebel forces with an infrastructure for film production that they lacked for obvious reasons tied to the war. At the end of 1937, the Hispano-Film Produktion company was created at the initiative of Norberto Soliño, an ex-delegate of the Cuban branch of CIFESA, with the intention of opening up new markets in Latin America while the Spanish Civil War was being fought. This project was warmly received by the Germans through the figure of producer Wilhelm Ther, and, without major problems, became part of a powerful cinematographic industry that had been expanding since Hitler's rise to power.

Hispano-Film Produktion produced five films for the Spanish-speaking market between the years of 1938 and 1939: two of them, *Carmen, la de Triana* and *La Canción de Aixa*, directed by Florián Rey, and the remaining three, *El barbero de Sevilla, Suspiros de España,* and *Mariquilla Terremoto,* by Benito Perojo. Furthermore, we know that at the same time Rey's *Carmen, la de Triana* was being filmed, a German version entitled *Analusische Nachte* was produced. Directed by Herbert Maisch, it featured the actress Imperio Argentina in the role of Carmen, surrounded by German male leads. The two versions cost 780,000 marks. A sixth film, a documentary exalting fascism produced by Joaquín Reig, was co-produced by Hispano-Film and the Ministry of Propaganda of the Third Reich under the double title of *España heróica/Helden in Spanien*. CIFESA distributed it in Spain, along with Florián Rey's two films.

Up to this point, the facts provided by most serious historians and scholars of the period coincide. The documentation furnished by Ramón Sala and Rosa Alvarez in the annual *Cine español (1896–1983)* and by Félix Fanés in *El cas Cifesa: vint anys de cine espanyol (1932–1951)* is practically identical. Doubts begin to surface, however, when one tries to discern CIFESA's level of participation in these films. Fanés indicates that even if the links between CIFESA and Hispano-Film are not very clear, there are reasons to suspect that Casanova's company could have had a relationship with the Berlin-based Hispano-Film.

Leaving aside the question of possible links between both companies, we are able to trace in *Carmen, la de Triana* both the continuity and the possible metamorphosis of a specific populist cinematographic model that Florián Rey had introduced at CIFESA in his two earlier films: *Nobleza baturra* (1935) and *Morena clara* (1936). The questions that surface in analyzing could be condensed into one: to what extent does *Carmen, la de Triana*, a film produced in 1938, present itself as a possible transitional model between the populist, pre–Civil War current and the fossilized discourses that dominated Spanish film in the 1940s?

In terms of its plot, *Carmen, la de Triana* is a recreation of Mérimée's *Carmen* (1845): a folkloric-racial archetype that today is subject to new readings ranging from those of Jean-Luc Godard to those of Francesco Rossi and Antonio Gades. The liberties that Florián Rey takes with respect to Mérimée's text leaves unharmed one aspect of the original rarely respected: the point of view that guides the narration of the plot. Mérimée conceived the story to be that which José Navarro, in jail awaiting a death sentence, tells an erudite Frenchman, much like Mérimée himself, traveling in Spain. Piero Faggione, in his production of Bizet's opera, which opened at the 1977 Edinburgh Festival, organized the entire dramatic plot of the work around the image of José Navarro awaiting execution.

In Florián Rey's version, the brigadier José Navarro's arrival at the barracks of Seville's garrison is preceded by a conversation between officials, looking at a map of the region and discussing the military strategies needed in order to capture the smugglers operating in zone 44. Commander Ramírez Alberto Romano tells the recently arrived brigadier (and the spectator) about the problem: "The Andalusian smuggler, who is our greatest enemy, is bold and brave. We must be better at everything than he is" (El contrabandista andaluz, que es nuestro mayor enemigo, es audaz y valiente. Estamos obligados a superarle en todo). In order to do so, the commander continues, " . . . one must make a supreme effort to be austere in behavior" (. . . hay que hacer verdadero alarde de austeridad en las costumbres). Another official echoes these words with a sentence loaded with meaning: " . . . and [have] very little contact with the [towns]people" (. . . y muy poco trato con la gente del pueblo).

In the film, the conflict that develops is clearly enunciated by the institution of the military: there is a war between the military and smugglers, and the smugglers, in the view of the military, become one with the popular classes. This is a war that will cause a split within the brigadier José Navarro, opening in him a conflict between his desire and his responsibility to obey orders. How, then, does the film characterize the popular classes? Led by the hand of Carmen (portrayed splendidly by Imperio Argentina), we begin by witnessing a curious scene: Carmen succeeds in getting through the iron gate of the barracks to visit the bullfighter Antonio Vargas Heredia in the prison cell. Visually, the spectator moves from the iron gate that isolates and separates the military garrison from the city of Seville (through a magnificent parallel tracking shot), to other gates that enclose the garrison's prisoners. The first song of the film, "Puerto de Santa María," is begun by a convict in his cell and continued by Carmen. Carmen is recognized and urged on as an emblematic, popular character by a town that is imprisoned and, moreover, repressed in its fervor by the official on duty. In the view of a colleague of mine, this scene, integrated — let's not forget it — into one of the first official films of the new Franco Spain, would have been violently suppressed, or at the very least its director admonished, had the film been produced in Spain after the victory of Franco's rebel forces.

We see a second instance of the film's characterization of the popular classes, when Carmen performs "Los piconeros" in a tavern in Triana, in which the popular masses that attend the show are displayed by the camera as being a part of the show itself. Only José Navarro's appearance at the tavern will provoke a significant displacement (through a parallel tracking shot from right to left, from the stage to his table), thus privileging his point of view and making it dominate the entire sequence. If, on one hand, the brigadier seems to have ignored the recommendation of his superiors not to associate with the townspeople, on the other hand, this enunciative frame, created by the movement of the camera, redirects his gaze (identifiable with that of the spectator) toward Carmen's suggestive dance. The interplay of the tracking shots from Navarro to Carmen (after which the camera pans the scene) during the song in which Carmen explains to the brigadier who Antonio Vargas Heredia is establishes a relationship between the two characters. This relationship is in direct contrast to the anonymous and mercenary presence of a Gypsy woman, whose explicit flirting with José Navarro is rejected, even visually, because of her obscenity and crudeness.

Even before the complex scenes in the *barrio* (neighborhood) of Triana in which José Navarro will be seduced by Carmen, the filmmaker places in Carmen's mouth the only word taken literally from Mérimée's narration: "I am a Gypsy, and I must die a Gypsy... and the man who loves me, must love me in my land" (Soy gitana y gitana tengo que morir... y el hombre que a mí me quiera, me ha de querer en mi terreno). Mérimée included this statement in such a way that emphasizes Carmen's fundamental freedom. From the moment of Carmen's arrest to the kiss of love that begins her passionate relationship with the brigadier, Florián Rey characterizes enunciatively the protagonist's assertion. What emerges here again is the basic theme of the first part of the film: the notion of a split within José Navarro. Let's analyze it in detail.

1. José Navarro notifies Carmen that he must arrest her. The close-up of both characters appears reinserted into a

mirror and from this virtual, reflecting image, the brigadier says, almost as if it were an excuse: "Understand Carmen, I wear a uniform, and although it wounds me deeply, I have no other choice but to fulfill my duty" (Compréndelo Carmen, llevo uniforme y aunque me llegue al alma, no tengo más remedio que cumplir con mi deber).

2. In the trip to Carmen's house, the filmmaker, assisted by Reimar Kuntze, the director of photography, creates a backdrop for the song "Triana" through the play of moonbeams reflecting on the river. In Carmen's bedroom, these reflections combine with her own reflection on the window pane. The kiss of the two lovers takes place at the same moment that the sound of the retreat is heard from the barracks.

We find that the mirror has a double function. In the arrest scene, the mirror has the role of reaffirming the uniformed brigadier's narcissistic image, his appearance of rectitude, and his integration into the military. At Carmen's house, the window pane is, from Navarro's point of view, the mirror of Carmen's femininity. Torn between the necessity of duty and his own desire, the brigadier will yield to desire. This, of course, is an act of transgression of the established order. However, through the reflection in the window, Carmen is given a ghostly appearance, a deceitful mask of seductive tricks. Thus the filmmaker characterizes Carmen's statement, "I am a Gypsy," by conferring on it all the attributes of duplicity. The later development of dramatic moments in the film demonstrates to what extent Navarro's dubious excuse, "I wear a uniform," is converted into an absolute and dogmatic vindication of the military imaginary, transmuted psychotically into the "real-coativo propio" of fascist thinking.

The entire second part of the film, in contrast to the first, will be dominated by the idea of the restoration of unity and the resolution of contradictions. In the majestic opening scene, José Navarro is humiliated and deprived of his signs of identity, his brigadier's stripes, whose recovery will be the distinctive seal of his personal crusade. In this scene, for the only time in the film, the voice of History emerges. Through the voice of Commander

Ramírez and after invoking the figure of the king, the incident is situated chronologically and spatially: "in Seville, the twenty-fifth of July, 1835." This is History as enunciated, created, manufactured by military authority, which when José Navarro is kidnapped by the smugglers plays off of the brigadier's almost existential being condemned to freedom (*condena a la libertad*). Before a smiling Carmen, who reacts with, "Isn't it true that liberty is good? The best thing that God has ever made!" (¿Verdad que es buena la libertad? ¡Lo mejor que ha hecho Dios!), José Navarro only responds with a frightened gesture and a comment that is as fatalistic as it is devoid of more pleasant connotations: "Do with me what you will!" (¡Haz de mí lo que quieras!).

Florián Rey continues Mérimée's parameters when he defines Carmen as a free woman, a flame alive with desire that blows wherever it wishes. But the way the film characterizes this desire, this freedom has repressive connotations. Thus, Carmen will not be the cause of her own death upon confronting the brigadier's rigid thinking about order: on the contrary, she will destroy everyone she loves. Carmen's visit to the witch is evidence of the curse that weighs upon her, canceling her desire to be free—that is, to choose—and placing her at the mercy of a metaphysical concept: Destiny's punishment of bad behavior.

From this moment on, not only does the visual aspect of this film darken (for example, during the second performance of the song "Los Piconeros," Carmen dances with her own shadow projected upon the wall), but also Carmen's role as female protagonist is diminished. Wounded in a skirmish with the dragoons, José Navarro, on his deathbed, will hallucinate about the military from which he has been separated. The army is a feverish delirium, but also, like all nightmares, it is the return of what has been repressed via the unconscious. The voices of command, the regiment's flag waving in the wind, and the scene of his humiliation in the patio of the barracks, constitute a "plus de real." They are a displacement in the imaginary register through which José Navarro enters and from which he never escapes, the virtual space of the primary identifications characteristic of psychosis. Later, at the smuggler's caves, the brigadier asks Carmen for the jacket of his old uniform to calm his pain, and he embraces it with tenderness worthy of a better cause. Before such an extraordinary return of the authentic object (the cause of his desire) to her lover, Carmen has no other option but to separate herself from him as a fallen object.

The wound needs to be healed, the error be redeemed. José Navarro chooses the military, denouncing the smugglers' dealings to the dragoons and dying at their hands. Again, as at the beginning of the film, war is established as the authentic liberator of History. The fact that nothing seems to be lost in the narration's economy of meaning—the same Order that engendered it is reinstated at the end to close the film—allows for the brief amorous interlude between Carmen and Antonio Vargas to be summarily dismissed. Perhaps this is because this interlude is a popular idyll between subjects from the same environment, and it is assumed, unquestioned, by the bullfighter to be "a cursed love," (un querer de maldición); perhaps it is due to Carmen's unconvincing prayer (so foreign to her very essence!) before the image of Christ. These populist bits and pieces are never given full form in the general body of the film.

For Mérimée, Carmen's only tragic destiny is the one based on her continual reaffirmation of liberty and independence in contrast to the timid and wretched José Navarro, who represents a bourgeois code of behavior, characterized by pure vacuity and having no desire beyond that which is not exclusively or narrowly determined by possession. This is the reading that, for example, Francesco Rossi attempts in his film version of Bizet's opera and that is also a substantial part of Teresa Berganza and Piero Faggione's clever version presented at the 1977 Edinburgh Festival. Mérimée establishes some enunciative frames critically distancing José Navarro's point of view which structures the entire narration. We remember the last sentence in which José tries to explain away her murder: "Poor girl! The Gypsies are to blame for her death, for having educated her this way!" (¡Pobre niña! Los calés son culpables de su muerte por haberla educado así"). A few pages earlier, José, incapable of explaining certain peculiarities of the feminine character, speculates in a generic tone: "Women are made that way, especially Andalusian women" (. . . Las mujeres están hechas así, sobre todo las andaluzas).

At the beginning of this essay when I stated that Florián Rey shows the brigadier's point of view, I did not mean that the filmmaker would also assume that critical distance. José Navarro's displacement of Carmen, very evident throughout the second part of the film, appears in the film's last images, so as to close the discourse. Carmen, excluded from the military funeral in which José is reinstated with all honors and his stripes are returned posthumously, leans on the iron gate of the barracks, the same gate that she slipped through at the beginning of the film in order to visit Antonio Vargas, and whispers the brigadier's name. In this split image we are tempted to see a foreshadowing of what later will be the dominant cinematographic model in Spanish film in the 1940s: a popular archetype—the figure of Carmen— reduced to an empty subject, fallen and dispensible, adorned in sorrowful mourning, at the gate of the barracks, contemplating the military funeral as a passive spectator. Florián Rey's film, a transitional model, proposes a compromise between the populist, dynamic, and liberal current, clearly outlined in *Morena Clara,* and a discourse of military order that the "New Spain" of Franco's Burgos government will try to create after the defeat of the Re-publicans. The films of directors such as Edgar Neville or Luis Lucia are testimonies of the difficulties of continuing or at least maintaining this populist current during the Franco years. But this is another story, although not another scene.

Notes

1. Translators' note: "Crusade" was a term used by the Franco forces in the Spanish Civil War (1936–1939) to refer to the war itself. The term embodied the intersection of their military and religious ideology and harked back to the me-dieval crusades as well as to the Reconquest of Spain, symbolized by the figure of El Cid, who was closely linked to the city of Burgos, the seat of Franco's rebel government.

Works Cited

Fanés, Félix. *El cas Cifesa: vint anys de cine espanyol (1932–1951).* Valencia: Filmoteca de la Generalitat Valenciana, 1989.
Mérimée, Prosper. *Carmen.* Paris, 1845.
Sala, Ramón, and Rosa Alvarez. *Cine español.* Madrid: Editora Nacional, 1984.

Part II
The Long and Winding Road:
Spanish Cinema Under Franco

◆   Chapter 4

Vida en Sombras: The *Recusado's* Shadow in Spanish Postwar Cinema

Jesús González Requena

(translated by Violeta Richards)

The *Recusado's* Shadow in Spanish Postwar Cinema

Spanish Postwar Cinema

For some time, Spanish film from the 40's and 50's was called "franquista." Today, nevertheless, time has passed. Above all, a certain consolidation of parliamentary democracy has brought increased critical distance with respect to the regime of Franco. A calmer historiographical reflection allows us to recognize the impropriety of the categorical adjective franquista. *Franquismo* of the early days was above all an extensive and rather confusing counterrevolutionary front. As such, differing from German na-tional-socialism or Italian fascism, it constructed a historically de-fensive movement, clearly conservative (in the literal sense of the word), lacking both a future historical project and, for itself, a strongly consolidated ideological discourse.

It couldn't be any other way. The very survival of the regime depended on the conservation of a heteroclite front—which had to be realized in the Bonaparte style, constituting the dictator as supreme judge—and it made impossible the adoption of any of the discourses of its diverse factions. This is a long paradox: the franquista cultural politics never maintained a solid ideological discourse. It was, on the contrary, a politics of the lowest common denominator, one that gathered ideological commonplaces of the conjoined factions at a level of abstraction that almost emptied them of meaning; one that furthermore saw itself obliged more than once to reformulate its positions in light of surrounding transformations in the international sphere.

Thus, in the absence of a well-bound sustained ideology, confusedly reuniting abstractions such as "family," "fatherland," and "God," franquista cultural politics, far beyond what the preceding terms had accomplished, exercised censorship for the explicit good of prohibition. Thus, in the absence of a well-consolidated ideological body, through the negation of everything related to the defeated enemy, the regime's diverse factions could find more or less operative conditions.

In regard to cinematography, the franquista cultural politics established a protective system of national cinema; by means of censorship it legitimized—albeit in a peremptory way—a universe of discourse. Such were the limits in which the Spanish cinema of the period had to develop. Narrow limits, to be sure, but limits traced in a negative manner, which in no way imposed or dictated what should develop within their confines. Strictly speaking, there never existed a so-called franquista cinema. Thanks to this elision, with a greater degree of politeness, we are able to speak of "Spanish postwar cinema." The formula alludes thus to an obvious historical context: that which makes a division between the conflagration of the civil war and the consequently profound transformations that the social body begins to experience in the 1970s.

And yet, it is necessary to note that a temporal demarcation is being made. Though benefiting from a sufficient historical validation, the dividing line still remains exterior to what it inscribes or justifies in the field of film history. The question before us is this: to what degree is it possible, in light of the sum of Spanish films from the forties and fifties, to recognize some common characteristics, seen from the point of view of content, that mark a certain temporal division? If we were to name this period "Spanish postwar cinema," would it be by chance that the imprint of the war leaves the impression of a key date that can permit the organization and the delineation of sets of pertinent traits before and after Franco? Everything seems to dissuade us from responding to the question: the civil war is found almost completely absent from cinema under Franco; very few films chose it as a theme, and only a few more managed to mention it in passing. But in its absence (understood in the manner of radical negation), we can ask what was it that endowed Spanish cinema of this period with such a strange coherence?

Civil War

Let's begin with an affirmation which is banal only in appearance: *a civil war is a war launched between enemy brothers*. The obviousness implied by this statement will disappear as soon as we undo the humanitarian metaphor and take it at face value: a war between brothers, between children of the same generation who share the same mother tongue but do not recognize any paternal word. If this condition of things existed, if it could be recognized or articulated, the paternal word would already exist on the grounds of the discussion that it actualized.

But there is none of this: the impossible restoration of a symbolic reference leads, finally, to a confrontation in the imaginary: to war, in its most lethal form. We must be sure that our remarks are not distorted: we cannot pretend to cover the reality of class struggle with a psychological veil, the historical dimensions of a combat in which one town on the border of the revolution was destroyed. But if what we must now seek is to establish the textual imprint of the Spanish Civil War in the space of cinema and its cultural environment, we should ground any debate about the same possibility of symbolic inscription, of conversion, in our discussion of a phenomenon that was, we must recall, ultimately settled with bullets. Neither psychologism nor an excess of sociology impedes us from glimpsing some specific problems of the textual nature of this history. At the very least the latter entails lending an ear to the paradox that the expression "civil war" maintains: war that escapes the well-codified confines of the military, that takes root within the fabric of civil life itself, tearing it apart or brutally deracinating the population. War, we have said, in which the factions speak one same (many? the same?)

mother tongue(s). And one, above all, in which each family knows amongst its dead members from both Republican and Francoist sides (although, in either case, they are found in the only side of the dead).

Such is the question that we want to formulate: when something has lost all its force of symbolic inscription, when it has unfolded in the purely imaginary order (of unmediated identifications and projections and through which pass lethal designs), how could it be articulated in the filmic discourse of survivors? Such is the essential problem that I shall take up in this essay, a problem that well exceeds the limits of cinema.

Refusal?/Repression

What is most surprising is that in Spanish cinema from the forties and fifties — that is, in the production by the survivors of the civil war — that same war is almost completely absent; in the great majority of films it is never even named; in others vague allusions are made in bold ellipses (it happens in this way, for example, in *Malvaloca*, by Luis Marquina, or in *Huella de luz* and *El fantasma y doña Juanita*, both by Rafael Gil). But it does not suffice to recall this silence. Rather, its relevance must be measured, and so too its incidence in the textual fabric in which we note its presence.

There are silences that speak in voices made manifest in texts through multiple forms of indirect allusion, by means of displacement, metaphor, or allegory. There are others, though, that perforate or punctuate the text in a radically absent manner, leaving openings that extend their effects throughout the entire textual fabric. Two very different textual economies depend on this type of punctuation. The first responds to the exercise of a determined censorship — the police, a repressive mechanism that excludes what is prohibited but at the same time facilitates its constantly camouflaged return; what is silenced resurfaces, despite all else, through metaphor or other allusive forms that have a positive presence: the prohibited inscribes itself in the text with the force of that which succeeds in mocking structures of censorship and prohibition. Second, there is the function of neurosis: "What falls under the action of repression returns, since repression and the return of the repressed are not solely the law? and the reverse of the same thing. The repressed is simply there, and is expressed in a perfectly articulated manner in the symptoms and multitude of other phenomena" (Lacan 24).

Spanish cinema of the seventies until 1975 responds in a precise manner to the discursive economy of neurosis. The symptoms are seen in the new comedy of this period (in popular farce we see reflected the accelerated transformations the civil society undergoes, especially in the area of a new Spanish middle class that suddenly wants to be "European" but suffers intense pangs of inferiority) and in the "cult" cinema — then called "new Spanish cinema" — that challenged censorship and defined positions that became increasingly and more overtly critical. In comedy the criticism was glimpsed in the wink of the players; in cult films, in metaphoric allusion. Without being allegorical, these traits characterize the dominant lines of this period of Spanish cinema that, as we have already observed, is prolonged until the biographical death of Francoism. The "biological times" also have here their relevance: in the broad picture we can affirm that this period's cinema is produced for a generation that did not fight in the civil war.

But a second economy, one of psychosis, still exists; it deals with the performance of a radical absence in a text, of a tearing of its fabric that signals a place that is present neither in an allusive nor in a metaphoric way. It is something, therefore, that does not attain a positive form: the presence of a black hole or a radical void that, nevertheless, in its negativity, is traced through determined effects. Lacan, in his re-reading of Freud, has recognized the mechanism of psychosis: "Freud admits a term of exclusion for which the term *Verwerfung* [in Spanish, *recusación*; in English, repudiation or foreclosure] seems valid, and that distinguishes itself from *Verneinung* [in Spanish, *represión*; in English, negation][1] which is produced in an ulterior stage. It can occur that the subject refuses the access, to her/his symbolic world, of something that is nevertheless experienced, and on this occasion is neither more nor less than the threat of castration. All continuation of the subject's development shows that it wants to know nothing about it, as Freud states textually, *in the sense of the repressed*" (Lacan 24).

This is the difference between *Verwerfung* and *Verneinung*, between *recusación* and *represión*: In the second there is denial of something that has previously acceded to the subject's symbolic world; in the first, on the other hand, such access has not taken place, thus producing a void in the symbolic whose effects, notwithstanding, could be verified in the chain of signifiers.

It is now time to make the principal argument of this essay: the absence of the civil war in postwar Spanish cinema cannot be understood in terms of repression. If censorship could explain a hypothetical muffling of the dominated groups of the Spanish population, this argument would in no case serve to explain the silence in the discourse that is being muted. We know, even, that franquismo tried to produce a martial cinema and that it was an unmitigated failure. It couldn't be any other way: the traumatic rupture that the civil war supposed remained latent in the imaginary. Thus, postwar spectators could not accede to its discursivization, its inscription in the symbolic universe.

Raza

We first spoke of exceptions. *Raza* is for this purpose the best example. In *Raza* the budding franquista state was overturned in the effort to speak about its origins. War origins, without doubt... And nevertheless it is precisely at this point where, in spite of everything, *recusación* imposes its play of absences in a determinate manner: in *Raza*, the Crusade's apology, the nucleus of the martial scene will never be shown, the armies' confrontation will never appear, nor will the hand-to-hand combat that has to end in death.

Regarding this blind spot in which the repressed figure marks its impression, the film is organized in the style of paranoid discourse. On the one hand, there is the performance of a constant method of production which constitutes the enemy's figure; *Raza* finds itself, in this sense, in the same register of the discourses that, in the immediate postwar period, spoke in the name of the dictator himself—for the rest, as we know, the scriptwriter stuffed his scenario with constant allusions to international, Judeo-Masonic, and other conspiracies. On the other hand, there is the articulation of a delirium of grandeur made manifest in a sacrificial key: its heroes are not characterized by their martial prowess, they are never affirmed in the deployment of some always absent phallic attributes, but rather in their capacity for suffering, in their constant offer to be sacrificed. This is the way in which the protagonist's brothers' deaths are portrayed, the priest as well as the communist-but-repented brother. The visual metaphors that enshroud these deaths espouse an openly mystical vocation: for the first brother, ocean waves illuminated by the light of dawn; for the second, a diegetically unjustified crescendo of light that unleashes an apotheosis of victorious flags.

The light, in both instances — and in many others that would be tiresome to enumerate — inscribes, in an always excessively explicit manner, the theme of illumination, of the access to a certain sacred resplendence of the Truth. Through it we witness a delirium of grandeur that will obtain its greatest expression in the execution and in the hero's subsequent resurrection: an old body that will be seen regenerated by death to give birth to a new, completely spiritualized body, capable of assuming a Messianic task.

This sacrificial constant will be projected even in the remote origins, such as those in which the hero's father lived, with the same sacrificial passivity, without the least real combative gesture, the fleet's curse in the Cuban naval battle: thus the castration is discovered, in a well-defined way, as the return of that refusal of the real which, as Jacques Lacan would say, characterizes psychosis. The film's rigidity is hardly surprising; it especially affects the staging and is notably concretized in the awkwardness of the actors' movements, but much less so in its dialogue. Everything is intended to serve those completely delirious moments in which the (impotent) bodies are sacrificed on the altar of history.

Balarrasa

No less exemplary for this purpose is *Balarrasa* by Nieves Conde. It tells the story of a valiant Legion captain who is tormented by a companion's death for which he feels pangs of guilt (occluded because he was substituting for his friend in a night guard that they had wagered in a card game). After the war ends, he enters a seminary, and while preparing to become a priest, he takes advantage of a vacation to redeem his corrupted family, a dissipated example of the high madrilenian bourgeoisie.

Also on this occasion, as we have seen in *Raza*, the martial confrontations are not all that is clearly excluded: even the enemy is perpetually kept from view. Thus, the bullet that kills Balarrasa's friend comes from a black space *off*, a kind of dark warning in front of which the hero will have to feel a sensation of interpellation.

The film devotes itself, at a ritualistic and ponderously slow pace, to the exchanging of the military uniform for the priest's cassock, of the regimental pistol for the crucifix. The guilt leads, then, back to sacrifice. We see all the characteristics of a castration ceremony. Captain Balarrasa renounces all emblems of masculinity with which the film had endowed him in its beginning (the uniform, the gun, but also drinking, swaggering gestures, his rank as sky champion, and, of course, his fiancée), in order to accede to definitive purification.

The regime's ultraconservative Catholicism is presented to us here as something more than a mere ideological screen or a comfortable commonplace of the ideologies arising from the different factions of the dominant power. In fact, as these films show us, it occupies a necessary place that defends the repudiated figure's dynamism. This can explain the intimate relationship between the period's military films and those of strictly religious stamp (such as *Misión blanca* by Juan de Orduña, *La guerra de Dios* by Rafael Gil, or *Molokai* by Luis Lucía), a relation to which certain films that situate themselves between some and others, without a solution of continuity (*Cielo negro* by Manuel Mur Oti, for example) are perfect testimonies.

Action Cinema/Melodrama

In light of these considerations, a general reconsideration of postwar Spanish cinema can be undertaken. Obviously, this is a task that exceeds the scope of this essay and would require the collaboration of many specialists. Yet, in the manner of a general hypothesis, we can sketch the broader outlines of the project. We can state, on one hand, that the absent *recusado* (the martial confrontations between which they fought in the civil war) tends to extend its presence over all of the period's cinema, thus making impossible the inner consolidation of those cinematographic genres that pivot around a phallic hero summoned to test his attributes in hand-to-hand combat. Thus, and differing not only from Hollywood but also from other traditions closer to Spain, such as French and Italian film, the absence of strictly war movies, cops-and-robbers, and adventure cinema is striking. In other words, the ensemble of genres that constitute what has been called "action cinema" is not evident.

Systematically, when the principal themes of these genres are reviewed, the forceful presence of the *recusado* leads to a slippage through which the sacrificial (and self-punitive, self-castrating) gesture occupies the place of the unnameable, the unrepresentable. This can be observed in an exceptional way in one of the most significant genres of the period: historical cinema. As Félix Fanés has indicated, the Spanish variant of this genre is populated almost exclusively by female characters. The mere enumeration of their titles is, in this respect, surprising: *Eugenia de Montijo, Inés de Castro, Reina Santa, La princesa de los Ursinos, Locura de Amor, Agustina de Aragón, Catalina de Inglaterra, Alba de América, Amaya, Jeromín* . . . If we remember that *Jeromín* has a child as its protagonist and that *Alba de América* presents a Columbus who is more of a mystic than a fighter, we cannot fail to note that wherever the spirit of the fatherland is glorified, something is opposed to the emergence of a virile hero. Ad hoc characters such as the Cid or Fernán González would have to wait for Hollywood to accede to filmic representation.

Slippage in the direction of the sacrificial, predominance of the feminine (which is extended to the folkloric atmosphere in its diverse manifestations: musical, drama, or comedy) leads, in a logical manner, to the almost absolute kingdom of melodrama. In a certain sense, melodrama can be understood as opposed to action narratives. If the latter is sustained by the virile gesture, by the test of the hero's power and audacity, the former is based on the lack, the loss, the suffering generated by the absence of the beloved. Hence it becomes a suitable field for the staging of guilt and its pacifying correlatives, self-renouncement and sacrifice.

A history of Spanish postwar melodrama is yet to be written. Its difficulty, which has led a studious few to undervalue its quantitative and qualitative dimensions, resides in its astonishing expansion, which leads it to penetrate, in an imperialist manner, all other genres. It happens thus in comedy, whose almost unsupportable softening (exception made from an absurd and banal tradition that sooner or later will have to be treated properly) and insanity do not respond so much to censorship as to the constant infiltration of the thematics of guilt—or its more immediate product, goodness. But we could say the same about many other genres, such as the musical (which is always folkloric), the historical, the religious, the martial, the so-called Levite cinema—cinematographic adaptations of nineteenth-century novels—and last but not least, the taurine cinema.

Next to these two great characteristics, apart from this complement, consistent in the impossibility of action cinema and hypertrophy of melodramatic films, we should still point out a last important characteristic of this period's Spanish cinema: the impossibility of including any historical discourse about the present. That is, the films based on historical topics are obliged to find their unexceedable limit in some, always diffuse, moment of the preceding twenty years. This impossibility of reaching the present exceeds its most significant evidence in the incapacity that franquismo suffers in staging its own history, that of its insurrection and of its national resurrection—exception made, of course, for the brief, delirious outbreaks such as *Raza* or *Caudillo, ese hombre*. It could not be otherwise, because in this story's origin we discover nothing other than the core of the *recusado*.

Vida en sombras

Vida en sombras (Lorenzo Llobet Gracia, 1948) is, for many reasons, an insolent film. It radically breaks away from the context in which it was produced. The motive of the crushing failure was surely not other than what made its premiere suffer in its delay, five years after its realization. It has only begun to be repaired after its recent rediscovery by the Filmoteca Española (that owes much to the arduous reconstruction work of the film carried out by Ferrán Alberich) and in its recent televised rerun on "Noches del cine español."

Insolent, in the first place, because, at a time when the regime had already renounced its vain project of making a cinema of the Crusades, it dares to speak about the civil war. In the second place—and this, of course, is much more surprising—because it portrays, in an implicit manner which is no less symptomatic, the story from the side of the defeated. And in the third place — perhaps this is the least noticeable difference for the unadvised spectator, but, in all, the most surprising for the cinematographic historian — because it proposes, when classical Hollywood cinema is still at the apogee of its glory and splendor, an exciting reflection about cinema both as the site of the producer's desire and that of the spectator. The film proposes a dramatic voyage through its imaginary dimension.

And nevertheless, in its radical eccentricity, *Vida en sombras*, whose title is already an admirable metaphor for the historical context in which it is born, is at the same time a reflection about cinema that at once puts forward and constitutes an exemplary place where the following hypothesis — that the *recusado*'s shadow is cast over postwar cinema — can be examined. What happens when the *recusado*, the civil war, the hand-to-hand combat between brothers, when all these elements strive, despite their absence, to be made present in the discourse?

We will thus try to respond to this question, knowing full well that the analysis that leads to it inflects our own discourse and that this inflection will make it incapable of giving a sufficient account of a film that, in our opinion, constitutes one of the most beautiful and dramatic masterworks that the cinema has known in its entire history.

And a last warning. It would be easy — and it will be necessary to engage the problem, at another time — to link what follows with the producer's stormy biography: combatant on the Republican side, active cinematographic critic, committed to a psychiatric hospital after his son's death, of which he fantasized himself a guilty party. But it is not our intention here to psychoanalyze the director; via textual analysis we will seek, instead, to read a filmic text and give an account of its discursive economy. If we appeal to certain psychoanalytic notions to do so, we are doing so for the purpose of studying discursive economy.

Impressions of Castration

At the antipodes of the paranoid discursivity of *Raza*, *Vida en sombras* constitutes nevertheless a discourse monitored by a psychotic economy at the very moment its discursive register is situated under the shadow cast by schizophrenia. Here the *recusado* is foreseen, by way of an evident void, in the center of the film. His impact is felt throughout the rest of the text, which in turn endows the figure with its thrilling, anguishing, and palpitating effects.

This nuclear void is constructed, newly, by the war, the object of an ellipsis inscribed at the center of the film. But a first difference should be noted: the two sequences prior to this ellipsis, through a notable displacement, inscribe in the text the most punctuated impressions of the *recusado*. In the first place something that, apparently, would call our interpretation into question: an armed confrontation, on the first day of the civil war, between Falangists and the workers in a street in Barcelona. And nevertheless here the war is presented to us as a war of "others." Individuals without names, simple extras, secondary figures, that will glide along another emergent track in the film, where combat is markedly theatrical. The outdoor street has been abolished by quite evident scenery—while the character, always exterior to the conflict, records street life with his cinematographic camera.

It is impossible, thus, not to note the terms of this opposition through which the war, as the *recusado*'s being itself, is projected in the form of a war of others: gun versus camera. This decisive opposition in the text thus signals, in a negative way, that which will be excluded by the ellipsis: we see a war of others in which the protagonist maintains a non-gun, that is, a camera; but then, during the war that we do not see, the character will try to maintain a gun—even though, in fact, no image will confirm the realization of this desire.

Further ahead, in the duration of a brief sequence in the producer's offices in which the character tries uselessly to speak on the phone with his wife—while her face accuses the persecutor who is firing a machine gun off-screen—returns home to find her cadaver. The war of others is found, then, at the site of her own death; the wife's cadaver is thus connected in a chain of signifiers that recognize in the castration the effect of meaning. Four links are evident:

1. The *recusada*'s war (projected in the war of others)
2. The cinematographic camera as a non-gun

3. The wife's death
4. The death of the child that she carries inside her

The last two links — but also, in a certain sense, the first — give a sense of the brilliant staging of this sequence. The camera shows us first the character in the shadow of the door, as he directs his gaze to an area *off* in which the cadaver is found, in order to abandon it right away, followed by a panoramic shot to the left that, combined with a tracking shot of approximation, arrests on a figurine of the Virgin of Montserrat (the wedding of the two protagonists took place in her monastery) that, only an instant later, will stand decapitated. Then a backward tracking shot combined with an accelerated ascent (a crane shot), will discover him in a tilt at the feet of the dresser on which the statuette is found, next to the woman's cadaver.

This enunciative gesture establishes as its objective a strong association between the decapitated statue of the virgin and the dead wife. We have here, therefore, a metaphor, but one of such density that it becomes the intersection of one of the strong points of the text's signification.

Ana (this is Carlos Durán's wife's name) is apparently presented as a metaphorized term for a metaphoric term for the Virgin. The common semantic elements, on which the metaphor is based, can be thus noted:

Ana = pregnant woman = Virgin
cadaver = death = decapitated body

But the meanings mobilized by the metaphor are not limited to these common sémic traits. Much to the contrary, we will be able to accede to its richness only if we consider the metaphoric effects of other sémic traits that we find in opposition. Thus, given that

Ana = Virgin

then:

Ana = (wife vs. Virgin) = Virgin
(pregnant = mother)

But this opposition that we just isolated in the interior of the metaphor (pregnant) wife vs. Virgin (and mother)

reminds us of another equivalent opposition that affects the paternal figure. Given that:

pregnant wife = presence of the male as father

and that

Virgin and mother = absence of the male as father

then

presence of the male vs. absence of the male as father.

And this is what we arrive at: the metaphorized term (Ana) is nourished not only by the meaning that it shares with the metaphoric term, but also with those that it finds in an anonymous position:

Ana, pregnant but virgin.

This statement's apparent absurdity will cease in the same instant that, discarding prevailing theories about the metaphor, we understand that a third term exists, exterior to the metaphoric statement (that only talks about Ana and the Virgin): the protagonist, Carlos Durán. All the pieces of the puzzle find their place when this third term leads us to the metaphor via the chain of signifiers of castration (noted above):

cadaver = death = (guilt) = decapitated body = castration = war of others = no-gun = no son = absence of the male as father.

Thus, finally, the impressions of the *recusado* emerge:

the civil war = castration = absence of the father

The Circle, the Mirror

And such is the power of the void being delimited in the film's center: the narrative, even when biographical, far from knowing any kind of progression, devours itself in a circular structure. It is not only because this film ends by returning to its beginning — that of ambiguous ciphered origins in the parents' wedding picture—that we discover how the last sequence will be, literally, the same one that we thought we had just seen end in a closed gyration that definitively introduces us to the anguish. But also, the film's overwhelming circularity is translated in its division into two halves. The pivotal point between the two is determined by the void that organizes the division. The axis is structured within the mirror.

Thus, the sequence in which the children go to the neighborhood theater will have its counterpart in Carlos Durán's return to the same theater, after the war, but this time without daring to go inside. At the entrance he will see, in the publicity photos, images from the love story during the first part of which he kissed Ana for the first time.

But this theater, where the kiss took place, will be the same one that he will accede to much later to contemplate *Rebecca,* another love story marked by its impossibility. Thus everything is split: the first childhood photographs will be found in an echo, in a similar mise en scène, including a very similar angularity, when he realizes the short film that he will prepare with Luis and Clara. In both parts of the film, a letter from the producer will arrive offering him a job. The girlfriend's picture that hangs happily on the wall will fall later in a necrophilic vision of a familiar movie in which Ana also will look toward the camera. The beach scene, where she confesses her pregnancy, will find its sinister reincarnation in the sequence in *Rebecca* in which Joan Fontaine, also on a beach, will decide to approach the abandoned house—the very house associated with Rebecca's death and another pregnancy that also had to conclude in death.

To prolong this relation would necessitate a minuscule structural analysis of the narrative that would offer us many surprises. But we do not have sufficient space for it now. We believe, in any case, to have brought sufficient data about this specular structure that denies the story all progress in order to constitute it as a circular discourse whose axis marks the *recusado*'s absent place.

Thus, two differences made manifest in the two halves of the film can be noted. On the one hand, the well-revealed absence in the second part of these historical marks that were constantly punctuating the narrative's first part. One of the *recusado*'s strong effects is the impossibility of all discursivization in the historical present. It cannot be surprising that, in this second part, the protagonist totally abandons the documentary in order to dedicate himself to directing fiction films.

On the other hand, nothing could be so consistent with the narrative's circular configuration. The story is abolished as history, but at the same time as biography: when the collective narrative becomes intimate, the status of the individual is problematic. Furthermore, therefore, from the dark ellipsis, Carlos Durán's biography is converted into a rapid regression toward an always doubtful origin.

A regression that, it must be admitted—and this is the other major difference that opposes the narrative's two parts—will be an *escorada* regression toward the sinister: Carlos Durán's dark pension room, inhabited by resistant ghosts, will occupy the pleasant, familiar house; *Rebecca*'s morbid beach—also clearly phantasmal—will substitute for the beach on the Costa Brava where the protagonist knew an ephemeral happiness. The end of the film is introduced by the reappearance of a calendar with the date July 19, which will remit us to the day of Ana's death and lead the character to her tomb, thus to mark definitively the presence of the sinister in the new film's beginning. In this penultimate sequence of the film, a disappearance of Carlos Durán takes place, which refers us, in the mirror, to his appearance—at his birth—in the second sequence of the film. Appearance, thus through the parents' wedding picture; disappearance, then, just before returning to that same wedding picture where the circle closes forever.

The Absence of the Father

None of this could, in any case, surprise us, because the sinister left impressions, even though less clear, in the film's first part. We should remember the content of many of the protagonist's filmed reports: skiing or race car accidents, floods, fires, including the first childhood film, even when interpreted by a child, that shows him hopeless, spilling his wine bottle in a state of intoxication.

More significant is the fact that all these traces of the sinister scattered in the film are attached to cinema—including the tragedy of *Romeo and Juliet*, present in Cukor's filmed version — and, more concretely, with Carlos Durán's camera. This is to say, with the camera that, as we already know, heads the chain of signifiers of castration. What can we say, then, about this camera that, as a fetishized object, the character carefully guards in the dresser on which the statuette of the Virgin rests? And later, in the film's second part, in another similar dresser on which the dead wife's portrait will be found — with which, a posteriori it insists on the metaphoric dimension, establishing a link between this object and the decapitated statuette? Fundamentally this: the camera deals with the father's heritage.

We see then how, again, all the signifiers that we already saw are organized around the metaphor of the Virgin and the dead wife. And the father, whose function we then noted as absent, reappears here as something other than father: far from being equal to what grants the phallus, he is presented as the figure who grants his negation, the condition of the no-gun where the character will remain trapped all his life.

This absence of the paternal function sends us back to the film's first two sequences: to the parents' enigmatic wedding picture — and that because of this it was shown to us inverted in the photographer's camera — that also will have to close the film; but, above all, to that admirable sequence in which the producer's birth is interwoven with the protagonist's own birth.

A little later, in the target shooting hut, the father practices his marksmanship. "My husband never hits the bullseye," exclaims his wife, as in passing. Nevertheless, this time, he hits the mark and receives as a prize a zoetrope. This is a curious prize that only ambiguously sanctions his marksmanship. We will better understand its sense if we remember that this precinematographic toy from the beginning of the century is no more than a popular version of the phenatiscope. *Phenakistikos* and *escopio*, that is, *escópico*, deceit, fiction of the gaze to which the character will always remain attached. It is not necessary to remember now the multiple occasions in which this toy appears throughout the film. It interests us more to note its circular form, which produces an illusion of movement that repeats itself indefinitely. The circularity — of the film, of the biography — is suggestive of the first paternal gift.

Thus there is something deceitful in this shot by the father. What wouldn't be decisive in itself if it weren't because in what follows, this father doesn't appear to render any role. In fact, all the staging, where the producer's magical and diabolical traits dominate the scenography, seems to indicate that Carlos Durán's enlightenment is the product of his mother's encounter with this beam of light from the projector, or with the Lumière brothers' unforgettable train entering the station at La Ciotat. It is, at least, what extracts the first breath of labor in a very beautiful close-up of the woman.

This birth's magical and at the same time diabolical side—that is, in all the senses of the word, an enlightenment—will be underlined by this fair magician that takes a baby from its top hat. Absence, then, of the paternal function that, at the same time that it multiplies the chain of signifiers of castration, certifies an essential deficit of symbolization that will make it impossible for the protagonist to escape the net of the imaginary—because it is what feeds his guilty passion for the cinema—and that will lead him at the film's end to return to the wife's tomb and to that already indecipherable image of the parents.

This is, then, what is at work in the whole film: the impossibility of breaking that circle traced over the *recusado*, the impossibility of escaping the mirror, the imaginary's dominion, the impotence, in sum, of acceding completely to the symbolic order. Perhaps from that the big roll of paper speaks to us, proceeding perhaps from an adjoining printing, but this white paper—like the documentary that the character films and that without a doubt will never be mounted, paper not written that Carlos Durán pushes and makes slide down the street through filming the cadavers of the street encounter. Absence, in sum, of a discourse that could introduce a certain order at the impasse of the imaginary.

The Kingdom of the Imaginary

The imaginary's kingdom: such is the lethal mark in which Carlos Durán's passion for the cinema is inscribed. It is now time to return to the sequence that constitutes one of the most brilliant stagings of such a kingdom known in the history of cinema. In his room, in the dark, illuminated only intermittently by the light

from an *off* where the theater that is showing *Rebecca* is found—
that same theater, let us remember, where he kissed Ana for the
first time, Carlos Durán alone and, in front of him, in a medium
shot that contains everything, the dresser—in whose closed
drawer we know the camera is found, the dead wife's portrait,
the zoescope, and above both, a mirror that reflects nothing.

He has arrived a few seconds ago, fled from the vision of that
other mirror called *Rebecca* in which he has seen himself intimately reflected. His hair acknowledges grey hairs identical to
those of Laurence Olivier; with the latter he has merged in a devouring shot/reverse shot that opposed his fascinated face to
the vision of the incarnated ghost in the film. And there is no
doubt that it is the ghost that returns: "Last night I dreamt that I
was returning to Manderley." Rebecca's ghost, which is none other
than that of the dead wife, of the non-existent son, of the absent
paternity, and of the impossible phallus. All is there, even though
in this game of mirrors that confronts *Vida en sombras* with *Rebecca,*
the point of view has been inverted: no longer Joan Fontaine's—
or Clara's, both confused with the dead wife, but, this time, Carlos Durán's—or, as it is given, Laurence Olivier's. The Joan Fontaine of *Rebecca* or the Clara of *Vida en sombras* incarnates the
woman-child, the companion for games—or the Ana from childhood, not the loved woman. She is designated by Rebecca's ghost
or by the dead wife and is only possible here as an inaccessible
and castrated woman.

Thus, the change in point of view that separates *Vida en sombras*
from *Rebecca* is not gratuitous. In the Hitchcock film the adoption of Joan Fontaine's point of view, at the same time that it permits a dosage of the narrative information on which the structure of the thriller rests, also makes possible sufficient distance
that separates the spectator of the persecution to which the ghost
subjugates Laurence Olivier. In *Vida en sombras,* on the other hand,
it is the experience of this persecution to which the spectator is
invited to accede: to accede, in sum, to delirium as emergence, in
the real, of the imaginary.

Thus, it is Rebecca's vision (that Carlos Durán has detained
there where it really ends, eliminating the residual comfort of deceitful explanations) which has been called the *recusado.* The immersion into the imaginary is then presented through that brief

flashback, proceeding from *Rebecca,* in which Fontaine and Olivier contemplate the familiar film that they shot during their honeymoon. But an added minimum is found: above the images from Hitchcock's film appears, intermittently, through lap-dissolves, the word "Rebecca," referring to the theater's illuminated sign whence Durán has fled: the signifier of the dead wife thus becomes engraved over the apparently jovial cadavers of the husbands.

The imaginary has been unchained: Durán turns on his projector and his shadow is cut off above the white screen. Necessarily, the screen that is marked by the character does not constitute a rescreening in the interior of the screen of *Vida en sombras.* Both screenings are merged, are mutually erased in order better to reveal the immersion in the imaginary. He then accedes to the hallucination, to the return of the *recusado* in the real: a foreshortened view of the character's face. In the center of the picture, invading the two screens, the image, in an extreme close-up, of Carlos Durán himself, manipulating a movie camera—the one with which he filmed those same images—that, finding himself logically in countershot, is now replaced, his place invaded by the already mentioned foreshortening of the character that gazes. And on the left, in the background, across Durán's large face, the dead wife. The subject, his specular image and through it, the ghost. No other element is necessary, since it would lack all sense of place. Time itself has been abolished in this absolute emergence of the unconscious. (Because of it, perhaps, the disappearance, with no justification of diegetic order, of intermittent light coming from the window that, against all anticipation, inscribes its sparkle only a few instances before the proceeding flashback of *Rebecca.*) If the camera and the projector have now been excluded from the picture it is because they already represent nothing, given that they are discovered by us as mere substitutes of the subject's gaze, subjugated to the register of the imaginary.

Such is this imaginary universe's pregnant implication, to which we accede through the shot's semi-subjective configuration, that subjugates us to the character's point of view; thus its delirious potency, when Ana's image leaves the picture for a minute ("Hey, hey, leave me but don't leave the picture," exclaim Carlos Durán's images in a paradoxical enunciation that admirably translates the syntax of the unconscious), the subject that looks in foreshortening by turning his head to the left, following the woman farther away, to the end of the screen, with his gaze. As we know, no spectator behaves like this, no one looks outside of a picture when a character leaves. It happens like this because the spectator knows and respects the law of framing—of segmentation—as the first operation in the symbolic that makes the filmic discourse possible. But here, in this moment, the symbolic laws aren't in force. Because of that, Carlos Durán's gaze that pursues the ghost outside of the screen proclaims that in the imaginary the *off* doesn't exist.

And from the deepest level of the unconscious, where the forms of the imaginary dwell, it is impossible to withdraw the gaze. Thus the subject's gesture in foreshortening marks the spot, from whose point of view, let us remember, we participate: separate his gaze from the screen—leaving his face in profile—and nevertheless he continues—we continue—seeing the ghost woman who asks, "What do you want me to tell you?"

It is not inappropriate to end here: the delirious metaphor has already been consolidated—he who doubts it should remember that sequence where Carlos Durán will smile at his dead wife's picture—where the subject will find his definitive, but precarious, equilibrium.

Notes

1. Translator's note: Included are English translations of the German terms, as found in Laplanche and Pontalis 1967: 13 and 112 respectively.

Works Cited

Lacan, Jacques. *Séminaires III (1955–56): Les psychoses*. Paris: Seuil, 1982.
Laplanche, Jean and Jean-Baptiste Pontalis. *Vocabulaire de la psychanalyse*. Paris: Presses Universitaires de la France, 1967.

◆ **Chapter 5**
Redundancy and Passion: Juan de Orduña at CIFESA

Francisco Llinás

(translated by Nicholas Spadaccini and Jenaro Talens)

The twelve films that Juan de Orduña directed for CIFESA Productions can be divided into two groups: the first comprises those
produced between 1942 and 1944: *A mí la legión, El frente de los
suspiros* (1942), *Deliciosamente tontos, La vida empieza a medianoche,
Rosas de otoño, Tuvo la culpa Adán* (1943), and *Ella, él y sus millones*
(1944). The second, those produced between 1948 and 1951: *Locura
de amor* (1948),*Pequeñeces, Agustina de Aragón* (1950); *La leona de
Castilla y Alba de América* (1951).[1] Between 1944 and 1948 Orduña
directed a half-dozen films outside of CIFESA, a break which can
be attributed to a sudden halt in production by the film company
during that four-year period.[2] While Orduña went on to work for
various producers, his more personal films were either produced
for Colonial AJE (*Misión blanca* [1945], *Serenata española* [1947] or for
his own studio (P.O.F.), for which he had already directed *Porque
te vi llorar* (1941). This latter had been distributed by CIFESA, just
like the second of the other films produced for P.O.F.— *Un drama
nuevo* (1946) and *La Lola se va a los puertos* (1947). Nonetheless all
of Orduña's other productions during the 1950s would be distributed by the CIFESA label. It may be assumed that some films
(the three from 1954: *Cañas y barro, Zalacaín el aventurero* and *El*

padre Pitillo) were also financed by CIFESA, following its policy of underground productions.[3]

The differences between the two stages of the Orduña-CIFESA collaboration cannot be reduced to a simple chronological problem. The films from the first group are all comedies — excepting the obviously mediocre melodrama *El frente de los suspiros* and *A mí la legión*, a curious mixture of musical comedy, film of intrigue, and patriotic-military exaltation that seems to be above all a crude outline for a certain fantasy in which the cineast will later indulge. In contrast with the films included in this group, his five later films belong to the genre of historic melodrama which, when seen as a whole, and in a somewhat reductionist fashion, has come to be the trademark of both Orduña and CIFESA. But the differences between them do not only affect the themes: the historical films, whether we like them or not, demonstrate a coherence, a homogeneity that is difficult to find in his earlier works. His comedies range between high comedy, sentimental comedy, slapstick and melodrama. When Orduña does not control the change of tone, he neglects technical aspects (breaks in editing and failed synchrony abound) and gets lost in tedious digressions. Above all, it seems that those films should constitute a stage of apprenticeship, and it is therefore not surprising that the last of the first series, *Ella, él y sus millones*, should appear as his most accomplished movie.

One of the basic problems posed by Orduña's comedies and which, to a great extent, mediates their possible impact, is rooted in issues that are external to the producer himself and which can be directly imputed to CIFESA's particular production policy, as well as to the Spanish cinema of the period: the lack of good leading actors, poorly structured scripts, and above all, a particularly unfortunate production design. In Orduña's contemporary films all actors dress alike, as if they had stepped out of a fashion magazine. On some cool, dull and lavish sets, actresses could exchange roles without the spectator noticing anything. The spectacular nature of the period (CIFESA's primary objective) seemed to be at odds with every possible attempt to endow the cinema with those elements that confer dramatic expressivity upon the action.

In the case of Orduña's films, the deficient production design is aggravated by the use of flat photography (generally by Goldberger) which washes the set with light, obliterating even the slightest hint of shadow, and showing a lack of interest for natural sources of illumination. But this is a question concerning the CIFESA look which results from CIFESA's imitation of the production policy of the large American studio. Thus, its production style is indebted to the most time-honored Hollywood traditions: lighting serves the stars rather than the narration. While at the end of the 1930s and the beginning of the 1940s, American cinema shows notable advances in the area of photography (one thinks of the works of Greg Toland, Arthur Miller, Nicholas Musuraca, and Stanley Cortez, among others) in films of independent producers (above all, Goldwyn) or of studios that were less focused on the great female stars (Fox, R.K.O.), in Spain CIFESA is committed to a traditional style. Even its best cameramen (José F. Aguayo, Alfredo Fraile, and the American Ted Pahle, to name a few) are anchored in a tradition that values faces rather than action.[4] For this very reason those directors of photography that were influenced by the new styles (Manuel Berenguer or Cecilio Paniagua) would not work for CIFESA.[5]

With a few exceptions, most leading men and women are inflexible, rigid and inexpressive: a good example would be Marta Santaolalla of *La vida empieza a medianoche,* with her monotonous voice and inexpressive gestures. Such rigidity is especially notable in a genre such as comedy, which requires a certain brilliance on the part of the actors. Moreover, within the tradition of Spanish film, the supporting actors are the ones who save the show and monopolize the best scenes. From Freire de Andrade, the eternal butler, to José Isbert, Guadalupe Muñoz Sampedro or Antonio Requelme, these supporting actors break the monotony of some fairly unimaginative scripts and give life to action that is generally dull and lackluster. When Orduña tries his hand at high comedy, disaster seems assured, while the quality of the film is automatically elevated when he allows himself to be dragged down to the domain of slapstick, and quits playing Lubitsch, who, already in 1943 was Orduña's favorite cineaste.[6]

Orduña is never successful in his quest for a certain sophistication because subtlety is not his strength, nor is he a cineast particularly given to constructing controlled mathematical action.

One might say that Orduña is a contemplative producer rather than a narrative one.[7]

It is obvious that Orduña knew Lubitsch well, even if he did not have a great appreciation for his brevity and indirectness. We can observe the significance given to the world of servants as indirect channels for their masters' actions (*Deliciosamente tontos, Ella, él y sus millones*) as well as the entire episode of the supplanted accusatory letter—which precipitates the definitive fall of the protagonist—in *Locura de amor* and which seems to be taken directly from a similar situation in Lubitsch's *Lady Windemere's Fan* (1925). Curiously, however, the most conspicuous and beneficial influence that is noticeable today is that of Howard Hawks, for the best moments of *Tuvo la culpa Adán*, with the seven isolated little dwarfs without Snow White, inevitably remind us of characters from *Ball of Fire* (1941).[8] In Orduña's movie there is also a jail sequence that seems to come directly from *His Girl Friday* (Howard Hawks, 1940). Something similar happens in *Ella, él y sus millones* (especially during its first half). As in Hawks's films certain dialogues quickly recited by secure actors stand out instead of fading into the background. Within the realm of the grotesque and the excessive, with some nearly always excellent performers, there are in *Ella, él y sus millones* outstanding scenes, as successful as the one in which a ruined nobleman (José Isbert) gives an absurd speech about Favila and the Bear—the characters of the founding myth of the origins of Christian Spain—to a secretary (María Isbert) who, while reading a novel, is periodically interrupted by all her family members entering to request money. Unfortunately, Orduña's comedies do not always follow this path.

In *Tuvo la culpa Adán*, the professional female thief who has attached herself to a man who has come from America on the same ship as she, leaves a train on a rainy night after grabbing the protagonist's suitcase which, coincidentally, is identical to her own. What is interesting is that upon abandoning the train she also abandons the movie: the story no longer accounts for her, even if the structure of the script seems to demand it. Earlier, however, in an energetic but barely convincing parallel montage, Orduña had followed her steps through La Coruña, with a meticulousness that foreshadowed a later character development. This sudden departure of a leading character reveals some significant aspects of Orduña's work: in the first place, his limited ability as scriptwriter accounts for the long and tedious explanatory scenes which are unnecessary to the central lines of development. If, for example, the lady thief had appeared directly in the same train car as the protagonist, and the audience had later discovered the truth (when the girl loses her memory and suffers an identity crisis after a regrettable accident), the spectator's interest in the story would undoubtedly have increased.

In the second place, the sequence is illustrative of the extent to which Orduña is a prisoner of melodrama. The unnecessary explanations in the earlier sequences lead to an elimination of suspense. From the point of view of an omnipresent god, the spectator always knows more than the characters, but his or her expectations are one-dimensional. And this absence of suspense, this always-knowing-what-is-going-to-happen, how the movie will end, in which situations are always predictable, constitutes one of the most peculiar characteristics of the genre. Only chance or fate can shatter these expectations. And chance is one of the trite mechanisms which Orduña abuses in the way that he arranges his stories. Except perhaps in *Ella, él y sus millones,* his characters never control the given situations; instead they end up being simple marionettes in the hands of a narrator who rescues them from awkward situations with casual appearances, unexpected developments or excessively detailed social gatherings in which a poorly ordered narrative clumsily brings together its characters.

The "historical" stories—*Locura, Alba de América, Agustina de Aragón*—are almost always based on flashback. The flashbacks are in all of them apparently unnecessary because they have no dramatic function: for example, in *Alba de América,* one of the Pinzón brothers relates the story of Columbus to some sailors who, tired of navigating in search of the Indies, are about to mutiny. The problem is that the sailors are presumably familiar with the Columbus story. Pinzón even relates some deeds of which they themselves are the protagonists. The flashback clearly emphasizes that the story is told to the spectators, who, in any case, know perfectly well that the story, that is, the official version of events, is being told to them. There is in this double redundancy an erasure of all suspense and a quest for complicity with the spectator. In *Agustina de Aragón* it is obvious that the flashback is being directed at the spectator. Here the protagonist arrives at the Palacio del Oriente, where he will be received and decorated by King Ferdinand VII. While he waits, the protagonist kills time by remembering the facts. While this is a rhetorical device of substantial tradition (in the best sense of the word), what is interesting here is not that Agustina tells herself her own story, but that she tells herself about moments and places in which she was not present, and of which she is therefore presumably unaware. This technique emphasizes the multiplicity of points of view that are present in Orduña's film, techniques which will be later analyzed in greater detail.

Some of these films, more thought-provoking than the comedies, explicitly insist on this complicity with the spectator. Although we might have known that the composer would marry the girl in *La vida empieza a medianoche*, or that Rafael Durán would end up falling in love with Josita Hernán in *Ella, él y sus millones*, a trace of suspense still lingered: there could always be a new and unpredictable accident that would modify the course of the story. But in *Alba de América*, no scriptwriter could possibly avoid Columbus's "discovery" of the Indies. Knowing that the spectator is familiar with the story that is being told, Orduña can take great liberties with the *pathos* that he so much enjoys. It gives way to a riotous theatrical incoherence that removes the cineast from the classical institutional American mode of representation.

As soon as the spectator knows what is going to happen, the facts are confirmed through cultural references which are external to the film and almost always portayed visually. It is no accident that the credits from *Locura de amor* are superimposed over the famous painting of Francisco Padilla, that those of *La leona de Castilla* pass over a Toledan landscape that directly refers to El Greco, or that one of Goya's famous pictures is produced on a *tableau vivant* in *Agustina de Aragón*. Or that before the credits of *Agustina de Aragón*, the protagonist appears amid smoke, backlit and firing a cannon. While in the classical model of the story there usually occurs, near the end, a recapitulation which gives way to the denouement, in each of these cases the initial image of the film announces the final moment. In contrast, the entire film is summarized at the beginning in such a way that interest will not be rooted in the story's future development, but in its intensity, indulged in by the producer's favorite type of character: the strong heroine, a tough and obstinate female, much in keeping with a certain gay culture in which most of Orduña's work can be inscribed. In some cases this amounts to pure and simple misogyny, as when a character from *Tuvo la culpa Adán* rhetorically asks himself: "What trouble do women cause in the world?"

In Orduña's films only God's point of view prevails. Both the hypothetical narrator (the director's double on the screen as narrator) and the hypothetical listener (the spectator's double as auditor) see everything from the best angle and possess a maximum of information. But Orduña, no friend of subtlety and so given to the obvious, goes even further and, opposing the classical (American) narrative code, explains the position of the spectator. There is a particularly exemplary sequence in *La leona de Castilla*.

María Pacheco, another tough heroine, receives the spokesman of the imperial army that laid siege to Toledo. It must be decided whether to maintain a suicidal defense or to surrender to evidence and lay down arms. The first scene shows a large room with a stage in the background, on which María Pacheco is found seated behind a table with other Toledan nobles. High above her is a great and ostentatiously displayed crucifix. When the ambassador enters Orduña makes the predictable countershot. Not, as might be expected, from María's point of view, but surprisingly, from the point of view of the crucifix. Throughout the entire sequence, the main character's point of view will be systematically obviated and assimilated, in clear and plain language, to God's point of view. And Orduña demonstrates that he is aware of this use of point of view at the end of the scene when Amparo Rivelles says, "With God as my witness." At this point the director abruptly returns to the crucifix's point of view, because Orduña's historical characters only respond to God and history. Even popular heroes like Agustina de Aragón are resurrected in a tyrannical conception of history: here the town functions in the name of its chief (Palafox) who, cinematically, defines it as "a legion of the deluded." In this case popular resistance is manipulated for the ideological needs of the moment: "And so Napoleon imposes his liberty on those of us who do not wish to understand it."

God and history are therefore identified with the spectator in such a way that the latter completely assumes the dominant ideology, not by way of a classical (American) model in which he or she might be obliged to identify with a particular positive character who fully embodies the dominant ideology, but by breaking in a certain way with the usual mode of representation, assuming the role of spectator, situated in the place of God, accepting, via a certain rhetoric at the center of the fiction, the creator who is staging the scene. In this sense Orduña's films, and especially the historical movies made for CIFESA, represent an unusual case in the history of film (and not only Spanish film), since what is today considered subversive within the traditional code is precisely what serves (in a non-Hollywood fashion) the interests of the dominant class. If Orduña was aware of this (and I believe that he was not), that degree of awareness is of little interest for further study.

Notes

1. This text, first read at a symposium on CIFESA that took place in Valencia in 1981, was published with some revisions in *Contracampo* 34 (Winter 1984). The study has been further revised and expanded for this publication.

2. See Félix Fanés, *El cas Cifesa* (Valencia, 1989). There is an abridged translation into Spanish (Valencia: Mostra de Cinema del Mediterrani, 1981).

3. After 1951 Juan de Orduña produces all of its movies (along with others).

4. See the comments of Aguayo and Fraile in Francisco Llinás, *Directores de fotografía del cine español* (Madrid, 1989).

5. Berenguer only worked on *Nada* (Edgar Neville, 1946), one of the most photographically notable films of the decade, for which CIFESA intervened as distributor. Some interesting photographic contributions (those of Emilio Foriscot in Iquino's films) may be seen in movies produced by CIFESA with Aureliano Campa in the role of an intermediary.

6. Interviewed by D. Fernández Barreira (*Primer Plano* 133, May 2, 1943), Orduña points to *Rebecca* (Alfred Hitchcock, 1940), *Angel* (Ernst Lubitsch, 1937), and *Bluebeard's Eighth Wife* (Ernst Lubitsch, 1938) as his three favorite films. When the interviewer requests that he name a director, Orduña answers: "The master, the master, Ernst Lubitsch!" This interview has been reprinted in pamphlet form by Filmoteca española, on the occasion of an Orduña retrospective in 1985. Years later, in an interview conducted by Antonio Castro in *El cine español en el banquillo* (Valencia: Fernando Torres editor, 1974) Lubitsch is the only American producer mentioned by Orduña.

7. It is important to note, however, that in Orduña's movies, as well as in most of the Spanish comedies of the time, the influence of Italian comedy of the late 1930s and early 1940s can be detected. Films such as Mario Camerini's *Il*

signor Max or those done during the early 1940s by Rafaello Matazzaro or Vittorio de Sicca, belong to a genre rooted in American comedy of the same period, but hint at substantial realistic detail. Since those films were produced at the height of the Second World War, they arrived to Franco's Spain more promptly than American movies. In a certain way, thus, the U.S. comedy genre's influence on Orduña, and on the Spanish films of the period, worked through the filter of Italian cinema.

8. When producing *Tuvo la culpa Adán*, *Ball of Fire* had still not been released in Spain (although *His Girl Friday* had been screened). However, the possibility that Orduña knew Hawks's film cannot be discounted. As shown in note 6, Orduña states that *Rebecca* (at a time when Hitchcock's film had not been released in Spain) was one of his favorite films.

Works Cited

Barreira, D. Fernández."Entrevista con Juan de Orduña." Primer Plano 133, May 2, 1943.

Fanés, Félix. *El cas Cifesa: vint anys de cinema espanyol (1932–1952)*. Valencia: Filmoteca de la Generalitat valenciana, 1989.

Llinás, Francisco."Entrevista con Juan de Orduña." Madrid, Filmoteca Española, 1985.

———. *Directores de fotografía del cine español*. Madrid: Filmoteca Española, 1989.

Chapter 6
Seeing beyond the Delicate:
Luis García Berlanga's *Novio a la vista*
Stacy N. Beckwith

As its title suggests, Spanish filmmaker Luis Garcia Berlanga's *Novio a la vista* (Suitor in Sight) (1953), turns, both as whimsical comedy and as serious social critique, on the dynamics of seeing and not seeing. The selectivity practiced by most every adult character in the film, while superficially amusing, admits into view only those elements of a circumscribed everyday that square with a dominant conservative imaginary. All that does not is automatically or forcibly screened from view, leaving only the actions, mimicries, and words of the children present to advocate a more inclusive praxis of perception. Indeed, were it not for them such commentary would be difficult to formulate, for in the few histories of Spanish cinema citing this particular work,[1] its function seems to be that of a musical tie, allowing a discussion of Berlanga's more reknown production, *Bienvenido Mister Marshall* (Welcome Mr. Marshall) (1953) to transit smoothly into an exploration of the equally celebrated *Calabuch* (1956).

What is more, the few lines of description accorded *Novio a la vista* cast the film as "delicate"; a treatment of "the difficulties encountered by adolescents as they seek to integrate themselves into the adult world."[2] Such trials may be experienced by characters "who serve as role models for the [Spanish] social situation of the moment,"[3] just as they may be played out in settings which do the same. In one paragraph, however, they are framed by an opening emphasis on "caricature,"[4] and although reference is made to Berlanga's deployment of sketches as a means of heading off the cultural censors instituted under then dictator Francisco Franco, there ensues little exploration of how or why this occurs. Instead, one moves on to a lengthy study of *Calabuch*, for example, still bathed in the lighthearted innocence that is *Novio a la vista*, when mentioned at all.

In the event, both picture and producer may appear under such chapter or section titles as "Francoist Spain: 1939–1975 ... Cinema as Witness,"[5] a heading from French film critic Emmanuel Larraz's general history of the industry in Spain. Unfortunately, the more deliberative tone set here hardly extends to Larraz's rapid overview of *Novio a la vista*. His ascription of entertaining, fast-paced content to the "difficulties of adolescents" at play in a generation gap connects slimly with the notion of witnessing, and brings to it an emphasis on the carefree. To other film analysts such as theorist Yvette Biro, however, "generation gap" as a phenomenon connotes a starker picture, and one that places the onus of action on the older parties involved. Indeed, "it is in this conflict," writes Biro, "that adults are pathetically compelled to formulate the worn-out lessons of their experience and superfluous wisdom of life and then to bequeath them, like a precious inheritance, to their children."[6]

Different here is not only the particular characterization of adult life experience and the direction of message transfer, but the underlying mode of witnessing, or seeing as well. According to Biro, "seeing, by its nature, is far more than passive reception; it is a creative, intellectual activity,"[7] and as such, entails

> the confrontation of perception and knowledge, but not only on the level of personal experience — collective knowledge also figures in the process. Perception is highly mobile and constantly fluctuating; there is always a different background or interpretive basis behind new and fresh impressions. Therefore we may claim that we do not know what we see, but rather the opposite is true: we see what we know.[8]

The claim is certainly true for the *mayores*, or grownups in *Novio a la vista*, who see only what they know in Berlanga's period setting (1917–18, an upper-middle-class city and resort in Spain, barely touched by the closing reverberations of World War I). Yet their patterns of perception, unfluctuating against a lateral shift in interpretive basis, from mid to early century, serve as more than mere decoys for State censors in 1953. The myopia espoused by Berlanga's adult characters constitutes a background in and of itself; a particular configuration of collective knowledge designed to arouse in the contemporary Spanish spectator, at least, a mode of viewing that is more creative and intellectual, more active than the walking blindness exhibited on screen. That the producer intended as much is underscored by Emmanuel Larraz himself, when he likens certain scenes surrounding an obsolete map of Europe and a dying, now defunct Austro-Hungarian Empire, to "winks"[9] at a 1950s audience from the cover of a not-so-distant yesteryear.

The moments to which Larraz refers involve a secondary school lad named Enrique, and his efforts, as the film opens and closes, to pass a panel examination in geography. Entering the classroom on the heels of a highly touted and successful colleague, the adolescent Prince of Spain, Enrique proceeds to bungle all descriptions of Hapsburg domains and their whereabouts. His charge over the summer is to study the requisite class text anew. When, during his retake, the student names and recites to perfection, however, all that comes down is the shrill exclamation of one of the elderly questioners:

> All wrong! Not one right! The kingdom of Serbia no longer exists, nor does the kingdom of Montenegro . . . nor the Austro-Hungarian Empire! There has been a war señor . . . Hurtado, Don Enrique. In fact, it's already over! — Or weren't you aware? What have you been doing all summer?

The irony, of course, is that all summer, Enrique's scrutiny of the out-of-date text has been supplemented by his study of adult social behavior, in an effort to free his friend/sweetheart Loli from the alchemic clutches of her mother and spinster aunt. Meanwhile, a panel of academics that in the spring seemed buried in a printed past, has apparently cast this aside by autumn—though the teen-ager's misfortune may only bear witness to a brief hiatus before the formulation of new geography books. Indeed, while these do not materialize with the close of the film, the conjecture remains a possibility as, according to *Cahiers du Cinema* contributor Pascal Bonitzer,

> the screen does not show us 'everything.' In other words... The cinematic image is haunted by what is not in it. Contrary to popular opinion, the filmic image is... characterized by absence [and] works (the story makes it work), ingrained with what is not there.[10]

Accordingly, Berlanga's screen may not show the deployment of new school books, but it does work with this as a potential. In supplement to Bonitzer's observation, however, the cinematic image in *Novio a la vista* is characterized not so much by absence alone, as by the space that absence creates for related projection. The latter is fostered by the story's cast of young protagonists; Enrique, Loli, and a sizeable group of extra companions—whether or not a *bandido de cafres*, or "herd of good-for-nothings," as the girl's mother would have it. Loli and her friends are in fact good for illuminating just how the producer's

> filmic scene 'plays' and works with what is not there, whether in its dynamics and its diachrony, on the level of the sequence and transition of shots, or in its architectonics and its synchrony, on the level of the frame.[11]

These dynamics, in turn, bolster the straightforward, plain talking adolescents who may appear to be at play, but are actually at work. Underwritten by the structure of the film, both in single and sequenced frames, Enrique, Loli, and their friends model the type of proactive seeing so atypical of their parents, and by extension, of the Spanish public in construct under Franco. Particularly effective is Berlanga's fragmentation of their discourse into episodes, "unfinished events," or scenes in which "a multitude of simultaneous stimuli keep[s] [a] series of images alive,"[12] from one shot to another and within disparate frames. More often than not, related sequences in the film are noncontiguous, separated by the camera's follow-up of youthful pranks and exchanges as these become parody through adult (mis)handling. Unawares, the grownups may also set the comic momentum on a new course, as different threads in the fabric of their cogitative closure come loose and avail themselves for the tweaking.

In this way, the process of generating both humor and commentary is unpremeditated on both sides, requiring little or no effort to initiate. The *mayores*, in effect, constitute a sitting duck for jibes coming from or via their offspring. They live only within the bounds of what is and has long been appropriate, while strayed perception, when not truncated, is interpreted to the specifications of an ideological window on the world around them. This, in turn, opens onto a panorama[13] held together through the congruency of passable elements and the inadmissibility of things unexpected. The waterfront, as a "public place,"[14] for example, cannot be appreciated as Biro understands it. Describing the film camera's interest in such locales, the critic writes that

> Restaurants, trains, post offices, and the beach are not simply scenes of certain events; they have acquired an additional quality: they are meeting places that hold out at least the promise that something extraordinary might happen.[15]

Her view is very much in tune with the teenage outlook, for the adolescents roam the beach communicating with one another through makeshift walkie-talkies and spy code names (X-13, X-27), in full expectation that just such a promise will be fulfilled. Their parents, meanwhile, live only for the ordinary, delineating and guarding it with showers of praise, in themselves extraordinary. Apt illustration is provided by the revving of tongues at the arrival of *los Villanueva*, exemplary family and vital component of the summer panorama at Lindamar. The clan could gain entry on the basis of surname alone — "villa" implies family, aristocracy and high living (beyond the dimensions of *casa* or *piso* [house/apartment]), while "nueva" points to success along the most desirable lines.

Indeed, the Villanueva presence is first detected through the lenses of a gentleman's binoculars and not through his eyes alone, as if to privilege modernity over the no-tech appeal of unaided seeing. Accordingly, as each family member alights on the hotel steps, he or she is caught in the double scope of Vicente's devices and thence relayed to the gazes of thronging admirers. Even those impossibly out of range add their clamor, as a beach event rooted in the status quo turns into a fanfare for more of the same. From the water come the shouts of disparate bathers: "They've grown more stout!" "No, they're much thinner!" and the volley continues until Vicente and his binoculars spot a true novelty. "There's one more!" "One more?" comes the echo. "He has a mustache—and he's very tall!" In the final analysis, however, the stranger counts for little. All speculations are checked as one woman cries, "*¿Qué importa? ¡Son los Villanueva!*" ("What does it matter? They are the Villanuevas!") The name, indeed, tells all.

It also absolves Vicente of any previous error in perception. In a sequence just prior to the commotion, he and his lenses are engaged in surveying the shore and reporting each find to a hawkish wife bent over knitting, but alert to the least incongruity. It will register on the cadence of her husband's voice: "*Una ola, otra ola, otra, otra, un niño con un cubo, otro niño con otro cubo...*" ("A wave, another wave, another, one more, a boy with a pail, another boy with another pail...") But what about this boy? "*Un niño con la mamá... la mamá... ¡la mamá!*" ("A boy with his mother... the mother... the mother!") Vicente has broken his litany and the swoon is picked up immediately. This time he is spared rebuke by detecting the Villanuevas—his last visual encounter with the "loose" single woman in revealing leggings and costume ended in: "Vicente! What nerve! I've told you a thousand times to tell me what you see, or I'll hide those twin lenses from you!"

The wife's knitting party has already dubbed the *soltera*[16] Russian, Catalonian, communist, or worse (divorced), and has dropped her from its needles along with other undesired stitches that point *al reves*, or backwards, instead of *a la derecha*, or to the right. It cancels even repeat anomalies seen through the binoculars, striking them from the record of a dutiful husband's shore survey. Only the obvious arouses excitement. As a ship moves across the horizon a cry goes up: "*¡Un barco! ¡Un barco! ¡Ay, un barco!*" ("A ship! It's a boat! Oh my, a ship!") Then there is quiet as a different onlooker, this time, squints through the binoculars and solemnly reads, "L-O-N—LON—DON...it must be British." Chatter resumes and the boat passes on, innocuous as the words on its side, but also a vehicle for tales spun by Loli the sequence before.

Indeed, the ship appears to move with the camera, crossing from one ideological frame into another. It seems an embodiment of Bonitzer's remarks apropos scene, architectonics and diachrony, with an emphasis on absence and its haunting of each. The course of the steamer seems also to concretize one line of projection such absence can spawn. Loli first sees the boat, for example, as an extension of one she imagines in conversation with Enrique, while the two take time away from their peers during an outing off Lindamar. She also peoples the phantom vessel with her parents, whom the British ship will reach in the next sequence. Their absence on this stretch of beach sees them reconstituted as royalty, and Loli's future prospects changed into those of a princess. From here, further conjecture fans out in strands, linking the seeing spectator to shots as the film opened, and to several ahead.

Loli might be related to the young Prince of Spain who so easily maneuvered the exam in geography, for example. Where the topography of his lineage included "Papa," her father now figures as a monarch as well, outstripping even Villanueva prestige in his rise from an everyday dentist. Unfortunately, his stature sinks along with the family ship as the girl's fantasy comes to a close, though not before she asks of Enrique, "Can't it be true?" His comeback is largely supplied by the real boat now appearing on the horizon. "Look! Another boat. Let's see if this one sinks with a queen on it too." The teen scoffs at Loli, but even in jest does not do away with her make-believe craft, as would his elders on instinct. Instead he confirms its existence as antecedent, referring to the new shape on the water as another boat, and connecting a possible queen with passengers verily felt to be on the first.

Where this sovereign becomes a figure of transition from one vessel to the next, however, there is not always a ship marking Berlanga's passage from one to another sequence in so clear a fashion. Still, images are sustained across disparate frames through the interweaving of absence and projection as viewed above, and as seen in a different case to do with the ocean. Three times throughout the movie, certain grown "ladies dressed in black and white," along with their mother, look out on a pair of hands waving frantically off shore: "Oh! Look! That person is waving to us! *¡Hola! ¡Hola!*" The women's oblivious greetings continue each time until a male voice suddenly interrupts: "But maybe he's ... what if ... someone is drowning!" In desperation at one point, the caller flings off his jacket and heads for the waves.

When the mother is finally made aware of a possible accident her only reaction is disdain for Lindamar: "Next year to San Sebastian!" She has no thought for a waterlogged victim, just as the loose "Communist" woman was quickly erased from Vicente's field of vision and reportage. Enrique, on the other hand, lets Loli's ship stand even imagined, causing these adults to appear not only short-sighted but perilously so, as the mother here might have presided over an actual fatality. She is clearly not prone to the adolescents' direct engagement with items they find or phenomena they discover in and around the sea; an involvement so uninhibited as to have physical repercussions for a head, a nose or a finger.

Leaving the hotel one evening, for instance, some of the youths gather on the rocks by the shore, and spot their friends through the fog, fishing for crabs. All but one, that is. A taller boy with glasses hesitates to reach into the water, though a companion urges him not to be a sissy, encouraging with "they're not going to bite you," and other such phrases. Yet the lad can hardly make out the crabs and fears dipping into the dark of the tide pool. When he does so at last he is the only one bitten, a consequence of some blindness despite the lenses over his eyes. By all accounts these should have enabled him not only to size up the crabs, but to locate the underwater hideout of each as well. Instead, both glasses and owner now relate inversely to a counterpart two-some not appearing in this scene.

The reference, naturally, is to Vicente, for in the adult sphere he looks through the impressive lenses to describe what he sees. Here, however, the youth gropes to directions from friends since his spectacles are useless. Taken again, Vicente's binoculars, mainly for show and not of critical importance, permit the man to see, while the teenager's glasses, truly a necessity, preclude just this. Finally, Vicente's perceptions are always held up to the familiar for acceptance, reinterpretation or rejection. What the adolescent encounters in the tide pool immediately bites back. There is no option to cancel, as with the swimmer waving or drowning, or the "Communist" woman threatening to unhinge social order.

Indeed, as if to portray the *mayores* as socialites with their heads in the sand, Berlanga uses the boy and his spectacles in another short sequence, this time during the outing in which Loli envisions her family ship.

The expedition is actually chaperoned by Enrique's father, who leads the teenagers in various activities and models a dive as many swim near the picnic site. *"Flexión, inspiración, y ¡al agua!"* ("Flex, inhale and into the water!") barks the middle-aged man, inspiring many, but not the tall lad in glasses who hangs back again. Finally, however, this one looks round, positions himself, and then hands his lenses to a cohort near by. *"A la de una . . . a la de dos . . . a la de"* ("And a one . . . and a two . . . and a")—by *tres* he has received a push from behind and dives headfirst, not into the sea, but into the sand. The camera catches him momentarily, legs on top, frantically treading water where there is none, and head submerged where his feet should have landed. Amazingly, the youth is righted, with nothing but a sore nose. He does stumble for a while, dizzy, perhaps, from now having bodily enacted his upside-down relation to Vicente and his binoculars.

Indeed, in terms of sustaining comparison, the adolescent's feat is capped only by another teen's handling of the lenses themselves, when they fall into young hands toward the end of the film. As a means of salvaging Loli from early conversion into a woman full fledged, her friends abscond with her to the ruins of a castle far up the shore, having already declared "war on the grownups." To prepare and provoke, they avail themselves by night of adult clothing, gadgets, and other accoutrements, including the pair of far-seeing lenses, by now generally associated with Vicente. On the morrow, their parents are roused by a piercing reveille, then obliged to assemble in the hotel lobby, defrocked, as it were. All they discover is a note from the escapees rotating above their heads on a ceiling fan. The effect is to suggest that the page contains a message revolving around a clear set of conditions, as indeed it does. It also galvanizes the recipients to organize into battalions, while one woman, in a panic, suggests running to the Guardia Civil for help. Indeed, the whole company appears juvenile as the film's soundtrack breaks into an instrumental rendition of a popular children's song:

Mambru se fué a la guerra/ Qué dolor, qué dolor, qué peña/ Mambru se fue a la guerra/ No sé cuándo vendrá/ Do re mi, do re fa/ No sé cuándo vendrá . . . (Mambru has gone off to war/ What sorrow, what sorrow, what pain/ Mambru has gone off to war/ I know not when he'll come back/ Do re me, do re fa/ Don't know when he'll be back . . .)

Through mature and coordinated effort, however, the real youths are by now well entrenched in the castle embankments, prepared to deflect attack with pine cones and flares. As the parents approach, Enrique and one troop of friends line the uneven ramparts and take stock of the valley, just as Vicente and other adults survey the sea, in frame after frame. And though suddenly there is movement, one boy protests: "¡*Pero si están muy lejos todavía!*" ("But they're still far away!") Predictably, the binoculars are with him, though not properly held. "¡*Pero si los tienes al revés, tonto!*" ("Stupid, you have them on backwards!") shouts Enrique, righting them promptly. Once again, in this final play on the lenses, the generational poles are skewed in their association with one another. Where Vicente holds the lenses correctly and encounters images which are then cut off by his wife, this youth looks through them wrongly, to counter that which his peers can see for themselves.

Meanwhile, after this series of examples, Berlanga's spectator may see both the binoculars and the boy's eyeglasses as vehicles for parody and ideological contrast on a par with Loli's imaginary ship. The objects take on this role incrementally, as they weave in and out of one and another sequence, now present, now present though absent. What is more, not all of the filmmaker's props turn on the visual, which variety enhances both the subtlety and the potential for analysis projection that underlie his twists to generation gap dynamics, as noted above. Other accessories to critique include hearing devices, such as an ear trumpet found by a heavyset boy when the children first appear on the beach at Lindamar. In a hurry to flee his friends, the lad stuffs the pirate's map they are after into the device lying near the chair of one Señor Almoro.

This man forms part of a group of elders who, according to the women on hand, "have been calling themselves generals for two years already" by dint of joint military service in Cuba.[17] From time to time Almoro attempts to join in their discussion, but finds this impossible with a hearing aid now blocked. After a brief glimpse at his efforts to unplug it, the device falls out of sight until the teenager's raid on their parents' hotel rooms toward the end of the film. As the looters settle in to the castle ruins, one of the girls brings out the hearing aid and attempts to blow through it. Putting it to her ear brings only frustration: *"Nada. No oigo nada."* ("Nothing. I can't hear a thing.") Her efforts must have dislodged the old plan somewhat, however, for when Señor Almoro defects to the castle once the "war" is underway, Enrique hands him the trumpet. All of a sudden he hears perfectly—and perhaps, because the paper is never seen to fall out, one might conclude that the gadget has become an extension of the children's own unblocked ears.

Further, when Almoro rejoins the "generals'" declaiming sessions after helping the youths to win their campaign, he brings them with him into the circle, via the synecdochal properties of the trumpet. When looked to for input, as befits a commander who has in fact won a battle, the old man graces his audience with such tautologies as: *"Tal vez sí, tal vez no . . . estratégicamente hablando ya lo decía . . . un buen dispositivo de covertura es un buen dispositivo de covertura"* (Maybe, maybe not . . . strategically speaking, as I was saying, a good cover mechanism is a good mechanism for cover"). The interjection not only highlights his comerades' oratory efforts as empty and nonproductive, but Almoro, a veritable adult/adolescent hybrid at this point, also relates inversely to this set of *mayores.* The man's nonsensical contribution to the discussion is closely attended by the "generals," *sans* ear trumpets, while he designates their prattle as such through his selective use of the hearing device.

Their ruminating may as well be screened, for it is regularly endured by vacationers outside the circle of veterans who have not the wherewithal to shortcircuit it with the acuity of Almoro. One "general," in particular, is prone to unleashing his opinions on people engaged in all manner of unsuspicious activities. Inside the hotel social hall, for example, he marches in protest toward a man stringing miniature international flags from one beam to another. The ex-captain demands they come down, to which the gentleman replies, "*¡Pero si son de adorno, mire!*" ("But look! They're just for show!") His interrogator is incensed.

¿Cómo de adorno? ¿Conoce Ud. alguna bandera de adorno? Hay banderas de batalla ... banderas de señales, banderas de desfile ... pero de adorno nunca ... (What do you mean just for show? Do you know any flag that is only for decoration? There are flags of war ... signal flags, flags for parades ... but for decoration? Never.)

The outburst itself seems more for show than for substance, as even the man holding the flags sees no point to the filibuster. In circularity and emptiness, then, the latter recalls Señor Almoro's brief pronouncement on war-time cover, and relates through this to the type of hyper-statement on the ordinary witnessed earlier with the delayed arrival of the Villanueva clan. Certainly, comments on the family were more positive in tone, but as they continue to swirl around the new, unattached nephew, they too come up as ragged and torn as the scrap of material flying above the children's castle encampment during the "war." This time, Loli manages to puncture the aura *de adorno* that has grown up around the stranger, literally rendering it "see-through" with some innocent questions one evening.

The bachelor's reputation has been steadily elaborated by the girl's mother, her aunt, and their gossipping friends, whose praises for him feed on each other:

Es un Villanueva Villanueva/De los pies a la cabeza/Sobrino de Don Adolfo/Y además muy guapo e ingeniero/Está en la hidroeléctrica/Formalísimo y muy buen hijo/ ... El mejor partido de todo el verano. (He is Villanueva through and through/From head to toe/Don Adolfo's nephew/And very handsome besides, and an engineer/He works in hydroelectrics/Very tailored, and a fine son/ ... The best catch of the summer).

With this level of enthusiasm it is little wonder that Loli is swept up by her mother as soon as the girl returns from the teenagers' expedition. She is dressed as a young lady for the first time, and then seen dancing with the new Villanueva at the hotel ball, to admiring bleats from her relatives. She is uncomfortable dancing, however, and the pair leaves the floor for the balcony. As the girl peels off her new high-heeled shoes, she curses the blisters they have given her feet on this, the first night she is wearing them. "I've been made up and dressed like a grownup tonight," she explains. "You're not grownup?" asks the Villanueva, surprised. "No," confesses Loli, admitting that she is only fifteen.

At this point, the gentleman may either continue to believe, or move to reject Loli's image, as go the typical adult options. Instead, in an unprompted tit for tat, the girl proceeds to pierce through his guise, as constructed by her family and most every vacationer at Lindamar. "So you're an engineer. What do you make? Bridges?" she asks innocently. "Well, no," he answers, "I'm in an office." The duties of a clerk or a bureaucrat are a good deal less glamorous than the Francoist ideal of erecting bridges or putting up power lines.

After all is said and done there is nothing to this man's title, whereas nicknames in the adolescent sphere are visibly substantive. One of the only youths besides Enrique and Loli to have a name in the film is a sizeable teenager called *Gordo*, or "Fatso." He is the character to whom the boy with the glasses hands his spectacles before his fateful dive, and Gordo is also caught gorging himself on everyone's lunches during the outing. When Loli slips out of the hotel one morning, she finds her friends in tower formation, holding up one member of the gang so she can spy into an attraction booth named "Salón Edén." Down below, Gordo is restless. "*¡Dejadme subir! ¡Quiero subir!*" ("Let me go up! I want to go up!") Impossible. "*¡Pero no peso nada!*" ("But I don't weigh a thing!") he cries, to be categorically denied once again.

Gordo's plea is only rejected, however, because the lad is exactly what he looks — an overweight teenager who will most likely topple the tower. Unawares, he also stands in direct contrast to a host of epithets and descriptions in the adult sphere that do not often accord with a corresponding image, figure or phenomenon. With this Gordo also serves as one last vehicle for commentary in a film which at every turn invites the viewer to see beyond the "delicate" in its content to an underlying matrix of social critique, both inherent and potential. As supporting structure, this relies on an interweaving of absence and projection, set up by Berlanga but set in motion by the spectator. The filmmaker provides some indicators to facilitate what is fundamentally an individual process

of object and agent association, but not all are depicted as graphically as Loli's ship, the British boat, or Vicente's binoculars.

Still, because *Novio a la vista*'s adults provide so entrenched a
backdrop of conservative ideological practices, even gadgets with
more subtle entrances and exits, such as Almoro's ear trumpet,
may be detected eventually and joined with one or more strands
of developing critique. In much the same way Spain in the 1950s
can be experienced through Berlanga's turn-of-the-century over-
lay, by active seers who engage with his smoke screen *comme
temoignage.*

Notes

1. Emilio C. García Fernández, *Historia Ilustrada del Cine Español* (Madrid:
Planeta, 1985) 205. Also Emmanuel Larraz, *Le Cinema Espagnol des Origines a nos
Jours* (Paris: Editions du Cerf): 144–145.

2. Emmanuel Larraz, 144.

3. García Fernández, 205.

4. Ibid.

5. Emmanuel Larraz, 136.

6. Yvette Biro, *Profane Mythology: The Savage Mind of the Cinema* (Bloomington: Indiana Univ. Press, 1982): 72.

7. Yvette Biro, 39.

8. Ibid., 40.

9. Emmanuel Larraz, 144.

10. Pascal Bonitzer, "Off-screen Space," *Cahiers du Cinema 1969–1972. The Politics of Representation.* Trans. Lindley Hanlon. Ed. Nick Browne (n.p., Harvard Film
Studies, 1989): 293.

11. Pascal Bonitzer, 293.

12. Yvette Biro, 64.

13. Adapted from Louis Althusser, "Ideology and Ideological State Apparatuses. (Notes towards an Investigation)." *Lenin and Philosophy and Other Essays.*
Trans. Ben Brewster (New York Monthly Press, 1971): 127–186.

14. Yvette Biro, 70.

15. single woman

16. Berlanga, it seems, takes added aim at the Franco regime and its military
apparatus here, as Spain lost Cuba in 1898, and these "generals" do nothing but
recreate old battle scenes and sing their own praises. When, during the children's
war on the grownups, they attempt to take command of the field, each is so caught
up in his own plan that the battle is lost despite an entire night of haggling over
leadership and high ground.

Works Cited

Althusser, Louis. "Ideology and Ideological State Apparatuses. (Notes towards
an Investigation)." *Lenin and Philosophy and Other Essays.* Trans. Ben Brewster.
New York: Monthly Review Press, 1971.

Biro, Yvette. *Profane Mythology: The Savage Mind of the Cinema.* Trans. Imre Gold-
stein. Bloomington: Indiana Univ. Press, 1982.

Bonitzer, Pascal. "Off-screen Space." Trans. Lindley Hanlon. *Cahiers du Cinema*
(Dec. 1971–Jan./Feb. 1972). *Cahiers du Cinema 1969–1972: The Politics of Representation.* Ed. Nick Browne. N.p., Harvard Film Studies, 1990. 291–305.

García Fernández, Emilio C. *Historia Ilustrada del Cine Español.* Madrid: Ed. Planeta, 1985.

Larraz, Emmanuel. *Le Cinema Espagnol des Origines a nos Jours.* Paris: Les Editions
du Cerf, 1986.

Chapter 7

Between History and Dream: Víctor Erice's *El espíritu de la colmena*

Santos Zunzunegui

(translated by Tom Conley)

> *Explanation is excessively uncertain in respect to the impression that is given by the event when it is described.*
>
> Ludwig Wittgenstein

Initial Questions

Most film critics would agree that Víctor Erice's work—more specifically, his two major works of fiction—are not only the zenith of the trajectory of Spanish film since its beginnings, but also one of the most pertinent expressions of contemporary Spanish art. But in order to get beyond overly general categorical assertions, we shall have to undertake an investigation of the delicate articulations of a creative work that all viewers agree is both extremely rigorous and coherent. In order to reach these objectives with some adequacy it will be necessary, at the same time, to look at each of his films in detail; locate the connections or ruptures in Erice's evolution as a director; establish, in the final analysis, the coordinates that mark his films. We shall argue that it is impossible to approach a film like *El espíritu de la colmena* (The Spirit of the Beehive) (1973) without first shedding some light on the position this work occupies within the textual circle from which it emerges. And if there is little doubt about the ties held between this work and its prolongation, ten years later, in *El sur* (1983), the causes appear less evident if we wish to link it with the work that Erice had completed throughout most of the 1960s as critic in his writings in the film journal *Nuestro Cine*.

In effect, the prevailing opinion tends to stress the fact that it is possible to identify clearly in Erice's career two periods of notably different orientation: an initial period that would include his work in *Los desafíos* (1969), joined with his trajectory as a student and critic of film throughout most of the 1960s; another, later, associated with his two full-length fiction films and completed critical works in the decade of the 1980s, that offer the crucial example of the monograph (written in collaboration with Jos Oliver, for the Spanish Cinemathèque) entitled *Nicholas Ray* (1986).

But probably these causes are much more complex. In this study I would like to put forward the following hypothesis: all of Erice's work, without distinction made about the medium he deploys, can be studied in light of the progressive desire to resolve what Erice himself called "this socially established contradiction between history and poetry." Or more precisely: as the will to found an aesthetics strong enough to reject this "hypertrophy of the concept of realism" that happens to "confuse the individual with society, eliminating all of a sudden the contradictions that exist between these two key points of reference," and clearly demonstrating that between history and dream there exists no real line of demarcation.[1]

Criticism and Esthetics

The hypothesis above requires a sub-hypothesis that might be expressed in the following way: Víctor Erice's critical trajectory that, upon cursory view, appears clearly inscribed in the tradition of "critical realism," of a heritage inflected at once by Gramsci and Lukács, is nonetheless marked by a series of "decisive encounters." Among them can be traced retrospectively (I shall immediately return to discuss this aspect) an entire series of elements that reappear a posteriori and that are precisely rewritten and cast in new shapes and forms in *El espíritu de la colmena*.

We can now wonder what may be the stakes in an interpretation of this kind. Are we confronting yet another of these operations destined to reconstruct a more or less secret kind of genealogy, by means of identifying in the remote past of an author the keys that will open the doors to the interpretation of his or her later works? Or yet another critical speculation that cannot be detached from necessity, inherited from the old system postulated by the so-called "politics of *auteurs*," so as to give a positive valence to a work that has been included in the pantheon of *auteurs*.

In my opinion, none of the former options is worthy enough to tackle the problems that have nonetheless been put forward. I believe that three clearly articulated lines of argument can be brought forth with this incursion into Erice's past in terms of his cinematic themes. The first refers to the sole possibility of taking up, without any preconceived ideas, the entire work of an author as if it were a global vision defined by determinant, formal "isotopias" (that can affect at once levels of content and of expression).[2] Directly linked with this, the second tries to demonstrate how an identical content can be embodied in different modes of expression. And the third, whose vector of meaning derives from the two preceding lines, posits that there can be no way of "reading the films in the light of the former critical writing," unless it be that of edifying a past that emerges when a series of morphological relations is established that can allow one to conclude, in the words of Hayden White, with what might be called "a retroactive adjustment of the past." Replacing the genetic hypothesis by morphology, rejecting the stages of an "evolution" gained from attention to the formal connections among facts, locating the historical explanation as "one way of arranging facts," it is possible to read in these old critical texts echos and crisscrossings that occasion the appearance of what Wittgenstein called an "intelligible representation" capable of "resuming the givens in a general image that does not take the form of a hypothesis based on chronological development." The operation as practiced allows one to

> draw attention to resemblance, to the connections among facts. In the same way that an internal relation is shown between a circle and an ellipse that transforms the ellipse into a circle, *but not in order to affirm that a given ellipse might have effectively turned into a circle,* but solely in order to make a formal connection appear before our living eyes. (my emphasis) The evolutionary hypothesis can be considered as the formal connection in disguise.[3]

In other words, if the critical texts do not signal a future necessarily written in them, it will be up to the later cinematographic criticism to illuminate them retrospectively. The latter will search for implicit connections, ostensibly secondary aspects, and bring them into focus merely for the sake of showing their authentic dimension.

Decisive Encounters

Following this line of inquiry, I believe that Erice's critical trajectory was marked by successive encounters with Visconti (1964), Pasolini and Mizoguchi (1965), and von Sternberg (1967). In the writings that he devoted to the study of certain works of these filmmakers, Erice will begin to build the basis of an aesthetics that shortly afterward will find its clearest articulation in *El espíritu de la colmena*.[4] In the first case, the encounter with Visconti's *The Leopard* (*Il gattopardo*) will set the stage for two kinds of relations. One, that will be called superficial and that can be followed through the deployment of distinctive figures (and I shall return to this notion below) exactly "disguised" (to use Wittgenstein's vocabulary) as in the case of this variation on contemplation that transforms Prince Salina's passion for astronomy into Fernando's study of beehives in *El espíritu*,[5] and that which—in reference to Erice's other feature-length fiction film—locates in the south the site of infancy, the space of happy memories (*Rocco and His Brothers/The South*).[6]

Deeper and further concealed, it appears to me, is the link that is made—by way of *The Leopard*—with Giorgio Bassani's work, especially in his *Garden of the Finzi-Continis*.[7] In the work already cited above on Visconti (1964: 13–25), Erice insists that in the work of the author one moves in the direction of "the study of *moral and affective climate* of a past lived under the decisive experience of fascism" (my emphasis) and that for the same reason one of the central themes asks how memories of the past can be transcended. To affirm these connections it would be useless to seek in *El espíritu de la colmena* the solutions that Erice indicates as belonging to Bassani. Beyond the shadow of a doubt the transcendence of the past is also one of the major themes of Erice's film, but the analogy does not go any further. Bassani's aesthetic proposal—when he crafts his novel by means of a narrative voice that in the gap of twenty years reconstructs in the first person a penetrating and elegiac memory of lost events—moves through a lucid historical conscience that according to Erice confers memory with an active, transformative character (in Erice's own words). It suffices to recall that in one of his last drafts our auteur eliminated the structure of the flashback, through which it was anticipated that all the later events in the film would begin from the memory of Ana who was going to Hoyuelos, then an adult, to have her father buried. In rejecting memory as a mediating device, a way to transcend the past was made possible—by directly joining the basic narrative world to a series of primitive or primary images whose combination proceeded to spring forth in the film (see below).[8]

Quite different are echoes from the article on Pasolini's film that are heard in *El espíritu de la colmena*. In his piece of writing on *The Gospel According to Saint Matthew*, Erice will clearly specify two fundamental aspects. The first refers to the way that Pasolini reformulates the heritage of realism (and more exactly, Italian Neorealism) by discounting the epic motives and the revival in the 1960s of themes concerning pain and death. The second is aimed in the direction of Pasolini's construction of a celebrated "cinema of poetry" through a play of equivocation between word and image, a reiterated use of grammatical elements as a function more of lyric than narrative, and a transcendental role assigned to metaphor. This use of metaphor is one of the favored mechanisms of *El espíritu*, where a traditional filmic syntax will be subjected to new aesthetic criteria (see below the treatment of space and of time), where images and words will be combined in respect to a degree of poetry that, without directly referring to Pasolini's statements, themselves encounter a lesson in creative liberty. What can ultimately be said about this "epic of resistance" that *El espíritu de la colmena* liquidates before it has a chance to be born? From this thematic dimension is constructed a diffuse background over which the figures of the story are seen clearly outlined. The film appears to invert the political priorities of the moment—1973, in the final stages of the Franco regime—in order to set in place a far greater degree of complexity.

In the same year (1965), at what was then called the Filmoteca Nacional, Erice attended a retrospective of Kenji Mizoguchi's films. His reflections about these features were set down in a long article entitled "The Itinerary of Kenji Mizoguchi."[9] If we stop to think for a moment, it is not difficult to identify, regardless of the confused information generated about the sociohistorical context that marked the Japanese cineast, Erice's points of connection. Thus I should like to qualify this emphasis on the idea of the liberating impact that stirs up Mizoguchi's heroes insofar as, in the manner of the endless experience of the subject in zen revelations, "a flash of lightning will illuminate the night of the soul," producing a "spiritual shock, an emotion that frees the soul from its everyday activities."[10] Or in the selection, among many others, of Mizoguchi's two exemplary films *The Life of O'Haru* (1952) and *Ugetsu* (1953).[11] In the former the protagonist is a "chosen one," a woman in rebellion who infringes upon the moral customs of her time, while in the latter there is the famous scene of the renewed meeting of the potter Genjuro and his wife Miyagi, who was previously killed by pirates. It would not be erroneous to emphasize the first of these references and its imbrecation with the themes of *El espíritu*. No less evident are the ties that bind the scene (noted above) from *Ugetsu* to the privileged moment of Erice's first feature film where Ana encounters the Frankenstein monster at the edge of the river. In both scenes imagination and reality are fused, exhibiting an erasure of boundaries between truth and falsehood (see below), between fantasy and reality.

Scarcely two years later, after encountering Josef von Sternberg's work, Erice published his last important piece of critical writing before going on to make films.[12] In the great director's work we can note the endless presence of characters, careening out of the past, lost and mystified inside, thus distinguished from other mortals. And we can remark that the mechanism of the transformation of reality that these unique heroes set in play is none other than romantic passion. But above all, Sternberg offers Erice the double lesson of a mise en scène twisted to the point of a sacralization of the imaginary and of discovery, attained from the moment Sternberg directed the Dietrich films, that followed a path leading to abstraction, opposed to the traditional mythification of the everyday purveyed in most films. This double lesson will not, as we shall observe, be easily lost upon Erice.

Continuing a Work

Up to now we have developed a position that from here will allow us to address directly, without further ado, *El espíritu de la colmena*. For this purpose I should like to take as a starting point some of the acuitous and terse reflections that will structure what follows, more than fifteen years after its writing, the best and most synthetic approximation of this unique film, Javier Aqua and Marta Hernández's study of the beginning of the film.[13] In this brief critical review the authors indicated that the spectator faces a strongly catalytic, firmly controlled film, brimming with noise, that moves according to abstraction, without redundancy, endowed with a highly elliptical structure, dominated by the notion of absence and tilted in the direction of metaphoricity.[14]

In the pages that follow my analysis will develop what is stated implicitly in these affirmations. It will then animate what, in turn, will remain inconclusive, continuously unfolding on the horizon proportioned by the textual space of Erice's film. At the same time, I claim to continue a labor following an analytical trajectory that, now more than ever, has to be continuously summoned and engaged.

Abstraction and Loss of Reference

If we take as a grounding element the assertion that a film such as *El espíritu de la colmena* develops through abstraction, we must attempt to explain the nexus of complex operations implied by this expression and that are led to endow the film with a particularly dense work or labor of meaning. In contrast to so many films that are based on a traditional structure, in which the design of the character and description of an action or a series of actions composes its narrative frame, *El espíritu de la colmena* from the outset rejects this possibility in order to assume as its point of departure a limited series of "primordial images,"[15] of figures conferred with a strong iconic density achieved through combinations made by way of juxtaposition. This phenomenon of the juxtaposed figures—at the same time that it gives birth to the elliptical character of a story in that, as we shall see below, causality becomes its primary mechanism—produces a structure reminiscent of effects produced by a number of artists in their work on canvases or walls.

I am thinking especially of a painter such as Zurbarán. It is common knowledge that the double pictorial reference that ought to be made in respect to *El espíritu de la colmena* includes Vermeer (through the anecdote noted in what Erice explained to Luis Cadrado as the visual qualities he sought to obtain for his film through the painter's images) or Rembrandt. Since pertinent traits are at stake, it does not matter what shimmers on the surface of things. It appears to me that reference to Zurbarán is located at another level of complexity.

Two dimensions allow a parenthesis to be opened between the seventeenth-century painter and the cineast of our time. A first, at a purely visual level, through the construction of certain images, as in the case of the brilliant shot in which Teresa combs Ana's hair while uttering the tautology that encapsulates much of the film's mystery, "A spirit is a spirit." Filmed in a mirror, this shot (while the image displays a carefully inserted reference to its construction)[16] shows, in its calculated composition, a formal structure that is identical to what can be discovered in Zurbarán's most famous still-lives of food: the abstraction of space on which bodies are located (as in the paintings in the Prado or in the Simon Norton Foundation in Los Angeles), in which vessels or chosen fruits are located, one next to the other, in a space free of everything except, in practice, luminosity. Vessels or fruits, we would do well to recall, do not fail to possess a symbolic value that can be added to the purely referential value without, however, annulling the latter. More profound, however, is the transposition that the film effectuates from the pictorial to the narrative organization of spaces of figures and themes mobilized insofar as they are patterned according to a law of juxtaposition, functioning through proximity and contact, in the very way objects are distributed over the surface of Zurbarán's canvasses.

This being stated, we must not fail to recognize that the sequence of the opening credits describes on a miniature scale the overall design of the film. We see twelve children's drawings that reproduce the emblematic figures that the film will immediately set in play: a beehive, a beekeeper with his face covered, a woman writing a letter, two little girls with their satchels next to a school, a train, a cat, a little girl jumping over a bonfire, a well, a little boy with a hat, a cape, and a stick; a mushroom, a pocket watch, and a twelfth image on which will be shown a slow tracking shot that will give way to a group of spectators lining up before a film screen on a tripod, on which will appear the scene at the river in James Whale's *Frankenstein*, which will soon play such an important role within the film.

In this scene there emerges another of the mechanisms destined to lead by way of abstraction to the reflexive labors of the film: on the last image of the credits (the screen) is inscribed an explicit allusion to the most basic of all narrative beginnings: "Once upon a time." At once promising an account and declaration of its intention, this text is immediately confronted with what comes to be superimposed over the first or primary, so to speak, image of the film (the "film truck" that follows a circuit, as do so many others, toward a little town): "Somewhere in Castille, about 1943."[17] Between the two texts, one situated in an overtly magical dimension that corresponds to the initial narration, the other of clear referential measure, is a connection reminiscent of an oxymoron: two semantically distant terms are linked to each other, however difficult the connection may seem to be. Under the guise of proposing a fusion, the moment deals with the combination of this world of myth — localizable, but forever elsewhere, or beyond any concrete space and time, with that of our at once everyday and historical experience. By all appearances, because of this fact, as of the very first shots, the second is subordinated to the first, as is shown by this movement of the camera that sets the child's picture under the unnameable power of the cinema. Cinema is called upon to be configured as an authentic mythical operator, capable of suspending an entire series of oppositions that the world of "common sense" would be inalterable and irreconcilable.

In this way the film undertakes the task of erasing all concrete reference, a task destined to reinforce the abstract dimension of the story being told. A labor of "dereferentialization" that in order to be clearly grasped must be situated in a conceptual frame adequate to its process. No doubt that in the same way the film makes figures of a high iconic density, it also does not fail to yield referential effects.[18] Yet, it seems to me that this is not essential, for an entire series of elements serve to orient the film in another direction. An example tied to the transformation shown by the work in its development from the first to the final version might be illustrative. In place of the sequence of the opening credits already noted above, the version imagined a very different beginning: the image of a beehive linked together with

> a general view of a town. Most of the houses are placed together in the bottom of a ravine, near a little river. On the inside, but especially along the outskirts of the town, we see a few dilapidated houses, and others, vacant, without inhabitants. Walls in ruins. Walls blackened. Windows with broken panes. A barn in the middle of the fields, abandoned. Next to it, the iron windlass of a waterwell. A piece of artillery, rusted, destroyed and crushed, converted into a *chatarra*. An abandoned trench. A pair of soldier's boots, at the bottom of a furrow, torn shoes. A common grave. A cross, next to the tomb, many wild flowers in bloom.[19]

In this fragment of the script are mixed a few of the elements that the film will deploy as narrative figures (the well, the barn in the middle of the field) with others that are intended to mark indelibly the idea that the story is located in the immediate postwar years. The "realism" of these "disasters of war" will be incidentally left aside in order to give way to the construction of a universe that, without being relinquished —through their absence— from the Civil War, will disallow explanation from this point of view so that the film can be oriented in other, more secret directions.[20]

If we wish to remain within the film, so to speak, we discover no lack of significant examples. We can cite, in the manner of a partial inventory, a few of the more noteworthy operations destined to disorient any schematic desire to anchor the film immediately in an overly external field of reference. Initially, a frontality of framing is chosen to film certain nodal elements of the story: Fernando and Teresa's house, the Cartel-House, the old municipal structure that is used for an improvised movie theater, the corral where the "spirit" lives and where the fugitive will take refuge. A frontality, in the same sweep of the camera, that refers to the child's vision displayed in the opening credits and in the duration and permanence that appear invested in everything that is shown in this concrete way.

This same frontality facilitates the anthropomorphization of specific emblematic objects. It is the extraordinary case of the *casa del espíritu* that, as is shown in the shot of Ana parading in front of and situated between the doors (authentic black filigree ironwork) that are opened in their frame, hold the power of vision. In this moment Ana will recognize the mirage that she herself has constructed in the immediately preceding sequence, over the inert face of Don José. A power of the gaze that is extended, in an immediate form, into one of hearing (the well serves as the ears of the bodily site) and going (the footsteps that Ana and Isabel discover nearby).

This anthropomorphization of the little barn will be developed later, in magisterially cinematic form, when Ana returns to this place after having discovered (in a shot that puts her in view with only one eye, the other concealed by the large bowl from which she is drinking) that the pocket watch has returned to the hands of her father: the mirage of the barn will have disappeared from the frame, much nearer than the one above, not being shown any more than one or another of the doors. With the death of the fugitive sheltered inside the barn, the mirage of the barn will become obscured.

Specifically, in opposition to this frontality—that, we have already stated, signifies immobility and timelessness—the film will set in play at least three perspectival figures. First, the furrows that cross the field emphasize the barn that is the *casa del espíritu.* The furrows that Ana will cross diagonally heighten the angular path she physically makes in leaving the barn after discovering the murder of the fugitive. Here we can appreciate how the film treats some of its expressive pictorial qualities with extreme care: frontality versus diagonality. Second, the double perspectival lines that are traced both by the circuit the cinema truck follows and the very rails of the train that arrives from an unknown origin and goes to unnamed places.[21] Third and most important, we meet the illuminated circle of the lens that projects light through the film projector, that will be cast, in the last image of the film, as the light of the moon. Streaming into Ana's room just as had the film projector on the screen, it will change the color — formerly a golden hue — of the hexagonal, beehive-like window panes. The transformative quality of the film is seen rising to the foreground, most of all in this shot that ends the film. It marks Ana's definite elevation within the profoundly inner dimension of her adventure.

But the frontality as vehicle of abstraction and dereferential-ization is seen reinforced through a series of mechanisms of scenic sites that help create a densely woven net of relations among all the given stylistic elements. The systematic repetition of identi-ties or very similar framings functions identically, each time that the camera shifts to record a familiar space from a different an-gle.[22] Or the lap-dissolves, marking changes of time (disengag-ing its immobility; see below), that hold the frame in place; the children's departure for school; the night that falls on the facade of Fernando and Teresa's house; Ana and Isabel's first trip to the corral; the death of the fugitive. Above all, this extraordinary image that after showing Ana's departure from the field in mov-ing to the left of the frame, contemplating her immediate entry through an identical doorway, during which time we can take note of the almost imperceptible change of the woolen stockings she has been wearing.

The task of anchoring this feeling of dereferentialization is due, on the one hand, to the fact that the film appears to begin over and over again, at different levels, with the probable effect of a progressive enrichment of the narrative material, while on the other, to the fact that the narrative is endlessly being established, of adopting a definite line of development.[23] Three beginnings are superimposed: the title credits, with its child's drawings, and this tracking shot with the film truck that leads the spectator to the heart of the film's imaginary figure of itself; the arrival of the film at Hoyuelos, made of already "realistic" images; the begin-ning of Whale's feature, *Frankenstein* (1931) of which we are shown the poster the assistants are putting up in the dark room, that might provoke a double impression of scandal and terror: Whose film? Is it Whale's? Or Erice's?

This approximation of the workings of dereferentialization (and abstraction) would be incomplete if allusion were not made to the same necessary complement that presupposes the stupen-

dous labor that the film exhibits in its own internal referentializa-
tion.[24] For that effect a thick tapestry of expressive allusions is woven, serving to bind the different levels of the story. Here is the
function of the abundantly binary figure that can be drawn
throughout the entire film. We can recall, for example, some of
the more obvious ones: the well next to the barn/the river near
which the final meeting with the "monster" will take place; the
seeming outer and inarticulate side of Ana into the depth of the
well/the final take, then inside and discernible, of Ana at the balcony; the shadow-figures that the two sisters make in their room/
the immense shadows that are drawn over Ana, seemingly im-
mobile, over a series of abandoned beehives, while her sister and
their classmates jump over the bonfire; Ana paying attention to
her boots prior to her nocturnal escapade/Ana tending to the fugitive's boots; Ana "visiting" Isabel who is playing dead/Isabel "visiting" Ana who is feigning sleep; Fernando, coming alongside
like a shadow, in Teresa's bed/Teresa's hands arranging the cover
over the shoulders of Fernando sleeping on the table of his office. In the same way can be understood the symmetrical effect
produced between the light of the film projector of the first sequence and the moon that flows into Ana's room in the last scene.

All these connections that subtend the narrative structure of
El espíritu de la colmena are responsible for what the film puts before the spectator as if it were something endowed with such a
strong stylistic unity that it could project onto a second level—
yet without denying them—the elements that we will call external references and that are primarily directed toward the creation
of an impression of reality. Without rejecting this dimension, Erice's
film is constructed as a self-referential universe, full and sufficient to itself, as a possible world, that is probably linked with
that of our direct or historical experience, but in which the elements at play are themselves endowed with an internal coherence capable of sustaining its full signifying force of production.

The Temporal Program

We can now move toward an exploration of what we have above
called the pure filmic articulations. In order to do so I shall work
on the level of the discursive practice that holds to the double

logic of the time and space of the story. Normally, "temporaliza-tion" means the anchoring of actions that compose the narrative into an order of time dominated by a dynamic of a causal type of consecutiveness.[25] Nonetheless the logic animated through *El espíritu de la colmena* is quite far from these definitions.

What kind of temporality is Erice's film inscribing or writing? One that directly takes as its model basic narratives (called forth through the initial statement, "once upon a time") in which the time-effect appears to be construction as a pure suspension, yielding a clear sensation of a pause in chronological flow; in a word, of a stationary time. A stationary time in which the realistic logic of daily activity is being drawn into view, produced by concatenations of cause and effect. It suffices to think of the difficulty of establishing parameters that would be adequate for the duration of the story that the film is undertaking to tell. Solely during the first part, the duration of the projection of *Frankenstein* provides the ground for a referential and realistic time that will definitely disappear throughout the rest of the narration. Significant will be the figure devoted to the power of creating the first sensation of chronological reality, in which is stated a truth that will be confirmed beyond all doubt (see below) in the scene where Anna, trembling and with her eyes closed, abandons herself to the arms of the creature surging out of Whale's film; there exists no time other than that of film, of the founding story.

It is no less strange, however, that the logic of causality that belongs to the chronological time of daily activities is, in this film, subordinated at every moment to another, far more abstract, temporality offered through the exemplary images of autumn (an intermediate season, in the middle, which the film appears to follow) or the beehive, the figure of movement immobilized, "perpetual, enigmatic, and crazy,"[26] that appears to swarm, in a swift movement that leads nowhere, along with the adult players of the story. A temporality, finally, in which every ending always returns to the point of departure.

This temporality—negated, suspended and checked—will be shown to be homologous to the murder and is nowhere more evident than its most hallucinatory figurativization—Fernando's pocket watch—that counts less its capacity to measure the discourse of time than to move along a circular course in which everything returns in accord with an endless rotation around an origin. Thus when it passes into the hands of the fugitive it will convey in itself the promise of his death. If, for the effect of extending analysis in this direction, we can select the conceptual doublet mobility/immobility in order to account for the temporal program of the film, then we should be able to explain better its significant articulation and show how the trajectories of some of the characters are organized as a function of this semantic category. This category can be represented according to the method of the semiotic grid,[27] whence the following configuration:

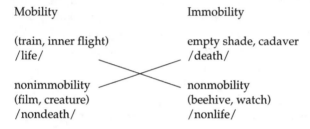

Mobility   Immobility

(train, inner flight)   empty shade, cadaver
/life/   /death/

nonimmobility   nonmobility
(film, creature)   (beehive, watch)
/nondeath/   /nonlife/

Now if in figurative terms we analyze the passing of the fugitive, we shall see that it can be visualized as a passage from mobility to immobility and, more precisely, as the following:

the train   empty shade, cadaver
                                        ↑
                                 wounded leg, watch

The fugitive (that critics generally identify as a resistance fighter) is shown originating from a space that is (ideologically) foreign to the "beehive," a space whence comes the train in which he arrives. In jumping off the train he will wound his leg, and will seek refuge in the corral where Ana will meet him. Killed in a shootout, his cadaver will repose—in a handsomely foreshortened persective that clearly recalls Mantegna—below the same shade that had earlier been cast on the creature created by Doctor Frankenstein.

Now Ana moves along the following itinerary:

inner flight   empty shade
    ↑
film

If Ana is *born* before our eyes in the scene of cinematographic projection, her anterior position — logically presupposed — can be defined as one of the absence of cinema (empty shade). For good reason it will be thanks to cinema that in her will be born this will to know destined to end in disembodiment — after the "false movement" of the desire to escape and in her last meeting with the creature in an imaginary space and time — in the ascension for which there is no other real exit than the "beehive" that is her "inner flight."

These simple grids allow us to visualize categories that pertain to figurative iconicity[28] (the train, the beehive, the film, the watch, and so on) that can be directed toward dimensions that, without already being figurative, are sensibly more schematic and that, above all, contain deep semantic categories that can be grouped into concrete relational configurations, the way they function in and about the local universe of meaning of the film. Thus we should now be able to propose that the emblematic image of the film — not the beehive to which the title alludes — is nothing other than what connects the figures of the empty shade and the lifeless body of the fugitive. This shot, an authentic center of gravity of *El espíritu de la colmena* makes manifest the way that leads all the signs of the activity of the "beehive" toward the elimination of all movement. Contact with the "beehive" implies death. But aimed alternately — hence it is a true hinge in the story — toward the fact that Ana, having contemplated in Whale's film the construction of a living being from the spoils of dead bodies, will have learned and internalized the decisive lesson: it may follow that she will be calling indefinitely to a spirit that cannot die as long as the human imagination continues to live.

At the same time, *El espíritu de la colmena* asks us to let causal logic give way to a magical logic in which the succession of causes and effects, liable to establish the same linearity of time, is abandoned for the sake of association by contact, a privileged mechanism for the explanation of happenings and events. The entire central episode of the film is specifically constructed according to this principle: while Ana closes her eyes the noise of the train floods the soundtrack, at the same time that a dissolve carries us over the tracks of the railway; the image of the fugitive arriving at the barn will dissolve into that of Ana returning to the bedroom. But the transcending moment corresponds to a tripartite structure where, in an exemplary way, the world of reality dissolves into the world of dreams: a shot of Ana sleeping is juxtaposed against another of the fugitive resting with his eyes closed, by means of a straight cut, and with exquisite respect for the match of the characters' gazes, and gives way to an image of Ana contemplating the sleeping figure. Imagination and reality are shown as two sides of the same coin, as two dimensions that cannot be separated from each other and between which there can exist no unassailable gap.

This interpretation that the film systematically explores — the area between reality and imagination — justifies what Ana finds in a "direct" meeting with the monster created by Doctor Frankenstein. And yet this meeting by the riverside can be explained, in strictly realistic terms, as being caused by her having eaten the poisonous bolete mushroom. To interpret the episode thus would be tantamount to a desire to ignore one of Erice's central points: the film explicitly refuses to distinguish between the two given levels.

And in this melding of reality and imagination the film occupies, as we have suggested above, the authentic position of a mythic operator, in the sense that Claude Lévi-Strauss has ascribed to this notion, that is, a median ending that can reconcile oppositions. The following schema might visualize this idea:

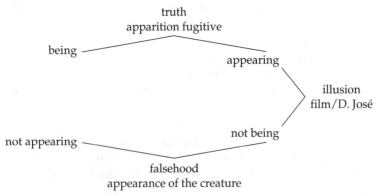

Expressed in discursive form, we may say that Erice's film shows how the commonly admitted opposition between truth and falsehood is allowed to float in suspension, a suspension principally given to the film in a first moment and, finally, in Ana's inner ascension with the "spirit." And we should recall that in this moment of the nocturnal meeting (the apparition of the creature), who already knows and whose choice has already been made, waits with her eyes closed, in a state wavering between fear and a desire to welcome the creature's embrace. It is with the same closed eyes that the apparition of the fugitive is invoked in an earlier scene of the film, that has the finality of detaching the child's definite acceptance of the necessity to interiorize a knowledge acquired at a much higher price. In this same instant the physical shadow of Ana will be at the point of arriving at its destination. And alone she will keep the inner shadow before her.

If we return for a moment to the level which, earlier, we called the figurative iconicity, we should be able to describe Ana's trajectory in the following terms: Ana, her eyes exorbitantly open, looks at, but without understanding, the cinematic projection → Ana, with her eyes closed, invokes the presence of the fugitive → Ana, with only one eye visible, discovers the watch in her father's hands → Ana, with her eyes closed, receives the monster's "embrace" → Ana, from the threshold of the balcony, with her eyes open and bathing in the pale blue moonlight, looks at—having understood—the spectator.[29] A symmetrical structure where emphasis is placed on the passage from the outer gaze to this inner gaze, a gaze uniquely capable of embodying Ana's choice of definition.

The Cartography of Things Becoming

In a parallel fashion, *El espíritu de la colmena* maps out a universe of disconnected spaces. It would be profoundly metonymical were it not because the whole is empty at the points to which its parts refer. To this end the film becomes the pure and systematic confrontation of a series of territories that are not exploited following a transitive model that would ultimately lead to a higher unity; rather, parts are subordinated to an exhaustive comparative operation by way of juxtaposition, at the same time they undergo a parallel movement of deterritorialization. A patent deterritorialization results from the disconnections that the film establishes among the diverse areas of the town and the house; in the absence of transitions between topographies whose proximity or distance is irrelevant beyond a merely textual contact. It is a quasi-Bressonian treatment of space, where fragmentation is a mobilizing principle. By means of this a first level of realism can be distinguished.

Thus, each character will live isolated in his or her space. Several examples can be cited: that of Fernando and Teresa who will only be brought together in the same visual frame when the former does not know where he is going. Two moments—already noted—offer the perfect illustration of this disconnection among characters and the spaces they inhabit: Fernando going to bed, outside of the field of view, next to Teresa who pretends to be asleep; Teresa's hands covering Fernando who sleeps over his worktable. Yet even more remarkable is the sequence in which Ana discovers that the pocketwatch has returned to Fernando's hands: the ordering of the same sequence show us how each character lives in isolation in his or her space without the latter being connected at any moment with that of the other characters; all the relations established among the figures are shown to be impossible; at stake are bodies (and spirits) that are at once proximate and profoundly foreign to one another.

A stylistic trait that the film exploits on various occasions works in an identical fashion: as in the films of Murnau or Hitchcock (especially *Rebecca*) the spectator is barely given a chance to witness even the slightest action of characters who move into a space, to cross a threshold or separation; the decisive moments of passing from one space to another are elided. There are two especially significant moments: we see Ana and Isabel entering into the movie theater only to discover them inside, after the projection has begun; Fernando will be seen approaching the barn following Ana but only, ominously, appearing at its threshold as if he had fallen from the sky.

Thus we see why Erice conceives all shots functioning as close-ups or primary shots.[30] Close-ups include those the montage will offer as a dense web of relations that are exchanged, echoed, and continually referring to one another. And if, as Bela Balasz has shown (by way of Gilles Deleuze), the close-up does not posit the separation of an object from a linkage with other shots of which it forms a part, then the close-up will be abstracted from its surrounding spatial and temporal coordinates. Now we can place emphasis on what is implied by the close-up and, in turn, consider all of the images of *El espíritu de la colmena* in this way.

Furthermore, it is important not to lose sight of the way, as Deleuze has shown, in which "the close-up is defined not for its relative dimensions, but for its absolute dimension or its function."[31] The remark enables us to grasp what is at play in Erice's style of framing. First of all, a "given space" is established, a space relieved of its referential weight, that moves toward the creation of a self-contained or monadic universe (see above). At the same time, we should not lose sight of the fact that when the notion of a given space is used, we do not mean an abstract space in the traditional sense of the word. Thus Deleuze insists that this type of space, made from disconnections, ruptures, fragments, separations, and isolations is

> a perfectly singular space, what has merely lost its homogeneity, that is, the principle of its metrical relations of the connection of its own parts, to the degree that matching shots can be made with an infinity of means. It is a space of virtual conjunction, as if seized by a pure site of virtuality. What effectively is made manifest through the instability, the heterogeneity, the absence of linkage of this kind of space, is a *richness of potential possibilities* or singularities that seem to be the preconditions to any actualization, to any determination.[32]

If we follow the path opened by Deleuze, we can note that these given spaces are constructed through various means: first, through the "shadow, the shadows" (we recall the photo in chiaroscuro of Luis Cuadrado, the extended play of the opposition between an opaque dark background and the illuminated beginning of the bodies extended over areas of obscurity). Then, through the colored image, the power that is granted by everything that is held in its scope, followed by this yellowish light that inundates the suspended time of the beehive. Finally, through the lyrical abstraction that is embodied in the principle of opposition, conflict or battle that the film acquires by means of an adventure of light understood as an expression of an alternative between the state of things as they are and the possibility, the virtuality that exceeds them.

Turning for a moment to the distinction between figurative iconicity and figurative abstraction, with the reference to lyrical abstraction (that we cannot fail to associate with von Sternberg's identical description of the films he shot with Dietrich in the late 1920s and early 1930s), we can sum up *El espíritu de la colmena* in terms of the substitution of one kind of light by another: the yellowish luminosity of the beehive will give way to a bluish moonlight that is at the same time the light emitted by the film projector. The figurative traits of the film are drawn into a sort of synesthesia at the double level where the luminous-chromatic dimension, a level that is situated in a higher logical category of profundity than the imagistic level, so to speak, in which the figures of the narrative are taking form.

Entities, Affects, Qualities

Having arrived at this juncture, we can now formulate the following question: What, in the last analysis, is *El espíritu de la colmena*? In (once again) paraphrasing Deleuze (who has paraphrased Charles Sanders Peirce in his own way), we should be able to synthesize the film as a field of tension established among the following points:

> There is Ana, the train, the film projector, Fernando the apiculturist: apparently real people with their individuated characteristics and their social roles, objects with their uses, real connections among these objects and these persons; in brief, an entire condition of everyday things. But there also is the sound of the train's whistle, the bluish light of the film projector, Fernando's apathy and resignation, Ana's stupor and marvel. To a certain degree these are pure qualities, that are potentially singular, pure "possibles." (1983: 145)

Erice's images cast us into an affective and conceptual space in which effects are probably set in rapport with determined causes, but in a unique way, without reference to another thing that in itself, in an identical fashion, allows causes to refer solely to themselves. If the latter constitute the "state of things," the former are configured as "the expression of the state of things." At stake is a work in which causes, in some way destined to explain effects, do not guarantee that they will make effects comprehensible. They are superimposed upon real connections, marking the force of the state of things, that is, their virtual connections. Apart from an immediate recourse to the calming effect of a rapidly identified meaning, image-affection (what is at stake) points toward the expression of complex entities that are situated quite far from individualization, in the territory of what, without being given a singular identity, is shown to be a point of connection, a meeting point of pure affect (Ana's gaze) expressed in a state of things where, nonetheless, nothing is confused.[33]

The intrinsic force of *El espíritu de la colmena* is surely to be found here. It overcomes a referential scheme that we might call essentiality, where all the images of the film are measured in accord with a view of spaces situated beyond a threshold.[34] In this way the disconnected, void space and the close-ups or primary shots would be oriented in the direction of the referent: the situation of the immediate postwar years in Spain with its at once physical and moral evisceration, with the real and mental destruction. But Erice's real contribution is not only one of understanding a unique way of accounting for this situation without putting it in words, but also one of abandoning the regime of an image-action that directly records this Peircian secondness. Thus, in the film there is actualized a path by which potential qualities become forces. In other words, there is actualized in states of particular things—partially geographical, partially historical—collective agents or individual persons (Deleuze 130).

In contrast, the images of *El espíritu de la colmena* are articulated under the category of firstness[35] ("a way of being that consists in a subject being definitely what it is"), where beings appear at the margin of all compromise, disconnected from all causes and effects. We can say that it resides essentially in what Peirce called a "quality of feeling."[36] For that reason it appears as a pure abstract potentiality written into the order of the possible and confirms, as the unique guarantee of its attraction, the problematic inscription of the observer in a kind of timeless instant. The singularity of this aesthetic experience set forth in Erice's film reaches the designation of firstness, far beyond that of a secondness (that is also clearly present), but that often sets between brackets—as witnessed by the exemplary scene of the impossible that has been quoted above—the contradiction met between Ana and creature accomplished throughout the cinematographic story.

Through its lacunary construction, through its juxtaposed figures, its disconnected spaces and ungrounded time, *El espíritu de la colmena* explores unknown territory wherever its qualities are shown as they are, in themselves, in an immediate and instantaneous conscience, felt by every real conscience that, from its own standpoint, is immediate and instantaneous. Perhaps it would not be farfetched to affirm that what this magical film produces is less of "a sensation, a feeling, than the possible quality of a sensation, of a feeling or of an idea."[37]

Notes

1. See in this respect Erice's two works entitled, respectively, "Entre la historia y el sueño (Visconti y *El gatopardo* [*The Leopard*]," and "Realism and Coexistence," published in *Nuestro Cine* 26 (Jan. 1964), 13–25 and *Nuestro Cine* 27 (Feb. 1964): 21–25.

2. On the concept of the isotope and isotopy, see A. J. Greimas and J. Courtès, *Sémiotique: Dictionnaire raisonné de la théorie du langage* (Paris: Hachette, 1979): 197–99. (*Semiotics and Language: An Analytical Dictionary*. Translated by Larry Crist, James Lee, Edward McMahon II, Daniel Patte, Gary Phillips, and Michael Rengstorf. [Bloomington: Indiana Univ. Press, 1982]. For isotopia and isotopy see 163–164).

3. Ludwig Wittgenstein, "Bemerkungen über Frazers *The Golden Bough*," *Synthese* 17 (1967), 233–253. English translation available in *Bemerkungen über Frazers Golden Bough/Remarks on Frazer's Golden Bough*. Ed. Rush Rhees. Trans. A.C. Miles. Atlantic Highlands, N.J.: 1979.

4. I am using the future tense merely for reason of simplicity. I would like to recall that what is at stake here is the identification of formal relations, but not a labor postulating their causal implications.

5. By means of the intermediate term of the image of "a man who contemplates the sunset."

6. These examples demonstrate clearly how certain "connections" are established. Direct influences are not at stake, except those, in many cases, of a subtle "impregnation." No longer are the remissions immediate for the text taken up in a concrete way: astronomy plays a much more important role in Lampedusa's novel than in Visconti's film, although Erice takes account of both works in his critical study. We would nonetheless be going too far to take into account the fate played by the conditions of production in order to assert, for example, a further connection between *Rocco* and *The South*. If the first begins already in the "north," the second will in no way be oriented toward the "south."

7. *Il giardino dei Finzi-Contini* (Turin: Einaudi, 1962). (*El jardín de los Finzi-Contini*. Trans. Juan Petit. [Barcelona: Seix-Barral, 1963]).

8. See the interview with Víctor Erice published in Angel Fernández-Santos and Víctor Erice, *El espíritu de la colmena* (Madrid: Elías Querejeta Ediciones, 1976): 153.

9. This is the moment to draw attention to the titles of the Erice's selected writings. Without underscoring the acknowledgement to Visconti ("Between History and Dream") that was selected as the title of my own work, I take pleasure in retracing the line that is drawn between the references that in themselves are made to "passion," to "itinerary," and, finally, to the "secret adventure."

10. Victor Erice, "Itinerario de Kenji Mizoguch," *Nuestro Cine* 37 (1965): 15–28.

11. *Saikaku Ichidai Onna* (1952) and *Ugetsu* (1953).

12. Victor Erice, "La aventura secreta de Josef von Sternberg," *Nuestro Cine* 58 (1967): 15–28.

13. Javier Maqua y Marta Hernández, "Los mecanismos comunicativos del cine de todos los días (*El espíritu de la colmena*)," *Comunicación* 21, no. 16 (1974): 89.

14. Following Roland Barthes's terminology in his "Introduction to the Structural Study of Narrative (originally appearing in French in *Communications* 8 (1966); the article is available in Spanish in a recent collection entitled *La aventura semiológica* (Barcelona: Paidós, 1990): 163–201. Catalysis is understood as a function of a finished nature, and is opposed to a nucleus defined as a cardinal function, in other words, that can establish alternate outcomes in the development of the story being narrated. Maqua and Hernández's text is the first in Spain to make use of concepts taken from narrative and narratological theory in filmic analysis. Thus a path is cleared for a cinematographic criticism stripped of "impressionistic" and "gossipy" obligations, and also as a means to engage the later work that develops in reviews, such as *La mirada* or *Contracampo,* between 1978 and 1987.

15. Erice stated it thus in the interview that accompanies the edition of the scenario cited above: "Angel Fernández-Santos and I had the feeling that we were not exactly going to tell a story. In a script of traditional size, when a character is created it usually suffices to think immediately of the role that he or she is going to play in the story itself.... We were working with a distinct form.... We were satisfied with having the unique, primordial image that, in a spontaneous, unconscious way we had glimpsed of the character: 'A man contemplating the sunset, a woman writing a letter.' Maybe that explains why the film, in a certain way, was made of fragments" (143).

16. See n. 99 (86) of the scenario quoted in n. 9 above.

17. [The English subtitle translates the reference as 1943, whereas in the Spanish original the subtitle is 1940 — ed. note.] This written intertitle locates the Quixotic motivation of the film that will open onto the path of "realism" that will be mobilized. We can say in passing that the beehive of the title presupposes a double allusion to the novel of Cela and to Unamuno (twice explicitly cited in the film: the photograph of Fernando with his teacher, the little hens [*pajaritas*] through *La tía Tula* in which is articulated the idea of the beehive, however with a distinctly different meaning (I wish to thank Professor J. M. Nadal for having drawn *La tía Tula* to my attention). Clearly Erice is working with the filmic adaptation of *La tía Tula* directed by Miguel Picazo (*Nuestro Cine* 34: 62–66).

18. The notion of iconicity is understood here as the juncture of discursive strategies aimed at producing an illusion of reference. See "Iconicity" in Greimas and Courtès, 147–148.

19. Angel Fernández Santos and Víctor Erice, 33.

20. We should recall that the only explicit reference to the war is located in the letter that Teresa writes at the beginning of the film ("... since we separated in the middle of the war").

21. We now begin to see a sketch of the cartography of the sites in the film, that is constructed around a double opposition inside/outside, in such a way that the specifically spatial *outside* will end up being homologous with the *inner space* within Ana.

22. A noteworthy example of this practice is seen through comparison of two scenes. In the first of these (that, surely, one cannot fail to recall in which Tancredi and Angélica pass through the loft of the Salina Palace in *The Leopard*), following Fernando's steps, the little girls play gleefully and open, one upon the other, a whole series of door into a depth that opens, where light floods the corridor before the scene darkens. This light is comparable to that of the film projecter of the initial sequence and with the moon in the last sequence. Immediately a lap dissolve brings us to the railway. In the second, Ana, who was hitting the keys of her father's typewriter, after hearing a noise, leaves what she is doing and exits through the corridor that she will then come back through in the inverse direction. At the end of the same sequence she will discover Isabel who is playing dead. A simple change of direction has been semanticized in a diverse way: in going through the light we take a voyage to the threshold of death.

23. It also helps to reinforce this sensation of the fact that until now the primary nuclear actions do not begin to become embodied in the film (in keeping with Maqua/Hernández/Barthes's terminology).

24. What must be underlined is the idea that "any discourse builds its own internal referent and establishes for itself a referential discursive level which provides a basis for its other discursive levels" (Greimas and Courtès, 261).

25. See "Temporalization" in Greimas/Courtès (337–338).

26. This expression appears twice in the film, in the two scenes in which Fernando, at the beginning and at the end, writes in his notebook his reflections as an observer of the world of bees.

27. On the notion of the "quadrant" or "semiotic square" see Greimas/Courtès (308–311).

28. To Ana's recourse to "false movement" of the physical escape corresponds the intermediate position (nonimmobility) in the trajectory from immobility to mobility. It is important to remember that Gilles Deleuze, following Henri Bergson, typifies cinema as that which produces a "false movement" (*L'image-mouvement: cinéma 1* [Paris: Minuit, 1983]).

29. Ana's trajectory can also be read more profoundly as whatever might invert all axiological polarities of social values. Sometimes Frankenstein's creature and the fugitive are invested with negative values in accord with the laws of the beehive: distant, primitive (connected with unconscious drives), incomprehensible, illegal; in a word, a different Ana will radically jostle this alignment of values.

30. There is a radical absence of establishing shots in the indoor scenes, a stylistic trait that further underscores the strongly metonymical dimension of the film.

31. "Le gros plan se définit, no par ses dimensions relative, mais par sa dimension absolute or sa fonction" (Deleuze 148).

32. Deleuze 155, with emphasis added. "Given spaces" translates Deleuze's *espaces quelconque* (154ff), in Spanish as *espacios cualquiera*—Tr. note.

33. We should recall that Deleuze [83–172], following Henri Bergson in *Matière et mémoire* (1896), proposes a typology of movement-images: image-perception, image-action, and image-affection.

34. A helpful comparison can be made with another film produced by Elías Querejeta in the same year (1973): Carlos Saura's *La prima Angélica*. See a first sketch of this comparison in Javier Maqua and Marta Hernández, "Los mecanismos comunicativos del cine de todos los días: *La prima Angélica*," *Communication* 21 no. 17 (1974): 71.

35. For the notions of firstness, secondness, and thirdness, see Charles Sanders Peirce, *Collected Papers* 1, ed. Charles Hartshorne and Paul Weiss. Cambridge: Harvard Univ. Press, 1978). See also Nicole Everaert-Desmedt, *Le processus interprétatif: Introduction à la sémiotique de C. S. Peirce* (Liège: Mardaga, 1990): 31ff.

36. I cannot resist quoting Peirce's famous passage where he typifies the notion of firstness. "There are certain qualities of feelings, as the color of magenta, the odor of attar, *the sound of a railway whistle*, the taste of quinine, the quality of the emotion upon contemplating a fine mathematical demonstration. I do not mean the sense of actually experiencing these feelings which, in themselves, are mere may-bes, not necessarily realized" (*Collected Papers* 1: 304). [The same passage is quoted in Deleuze 150—Tr. note.]

37. Paraphrased from Deleuze 145 and 149.

Works Cited

Barthes, Roland. "Introduction to the Structural Study of Narrative (originally appearing in French in *Communications* 8, 1966).

Bassani, Giorgio. *Il giardino dei Finzi-Contini*. Turin: Einaudi, 1962.

Deleuze, Gilles. *L'image-mouvement*. Paris: Minuit, 1983.

Erice, Víctor. "Entre la historia y el sueño (Visconti y *El gatopardo* [*The Leopard*])." *Nuestro Cine* 26 (January 1964): 13–25.

———. "Realism and Coexistence." *Nuestro Cine* 27 (February 1964): 21–25.

———. "Itinerario de Kenji Mizoguch." *Nuestro Cine* 37 (1965): 15–28.

———. "La aventura secreta de Josef von Sternberg." *Nuestro Cine* 58 (1967): 15–28.

Everaert-Desmedt, Nicole. *Le processus interprétatif: Introduction à la sémiotique de C. S. Peirce*. Liège: Mardaga, 1990.

Fernández-Santos, Angel and Víctor Erice. *El espíritu de la colmena*. Madrid: Elías Querejeta Ediciones, 1976.

Greimas, A. J. and J. Courtès. *Sémiotique: Dictionnaire raisonné de la théorie du langage*. Paris: Hachette, 1979. (*Semiotics and Language: An Analytical Dictionary*. Translated by Larry Crist, James Lee, Edward McMahon II, Daniel Patte, Gary Phillips, and Michael Rengstorf. Bloomington: Indiana Univ. Press, 1982.)

Maqua, Javier and Marta Hernández, "Los mecanismos comunicativos del cine de todos los días (*El espíritu de la colmena*)." *Comunicación* 21, no. 16 (1974): 89.

———. Los mecanismos comunicativos del cine de todos los días: *La prima Angélica*," *Communication* 21 no. 17 (1974): 71.

Peirce, Charles Sanders. *Collected Papers* 1. Ed. Charles Hartshorne and Paul Weiss. Cambridge: Harvard Univ. Press, 1978.

Wittgenstein, Ludwig. "Bemerkungen über Frazers *The Golden Bough*," *Synthese* 17 (1967): 233–253. English translation available in *Bemerkungen über Frazers Golden Bough/Remarks on Frazer's Golden Bough*. Edited by Rush Rhees. English translation by A. C. Miles, revised by Rush Rhees. Atlantic Highlands, N.J.: Humanities Press, 1979.

Part III
The First Steps of Transition

♦   Chapter 8

Pastiche and Deformation of History in José Luis Garci's *Asignatura pendiente*

Oscar Pereira

(translated by Francisco J. González)

This essay will analyze how *Asignatura pendiente* works out the historical experience to which it refers: the period around Franco's death. I propose that this working-out constitutes a distortion and a concealment of that past—achieved by way of pastiche as a means of composition, and of nostalgia as the unifying emotive structure.

I

The term *pastiche* seems appropriate for a strategic approach to the text. It would be well to begin by stating its precise meaning. The *Pequeño Larousse ilustrado* defines it as "imitación servil. Plagio" (servile imitation, plagiarism)—no doubt a highly ambiguous definition for what I have in mind. Still, I am interested in the second part, *plagio*, not in terms of the pejorative connotation that surfaces when associated with the value-laden concept of creation, but rather in reference to the act of recycling fragments from previously created cultural products—which have been stored in the most diverse ways—in order to make a new (the same?) product. We are moving closer, but new indeterminacies arise. The definition I am using seems to imply a comparison between two unique and already finished products, and therefore it does not refer to the process of elaboration of the plagiarizing product.

The *American Heritage Dictionary of the English Language* gives the following entry: "**pastiche. 2.** A hodgepodge of borrowed elements from various sources; pasticcio." Such a definition offers certain advantages. First, a pastiche would be a "new" product made out of quotations from different sources. Second, the structure of the end product is characterized as a heterogeneous mixture or jumble. In a hodgepodge, the whole—the result—is blurred by the presence of its elements. The display of the fragments becomes more important than their incorporation into an integrating design. A look at the word "pasticcio" confirms this and provides something else: "**pasticcio.** A work, especially of music, produced by borrowing fragments or motifs from various sources; potpourri." That is to say, a pastiche would be a work—in our case a film—produced out of fragments from different sources. In order to make the definition coherent we must think of a "work" in terms of container and contents. Potpourri = vegetables and meats gathered within the space of the pot—or let's think of Julio Iglesias singing the longest song made out of fragments from the best songs of the past. It appears that, in order for a pastiche to work well, what matters most is the viewer's immediate and flattering recognition of its fragments, the sudden identification and stirring of memories. Time undergoes a striking compression in which the viewer seems to live between present and past with each fragment, feeling again and again a simultaneity that leaves no time to examine in depth the personal experience of what was—and so on till the end of the next song.

Another point to consider: a pastiche is a simulacrum, which Plato understood as a copy of copies, an image of images. It signifies by allusion, by the connotative value of the fragment; hence the importance of the cliché, the commonplace, the stereotype. Should the viewer have any difficulty in quickly recognizing the fragment, the pastiche would fail to carry out its purpose since the viewer would miss the allusion, even distance himself from it, and identification would not be possible.

As we will see in the next section, *Asignatura pendiente* is a pastiche—the result of lumping together, in the form of a film, a heterogeneous set of cinematic, visual, and sonic fragments — all highly stereotyped and therefore devoid of depth — turned into mere simulacra in accordance with the models of mass communications. I would say, in addition, that the pastiche is a redundant structure in this film.

II

The Apertura

We are moving along the second half of the movie. Franco has just died and Christmas has arrived. New year, new life: it's the beginning of 1976, the time of the *apertura*. With the song *Como ayer* (like yesterday) by the Dúo Dinámico in the background, there unfolds a photographic montage whose sequence I will examine as the prototype of the use of pastiche in the film.

The purpose of this montage is to transmit a random series of fragments in an attempt to reproduce somehow the chaos of images that besiege an average city dweller: television, static publicity, posters, tracts, newspapers, and the like. Through this procedure, all the images automatically take on the status of simulacra. This is to say that all the images are treated as copies of copies, regardless of whether they are documental or fictional in nature. Thus, with no decipherable continuity, we go from pictures of half-naked women to portraits of politicians (such as Arias Navarro) to a Forges comic strip, images of demonstrators asking for amnesty, strikes, burials, and more — all of it at a fast enough speed to prevent any kind of perceptive reading, that is, aiming to summon up remembrances and hinder a critical detachment from them.

Another feature worthy of attention is the use of the Dúo Dinámico's song that puts a temporal frame on the photographic pastiche. To begin with, we are struck by the anachronistic use of a song right from the time of the economic boom of the late 1960s. This seems to imply an attempt to associate the *apertura* with the radical transformation of Spanish society in that decade. The "apertura" could then be seen as a sort of continuation of this process — and so could, indirectly, the political transition itself. On the other hand, the playing of the song throughout the photographic montage affects the reception of the montage. My own impression is that it manages to trivialize the dramatic potential of some of the images.

From all this I would conclude that the model of communication being used here is that of commercial television, in which, with no hint of continuity, we go from news to advertisements to a film, and to anything at all. It might even be possible to propose more specific models, such as those New Year's Eve programs that summarize into images the events of the last twelve months.

Social Microcontexts and Macrocontexts

Through the mechanism of pastiche, fragments that allude to specific historical events are put in contact with fragments pertaining to everyday life.

All the historical events alluded to come from the political arena, the main one being Franco's death. Let us consider the most significant among them. The first meeting between José and Elena takes place in a café during a speech by the dictator that can be heard in the background. A scene at José's home—with the family sitting at the table discussing what measures to take in regard to their son's using the word *coño*—also gives, in the background, news about Franco's illness and the existing provisions for the succession of the head of state. A phone call in the middle of the night brings them the news of Franco's death. Then, on the radio, they listen to the official press release of his death.

The presentation of the characters' daily life centers around the affair between Elena and José, which follows the narrative structure of Hollywood melodramas. We find, therefore, none of the dramatic intensity that marks so many characters in nineteenth-century novels, where adultery is a key to the possibilities of a new life. There is none of that, at least from the perspective the film takes, which is also José's—an affair which will end, like all the others, because "love" is a matter of time and "falling in love" is a transient state and then "there is no more of it." And the former has to do with one's wife, not with one's lovers.

What matters, in any case, is the way in which the film establishes a connection between the sphere of daily family life (the social microcontext) and the world of politics (the social macrocontext). As I have suggested earlier, such connection is carried out by mere simultaneity and contiguity. There is no detailed elaboration that can be said to articulate both worlds in the manner of Galdós's *Fortunata y Jacinta* or Clarín's *La regenta*. In fact, there can't even be any talk of an allegorical relation between the two worlds, since that would have meant an exhaustive work on their homology, a thorough search for the adequate correspondences— not only between elements, but also between the respective relations among those elements.

In the absence of such links, the film uses a simile to establish the connection, with the help of a third item: "...dictatorships are like bicycles: they come to a standstill and fall, just as love does." A dubious statement, not confirmed by historical experience though well in keeping with the conservative ideology of the film.

In the first place, the lack of articulation I have noted between the spheres of daily life and politics only reproduces the divorce between the state and the civilian population that characterized Franco's Spain. In addition, this lack of articulation is the defining element in the ideology of the *desencanto*, which marked the reform process undertaken by Franco's government after his death. In this sense, Rosa Montero's words convey with precision what is meant by *desencanto*: "Desencanto is a state of mind that makes us suspicious of all political options and social movements, forcing us to resign ourselves to our lot. This disenchantment that leads to a meek acceptance of one's miseries is also very favorable to the government [presided over at the time by Adolfo Suárez]: it is easier to govern a disenchanted country than a country full of combative and vindictive citizens. In this sense, I believe that the concept of *desencanto* as social discouragement is promoted by the government itself" (53). By the government and by *Asignatura pendiente*. Let us remember the clear expression of this disenchantment in José's words during a conversation with his wife in the second half of the movie, after the photographic montage about the *apertura*, when it is already clear his affair with Elena has begun to founder: "For so many years I've thought this was going to be different, but everything is the same." The word "this," thanks to the bicycle simile, refers both to the dictatorship and his affair with Elena.

The *desencanto*, then, promotes a passivity toward the political situation of the country. The bicycle simile itself contains the association—because, what does it mean that bicycles "come to a standstill and fall"? The use of the passive ("se paran y se caen") allows the absence of an agent. The only way to visualize the situation is this: a bicycle, moving with a certain amount of inertia and without a driver, comes to a stop due to friction and gravity, and then falls. But are dictatorships affected only by natural forces? What of the social agents who fought with determination, some in order to overthrow and others to maintain the dictatorship? The film ultimately silences them, thus reifying the dictatorship as if it were a structure devoid of subjects, subject only to its own laws, and beyond human control.[1]

This reification of political structures, and the subsequent passivity of social agents, also explains the manner in which the film works out the connection between social micro contexts and macro contexts. We have already seen that this connection is carried out through different media: television, radio, newspapers, and telephone. This could be understood simply as a reproduction of the real circumstances of daily life. Nevertheless, what the film emphasizes is not so much the interaction between individual and medium, but rather their mere coexistence side by side, leaving us in the end with the impression that such interaction is impossible. The pastiche reifies this impossibility since, as we have seen, at no point in the film is there a dialogue or an articulation between the spheres of politics and daily life. *Asignatura pendiente* uses, then, the relation between the individual and the media of mass communications as a model of relations between social microcontexts and macrocontexts, emphasizing the fact that information flows one way, with no return.

It is clear that this one-way flow reflects a factual situation. We must remain mere spectators of the media. However—and here I appeal to my personal experience at the time—news about the political transition was a constant subject of discussion among viewers. Not in the film, though. As we have seen by the examples I have given, the reception of such news never gives rise to a discussion about them; they usually remain in the background and have no effect on the narrative. A different treatment is given to Franco's death, but the result is identical: the phone rings, and someone gives the news of his death. There are no comments. They turn the radio on and listen to the official press release. No comments. Fade-out. Change of scene. Christmas has arrived and nothing has changed. The boys of the San Ildefonso school sing the winning numbers of the lottery, as they do every year. Everyone knows that Christmas is a time of peace, harmony, and new millionaires.

What are the results, then, of using pastiche as a means of connecting the world of politics with the world of daily life? I have already pointed out several: the reification of politics and its divorce from social microcontexts; the disappearance of the social agents from the political macrocontext, and therefore the reification of the context; and the application of the model of mass communications to the political community. To these we should add two more that bear special importance insofar as they stem from the mutual contamination that both the world of politics and the world of daily life sustain by the mere fact of their being put in contact with each other. On the one hand, we have a historicization or defictionalization of daily life melodramatically narrated; on the other, we have a melodramatization or fictionalization of political events. The first phenomenon allows us to view the film as a sort of documentary. The trivial love story is thereby contaminated with the prestige of the historical, the real. Conversely, the second phenomenon allows for an emotional reaction to the political events, a reaction shaped by the long exposure to melodramatic narrative structures. The end product is, quoting R. Hewison, "a shallow screen that intervenes between our present lives, our history. We have no understanding of history in depth, but instead are offered a contemporary creation, more costume drama and re-enactment than critical discourse."[2]

The Generation

I have pointed out how the social agents remain hidden in the film. I have also noted how daily life is melodramatically structured. In this section we will see how both of these aspects are subordinated to generation ideology.

A generation is *constructed* by joining fragments from the past. These fragments come from the media of mass communications, that is, a series of images, sounds, commonplaces, clichés, stereotypes, and so on, are first selected and put into circulation by the media; then they are all put together in a pastiche. Their extraction from the media allows for easy recognition by a large audience. Thus, thanks to the ideology of generation, the pastiche acquires a collective social projection.

The idea is a simple one: *Asignatura pendiente* constructs a generation—a generation defined by men and women who reached adolescence in the mid 60s, when the model of consumer society was successfully implanted in Spain. José and Elena conform, then, to a generational type, as do *Trotsky* and la Pepa. Hence the constant fluctuation between the "I" and the "we," the "we" used by the characters and the "we" that closes the film.

In order to deepen our understanding of the elements that make up this generation, as it is constructed in the film, the following example, which I consider one of its key codes, will suffice: "We are not the ones we once were" (Robert Redford).

So reads the card sent by José to Elena with a bouquet of red carnations after their first chance meeting. It contains a fragment from a poem by Neruda[3] and a reference to the star system of American cinema. They are structured by contiguity. The fragments come from different sources, but the treatment to which they are subjected does not take this into account: "The producers of culture have nowhere to turn but to the past: the imitation of dead styles, speech through all the masks and voices stored up in the imaginary museum of a now global culture" (65).

Both fragments are inert materials stored in that imaginary museum that Jameson talks about, ready for their incorporation into a pastiche. The selection of these materials, however, is never innocent, whether it follows a conscious or an unconscious scheme. The reference to Neruda functions as a representative symbol of that leftist culture which, existing underground at the time, did not have access to the media. Placing it next to an eminent symbol of popular culture shows an attempt to imply its triumphant ascent to the surface—yet a fundamental element is lost in the process: the fact that this leftist culture held a critical stand regarding mass communications. The ontological equalization of both fragments, brought about by mere contiguity, becomes possible because the culture of the left is being used as a mask.

The presence of Robert Redford in the card serves several purposes. On the one hand it is one among the various references made to cinema in the course of the film. These, in turn, serve several purposes. Some provide a means to make the scope of fiction and films go beyond the film itself; they endow the narrative with an aura of reality, as happens when José tells Elena that "people in movies just don't say things like 'I'd like to go to bed with you'," although such allusions can also serve the function of inducing the viewer to think he is seeing a new film that corresponds to a new period, a period in which censorship and certain taboos have disappeared. In any case I would say that, in general, the final effect of all these allusions is none other than to blur the boundaries between fiction and reality — and this blurring, as we have seen, is a necessary condition for the production of a pastiche — since all the images are treated as such regardless of their referentiality, that is, regardless of their fictional or documentary nature.

On the other hand, the association José–Robert Redford is a recurrent motif throughout the film. As a motif, it mimics the penetration of American cultural productions into Spanish society, a penetration that cannot be dissociated from the internationalization of Spanish economy during the decade of the 60s and the presence of multinational corporations and American military bases in the daily life of Spaniards — all of which stemmed from the treaties that were signed between the United States and the Franco government in 1953, and served, without a doubt, the purpose of consolidating the dictatorship. This being so, the association between a "red" José (who has been in prison because of it, according to Elena) and an American symbol can only come as a surprise, given the manifest antiamericanism of the Spanish leftist culture at the time. This can only be explained in terms of an eclecticism that permeates the whole film and is inseparable from its mode of composition: the pastiche.

José, then, is an eclectic product: the converging point in a hodgepodge of fragments taken from here and there; fragments which, in addition, stereotype a generation defined by a series of common experiences, such as going to the same places, seeing the same movies, having the same anxieties, and so on. These experiences have been previously shaped by the media in order to make them indistinguishable from certain habits of consumption. In this way, every historical content is reduced to the dictates of fashion; individuals are reduced to generations, and generations to a set of fashionable items.

Finally, I will say a few words about the long dedication that closes the film—first in order to point out that it is a pastiche, and second in order to call attention to its content. The text of this dedication is divided in two parts. The first, shorter one, is addressed "to us." The second, "to those who made us like this." The first part is linked to a conversation between José and Elena in the first part of the film, during their trip to Miraflores de la Sierra, since in both cases the "we" is used in connection with the same idea: having "arrived at everything too late." I have already mentioned that José and Elena are generational types. Now, the second part puts together a series of commonplaces that construct this generation, hence the "made us like this." The list of items may seem whimsical, but most of them come from the media of mass communications: comics, popular novels, radio, music, films, and the like. The last two items seem to me especially worthy of consideration due to their reproduction of the allusions in the association Neruda–Robert Redford: Marilyn Monroe–Miguel Hernandez—a communist poet and a Hollywood star.

III

Potpourri

Despite the heterogeneity of the fragments, we perceive the film as a unit. The frame, the pot, that counters the dispersing effect of Garci's mode of composition, is provided by the skillful manipulation of time in the film. This occurs at two levels: first, through the reduction of historical time to an emotional temporality melodramatically structured; second, through the translation of this emotional temporality into nostalgia, which thus becomes the unifying emotional structure of the entire film.

We have already seen how, thanks to the mechanism of pastiche, fragments alluding to specific historical events are put in contact with fragments alluding to a highly stereotyped daily life. The simultaneity of these two sets of fragments, along with the guiding function of the love story, reduce the historical time to the emotional time, thus establishing a parallel between the outcome of the love story and the melodramatization of political events.

This reduction of historical time to the emotional time of daily life is reinforced by the roles of the couple *Trotsky*-Pepa, and the labor unionist Rafael García. All three are hollow characters referred to as "reds." Their drama consists in their having been unable to reconcile private life with politically engaged public life. This rift reproduces the separation I mentioned earlier between social microcontexts and macrocontexts, and implies that a political dimension is absent from the social microcontexts. Thus, in the case of the "stainless steel worker," his problem consists in having failed to be a good father to his children: "I don't want to be anybody's idol; I want to be a father to my children." In the case of José's subordinates, the source of the conflict lies in the belief — apparently on *Trotsky*'s part only — that his love life is susceptible to a political appraisal. It would seem, then, that his strong engagement in public life questions the traditional family structures of private life, but such a reading is vehemently rejected by the film, since the models it offers of women and of man–woman relations are openly and unmistakably reactionary. The drunken conversation between *Trotsky* and José — male bosom pals — seems to put things back in place: a father's responsibility with regard to his children prevents any progressive experiments in man–woman relations. Because of this, *Trotsky*'s stag party indirectly implies a retreat from public to private life — the adoption of a passive attitude regarding political events.

The second level of temporal manipulation has to do with the love story's mode of narration: the flashback. The film ends at the same (present) time it started. In this way the narrative turns onto itself and is reduced to a single moment — not just any moment, but rather one of those crucial short spells in a person's life (the last, disenchanted meeting between José and Elena) during which the past seems to fly swiftly by, leaving but a wistful sediment of nostalgia, a sense of its irrecoverable loss. This past is defined, as we have seen, by the fragments associated with the generation that *Asignatura pendiente* constructs — not only through the course of the narrative, but also, and very obviously, in the closing dedication: "To us, who have arrived at everything too

late: to childhood, to adolescence, to sex, to love, to politics..."
(in the background we hear *Luna de miel* [Honeymoon] by Gloria
Lasso).

IV

Conclusions

Perhaps *Asignatura pendiente* was a prophetic film. Considered
with the hindsight of the present, some of the views it offers became the defining tendencies of the so-called "democratic transition" in Spain. Such is the case with the view of an essential, un-
broken continuity between the Franco and post-Franco periods,
a view made possible by the consumer society promoted in the
late stages of the dictatorship. This view is clearly alluded to in the
film. If one wonders what distinguishes the José before Franco's
death from the one after Franco, the answer is obvious: he drives
a Seat 1430 at the beginning and a Citroën GS at the end.

The same may be said about the generalized growth of political
apathy among former leftist militants and their subsequent transformation into yuppies. All this was clearly visible once the PSOE
won the elections in 1982. Let us remember José's feverish work,
midway between labor lawyer and earnest defender of an insur-
ance company's interest. Let us also remember his brisk, precise
style (even in bed) when it comes to making decisions that are to
be carried out by others—by his employees. We are dealing, in
short, with the prototype of what will later become the Madrid
yuppie.

Let us now go back to the hypothesis this work proposed. The
success of this movie lies in its offer of a conservative solution—
disguised under a certain progressive tone—to the grave political
problems of the time. In colloquial Spanish parlance, one would
say that the film offers a *progre* solution. The first key to this success should be looked for in the treatment the film makes of leftist culture. Such culture, being as it was still very much alive at
the time, though deprived of access to the great media of communications, is presented in the film as a "dead style" ready to
be manipulated according to the fashionable conventions of mass
culture, that is, ready to be consumed as one more item of fashion.
In connection to this we should remember *Trotsky*'s apartment, a

place where a great number of objects connoting progressiveness are accumulated. Once leftist culture has become a simulacrum of itself, it is susceptible, thanks to the mechanism of pastiche, of being combined with other simulacra. The rest of the privileged simulacra in the film come, as we have seen, from the Hollywood star system and from the Spanish mass culture of the 60s. It is with these three groups of fragments that Garci constructs the generation of *desencanto*.

The second key to its success, inseparable from the first, is the use of a sensibility akin to the *mode rétro* in conjunction with a melodramatic structure. The former is attained by the skillful use of musical themes from the 60s, although the narrative itself incorporates the topic of recovery of a past. The result is what we normally call a nostalgic film, yet, unlike other typical examples of its kind (*American Graffiti*, *Il conformista*, and others), *Asignatura pendiente* does not attempt to recreate a period removed in time by several decades, but uses similar mechanisms in order to narrate a story from a very recent past. The film came out in 1977 and the story takes places in 1975–76, with the 60s in the background. The result is a curious one: the projection, over a minimal chronological distance (1 to 2 years), of feelings which, according to the conventions of the genre, would be more pertinently applied to a more distant past (the 60s), caused the Spanish viewers of 1977 to feel their own historical moment (the political transition) with the nostalgia normally reserved for an irrecoverable distant time of papier mâché—a time one can only contemplate, not modify.

Thus *Asignatura pendiente* establishes itself as a limpid example of the ideology of disenchantment. This ideology, far from being a peculiarity of Spanish democracy, is a fundamental pillar of all western democracies, promoting and sustaining the passivity of social agents and the reification of the structures of domination.

Notes

1. For an analysis and criticism of the Foucauldian concept of "context strategy," see Charles Taylor, "Foucault on Freedom and Truth." *Philosophy and the Human Sciences. Philosophical Papers 2.* Cambridge: Cambridge Univ. Press, 1985, 152–184. "Strategies without projects; this would be a good formula to describe Foucault's historiography. Besides the strategies of individuals, which *are* their projects, there is a strategy of the context. The whole constitution and mainte-

nance of the modern system of control and domination is an example. Foucault speaks of its growth and self-maintenance in strategic terms" (169).

2. Quoted by David Harvey, *The Condition of Postmodernity*. Oxford and Cambridge, Mass.: Basil Blackwell, 1989, 87.

3. From poem 20 in *Veinte poemas de amor y una canción desesperada*. Barcelona: Bruguera, 1984.

Works Cited

Harvey, David. *The Condition of Postmodernity*. Oxford and Cambridge, Mass.: Basil Blackwell, 1989.

Hewison, R. *The Heritage Industry*. London: Methuen, 1987.

Jameson, Fredric. "Postmodernism; or, The Cultural Logic of Late Capitalism." *New Left Review* 146 (1984): 53–92.

Montero, Rosa. "La marginación de la mayoría." *España 1975–1980: Conflictos de la Democracia*. Ed. José L. Cagigao, John Crispin, and Enrique Pupo-Walker. Madrid: José Porrúa Turanzas, 1982. 41–58.

Neruda, Pablo. *Veinte poemas de amor y una canción desesperada*. Barcelona: Bruguera, 1984.

Taylor, Charles. "Foucault on Freedom and Truth." *Philosophy and the Human Sciences*. *Philosophical Papers 2*. Cambridge: Cambridge Univ. Press, 1985. 152–184.

Chapter 9

Eyeing Our Collections: Selecting Images, Juxtaposing Fragments, and Exposing Conventions in the Films of Bigas Luna

Ann Marie Stock

Bigas Luna collects disparate fragments in his films, much the way teacups and ceramic tiles comprise Antonio Gaudi's monumental temple *La sagrada familia.* In gathering fragments and conjoining them in his films, Bigas Luna moves among film industries, genres, and moments in the history of cinema; he casts actresses and actors from Spain, Italy and the United States, relies on conventions of numerous genres, and conjoins sounds and images from "classic films" and "B" movies. The filmmaker, moving as deftly as an art historian moves among rare objects or an ethnographer moves among "exotic" cultures, acknowledges his role as collector. The films enable us to interrogate the process of collecting inherent in making, viewing, and critiquing films.

Jos Bigas Luna brings to the screen the stuff of the tabloids. Neurotic figures, "deviant" relationships, scandals, and blood figure heavily in his films: a man's obsession with a prostitute leads him to kill her in *Bilbao* (1978); the passion a brother and sister share for one another and for their poodle results in the death of all three in *Caniche/Poodle* (1979); a TV evangelist falls in love with an Italian visionary in *Reborn* (1981); a man kills his former wife during a quarrel about their child just as the new wife returns

home in *Lola* (1986); and a psychotic mother encourages her obe-
dient son to gouge out eyeballs in *Anguish* (1987). These "popular" themes work themselves out in the filmmaker's self-conscious
pastiches.[1]

Bigas Luna insists upon identifying, analyzing, and revealing
the operative mechanisms of cinema. Films privilege a present
and dispense with a past, thus obliterating the historical conditions of their making. Representation is arbitrary; images are carefully selected and conjoined by filmmakers. Our own expectations about what the screen should and shouldn't contain, about
the "meaning" of a particular image in the film, and about the
functioning of certain conventions, determine in large part what
appears on the screen. At the same time Bigas Luna encourages
us to look at our own practices as critics, to interrogate some of
the assumptions informing our activities: first, that nation constitutes a meaningful category from which to analyze the filmic
production of a particular filmmaker; second, that genre conventions constitute standards against which to judge films; and third,
that auteur analyses can isolate the films of one director from
another. For a director disregarded as "thoroughly nauseous"
and for films dismissed as "depraved," "kinky" and "sick," this
feat is no small one.

Narratives of Collecting

Narratives of collecting structure *Bilbao* and *Anguish. Bilbao,* sometimes subtitled "A History of Love," centers around three figures: a prostitute named Bilbao (Isabel Pisano), the man obsessed with her, Leo (Angel Jove), and his mistress/mother, Mara
(Mara Marn). The film traces Leo's pursuit of Bilbao—he follows
her whenever he can, lingers outside her apartment, peeps in the
window, and mumbles "Quiero una foto" while fingering the
camera in his pocket. As the woman continues to elude him, Leo's
obsession to possess her grows. He seeks out any item related to
the word, the place or the woman. So panties like those worn by
the woman share space in Leo's collection with postcards depict-
ing the city. These collected objects, unrelated except in Leo's
terms, serve as metonyms for the woman. The woman is out of

his reach so bits and pieces of images and objects provide a substitute for her. With Bilbao scrapbook in hand, Leo masturbates.[2]

Obsessive collecting prevails in *Anguish* as well. John (Michael Lerner) is after only one thing: eyeballs. Controlled by his psychic and apparently psychotic mother (Zelda Rubenstein), he stalks victims and brutally mutilates them. He carves out their eyes, ever increasing the number of vacant stares in his collection. Neither scientist nor appreciator of beauty, he selects victims randomly and then clumsily hacks out their eyes. Floating pairs of eyeballs stare out from the jars in which they are stored; John squints back at them from behind thick glasses. These eyes can never compensate for John's failing vision; nevertheless, their accumulation drives John to mutilate victim after victim.

Good Collecting, Bad Collecting

John and Leo are very "bad" collectors within the structure set up by James Clifford. A good collector makes treasures public, sharing them with an interested audience. A good collector labels and organizes the components. A good collector distinguishes copies from originals. A good collector is tasteful and reflective. A good collector has a "proper" relation to the collection. Finally, a good collector perceives the task of collecting as one of many drives, interests and goals (219).

Bigas Luna's figures break the commandments of good collecting. Rather than show off his collection of eyeballs to the public, John keeps the eyes to himself. Rather than organize the eyeballs according to color or size or any other distinguishing feature, he simply preserves them in jars set randomly on shelves. No label relates the eyes to their former owner. Leo never labels and organizes his collection, either. Items are shoved at random into a scrapbook. Because of the nature of their respective pursuits, neither John nor Leo obtain "the real thing." Both must settle for substitutes of an elusive original, so while John relentlessly pursues perfect vision, he only manages to gather up other people's eyes, and while Leo pursues the woman, he amasses only objects related to her and images representing her. John and Leo are not tasteful and reflective but miserly and obsessive. The relationship between the men and their respective collections is not at all "proper"; rather, the collecting becomes a fixation, an all-consuming passion. Both Leo and John live to collect. Clearly, these are a couple of "bad" collectors.

Bigas Luna is not content to merely label the activities of these collectors as "bad" or "improper." Instead, he interrogates the process of collecting. Three fundamentals of collecting, gleaned from the work of Walter Benjamin, James Clifford and Sally Price, inform the following analysis of the collecting inherent in the cinematic apparatus. First, collections inevitably erase the individuality of their members, privileging instead the composite. The focus on the collection rather than on individual components erases unique histories. Discrete elements from the past are re-worked into a temporal present. Second, while the activity of collecting may appear as arbitrary or "objective," it is actually a very controlled process. Some individual carefully selects the bits and painstakingly combines the pieces in fabricating a collection. The selection of elements and the manner in which the collection is displayed are not "natural." Third, expectations determine the contents of a collection. Elements that compose the collection, by virtue of their inclusion, reinforce prevalent notions. The films of Bigas Luna enable us to probe the collecting inherent in the making, viewing and critiquing of films. His films identify the mechanisms that permit representation, name the conventions which effect expectations, and explore the space perceived to separate film from maker from viewer.

Collecting Fragments and Historical Moments

Like an anthropologist who gathers observations and details about a culture, Bigas Luna amasses fragments from other filmic texts. The familiar yet horrific image of a sliced eyeball appears in *Anguish*, immediately calling to mind the equivalent image in *Un Chien Andalou* (Luis Buñuel, 1928) and perhaps in the lesser-known *Eyeball* (Umberto Lemzi, 1977). The image signals that certain traditions, conventions, and codes inform *Anguish*; it posits Bigas Luna alongside another transnational figure, Buñuel; it comments on the filmmaker's debt to Surrealist aesthetics; it locates *Anguish* within the horror genre; and it perpetuates the association of blades and eyes in the history of film. In the tradition of the Surrealists, whose collecting during the 1940s "was part of a struggle to gain aesthetic status for... increasingly rare masterworks [of American Indian art]" (Clifford 238–239), Bigas Luna imbues new life into the images and films by virtue of their appearance in his films. At the same time he acknowledges his connection with other directors, other films and other moments in the history of cinema.

In adopting fragments of other films, moving them from their "original" context to the text of his films, Bigas Luna irrevocably alters the "original" images and sounds. A new "authenticity" results, one "produced by removing objects... from their current historical situation" (Clifford 228). In the process, their status as remnants of particular works created by individual directors, products of specific genres, and examples of certain national industries is challenged. The moving lips of *Rocky Horror Picture Show* (Jim Sharman, 1975) and the monster in *The Last Adventure* (Sir Arthur Conan Doyle, 1925), appearing together in *Anguish*, condense 50 years into a few frames. The result is what Sally Price terms the "ethnographic present" in which "cultural expression... [is abstracted] from the flow of historical time." Removed from their respective histories, "individuals and whole generations" are "collapsed... into a composite figure alleged to represent his fellows past and present" (57). Price's description of what happens to an artifact that "has been removed from 'the field' " is fitting to understand what happens to a film fragment that is restaged in a new work: "The pedigree of such an object does not normally provide detailed information about its maker or its original (native) owners; rather, it counts only the Western hands through which the object has passed" (102). The emphasis on the fragment's inclusion in the collection manages to occlude the past context, the fragment's existence in another film created by a different director in a distinct national and temporal space. The status as a part of the collection usurps the former history of the image. Like the books in Walter Benjamin's library, the fragments are meaningful primarily as members of a collection: The most profound enchantment for the collector is the locking of individual items within a magic circle in which they are fixed as the final thrill, the thrill of acquisition, passes over them. Everything remembered and thought, everything conscious, becomes the pedestal, the frame, the base, the lock of his property. The period, the region, the craftsmanship, the former ownership—for a true collector the whole background of an item adds up to a magic encyclopedia whose quintessence is the fate of his object (60). So while each bit carries connotations and invites associations with past images, the fresh writing ends up obscuring and ultimately obliterating past markings.

Bigas Luna removes these fragments from the static collection of film history and reactivates them in a new context. From the dusty shelves of an archive, they move to a dynamic assemblage, restaged in a new period, a distinct region, under different direction, often using unique techniques. The preservation and transformation of these images within a new context has the effect of occluding the historical relations of each fragment: what came before and after a particular frame, who was responsible for "collecting" the image, and which national or temporal framework made up the environment of the consumers of the image. So while a history puts the past in order, fitting events into a narrative, films "jumble up" that sequence. The new logic draws not from some neatly ordered past; rather, it emerges out of the texture of the fabric at hand, from the weaving of various filmic threads into the new work. Films, like collections of objects, absorb and erase features of individual items in the collection.

The Filmmaker as Selector

Collecting, as traditionally practiced, presumes an informed authoritative collector or connoisseur engaged in an objective activity. The person simply gathers the elements or truths which will constitute the collection without intervening in any way. Bigas Luna exposes the myth of "natural" or "innocent" collecting by revealing the active role of the filmmaker in the selecting and ordering of images. Careful decisions determine what is included and what is excluded. Clifford acknowledges this process in ethnographic actives: " . . . the concrete activity of representing a culture, subculture, or indeed any coherent domain of a collective activity is always strategic and selective. The world's societies are too systematically interconnected to permit any easy isolation of separate or independently functioning systems" (231). The "concrete activity of representing" in cinema is equally "strategic and selective" even though representations appear natural. Bigas Luna reveals how this transparency is achieved by calling attention to the filmmaker's intervention in selecting, framing and incorporating images and sounds into the filmic text. He includes "inappropriate" items and plants clues that lead nowhere. These techniques call attention to the framing and selecting germane to filmmaking, revealing that the process of collecting images and sounds on film is not at all natural, that it is carefully controlled by the assumptions, tastes and desires of the collector. (Ways in which viewers and critics share this control will be discussed in subsequent sections.)

Bigas Luna brings into his collection images which appear not to belong. The inclusion of images once relegated to that space off the screen highlights the process of selection in the making of films. In *Bilbao* the prostitute's genitals appear on-screen not during a sexual encounter but as she squats over the bidet between jobs. We see Leo ejaculate not in the arms of a beautiful woman but from the movement of his own hand in a grimy restroom. Such images, generally not projected on the screen, call attention to the fact that they have been selected and ordered, that the filmmaker's collection is not an arbitrary one.

Other images seem inappropriate not because they appear on the screen but because they fail to perform some expected function. In *Bilbao,* for example, the camera zooms in on a license plate as the car drives off. According to the conventions of thrillers and detective films, the privileged close-up would constitute a clue. That "establishing reference" only masquerades as such in *Bilbao,* however, for the license plate never reappears. In the same way the camera's attention to the scissors in *Bilbao* calls attention to its seemingly innocuous appearance. Generally a sharp blade stabs or at least punctures in a horror film. Instead of participating in the ensuing bloodshed, however, the scissor blades cut pictures out of magazines while saw blades and an electric razor cut up human bodies. Some viewers and critics react with irritation when their expectations are not met. Peter Besa notes in a review of *Caniche* that, "It's all seemingly leading up to something, but…the ambiguous ending is a disappointment and

nothing violent is ever seen to really happen, leaving the spectator irked at all the gratuitous false leads" (*Variety*, 16 May 1979).
What appears to be nothing more than a "false lead" is actually
a flag which enables the filmmaker's intervention to be recognized and named as such. Moments like these foreground the
active participation of the filmmaker in the selecting and conjoining of images. (Incidentally, they also reveal the "rules" gov-
erning critical responses, to be discussed in greater detail in the
following pages.)

The sounds and images selected, ordered and reproduced on
the screen seem to appear "naturally." Since the splice joining
two frames often eludes notice by even the most careful of viewers, connections are transparent. In the work of Bigas Luna, however, this "natural" appearance is unmasked. The filmmaker is
quick to remind viewers of the arbitrary selection and organization of the "collection." In doing so he acknowledges his own
role as collector. As Richard Handler notes in writing about Que-
becois culture, "the collection and preservation of an authentic
domain of identity cannot be natural or innocent. It is tied up
with national politics, with restrictive law, and with contested
codings of past and future" (Clifford 218). Bigas Luna reveals
the impossibility of innocent collecting, of arbitrary ordering, of
a "natural" sequence. Instead, he insists upon his own intervention implicit in choosing and framing images and splicing them
in his collections.

In foregrounding his relationship with the collection, Bigas
Luna differs from those collectors of art objects and cultures who
perceive themselves as occupying a space distinct from their collection. Separated by language or experiences or national origin
from the object or culture collection, some art historians, ethnog-
raphers and filmmakers collect and contain some Other. Bigas
Luna's collecting parallels the activities of postmodern ethnog-
raphers who take as the object of inquiry not some isolated Other
but their own relation to that Other, their own activity of collecting cultures. His goal, then, is to underline the interaction of the
collector with the collected. This exploration enables Bigas Luna
to establish a dialogue with his texts, acknowledging his relationship to the national industries within which he works, to the
conventions upon which he draws, and to the film history in

which he is implicated. Furthermore, it enables him to articulate a space which embraces the collecting Subject with the collected Object.

This space encompasses various "realities" or "worlds" in which dreams intersect with fantasies which in turn overlap with news stories. In maintaining that the roles of collector and collected are not so easily delineated, in fact that they are inextricably linked, Bigas Luna probes the space within which the projected images react with their receiver. The filmmaker alludes to his interest in exploring this space when describing two of the concepts which motivated the idea behind *Anguish*: "[First,] the possibilities in going beyond the limits — as several painters and film directors have already done — of the almost arbitrary ends of a visual work of art dictated by the frame in a painting, and by the edge of the screen in a film. . . . [Second,] my own love of the movie theatre and the idea of integrating such a physical and real space into the story that is happening on the screen. . . . making the space within which you are watching the movie become a psychological part of it." ("Notes on *Anguish*") In the same way that the spaces merge in *Anguish,* the distinct spaces perceived to separate collector from collected all merge in his work. For Bigas Luna, the film and the maker as well as the film and the viewer simultaneously interact.

Collecting Genre Conventions and Expectations

The collector's activities are dictated in great part by a set of expectations, those of the filmmaker as well as of viewers and critics. Rarely articulated as such, these expectations determine what is or is not acceptable for inclusion in the collection and influence the classification and display of the collected objects. Price notes that "[t]he mode of presentation for a particular art form from an 'exotic' setting is . . . often selected on the basis of its compatibility with received ideas, on its lack of abrasion with what an audience already has in mind" (118). Items in a collection are selected because of their conformity to certain preconceived notions. Not surprisingly, then, their appearance in the collection serves to perpetuate the very norms which enabled their inclusion in the first place.

Bigas Luna identifies the role of expectations in cinematic collecting by invoking genre conventions. He then deviates from them, an act which calls attention to viewer expectations. Because we are accustomed to genre "clues" planted by the director, we feel "duped" when Bigas Luna departs from them. While his films draw upon a number of genres — pornography, the suspense thriller, the musical comedy and the melodrama — the horror genre as developed in *Bilbao* and *Anguish* will be treated here.

That Bigas Luna demonstrates an interest in the conventions of the horror film comes as no surprise. After all, the filmmaker has looked to the painters, writers and filmmakers of the Surrealist movement in defining his aesthetic. These individuals took Hollywood-style horror films very seriously, considering them legitimate modes for exploring various states of human consciousness (Wood 203). The horror genre also lends itself to Bigas Luna's interest in creating "credible subworlds," in doing "imaginative things" (Anderson). Furthermore, Bigas Luna has been dedicated to identifying and recuperating marginalized forms of cultural expression, and horror films, overlooked by many serious viewers and most film critics until recently, constitute one such marginalized form.

Wood explains that "the horror film has consistently been one of the most popular and, at the same time, the most disreputable of Hollywood genres.... [the films] are dismissed with contempt by the majority of reviewer critics, or simply ignored" (202). Bigas Luna appears interested in exploring the reasons for the popularity of these marginalized genres, films dismissed as "just" horror. It is from within the horror genre, then, that we can examine how Bigas Luna identifies genre conventions and employs them to underline viewer expectations.

No standard horror recipe exists; conventions shift from film to film and director to director, within distinct cultural contexts and during different time frames. Still, some general characteristics of films produced within this genre can be noted. A basic formula for horror films, as expressed by Robin Wood, is one in which "normality [a heterosexual monogamous couple, a nuclear family, a social institution] is threatened by a monster" (203). Dennis Giles maintains that a "delayed, blocked or partial vision" is "central to the strategy of horror" (41). For Gregory Waller, "violence is a major element in the genre" and horror films offer "the representation of violence—violence embedded in a generic, narrative, fictional, often highly stylized, and oddly playful context" (6). These criteria locate a number of Bigas Luna's films alongside thrillers.

Bigas Luna names the genre within which he begins *Anguish* by incorporating explicit references to horror films. Hitchcock allusions abound: the chaotic bird scene calls to mind *The Birds* (1960); images of spirals, predominant in *Vertigo* (1958), produce the same dizzying effect; and the music from *Psycho* (1960) intensifies the mounting suspense. *Bilbao* incorporates "quotations" in the same way, serving up generous portions of blood, flesh and blades. A gory soundtrack accompanies these images, one which conjoins the repeated shriek of a table saw with the screams of dying pigs and the cries of a baby. This scene invites association with other blade-happy blood-soaked films, like the first two installments of *Texas Chainsaw Massacre* (Tobe Hooper, 1974 and 1986) and *Motel Hell* (Kevin Connor, 1980). By selecting and combining elements evoking a number of films, directors and national traditions, Bigas Luna's work leaves no doubt that the images flicking in front of us make up a horror film. Or so it seems.

Even without the textual fragments which "quote" other horror films, *Anguish* promises terror. The film opens to reveal a chaotic pursuit in a cluttered room. A bird has escaped from its cage and Alice shuffles from one Gothic corner to another while her son, John, traipses along behind. The frenzied flapping ceases when the creature becomes trapped behind a bookcase. "Careful," croons wrinkled "Mommy" in her little-girl voice as John attempts to capture the fearful feathers, "don't hurt it." John carves out a piece of the wood while his mother reiterates the raspy warning. She then praises him for catching the bird. John grins shyly upon hearing what a "good boy" he is. In this opening sequence, Bigas Luna wastes no time in saying "this is a horror film; prepare for a scare."

As soon as Bigas Luna has us convinced that we are watching a horror film, he deviates from the very conventions to which horror films supposedly adhere. Rather than conform to norms of the horror genre he introduces innovations which call attention to the mechanisms which permit, promote and perpetuate the operation of certain conventions within the genre.

So while *Bilbao* indeed contains elements common to thrillers, a number of events appear out of place or "incorrect." The terrifying "Monster," Leo, turns out to be a bumbling victim of some emotional disorder. He kills *Bilbao* not with a knife or a gun but by accident; he unintentionally lets her head hit the floor when he drags her off the bed. The "murder" actually occurs off-screen; no graphic violence accompanies the death. The film is spattered with blood, although it gushes not from the murder of a human but from the slaughter of pigs. Important pieces of the horror puzzle are missing in *Bilbao*.

The deviation from the horror norms is even more pronounced in *Anguish*, which draws upon the movie-within-a-movie technique.[3] After the bird scene described above, John's antics as an eyeball stealer begin. As our eye-gouging-tolerance limit approaches, the camera recedes to reveal two teenage girls, Patty (Talia Paul) and Linda (Clara Pastor), as they munch on popcorn in the dark theater. So we are watching the girls in a movie theater watching John and his Mother on the screen. Upon finding out that the violence is a representation, that the blood and eyeball business is "just" a movie, our reactions shift dramatically. At this point we can separate ourselves from the collection on the screen. So while the relentless violence affects us when presented directly, our anxiety dissipates once we recognize the convention and are able to separate ourselves from the events. The frame-within-a-frame technique delivers what is expected until this point.

Before long, however, we cannot separate the space which contains John and Mommy (the figures in the eyeball movie) from that which holds Patty and Linda (the girls in the movie theater on our screen). A woman catches John in the women's restroom as he waits to extract yet another pair of eyes from their sockets. This scene is conjoined with shots of Patty crouching in the restroom of the movie theater, hiding from a killer (Angel Jove). Events in the two movies continue to merge until by the end of *Anguish* the places and faces are inseparable. Patty is in the hospital, recovering from her injuries at the hands of the killer who entered the cinema. Her parents attempt to allay her fears and reassure her that "Like the doctor said, it's all in your imagination." As she is resting comfortably, the doctor enters the room. Our gaze matches Patty's as the doctor—who is actually John—

looms larger saying, "Like they said, I really don't exist." Here the figure from the screen enters Patty's reality. The movie-within-a-movie technique, with encouragement by Bigas Luna, gets out of control in the film. It exposes the workings of the conventions, dependent for their success upon our expectations. At the same time it leads us to acknowledge the importance of the frame in structuring our perceptions, in separating "fiction" from "fact" and "reality" from "fantasy." While Bigas Luna has carefully integrated elements evoking anxiety and invoking the horror genre, his representations are never transparent. Bigas Luna appears more interested in identifying what makes the horror clock tick than he is with simply using it to mark time in developing a "classic" horror flick.

Critical Implications

The films of Bigas Luna challenge us to examine extant critical categories within which we select, classify and evaluate films for our historical, theoretical and critical collections. By straddling national industries, combining conventions from distinct genres, and re-vising notions of a linear history of cinema, Bigas Luna and his films resist containment within these traditional boundaries. The filmmaker frustrates critics who work from within carefully delineated categories since the man and his work cannot be neatly contained within categories of nation, of genre, and of auteur which have heretofore enabled critical collection and classification.

Jos Bigas Luna stands with one foot firmly planted on Spanish soil and the other strongly positioned in the United States. He successfully straddles two film industries, having worked within Hollywood and Spanish production circles. By demonstrating the ability to cross national boundaries — shooting scenes in Barcelona, Texas and California, pleasing audiences in festivals in Los Angeles, Cannes and San Sebastian — Bigas Luna indeed constitutes a transnational figure. These crossings have enabled Bigas Luna to elude classification as a "Spanish" filmmaker. His work cannot be contained within the confines of a "national" cinema, since it incorporates elements from a broader arena and never relies on "national" themes. Critics are apt to focus on such

"Spanish" themes as the love-death equation, and then rely on the work of "Spanish" filmmakers—*Bodas de sangre* (Blood Wedding) (Carlos Saura, 1980), *Matador* (Pedro Almodovar, 1986), and *Amantes* (Lovers) (Vicente Aranda, 1992), rather than draw from the work of the transnational Bigas Luna.

Critics have been quick to evaluate the filmmaker's work in terms of genre. *Bilbao,* generally considered a "sex film," is termed the "Spanish sex film of most note" by John Hopewell (219) and a film "in which sexuality is treated intelligently" by Román Gubern (20). *Bilbao* was released in Spain with an "S" rating (comparable to an "X" in the United States), a rating reserved for a "sexually explicit" film. *Anguish* was received as a suspense thriller following advance publicity which set the film up as "a psychological horror thriller." Bill Warren terms *Anguish* a "slasher horror film," Deborah J. Kunk treats the film as a "horror drama," and Kyle Counts notes that *Anguish* "has a face only a horror fanatic would love." Critical expectations were further shaped by the publicity poster of the film featuring the image of a crazed woman in front of a gigantic eyeball under the words: "Zelda Rubenstein of 'Poltergeist' Returns to Create a Horror Classic". Because he strives not to meet expectations but to underline them as such, the films of Bigas Luna miss the mark for critics who disregard them as genre "failures." Kevin Thomas notes that "as a thriller [*Anguish*] doesn't really work" (10). Kunk concurs, "From the standpoint of horror parody alone, *Anguish* would be disappointing" (10). A disappointed Peter Besa comes to a similar conclusion about *Lola,* noting that the film is "billed as a suspense thriller, which it only in part is" (*Variety,* 28 May 1986). Critics dedicated to policing the boundaries of a particular genre perceive any deviation as a failure. Since self-conscious deviations recur throughout Bigas Luna's work, the negative responses to his films come as no surprise.

Bigas Luna's collection transcends not only national spaces and film genres but filmic texts as well. The filmmaker highlights images, sounds, and techniques recognizable to filmgoers. Fragments from a number of films invite association with other filmic texts produced over nearly a century. Since these fragments make up the fabric of Bigas Luna's films, it is difficult to identify a "Bigas

Luna image" or a "Bigas Luna technique." The filmmaker is consistent only in the innovative way he treats conventions. The carefully selected and positioned fragments which compose his films provide instruments for dissecting and scrutinizing notions of linear historical narratives, of discreet moments in the history of cinema. They do not, however, aid auteur critics in establishing a list of traits unique to the filmmaker.

What must we infer about such categories that obligate us to marginalize films which do not fit neatly? What are we to make of co-productions, for example, that straddle national boundaries? Or of films that combine conventions from various genres? If extant critical practices inevitably marginalize the very films and filmmakers most apt to imbue new life into cinema, how do we reckon with our role in perpetuating certain expectations and creating certain collections?

Bigas Luna encourages us to reflect on those assumptions which inform our own critical activity. He manages to achieve this by gathering fragments and introducing them into the collections making up his filmic texts. His collection attests to the arbitrary nature of the boundaries presumed to separate one film from another, one moment in the history of cinema from another, one genre from another, and one national industry from another. By gathering images and sounds from numerous films, he denies the possibility of an independent filmic text. By juxtaposing these bits and pieces in his films, he unmasks expectation-producing conventions and exposes the mechanisms of representation. And by exploring the cinematic space — that area perceived to lie between the image projected on the screen and the image projected on the retina — he draws attention to the impossibility of isolating a film from its maker and viewer.

Bigas Luna moves us beyond debates of where the lines should be drawn toward addressing the consequences of drawing such lines, of engaging in a critical practice that embraces only those films which fit within the categories we have constructed. By swimming, as he does, in the fluidity of the very boundaries within which films are produced, catalogued, consumed, and evaluated, Bigas Luna takes our eyes and invites us to see the implications of our practice.[4]

Notes

The research for this paper was made possible in part by support from the Harold Leonard Memorial Film Fund and the Department of Comparative Literature at the University of Minnesota.

1. Bigas Luna is currently working on *Jamón, jamón* (Ham, Ham) with completion expected in late 1992. The "road movie" takes rural Castille as its locale.

Kevin Thomas finds Bigas Luna's work "totally nauseous" at times ("Credible Subworlds"). The Animal Humane Society, after being contacted by an agitated viewer of *Caniche,* wired the FILMEX festival calling the film "depraved" (*Hollywood Reporter,* 11 April 1980). Peter Besa notes that the feeling in *Caniche* is "decidedly kinky and sick" (*Variety,* 16 May 1979).

2. For a detailed discussion of *Bilbao* and its treatment of detective, thriller, melodrama and pornography conventions, see my article entitled "Deconstructing Cinematic Conventions and Reconsidering Pornography in Bigas Luna's *Bilbao.*"

3. This screen-around-a-screen convention has a long history. Characters sometimes step off the screen as in *The Purple Rose of Cairo* (Woody Allen, 1985) and *Mi querido Tom Mix* (My Dear Tom Mix) (Carlos Garca, Mexico, 1991). The narrative sometimes revolves around the making of a film as in *La tarea* (Homework) (Mara Rojo & José Alonso, Mexico, 1990) and *Adorables mentiras* (Adorable Lies) (Gerardo Chijona, Cuba, 1991). And the movie house sometimes provides the focal point as in *Cinema Paradiso* (Giusseppe Tornatore, Italy, 1988). This technique, successful in a number of genres, appears particularly effective in horror films. Robert Schirmer, a Screenwriting Fellow at Universal Studios and author of *Living With Strangers* (New York: New York Univ. Press, 1992), pointed out a number of titles which draw their themes from the cinema: *Demons* (Lamberto Bava, Italy, 1985), *Demons 2* (1987), *Return to Horror High* (Bill Froelich, 1987), *Stage Fright* (Michael Soavi, Italy, 1987) and *Targets* (Peter Bogdanovich, 1969).

4. Bigas Luna straddles other boundaries as well. In addition to a reputation as a filmmaker, he is a renowned artist in Spain. His paintings are on display in Figueras at the Dali Museum.

Works Cited

Anderson, Brian. "Caniche." 1980 *Filmex.* 1980.

Benjamin, Walter. *Illuminations: Essays & Reflections.* Ed. Hannah Arendt. New York: Shocken Books, 1955.

Besa, Peter. "Review: Caniche." *Variety,* 16 May 1979.

———. "Review: Lola." *Variety,* 28 May 1986.

Bigas Luna, Jos. "Notes on *Anguish* from Director/Writer Bigas Luna." *Spectrafilm News Release,* 28 Dec. 1987.

Clifford, James. *The Predicament of Culture.* Cambridge, Mass.: Harvard Univ. Press, 1988.

Counts, Kyle. "Film Review: *Anguish.*" *The Hollywood Reporter* 4 Feb. 1988: 10.

Giles, Dennis. "Conditions of Pleasure in Horror Cinema." *Planks of Reason: Essays on the Horror Film.* Metuchen, N.J.: Scarecrow Press, 1984.

Gubern, Román. "Tendencies, Genres and Problems of Spanish Cinema in the Post-Franco Period." *Quarterly Review of Film Studies* 8, Spring 1983.

Hopewell, John. *Out of the Past.* London: British Film Institute, 1986.

Kunk, Deborah J. "You'll Get an Eyeful of *Anguish* in a Hurry." *Los Angeles Herald Examiner*, 29 Jan. 1988: 10.

Price, Sally. *Primitive Art in Civilized Places*. Chicago: Univ. of Chicago Press, 1989.

Stock, Ann M. "Deconstructing Cinematic Conventions and Reconsidering Pornography in Bigas Luna's *Bilbao*." *Cine-Lit: Essays on Peninsular Film and Fiction*. Ed. George Cabello Castellet, Jaume Martí-Olivella and Guy H. Wood. Portland, Ore.: Portland State Univ. Press, 1992.

Thomas, Kevin. "*Anguish* Turns a Mirror on Its Audience." *Los Angeles Times*, 29 Jan. 1988: VI-10.

———. "Credible Subworlds of Luna's *Bilbao*," *Los Angeles Times*, 17 Aug. 1983: VI-4.

Waller, Gregory A., ed. *American Horrors*. Urbana: Univ. of Illinois Press, 1987.

Warren, Bill. "New Edge for Slasher Film." *The Enterprise*, 29 Jan. 1988: 21.

Wood, Robin. "An Introduction to the American Horror Film," *Movies and Methods*. Vol II. Ed. Bill Nichols. Berkeley: Univ. of California Press, 1985: 195–220.

◆   **Chapter 10**

Mother Country, Fatherland: The Uncanny Spain of Manuel Gutiérrez Aragón

Teresa M. Vilarós

In a series of conversations with Augusto M. Torres, Manuel Gutiérrez Aragón said the following about his film *El corazón del bosque*: "Puesto que [la película] es difícil por fantasmagórica, por lo menos que el tono general sea fantasmagórico, aunque tenga lagunas argumentales" (109). The gaps ("lagunas") to which Gutiérrez Aragón refers, and which in *El corazón del bosque* correspond to the many scenes filmed but not included in the final cut because "bajaban el tono general" (109), are by no means exceptional within the totality of his filmic *oeuvre*. His films have often been labeled barely comprehensible, and Aragón himself explains: "La gente decía que con el fin de la censura [cinematográfica en España] deberíamos hablar claro. Pero... mi cine... no era cuestión de camuflaje."[1] Aragón's words imply that "not to speak clearly" ("no hablar claro") is a stylistic characteristic. This refusal to speak clearly corresponds to a certain "dark mode" ("modo oscuro") which, in the majority of his films, is associated with the sleight-of-hand of a magician cloaking the obvious and quotidian to make it reappear as strange, phantasmagoric, or dream-like. Here I would like to present, in the Freudian sense, the uncanny side of that dark mode, taking into account the representation of Spain made by two of his films which I consider to mirror each other: *Camada negra* (1977) and *El corazón del bosque* (1978).

These films treat, respectively, the years immediately after the death of Francisco Franco and the effects of the national conflagration during the years following the Spanish Civil War. The two films respond in a complementary fashion to a representational style that reveals the uncanny, as the director himself suggests: "En mis películas trato que las cosas más obvias parezcan extrañas y las más extrañas obvias" (*Conversaciones* 80). Gutiérrez Aragón conceals the obviousness of the domestic and familiar in order to estrange it, while at the same time making the unfamiliar appear quotidian. This simultaneous reciprocity evokes the paradox that Freud points out in the confusion of two German words, *heimlich* (the familiar) and its opposite *unheimlich* (the strange, the uncanny, the unfamiliar). As Freud explains in an example about the origin of these two words: "[A]mong its different shades of meaning the word *heimlich* exhibits one which is identical with its opposite, *unheimlich*. What is *heimlich* thus comes to be *unheimlich*" (224).

In both films, the familiar becomes terrifying and the terrifying familiar. The films are representations of the uncanny because they reveal "that class of the frightening which leads back to what is known of old and long familiar" (Freud 220). Both the strange and familiar are confused in the two films and the particularities distinct to each film can be called complements or reflections of each other, rather than differences. Insofar as *El corazón del bosque* exemplifies the uncanny through darkness and austerity, it is the reverse of *Camada negra,* which allows for an outcropping of the uncanny by means of the excessive and the caricaturesque. In *El corazón del bosque* the uncanny emerges in a partial and veiled manner; in *Camada negra* it erupts like magma. The grotesque nature in *Camada negra* manifests itself through the exaggerated depiction of its characters who, with the exception of Rosa, the girlfriend of the adolescent Tatín, seem more like quick sketches than profound psychological studies. The grotesque also produces the profusion of symbols that appear in the film: horses, dogs, allusions to violence and mutilation, and the use of an institute of serology as a familial enclave. *Camada negra* openly reveals all, unlike *El corazón del bosque,* in which everything is insinuated and suggested. In one way or another, partially or completely, what is revealed in both films is always an uncanny something: the intimate and personal which becomes unknown, as in *El corazón del bosque,* or the unknown and monstrous becoming familiar and recognizable, as in *Camada negra.*

The typical veiling/unveiling of the familiar and the terrifying present in these two films by Aragón has to do with the depiction of the so-called "two Spains." In different forms, the two films refer to an earlier Republican or Francoist Spain as a painful loss, manifested through both nostalgia and conflict. *El corazón del bosque* focuses on the Maquis, the Republican soldiers who continued to resist in the woods of the northern part of Spain in the years following the Spanish Civil War. *Camada negra* tells of an ultra-right group in the late seventies and of its will to resist the new democratic Spain. In both films, Maquis and fascists inhabit a space that, from a familial place, becomes for them an ominous enclave.

In *El corazón del bosque* the end of the Civil War and Franco's victory force the withdrawal of the Maquis from their families and towns to the nearby woods and mountains. Their entrance into the woods implies an irremediable loss of home life identified with the loss of Republican Spain. While in *El corazón del bosque* the loss of the particular becomes a more general loss, *Camada negra* goes from a general to a particular loss. Here, Franco's death and the instauration of democracy signals the end of a whole era, forcing the Republican force and its young protagonist, Tatín, to resort to terroristic actions. Yet their violence will not give them back the old Spain. Even the ultimate sacrificial ritual performed by Tatín, which signals the loss of the private, will remain ironically useless, as post-Franco Spain will be forever hostile to all of them. Caught between two Spains, the ultra-right group lives in an old Instituto de Serología, a place which easily becomes associated with Francoist Spain. Living under the care of an authoritarian and despotic maternal figure, the institute serves as a hiding place and as a center of operations.

Although the two groups in the two films are situated at opposite ends of the political axis, we find a similar displacement, a similar movement and interchange of spaces corresponding to an uncanny feeling of loss of a *madre patria.* The loss will produce in both movies a certain resistance, a force that will attempt the political recuperation of the lost country as well as the psychological construction (or destruction) of an identity associated with it. In *El corazón del bosque* and *Camada negra* dissolution and individual loss remain associated with the loss of the mother country. Yet, the construction of identity of resistance to this loss will necessarily move on to configuring itself in political terms, as a representation of a fatherland. Aragón shows in both films how each specific political loss can be translated into and refer to profound psychological losses, to old and primeval Oedipal mournings, and vice-versa. Crossing into the realm of both the political and the psychological, Aragón points out the particular and specific quality of displacement of the resistance to loss, a move that unveils the terrifying and the uncanny in the two films.

The process of resistance in *El corazón del bosque* acts against the progressive deterioration that collective memory (represented by Spanish post–civil war society) exercises upon individual memory (represented by the Maquis, and above all by their boss "El Andarín"). In *Camada negra,* the process of construction and resistance of an individual memory (represented by the ultra-right group and by the young Tatín) acts against a collective will of forgetfulness (that of the Spanish people in the post-Franco years). In both films, and from both sides of the political mirror, the representation of this resistance becomes uncanny upon making the will to destruction and/or the conservation of an identity coincide with the will to retrieve an unrecoverable mother country, a forever lost *madre patria*. In doing so, the terrifying familial demons become unleashed.

In *El corazón del bosque,* the time that the Maquis and "El Andarín" spend in the mountains marks a regressive space inescapably dedicated to a search for the recuperation of that *madre patria* (here a Republican one), a search that must necessarily pass through the equally impossible recuperation of an identity destroyed by the civil war. Thus, the magic forest that Aragón shows in his film is the uncanny space in which a journey takes place in the form of a quest.[2] The film portrays the initial post–civil war years as an incision that leaves exposed and in momentary contact a "before," related to the domestic space, and an "after," referring to the experience of living in the forest. The forest is not merely scenery, nor is it simply the place where the story occurs; it is, on the contrary, the true protagonist of the film.[3] The forest is for the Maquis their only shelter and sure home; but it is, at the same time, the uncanny place, the bearer of secrets and the heart of the film.

The forest is an atemporal and abysmal *locus* in which the last of the Maquis hide, and in which the *heimlich* and the *unheimlich* become confused; it is the force that sets the veiling mechanism into motion. Enshrouding the Maquis in its fog, the forest guards and protects them from indiscreet gazes, especially from those of the Guardia Civil. But that which is *heimlich* easily becomes *unheimlich* since, although offering them their only place of refuge, the forest also conceals the demon that destroys "the *Heimlichkeit* of the home" (Freud 222). No longer a safe haven, the forest will expel one by one the lifeless bodies of the last Maquis.

El corazón del bosque centers on the search that Juan, a former Maqui, undertakes for "El Andarín," the only surviving inhabitant of the forest. "El Andarín," former leader of the group and Juan's ex-boss, alone and sick, refuses to give in to Franco's victorious Spain. The treatment of this character is again characteristic of Gutiérrez Aragón's representational "dark mode." The director destroys any idea or notion of the familiar with the portrayal of "El Andarín"; he is not a recognizable person, but a confusing image, much like the secret of the forest. Covered in rags and hooded, physically indistinguishable through the mist and darkness of the trees that surround him, "El Andarín" remains visually incorporated into the forest that hides him. The visual destruction of the character, taken to such an extreme that Gutiérrez Aragón himself has called "El Andarín" "moldy" ("mohoso"), responds to the demands of the forest's demons.[4] The demons filter through the fog and partially efface the character of "El Andarín"; they also erase and disfigure all memory of those who once knew or heard of him. The nearby town, the only previous contact "El Andarín" has had with the outside world, estranges him more and more until his persona fades into a collective and ancestral memory which then transforms him into a mythical figure. A character out of time, "El Andarín" 's real and concrete humanity remains forever part of a universal "El." As a young girl tells Juan, no one in the area talks about "El Andarín" any longer; everybody simply speaks of "El."

The character's transformation into myth implicitly carries with it a process of destruction of identity. It parallels the loss of the fatherland, which corresponds to the process of destruction of the proper name. El Andarín was a former Republican soldier whom the viewer never comes to know as such. Forced by the course of the war, he loses his first and last name upon forming a Maquis group. As a member of such a group, the nickname "El Andarín" will quickly substitute for his proper name; a general name which, following the process of loss, later gives way to the universal "El." For "El Andarín" the loss of the name supposes the definitive loss of Republican Spain, the loss of the country. "El," unlike when he went by his first and last names, is no longer a former Republican soldier. "El," without a name, a fatherland (*patria*) or an identity, becomes something like "un bicho al que habrían que matar" (*El corazón del bosque*), something that must remain hidden.

The process of destruction of identity presented in *El corazón del bosque* mirrors the resistance to loss presented in *Camada negra*. In the latter, the process of destruction is related to the process of construction or access to an identity. If in *El corazón del bosque* Juan as well as "El Andarín" were ideologically formed and po-litically placed in the moment of their entrance into the forest (the destruction thus follows a previously established identity), in *Camada negra* Tatín is a young man who has still not entered adulthood and who, because of his youth, is refused entry into the para-fascist group. To obtain both identity and membership, Tatín must face destruction. To construct his identity, he must le-gitimate with blood his association with the fascist group. He ac-complishes this through the brutal murder of his girlfriend.

This violent murder harvests in its own immoderation the ter-rifying contradiction generated by the pairs *madre* and *patria*, the private and the public, the psychological and the political. The two films narrate the attempt to cover, conceal, or destroy an otherness hostile to the preservation or acquisition of identity. However, in the very process of concealment, both narrations turn into a text which keeps expelling its demons and ghosts into the open. The veiling motion unveils and the *heimlich* becomes *un-heimlich*; the hidden emerges partially and uncannily.

Quoting Schelling, Freud reminds us that "*Unheimlich* is the name for everything that ought to have remained...secret and hidden but has come to light" (224). In *El corazón del bosque*, Juan penetrates the forest in search of "El." This move forces the phantasmal and demonic "El," reduced to obscurity, to come out of the darkness. When Juan enters the forest he begins a process of (un)veiling, a process that, as I have said, is revealed as uncanny and is, in the last instance, destructive. In *Camada negra*, Tatín leaves the familial space in which he is secluded. He heads into the city to perpetrate terroristic acts. But these actions will not benefit the group. Instead, they will endanger it through public exposure. As Juan did in *El corazón del bosque*, Tatín also moves forward, though in an opposite direction. Juan directed himself toward the interior of the forest, while Tatín advances toward the urban exterior. However, the movement of both characters is circular, since the two move toward a point without exit, a zero point, a fissure-space portrayed as an enclave of an uncanny encounter with "the other."

The violence and the traumatic rupture produced by the civil war demand the denunciation of the "other." Any notion of otherness, however, requires the notion of an ego and vice-versa. The "other" is part of the ego; the "other" is, in a certain sense, a double for the ego, its mirroring figure. In both films the characters are presented as mirrored reflections of one another. In *Camada negra* Tatín's exit from the secluded Instituto and subsequent movement into the outside, urban world becomes the search for and construction of his own identity. The youth's initiation assumes an uncanny character by virtue of his being part of a family body that paradoxically insists on the negation of his existence. Tatín is caught up in this contradiction. "Somos un cuerpo" and "formamos una piña," together with "no existimos para afuera" or "no existimos ni para nosotros mismo," are expressions constantly repeated, and in a number of variations, by his tyrannical mother, Blanca. In order to be, in order to become a man and part of the group, Tatín must paradoxically become a non-being, an unsolvable conflict that necessarily ends in destruction and violence.

The non-being, on the other hand, concerns all characters in the two films. In *El corazón del bosque*, "El Andarín" is no longer "El Andarín" but "El"; while Juan's being is a "Maquis-being," a status not officially recognized as such in the Spain of 1952.[5] The civil war begins to fade away, history has been written and the Maquis' reason for fighting, and indeed being, gradually becomes diluted. The destruction of the being parallels the process of transformation from a familiar Spain to an uncanny one. For Juan, ten years after the Republican defeat, Franco's Spain is *unheimlich*. The family home, a recurrent image in Aragón's film, is populated by ghosts; furthermore, Juan doesn't know the new people, such as Suso, the boyfriend and future husband of Juan's sister Amparo, just as he doesn't know who has died in the village: "No sabía que había muerto" (*El corazón del bosque*), Juan says to his sister when she informs him of the death of a neighbor and family friend.

In *Camada negra*, Tatín also inhabits a familial space populated by ghosts, an "uncanny" household. Freud tells us that "*Heimlich* is . . . a place free from ghostly influences" (225), but is this space possible? It no longer is for Juan, as his home is lost forever. Nor is it for el Andarín, marked by the demons from the forest; nor is it for Tatín, for whom the home/institute, represented above all by his mother, Blanca, is always depicted as being hostile.

The acquisition of the ego requires the loss of the mother, at least partially, in order to incorporate the father. In political terms, this means that the "mother" of *madre patria* must yield its privileged place to the "father," the *patria*. In the two films, a reconciliation of the terms *madre* and *patria* will always prove to be impossible. If, as Freud said, what some call *heimlich* others call *unheimlich*, what some call "mother country" others call "fatherland," and vice-versa. Signs and symbols duplicate, double and become confused with each other. The mother hides the father and the father the mother, while weakness and/or force shifts from one to the other. The masculine *patria* is represented in *El corazón del bosque* through the image of a powerless bull, tied up and blindfolded. *Camada negra* shows us sickly horses from the serological institute, wretched horses useful only to provide an already obsolete serum, while at the same time portraying violently masculine images that relate as much to the watchdogs as to the militant-fascist paraphernalia of the all-male group.

In *El corazón del bosque* the images of the wounded bull (which together with the images of the wounded horses in *Camada negra* bring to mind Picasso's *Guernica*), are images-symbols that supplement and/or complement those in which the maternal figure is diluted and partially effaced, as in the scenes of the cow losing its milk, the old family house, Juan's sister, and even the forest itself as protective space. As images of the father and mother, all evoke the feeling of loss, nostalgia and disintegration. In *Camada negra*, on the other hand, the maternal symbology is opposed to the paternal one; this opposition occurs as much between these symbols as mutually within them. The open-minded and youthful Rosa, Tatín's girlfriend, is counterposed with the image of the wicked and dictatorial Blanca, Tatín's mother. The macho glorification of the group is opposed to the weakness and uselessness of Blanca's husband, and the wounded and broken horses are opposed to the violent and aggressive dogs.

Everything in the two films presents its two sides. *El corazón del bosque* portrays a familiar nostalgic perception of a pre–civil war Spain, to which the soldier would like to return. It is a nurturing and maternal Spain longed for in the exact moment that it is lost, that is, in the moment of entry into this forest which offers protection and shelter as well as death and destruction. *Camada negra* emphasizes the other side of the idea of the mother, the repressive mother, punitive and castrating—represented by Blanca—from whom the young adolescent male must free himself. Head of the grotesque familial and political body, Blanca is clearly the phallic woman described by Freud, as illustrated in the scene where, in a booming voice and with outstretched arms laden with rifles, she exclaims: "las armas las tengo yo." In hackneyed Calderonian style, the code that she imposes is a virile one based on honor and revenge.

However, despite the depiction of Blanca as the phallic woman and an uncanny ghost, Gutiérrez Aragón also portrays the *heimlich* as "feminine" by relating it, above all, through the characters of Rosa, in *Camada negra,* and Amparo, in *El corazón del bosque.* The fresh and contagious smile of the young Rosa counterposes Blanca's fanatical and exalted exclamations: "hay que vengar al hermano, guardar silencio y sacrificar lo más querido," the three tests that Tatín is going to impose on himself as rites of initiation and beginning and end of his quest. In *El corazón del bosque,* that which sends Juan on his quest is the sound of Amparo's voice and the soft, childlike voice of a young girl singing a popular song.

That symbolic fragmentation can be taken as a representation of the conflictual fragmentation and impossibility implicit in the terms *madre patria.* In Aragón's films, this fragmentation corresponds to the notion of a wounded Spain divided by the civil war. The mother/fatherland releases the paternal and maternal in uncanny form. As a father, Spain turns into Saturn, devourer of his children, and as a mother, she remains lost forever. However, Gutiérrez Aragón never lapses into clear-cut simplifications, as he reveals in the two films the uncanny side extant in the two discursive constructions. After the civil war, Spain has been neither "mother" nor "father." While on the one hand, Spain is felt as protective shelter, on the other hand she is the wicked mother who rejects her children. As *patria,* Spain assumes the father's authority, refusing to name many of its children. Over and over again, the post–Civil War fatherland denies his citizens the filial right to the paternal name, calling instead for silence and darkness.

In this game of doubles and mirrors, silence and darkness will be, paradoxically, the elements which permit the unveiling. The end of the civil war allows the nostalgia for an earlier Spain, Nationalist or Republican, to break through. Yet, it is a nostalgia which will turn terrifying, forcing that which wants darkness and concealment to come to light. In *Camada negra,* Tatín exposes himself publicly through desperate acts, and by doing so endangers the security of the neofascist group, a security based on silence and secrecy; as Blanca says: "Nuestro mejor arma es el silencio." Silence and secrecy are also necessary for the survival of the characters of *El corazón del bosque,* a secrecy which isolates them from the outside world, just as the group from *Camada negra* is isolated from the Spain of the late 1970s. In the darkness or in the forest, we cannot feel protected and sheltered. In *Camada negra* every member of the group turns into a stranger to the others. In *El corazón del bosque* those who wander into the forest become strangers: the civil guards are strangers to the Maquis, the Maquis is a stranger to "El Andarín," "El Andarín" is a stranger to Juan, and Juan is a stranger to himself and to his family, specifically to his sister Amparo and his brother-in-law Suso. For each other, for everyone, the exit is hidden, as one of the guards in the forest sings one night while on duty: "Oscurece la salida el bosque" (*El corazón del bosque*). The home and the familial haven were at the exit but are no longer accessible. The forest occupies their places now as an uncanny place that darkens the external.

Juan turns the search for "El Andarín" into a personal quest for his own identity. But in the middle of the forest the "one" and the "other" lose their meaning, just as the civil war loses its meaning as does the political fight of anti-Francoist resistance. The forest is now uncanny, "un lugar horroroso que se acerca más a la visión que dan de él los cuentos infantiles . . . morada de las brujas, los ogros y, en definitiva de la muerte" (*Conversaciones* 113). The process of "El Andarín"'s disfiguration and demonization begins to reproduce itself in Juan. The images of his childhood, a childhood lived in pre–civil war Spain, appear in the forest, confused and disoriented. In this scene, Juan is chatting with his friend Atilano, a ghostly figure whom we cannot discern as either dead or alive.[6] Juan, puzzled and frightened, sees how his childhood memories fuse with those of Atilano. Their memory images flow together in the heart of the forest: the bull with his eyes blindfolded, a boy ignored by his playmates on the day of the proclamation of the Republic, a cow leaking milk from its udders. The forest never answers its own riddles. These disturbing images demand that the viewer guess their meanings. Just as the blindfolded (and therefore metaphorically castrated) bull is not a bull, just as the child that cannot play is not a child, in the heart of the forest Juan is not completely Juan, Atilano is neither completely alive nor dead, and "El Andarín" is nothing more than an empty shadow who will continue diluting himself in the forest until he dies in it. The forest is lived through nostalgia, through the primeval memory of the home, thus exemplifying Freud's following words: "From the idea of 'homelike' . . . [the uncanny] is developed of something withdrawn from the eyes of strangers, something concealed, secret" (225).

Camada negra is also an example of Freud's previous words. Tatín develops the concept of the hidden and the secret through his notion of the domestic. The Instituto de Serología that hides the ultra-right group is as populated with ghosts as are the years of post-Franco Spain, or the Spain of 1952 in *El corazón del bosque*. The uncanny is born from the fissure established by the civil war and re-established by Franco's death. In Gutiérrez Aragón's films, the forest and the institute are representations of the uncanny, and they bring about nothing but destruction. They leave us defenseless and blind. The forest and the institute are the realm of darkness, a realm that renders the eye useless.[7]

The forest from *El corazón del bosque* veils "El Andarín" in rags. Shadows form and become indistinguishable, while images are revealed in their partiality, dark and nocturnal. To walk the forest in circles is, in a certain way, to be blind to the exit, to be incapable of discovering it; Juan, who penetrates the forest in search of "El Andarín," in search of the conclusion of the war (and therefore in search of the closing of the fissure), follows a circular path that is going to leave him opposite an "El" which is himself. In the last scene, he finds himself opposite the blindfolded bull, in the same way that Tatín's path is going to leave him opposite the statue of the horse that, as a statue, also stares without seeing.

In *El corazón del bosque*, Juan rewrites step by step the path of "El Andarín." Driven by the feminine voice, throughout the film he goes about filling the tracks left in the forest by "El." He travels a road back to the origin until, in one of the final images, his own image becomes confused with that of his ex-boss, superimposing the shadow of his body upon the disembodied shadow of the already-dead "El Andarín." At the end of this journey, each one is nothing but the shadow of the other. Juan's journey leads nowhere other than to his own veiled and doubled encounter. "El Andarín," a former personification of the real and concrete story of the Spanish Civil War, is, at the time of his encounter with his double, an "El" that seems to carry with it the echoes of Juan's unconscious id, the universal Id that resists history and its writing.

When, in *El corazón del bosque* "El Andarín"'s shadow is "filled" with the shadow of Juan's body, there is an uncanny space and moment, one of confusion between the conscious and the unconscious, between reality and dream, between the previous and the immediate, between absence and presence, between the ego and the id. The shadow-image of "one" corresponds to the shadow-image of the "other" (and vice-versa), which corresponds at the same time to the elusive images of the blindfolded bull and the cow leaking milk. These images are, in an uncanny sense, connected with the vision of the double. As floating signifiers, the cow and the bull without eyes become associated in the filmic narration with the moments of nostalgia and memory of Juan's childhood. The first time we see Juan is at night, hiding out in a milk truck. Surrounded by tall milk containers—another sign that makes reference to the cow and therefore to maternal nutrients and care, to the Spain of his childhood prior to the civil war— Juan, crouching and in the dark, is also a blind bull, a product of the war. Amparo, together with her house situated at the edge of the forest and her meaningful name, is the embodiment of the previous Spain. She, in the images of her sitting on the floor shrieking spasmodically, and the girl whose song gives Juan clues about the hiding place of "El" form a feminine chorus, a primitive and familial voice that sends Juan on his journey into the forest. This voice will lead him into the heart of the forest where he will meet the paternal figure of "El Andarín." Amparo and the girl are the "feminine," the echo and lure of the maternal land from which Juan can contemplate the defeated bull, the castrated bull into which "El Andarín" has been transformed, the blindfolded bull that is now the *patria* and Juan himself.

The final point of the regressive circular path effaces the notions of difference and absence. El Andarín is "El" and "El" is Juan. "El" is the bull and the cow full of milk; "El" is the id and the ego, the feminine and the masculine, the *heimlich* and the *unheimlich,* the victorious Spain and the defeated Spain. The vision of "El Andarín" in the heart of the forest is the uncanny vision which Freud, evoking Nietzsche, calls, "the constant recurrence of the same thing" (234). There is always a recurrence, as in the case of Tatín, who leaves the institute only to return to it in the final moment of the film. Although Tatín doesn't find his double (just as Juan doesn't in *El corazón del bosque*) he does however confront the "other" that Rosa represents. The two final moments of double encounter in the two films—Juan with "El" and Tatín with Rosa—mark the narrative circularity between the two movies, that is, the circular path, a moment without time or history, coinciding with the circle which Freud describes for the uncanny: "*Heimlich* is a word the meaning of which develops in the direction of ambivalence, until it finally coincides with its opposite, *unheimlich*. *Unheimlich* is in some way or other a sub-species of *heimlich*" (226).

Freud also writes that the fact "that man is capable of self-observation...renders it possible to invest the old idea of a 'double' with a new meaning" (235), a meaning which will be always profoundly familiar to us, always recurrent, always one and always uncanny, always known and unknown. It is a path that will always be a permanent return to the same, and which *Camada negra* depicts as limited and without possible hope. The uncanny and the unfamiliar definitively displace the intimate and the known. The familiar is now going to remain hidden; it will be returned to the land in the form of Rosa's lifeless body. A violent and unexpected scene, the murder of Rosa at the hands of Tatín, and her burial in a newly planted forest, is an uncanny return which reproduces "El Andarín"'s death at the hands of Juan in the other film. Rosa's murder and burial represents the loss of all familial place and space, the loss of a country free of ghosts, the loss of the (mother)land. Once the *heimlich* body of the young girl is buried, a sapling is planted. As a sad and pathetic phallic example, this small tree is a mirror of the real Spanish deforestation, of a Spain that, more than forty years after the end of the civil war, lived—and may still be living—like a fissured *patria* populated by uncanny ghosts, memories, and unsettling nostalgia.

Notes

1. This statement is from an interview given to *Lui* (Hopewell, 264, n. 7).

2. Gutiérrez Aragón explicitly affirms that his film is not a direct adaptation of Joseph Conrad's novel *Heart of Darkness* (*Conversaciones* 103). However, the journey as quest which the film offers is similar to the novel, as the director himself affirms: "Esto [*El corazón del bosque*] es como *El corazón de las tinieblas*" (103). The affinity with the theme of the journey made Gutiérrez Aragón decide to give his film a title in homage to Conrad's novel. *El corazón del bosque* would belong then to the group of films that, more or less explicitly, are related to the novel, like, for example, *Apocalypse Now*, the film by Francis Ford Coppola, or *2001: A Space Odyssey*, by Stanley Kubrick. Gutiérrez Aragón, however, has not taken these texts as explicit references.

3. Gutiérrez Aragón says exactly: "El verdadero protagonista es el bosque... El que vive, destruye, da de comer y aniquila es el bosque" (115).

4. The director says: "Me gustaba que El Andarín, el supuesto mito, fuera un poco mohoso" (*Conversaciones* 113).

5. The Maquis-being in 1952 was equivalent to a non-being from the point of view of the Franco regime, since from the end of the civil war they were not considered as a possibility within the system. The only official recognition of their existence was dedicated precisely to their extermination. Curiously, although in the film the character of Juan is a Maquis, Gutiérrez Aragón says jokingly: "Juan no es maqui, más bien es Jorge Semprún. Aunque Semprún nunca se hubiera metido en un bosque como ése" (*Conversaciones* 115).

6. In *Conversaciones,* Manuel Gutiérrez Aragón says about Atilano: "Se quitó una escena donde el personaje de Atilano . . . era fusilado, luego se veía que revivía y acompañaba un poco a Juan . . . [En la versión final de la película] no se cuenta si está muerto o no, pero como no se ha visto que ha sido fusilado siempre estará vivo, aunque tiene el tono de un personaje fantasmagórico. [La escena del fusilamiento] se suprimió porque una vez que tenía este acorde fantasmagórico, no estaba bien incluir una escena política de fusilamiento" (110).

7. The uselessness of the eye is also suggested in the movie poster for *Camada negra,* which depicts a group of men with their eyes covered.

Works Cited

Camada negra. Dir. Manuel Gutiérrez Aragón. With José Luis Alonso and Angela Molina. El Imán, 1977.

El corazón del bosque. Dir. Manuel Gutiérrez Aragón. With Norman Brisky and Angela Molina. Luis Megino, 1978.

Freud, Sigmund. "The Uncanny." *The Standard Edition of the Complete Psychological Works.* Trans. James Strachey. Vol. 17. London: Hogarth Press, 1964. 217–252.

Hopewell, John. *Out of the Past: Spanish Cinema after Franco.* London: British Film Institute, 1986.

Torres, Augusto. *Conversaciones con Manuel Gutiérrez Aragón.* Madrid: Fundamentos, 1985.

◆ **Chapter 11**

Images of War: Hunting the Metaphor

Antonio Monegal

It is well known that in an attempt to escape the control of the censors during Franco's dictatorship, Spanish cinema developed a remarkable tendency to disguise its political message by means of a highly codified symbolic discourse. It is not my intention to retrace that history, but to analyze the operation of cinematic rhetoric under those anomalous expressive demands. Under those particular circumstances, the political context required that film be made into the vehicle of a message that runs parallel to the narrative and is only accessible by recourse to what we could call a poetic reading. The causes, contexts and intentions which originate this type of discourse are extremely diverse, as it is not restricted to films produced under dictatorial regimes.

Even after Franco's death, it has also been the case that the civil war of 1936–1939 has only rarely been the subject of a film that represented the war *as such*. After the constraints of censorship were lifted, there have been many films made that were (supposedly) about the war, or about the tough times during the dictatorship. But the treatment of the topic was mediated by some form of indirection. In order to make it available for a specific kind of cinematic approach, the collective experience of the most crucial event in contemporary Spanish history had to be transformed into a private experience. Spanish cinema has, in a way, preferred the dramatic and lyrical modes over the epic. The everyday conflicts within the family or the small community, the memories of the individual were the formulas of choice. Marking one of the turning points for political films, Carlos Saura's *La prima Angélica* (Cousin Angelica) (1974) illustrates an indigenous *recherche du temps perdu*. At the same time the narratives often incorporated an allegorical reading, which allowed for the transference between private and collective experience, and was open to political interpretation. In Monterde's diagnosis, "History was channelled through 'stories,' which were all basically the same one" (48).

As the main examples which will bear the burden of my analysis, I have selected two films, *La caza* (The Hunt), directed by Saura, and *Furtivos* (Poachers), directed by José Luis Borau. They share their organizing allegorical motif: "the same broad metaphor — human relations as a hunt — which runs from *La caza* to *Furtivos*, *Escopeta nacional* ('National Shotgun,' Luis Berlanga, 1977), and *Dedicatoria* ('A Dedication,' Jaime Chavarri, 1980)" (Hopewell 27). They also share a classical antecedent produced within a very different national and historical context: the sequence of the hunt in Jean Renoir's *La règle du jeu*. The Spanish Civil War and the Francoist dictatorship constitute the unavoidable interpretive framework from which to address these films by Saura and Borau, though I will not try to decipher *what* they mean, but *how* they mean. The objective is to isolate in these two films the rhetorical devices that, in spite of being incorporated into the narrative and participating in its development, generate a discourse that is not ruled by narrative economy. Such a discourse is "extravagant," in the sense that it is narratively uneconomical and cannot be consumed simply as story. We may identify those devices as figural operations, equivalent to metaphor and metonymy, which, when combined, make up the allegorical texture of the film.

Film is a medium that creates very effectively an illusion of reality. The spectator tends to confuse the process of reading, of decoding the film, with the process by which we perceive reality, and to assume that the pertinent codes of interpretation — following which we assign meaning to reality or to film — are similar in both cases. As film is an analogical system of representation, it is too easy to assume that things are what they appear to be, and that they mean what they are. The cinematic equivalent of the poetic figure makes relevant to the reading of the film codes of extradiegetic import, as it triggers mechanisms of association with semantic fields that are alien to the literal reading of the sign. The operation of reading a sign as if it meant something different from what it appears to be is contrary to the law of inertia that rules the cinematic phenomenon. The powerful illusion of reality drives the spectator to take the representation — the image or sound — for the object itself. The representation is perceived, immediately, as presence. Thus, the separation between thing and sign becomes so tenuous as to impose, also immediately, a literal, denotative reading of the sign. In this first step of the reading, any attempt to separate the sign from the object seems to lead to a tautology: A means A. That is why in film the figural reading of the sign very seldom achieves the complete substitution of the literal reading. In verbal statements, such as "I am dying of thirst" or "He has a heart of stone," the metaphorical meaning erases the literal one. In a visual composition, the object that functions as the vehicle of the metaphor continues to be seen as what it is. For the spectator to perceive a figural operation in the cinematic text, there must be a call to attention inscribed within the figure itself, so as to identify it as such. We can apply to film, probably better than to any other art, Nelson Goodman's definition of metaphor as "an affair between a predicate with a past and an object that yields while protesting" (69).

The two films I am discussing are organized as narrative fictions, and ruled by principles of verisimilitude. They could be described as realistic, although this label would say very little. In *La caza* (1965) a group of former civil war combatants spend a day hunting rabbits, and end up killing each other. *Furtivos* (1975) describes the deer hunting expeditions of a Francoist governor of a small province, and is focused on the relationship between a poacher, his wife, who had been the girlfriend of a criminal wanted by the police, and a possessive mother, who murders his son's wife and is in the end killed by her own son. Both films are linked, by the cruelty and violence they portray, to a cinematic tradition that Gilles Deleuze has called "naturalism," designating Luis Buñuel as one of its main representatives (176). Buñuel and Renoir are the indispensable points of reference to approach Saura's film, and it is through the latter that they connect with Borau's. We can thus trace something like the outline of a tradition. Film lacks a predetermined grammar. What it has, as Pasolini acknowledged, are stylemes that become conventions (546). Although this process allows for each film to create its own idiolect and to authorize the pertinent interpretive codes, for the film to be legible the spectator must find some common ground, must share at least some of those codes. To identify a tradition, an act the spectator performs automatically when he or she assigns, for example, a film to a genre, involves recognizing a paradigm of operating codes both at the semantic and at the rhetorical level.

In Saura's *La caza*, Renoir's contribution can be easily detected. The only sequence in which a rabbit hunt is actually taking place displays an obvious parallel with the syntax of the hunting sequence in *La règle du jeu*. Everything in Saura's film is degraded in comparison to Renoir's: the landscape, which has become nearly a desert; the social class of the hunters and the rituals they practice; the number and quality of the servants, which in *La caza* have been reduced to the crippled keeper of the property, Juan, his sick old mother, and his teenage niece. There are not even any pheasants, only rabbits. But the structure of the sequence is very similar, reproducing an editing pattern that is now nearly classical: quick rhythm in the succession of gunshots and in the falling of the game, alternating shots of the hunters and the hunted, focus on the death of the animals. Without repeating details such as the close-up of the dying rabbit with which Renoir punctuates his sequence, Saura records equivalent moments at medium distance, without getting closer than the group shot. The message conveyed is similar. Of all the possible connotations associated with the activity of hunting, both Renoir and Saura choose to emphasize images that are charged with violence, violence that is presented as gratuitous, at the same time that we are made aware of the disparity between the means employed and the size of the victims. The context, and thus the implications of the message of the sequence, is completely different in both films.

We could establish other parallels, either thematic, about the critique of a particular class, or structural, as both scenes anticipate later deaths. But the comparisons are so remote that they would not even occur to us if we had not perceived the more direct link between the two sequences.

In any case it would be very difficult to claim that, by themselves, these hunting scenes invite a figural reading. They suggest, in addition to telling. They charge the action with connotations of violence and cruelty. But that is not enough to identify a poetic figure. As long as there is no proof to the contrary, the killing of rabbits is simply a killing of rabbits, presented from either a positive or a negative perspective. Saura's film contains an allegorical reading that is not merely suggested, but dictated by the film itself, as the film itself holds the key to its own interpretation.

To trigger the metaphorical operations Saura employs what Christian Metz calls *metaphor in syntagma* (227–229). It is a poetic figure constructed so that the vehicle of the metaphor does not replace the tenor, but in which both are present simultaneously and contiguously. This is the procedure more often used in film, as it satisfies the requirement of warning about the presence of the poetic figure and contributes to its reading. Very seldom is an extradiegetic element employed as vehicle of the metaphor, because any information that does not fit the criteria of verisimilitude would spoil the illusion of reality. Thus, if the vehicle is part of the diegesis, it is easier to perceive exclusively its immediate referential function. By establishing an association—the terms of which coexist in the film—by inscribing the sign in a relation of equivalency along the syntagmatic chain, one can construct a readable poetic figure.

The first warning, or clue, in *La caza*, is provided by the information that the three older hunters, José, Paco and Luis, had been together during the civil war, and had fought in the same area where they are now hunting. We can tell they were on Franco's side because of their social and ideological position. There are a number of other clues incorporated into details, for example the fact that Paco is played by Alfredo Mayo, who also played the hero in military epics such as *Raza* (1941), which was based on a script written by Franco himself. The association between the hunt and the war is made right away at a double level, with both sound and image. A comment by Luis, "Many people died here. It's a good place to kill," is echoed by shots of the caves where people used to hide during the war, followed by shots of the rabbit holes. The association between killing people in the war and killing rabbits in the hunt has already been formulated.

There is a verbal reiteration of the same association when, in a discussion about the lack of incentive in killing animals as defenseless as rabbits, Paco replies, stating his contempt for the weak. In a sententious tone, he becomes the spokesman of Nazi ideas about the survival of the fittest. In this exchange, shot in a succession of close-ups, there are two overlapping discourses—one is ideological and the other one is about hunting—which finally merge in a reference to manhunt.

That is why by the time the actual hunting starts, when one of the participants says that "it is not a military operation," the spectator knows very well that the valid message is the opposite one: it *is* a military operation, in the sense that there is an implied equivalency between what the spectator is watching and a war. The sentence is also contradicted by the image of the hunters advancing dispersed across the field.

When we see a ferret chasing a rabbit inside its hutch, the analogy established is between the ferret and the hunters. The figure that associates the pair hunters/prey is reformulated so that both parties belong to the animal kingdom, skipping the common denominator between tenor and vehicle that has allowed for the identification of the metaphor: the same characters participated in the war and in the hunt. The ferret occupies the same symbolic position as the human hunter, so when Paco kills the ferret the film shifts: the violence that was directed toward the other, the enemy or the prey, turns against the hunters themselves. Paco's gesture anticipates that of José, who kills him. In the final act of mutual destruction the executioners are fused with the victims, and the violence of hunting merges with the violence of war. The film has stopped narrating a hunt to become a symptom of the decay of a society (both Spanish society and that small society of friends) born of the war and founded on the memory and the perpetuation of that violence.

If Saura's attention is turned toward the origin, the civil war, Borau's is focused on a synchronic view of the final period of the dictatorship. *La caza* has an allegorical reading that encompasses the whole film, while in *Furtivos* allegory is a recurring temptation that never dominates the reading. Borau takes advantage of the precedent established by Saura. He uses some of Saura's rhetorical devices, and conducts an intertextual dialogue with *La caza*, in which it is very easy to recognize the repetitions and variations. Angel, the poacher, and his mother take the place of Juan and his niece; they are also at the service of the "masters" who go hunting. In Saura's film there was already the suspicion that Juan used to hunt in secret. The focus of the later film has thus displaced its focus toward the group that in *La caza* was restricted to a marginal role: the people who lived on and off the land.

The references are no longer to violence associated with the war, but with the oppression of the dictatorship. The act of hunting has lost its connotations of gratuitous cruelty to mirror the whole coercive system: the problem in *Furtivos* is who is entitled to hunt in the woods and who is not, something that Saura had only hinted at. Borau exploits this loose end, the metaphor of the nation as a *coto vedado* (a forbidden hunting preserve). He presents the violence of hunting as gratuitous only when it is practiced by the governor and his friends, while Angel, like Juan, hunts to survive. Except for the powerful, under a dictatorship everybody is a *furtivo*, in the sense of living clandestinely.

There has also been a decline in the caliber of the hunters, and a dignification of the prey, as they have gone from hunting rabbits to hunting deer. The hunting sequences imitate Saura's and Renoir's formally, but, with the exception of Angel, the hunters in *Furtivos* are inept and lack the good aim of their predecessors. In consonance with its synchronic perspective, in *Furtivos* the governor and his team are not replicating in their hunting an experience from the past, but their daily job. The first sequence in the film, in which the governor shows up in his hunting gear in the middle of a raid by the police, already suggests his function as a hunter of men. The fact that he is incompetent in both types of hunt helps to confirm the association.

While in *La caza* the metaphorical connection between the animal and human worlds is of a generic scope, covering a whole group, in *Furtivos* the procedure is applied to individual characters. In the raid the police are looking for El Cuqui, who the governor calls "a rat," an animal that is at home in the city, as opposed to his poor performance when he is being chased a second time, in the forest, where he loses his confidence and skill. His girlfriend, Milagros, arrives with Angel at the forest at the same time that his mother has just found a she-wolf that has been caught in a trap. When Angel drags his mother out of her own bed, so that he can share it with Milagros, the mother reacts by killing the wolf, anticipating in this act the murder of Milagros. These associations are provoked by the film itself, based on a code generated by the organization of the film's discourse. The references to predetermined conventions are extremely remote. There are, though, associations in this film which echo some commonplaces of colloquial speech: when Angel is looking for truffles with the help of a pig, to offer them to the governor, we are encouraged to see the analogy between the governor and the animal, through a traditional expression, "Dar trufas a los cerdos" ("To give truffles to the pigs," an example of terrible waste, equivalent to "to cast pearls to swine"). Later on, Angel is considering the possibility of catching El Cuqui, his rival, and surrendering him to the police, and he says, "Muerto el perro, se acabó la rabia" ("After the dog is dead, there is no more rabies"). Without realizing it, he is formulating, metaphorically, the reason that leads his mother to kill Milagros. Milagros may not be directly associated with the dog, but the connection is possible through a change in gender that reflects the mother's view: *perra* (bitch), which also invites another variation, still among the relatives of the wolf, *zorra* (vixen).

Another novelty in relation to the symbolic structure of Saura's film is the reworking of the pair hunters/prey, because of the special relationship that the poacher, Angel, enjoys with the animals. As a consequence of being a poacher, he belongs to both sides. He hunts but is also hunted. He also enjoys a special relationship with the powerful, because both Angel and the governor were breast-fed by Angel's mother at the same time. Of course, the governor is a very well-fed individual who does not stop eating throughout the film. Angel is leaner, and poorer, and his mother comments, jokingly, that the governor used to be a voracious baby, who sucked all her milk.

Angel marries Milagros to get her out of the correctional facility, and he lets El Cuqui escape, the same way he forgoes the chance to kill the oldest and most beautiful stag, the leader of the herd. The gamekeepers call this animal *el ciervo del gobernador* (the governor's stag), because it is his most wanted prize. We cannot miss the phonetic similarity with the expression *el cerdo del gobernador* (meaning both "the governor has a pig" and "the governor is a pig"). But the manifest contradiction between the connotations associated with the character of the governor and the traits that typify the stag leads us to read in the stag a figure associated not with the governor but with Angel. When, after Milagros disappears, Angel is desperate and kills this same stag in a completely gratuitous gesture, the implications are at the same time of rebellion against authority, and of self-destruction. As he does not take any precaution to avoid being caught by the gamekeepers, those who are in pursuit finally catch him. Thanks to the governor's influence, he avoids going to jail by becoming one of them, a gamekeeper, who now serves the system in what for him had been the most hateful job. The stag could thus be read as a sign of Angel's freedom, which introduces a new phonetic displacement: by killing the governor's *ciervo* he becomes the governor's *siervo* (serf).

Independently of the lexical evidence, which merely confirms the associations, figures such as the one just mentioned are unreadable outside of the idiolect of the film. They are customized to fit the discursive needs of the film, and they can hardly be translated into verbal language. The film poses analogical relations; it designs associative patterns. It is up to us to fill in the gaps in the webbing by means of a poetic reading. *La caza* and *Furtivos* share the same motif and the allegorical formulation of a political discourse, but they are not films *à clé*, if by that we mean that their message is codified and there exists, independently of the film, a code to decipher it. These films cannot be reduced to an equation. The key to their meaning is within the film itself, where the so-called hidden or underlying discourse is in fact a parallel discourse, which runs alongside the narrative, openly co-existing with it. Nothing is hidden, in the sense that nothing is concealed from the eyes and ears of the spectator. On the other hand, we can acknowledge that the message is screened, in the double meaning of the word, being both veiled and displayed (the way a film is screened); a double meaning which reflects very accurately the symbolic role of the cinematic screen. This double operation, of veiling and displaying, also synthesizes the conditions which ruled the political rhetoric of this specific period in Spanish cinema. It had to comply with a paradoxical double requirement: to be clear enough to be understood by the audience, and obscure enough to be approved by the censors.

I would like to comment very briefly on the evolution of this allegorical trend, or tradition, after Franco's death, when the representation of recent history became not only possible, but timely. We must take into account that in Spain the transition to democracy was made by consensus, under the banner of reconciliation, that encourages a revision of history now proclaiming that nobody is guilty. The point was to ensure a peaceful transition, and to safeguard the new-born democracy. The film industry became, to a large extent, an accessory in this strategy, and one of the ways to subscribe to the moderate position was to present the events from the viewpoint of the middle class, as if this group had been the innocent victim of the war (Monterde 56–59). The most emblematic example of this tendency, focused on the subject of the family saga, is probably *Las bicicletas son para el verano* (Bicycles are for the summer) (1984), Chávarri's adaptation of a successful play by Fernando Fernán Gómez. Even films that do take sides more explicitly, such as Jaime Camino's *Las largas vacaciones del 36* (The long vacation of 1936) (1976), adopt the bourgeois viewpoint. And when this last director addresses the role of the dictator himself in *Dragon Rapide* (1986), a film about the plotting of the coup that started the war, the topic is treated more in terms of individual dilemmas and family environment than of the social forces in play.

In a less predictable development, Spanish cinema not only embraced the conciliatory agenda of the period and a middle-class viewpoint, but also seemed to enact the experience of the war and the dictatorship as it was perceived by the kind of people who are involved in the making of films. I am not referring to the obvious fact that a film is subjective, and determined by the views of those who make it. What happened is that the lives of actors, actresses, singers, dancers—all sorts of performers, during and after the war—became the topic of several very influential films. But it was not simply a matter of satisfying a need to express the experience of yet another group that certainly had access to the control of the medium. We were also witnessing the advancement of a new symbolic paradigm: entertainment became the allegorical motif of choice. Two films by two of the most illustrious representatives of oppositional cinema under Franco would be enough to prove the point: Saura's ¡Ay, Carmela! (1990), about small-time itinerant entertainers caught on the wrong side at the wrong time, and Luis García Berlanga's La vaquilla (1985), a dispute at the front about what side gets a small bull for a bullfight (Spaniards being perfectly aware that bullfighting is not a sport, but entertainment). Both films have an unmistakable allegorical reading, and in the case of Berlanga's the spectator is hit on the head with its message at the end, when the bull, representing Spain, lies dead between the two frontlines, with both sides being equally responsible.

While in Manuel Majti's La guerra de los locos (The madmen's war) (1987) war is equated with madness, by employing entertainment as a vehicle the representation of the war is wrapped up in, or at least accompanied by, the notion of the simulacrum, of make-believe. It could be interpreted as an interesting postmodern move, but it is more likely just a delicate treatment of a ticklish subject. In any case, the move has serious political implications, in particular when we compare it with the oppositional value of the allegory organized around the hunting motif and the issue of violence. Several other films deal with entertainment during the early postwar period, even if their allegorical function is less obvious; for example, Chávarri's Las cosas del querer (Matters of love) (1989), Fernán Gómez's Viaje a ninguna parte (Journey to Nowhere) (1986), and José Luis García Sánchez's La corte del faraón (The Pharaoh's Court) (1985). But one common denominator among the products of this trend seems to be the idea that adaptation to the ruling regime becomes a matter of survival, and the films make it look as if it were even more so than in the case of the family sagas, as if entertainers were necessarily more defenseless. This kind of discourse applies even to the films where it is questioned, such as *¡Ay, Carmela!*, because here the person who resists ends up being killed. In the case of *Viaje a ninguna parte*, the story of the survival of a small dramatic company (also itinerant!) is directed by an actor who has managed to thrive within very different political contexts. The message of the films seems thus to agree with recent Spanish history: pragmatism pays off.

Three issues get mixed up in the subject I have discussed. In concluding I should try, if not to settle them, at least to delineate them. The first involves how a certain faction within Spanish cinema has dealt with the representation of a specific kind of historical event, under two different sets of political circumstances. There are a number of other films about the war, which are covered in more exhaustive studies, such as those by Oms, Gubern or Ripoll. I have left out probably the most consistently interesting segment of the corpus constituted by films that use documentary material. My selection was not exclusively thematic, but based on a tradition of allegorical discourse, precisely because it is one of the defining traits of Spanish cinema of the period, and probably the source of its most effective products. The metaphor of the forest, for instance, has inspired films as appealing as *El corazón del bosque* (Heart of the Forest) (Manuel Gutiérrez Aragón, 1979). The second issue entails to what extent the representation of the collective event by means of the private experience, of the universal by means of the particular, is predetermined by the medium itself, or whether it is a requirement of cinematic discourse. The third, and more transcendental issue is whether the experience of war can ever be represented as such. War may be recorded in documentaries, but the experience of war may exceed the representational potential of *any* language. If war as such falls under the category of what Blanchot calls the *disaster*, by definition it escapes representation. To make a film about a war, any war, may involve the challenge of representing the unrepresentable. When we consider the first and second issues, we might see some of the films discussed under a different light: not simply as an answer to political conditions in a particular nation during a particular time, but also as a more or less successfully resolved answer to a formal challenge. Poetic figuration emerges as an inescapable element in the work of analysis, because only poetry can meet the challenge of exceeding the limits of representation.

Works Cited

Blanchot, Maurice. *The Writing of the Disaster*. Trans. Ann Smock. Lincoln: Univ. of Nebraska Press, 1986.

Deleuze, Gilles. *L'image-mouvement*. Paris: Editions de Minuit, 1983.

Goodman, Nelson. *Languages of Art*. Indianapolis: Hackett, 1976.

Gubern, Román. *1936–1939: La guerra de España en la pantalla*. Madrid: Filmoteca Española, 1986.

Hopewell, John. *Out of the Past: Spanish Cinema After Franco*. London: British Film Institute, 1986.

Metz, Christian. *Le signifiant imaginaire*. Paris: Christian Bourgois, 1984.

Monterde, José Enrique. "El cine histórico durante la transición política." In *Escritos sobre el cine español 1973–1987*. Ed. Vicente Bonet et al. Valencia: Filmoteca Generalitat Valenciana, 1989. 45–63.

Oms, Marcel. *La Guerre d'Espagne au cinéma*. Paris: Editions du Cerf, 1986.

Pasolini, Pier Paolo. "The Cinema of Poetry." In *Movies and Methods*. Ed. Bill Nichols. Vol.1. Berkeley: Univ. of California Press, 1976. 542–558.

Ripoll i Freixes, Enric. *100 películas sobre la Guerra Civil Española*. Barcelona: CILEH, 1992.

Chapter 12

Homosexuality, Regionalism, and Mass Culture: Eloy de la Iglesia's Cinema of Transition

Paul Julian Smith

The cinema of Eloy de la Iglesia is by no means academically re-spectable. One standard reference work rehearses the majority view that the criteria motivating his films are wholly commer-cial: sensationalism, crude topicality, melodrama.[1] Yet de la Igle-sia's films of the middle 70s and early 1980s not only mark the first extended representation of gay men in Spanish cinema, they also stage an explicit and complex examination of the interplay between homosexuality, Marxism, and separatism.[2] Thus *Los plac-eres ocultos* (Hidden pleasures, 1976) has its bourgeois hero fall in love with a working-class youth; *El diputado* (The MP, 1978) has a Socialist politician engaged in a similar affair with a youth in the pay of the ultra-right; and *El pico* (The shoot, 1983) plots the complex relationships between a bisexual youth, his friend and fellow heroin addict, and their respective fathers (a Civil Guard and a Basque separatist politician). Homosexuality is thus in-variably qualified by factors such as class, national politics, and regional identity, and not exiled to some ideal space outside his-tory. Moreover, these works were the most successful Spanish films of their day at the box office. They represent what is per-haps a unique moment during the transition to democracy when the topic of homosexuality and the mass audience coincided in the Spanish cinema. De la Iglesia's exclusion from both national and regional histories of film is thus all the more troubling. As we shall see, his very visceral films raise questions of taste and value that must prove unsettling to those who would promote cinema as "the seventh art". In order to address such a body of work at all we must confront problems of genre (exploitation) and historicity ("shelf life").

In a 1983 interview, de la Iglesia himself called for a cinema that would be "like a newspaper."[3] And it is clearly impossible to consider his films outside the immediate context of the transition to democracy within which they were made. The model of the newspaper, however, has further implications. First it suggests an ephemeral medium, one that does not aspire to lasting value; second, it suggests actuality, the immediate irruption of the real into the text; and finally, it suggests political engagement: the film will not flinch from editorializing, from making wholly explicit its political bias.

In spite of his espousal of the newspaper form, de la Iglesia's treatment at the hands of the press during this period was brutal. While the initial banning of *Los placeres ocultos* may have motivated relatively kind reviews from those (such as Fernando Méndez-Leite,)[4] opposed to the continuing censorship one year after the death of Franco, later films received bitter attacks from all sides of the political spectrum. To read the accumulated press files in the Filmoteca is to be exposed to an extraordinary catalog of abuse, some of which is clearly homophobic. Interviewers constantly circle around the question of the director's own sexual preference (the secret that would "explain" the films) and repeatedly ask why he is so interested in homosexuality.[5] Some of the abuse is also motivated by anti-Basque racism: one squib mocks de la Iglesia for a project (later to metamorphose into *El pico*) featuring a gay love story set in the Basque country complete with dialogue in *euskera*.[6] The anonymous journalist states that other countries seek to conquer the international market, implying that Spanish directors waste their time on such minority projects. This was a curious complaint to make against the most commercially successful director of his time: homosexuality and regional identity would thus always seem to be marginal even when placed at the center of a mass culture.

Fernando Trueba's review of *El diputado* in *El país* (27 January 1979) is a good example of vitriol from the socialist side. Trueba begins by accusing de la Iglesia of a double servility: to leftist propaganda and commercialism. The boldness of the director's themes is no defense for this "cinema of excess," which tolerates the grotesque and ridiculous just so long as they are profitable. The film's overt references to actuality (recent political events) fail to disguise a story which is wholly false. This is not cinema: the characters are inauthentic, the dialogue unintentionally humorous, the aesthetics amorphous. The main character is nothing but a puppet. Trueba claims that de la Iglesia has not made one good film. Not only is he a bad director, he is also a bad trickster (no one will be taken in by this film).

The title of Trueba's review is "Sex and Politics: A Cocktail that Sells." Confronted by this very physical cinema, critical response is often physiological, evoking food and drink: ingestion, digestion, or expulsion. More noticeable here, however, is the stress on the inauthentic: references to falsity, disguise, trickery. And if we briefly compare this review with one of *El pico* from the extreme right *El alcázar* (15 October 1983), much of the same language and arguments recur. Thus Félix Martialay stresses the lack of "art" in the film, which is linked to its mendacity: it contains no truth or authentic feelings, but rather reflects the "deficiencies" of its director. Martialay finds particularly offensive the scene in which a father takes his son to a brothel in order to celebrate his coming of age. Such a scene reveals that the director knows nothing about what it really means to have a son. Disturbance in the reproduction of familial relations is indeed a recurrent theme in de la Iglesia's work, and one which this hostile critic clearly finds worrying. For Martialay, the characters are wholly "unreal," subject as they are to the threefold political program of the director: attacks on the army, scorn for the Civil Guard, praise for the queer (*maricón*).

As in the leftist critique, then, the question of aesthetics is also immediately a question of ethics: there is an unacknowledged shift from formal inadequacy to moral turpitude (the director is motivated either by base commerce or culpable anti-militarism). Yet the extremity of language used in both cases suggests something more is at stake: the attempt to expel the abject, that which the body cannot tolerate. One critic accuses de la Iglesia of the "aesthetics of the Y-front" (*estética del calzoncillo*). It seems likely, then, that what threatens critics in these films (in which naked male bodies are exposed to the viewer, in which the same youthful actors constantly recur) is the unmediated irruption of homosexual desire into the mass form of commercial cinema. It is this desublimation that is intolerable.

John Hopewell has recently given a brief but suggestive account of the emergence of new forms of sexuality in Spanish cinema of the transition.[7] The early 1970s saw a curious combination of Catholic morality and European-style consumerism in Spanish film. Extramarital sex was permissible only in certain special circumstances: if the female character was raped, if she was the object of a classical "Spanish passion" (as in a biopic of Goya), if she was an actress, foreigner, or prostitute (165–167). After the death of Franco, sex was no longer the other and three shifts took place: the gradual abandonment of the virgin/whore dichotomy; the shift from the family to the couple as the basic narrative and ideological unit; the emergence of active (heterosexual) women and gay men as subjects of desire. While the first films in this final category tended (like Hopewell himself) to confuse homosexuality, transvestism, and transsexualism, they adopted a liberal viewpoint, claiming that gays were "just like you and me." For Hopewell both *Los placeres ocultos* and *El diputado* display a fatally abstracted representation of homosexuality, which is conceived as a democratic right but not a democratic desire. Citing Steve Neale's *Genre*, Hopewell suggests (after Freud) that the occultation of homosexual desire is the basis of the scopic drive, and hence of dominant visual narratives. To desublimate homosexual desire would thus be to challenge the basis of mainstream cinema, to assert that gay men have a specific difference and cannot be represented by the liberal tag "the same as you and me."

In one of the very few articles on the representation of homosexuality in Spanish film after Franco, Eduardo Haro Ibars also rejects de la Iglesia's formulations in these films.[8] In *Los placeres ocultos* he finds not a Marxist analysis of sexual repression and class struggle but a novelette (*folletín*) full of stereotypes: the rich queen and castrating mother (88). In *El diputado* José Sacristán, who plays the eponymous hero, is "unrealistic," a "cardboard cutout." No one, Haro complains, has told the life of the true homosexual, he who is neither rich nor a politician, but is forced to live his life as best he can (91). Haro argues for the same criterion of authenticity as the straight Spanish critics, albeit from a different position: the characters must be (felt to be) real. Hopewell, on the other hand, in his sympathetic account of de la Iglesia, argues that the films reveal a subtle account of homosexuality and the ambivalence of familial relations (236–238). While most Spanish filmmakers are localist, trusting to the domestic audience's knowledge of the historical background of their work, de la Iglesia problematizes the relation of his work to the real by directly discussing that relation within the fiction: thus when the Civil Guard father in *El pico* speculates as to the frequency of corruption in the force, the question of whether this highly colored narrative can serve as an allegory of the national predicament is openly confronted (240). Hopewell argues that the film's relation to the real is thus necessarily mediated by its genre, in this case melodrama. Just as in melodrama the social stability of the family is undermined by a sexual desire which reaches beyond it, so in the narrative of national history minority groups (ethnic or sexual) can be absorbed only with difficulty into the new democratic order. Critical abuse of de la Iglesia has thus been motivated by an inability to read his use of genre: the rough texture of the film surface is taken to be neorealism, and the films are criticized for failing to live up to criteria that they do not themselves recognize. More particularly, Hopewell argues, the depiction of gays as "queers" (*maricones*) in these films is also determined by the melodramatic genre, which requires stock characters, not documentary style representation of the real (240).

Hopewell goes on to make an interesting point about de la Iglesia's preferred hero, the youthful hooligan. Such figures both concretize class conflict in the films and, by representing a life lived only in the present, comfort Spanish audiences of the period, who were equally afraid of past suffering and future uncertainty (242). However, Hopewell's insistence on the determining nature of genre (the fact that we should not "ask for pears from an elm tree") seems overly schematic. The particularity of de la Iglesia, I shall argue, is precisely that he subverts classical genres in *auteuriste* fashion while remaining within the confines of mass culture. Indeed the very choice of a homosexual hero in these films must pose a challenge to those codes of representation and structures of identification inherent in dominant cinema practice. Moreover, in the films I treat, de la Iglesia explicitly rejects stereotypical images of gay men, who are invariably described in the scripts as "worthy" or "manly." I shall call these figures (played by sympathetic actors such as Simón Andreu and José Sacristán) "Good Homosexuals."

What Hopewell does sketch out, briefly, is the possibility of a reading of these films which addresses both formal and historical questions; indeed, which relates the former to the latter through the mediation of narrative genre. During the period the films were being made the only comparable critical account they received was from an unexpected source: the pioneer journal of film theory in Spain, *Contracampo* (Countershot). In 1981 the pages of *Contracampo*, more accustomed to Godard or Ozu, ran a special feature on de la Iglesia.[9] It consists of a dense article by Javier Vega, a lengthy interview by Francisco Llinás and José Luis Téllez, and a fragment of the script for *Galopa y corta el viento* (Gallop and cut through the wind), the unmade feature on the affair between a Civil Guard and a Basque separatist.

Javier Vega's "The (Ideological) Apparatus of Eloy de la Iglesia" (22–26) is the most developed of successive *Contracampo* pieces on the director. As its title suggests, Vega's position derives initially from Althusser: cinema is one of those institutions through which the dominant class inoculates its ideology into the subject masses. The role of an engaged cinema would thus be to eschew avant-garde aestheticism and challenge the apparatus through a "direct engagement with temporal reality." This politicized cinema will reject all pretensions to art, and thus risk rejection by those critics of the Left who prize cinema most highly (21). In a culture of mass spectacle such films will no longer be of interest as an object of pleasure, but only as an object of struggle; the aesthetic criterion will cede to that of political efficacy. De la Iglesia's transgression of codes of dominant cinema will thus prove as challenging as that of the more rigorous (and intellectually respectable) formalists. Hence the angry responses his cinema has inspired (22). It does not express the viewers' feelings (their desires, fears, or obsessions); rather, it forces them to take up a position for or against the thesis of the film. The latter's power is thus based not on exquisite images, but on the exposition of ideas. Mise en scène is reduced to the strictly functional.

Citing an earlier piece by his colleague José Luis Téllez, Vega compares de la Iglesia's films to pamphlets. Their exalted tone, conjunctural discourse, and Manichean approach to characterization resemble written tracts (24). De la Iglesia's originality lies in adapting this medium to the cinema; but unlike in the case of the printed pamphlet, the aesthetic poverty of his films does not result from lack of finance. The peculiar expression of the genre he has created thus makes it particularly difficult to read. These tendencies have been stripped down, refined: in his later films clarity of exposition and the use of emblematic characters prevent the spectator from getting lost, in spite of unexpectedly intricate plots; references to the real are increasingly emphatic and dialogues openly schematic; the acting, apparently naturalistic, is strewn with redundancies and repetitive gestures pointing unambiguously to the function of the character in the plot. Such apparent clumsiness or vulgarity serves to prevent the viewer from being distracted from the topic at hand. These are closed films, without noise (superfluous interference in the transmission of the narrative message) (25). They constitute a shameless manipulation that (because of its very transparency) Vega can call honorable, even ethical. De la Iglesia, cineast of the people, is thus an *auteur malgré lui:* through theoretical reflection on the cinematic medium, he has evolved his own narrative style, which subverts conventional forms and conflates disparate genres (*film noir,* melodrama, agitprop, pornography). He thus reveals that auteurism is just another genre (26). Through this final theoretical twist, Vega ensures that the Marxist director is not reinstalled in the privileged place of the bourgeois artist.

As we shall see, *Contracampo'*s willfully perverse and sometimes ironic praise of de la Iglesia extends to specifics of filmic practice, such as the use or abuse of the close-up. More generally, however, their important account provides a precedent for the analysis of the central paradox of the director's work: the curious combination of mass technique (sex and violence) and personal, indeed idiosyncratic, obsessions. In the rest of this chapter I hope to chart the strange configurations that occur when the homosexual hero takes up his place in three of Eloy de la Iglesia's films. In the final moments of the fragment of the script for the unmade *Galopa y corta el viento*,[10] Basque separatist Patxi and Civil Guard Manolo, stranded in the countryside, are caught in the lights of the other's motorcycle and car. "The image," we are told by de la Iglesia and co-writer Gonzalo Goicoechea, "starts to take on a magical hue" (41). It is a fitting icon of the emergence of the gay man into Spanish cinema: caught in the light, exposed to view, illuminated by his relation to the other.

Los placeres ocultos: The Erotic Triangle

A medium long shot of a naked youth in the shower; the camera follows him to the bedroom, where he starts to dry himself. Cut to medium shot of a middle-aged man in dressing gown, looking off-screen to the right. A framed photograph can be seen behind his shoulder. Cut again to a medium long shot of the boy dressing with his back to the camera. Crosscuts between watching man and dressing youth lead to a medium shot of the man taking money from his dressing gown to give to the youth. The camera follows them in medium close-up to the door. As the youth leaves, the credits start to roll. The camera then follows the man back from the door and cuts to a low angle, long (establishing) shot of the room. We look up at the man as he relaxes in a chair, listening to choral music. A slow pan over framed photographs in a curious ghostly light leads to a close-up of the man wearing eye goggles: he is basking in the light of a sunlamp.[11]

The dialogue in this first sequence of the film is as follows:

CHICO: ¿Estará abierto el portal?
EDUARDO: Sí . . . se abre por dentro.
CHICO: ¿Me puedes dar algo suelto para el taxi?
EDUARDO: Venga, toma . . . A ver si nos vemos otra vez . . .
    ¿eh?
CHICO: ¡Vale! . . . Dame tu teléfono y te llamo . . .
EDUARDO: No . . . es que yo casi nunca estoy en casa, ¿sabes?
    Bueno . . . ya nos veremos por aquí.
CHICO: Yo paro mucho por los billares. Así que ya sabes . . .
EDUARDO: De acuerdo. Un día de estos me pasaré.

BOY: Will the front door be open?

EDUARDO: Yes... it opens from the inside.

BOY: Can you spare some change for the taxi?

EDUARDO: OK... here you are... Maybe we'll get together
again some time.

BOY: Fine... Give me your phone number and I'll call you.

EDUARDO: No... the thing is, I'm hardly ever at home. Well,
see you around.

BOY: I hang around the billiard halls a lot. So you know...

EDUARDO: Agreed. One of these days I'll drop by.

The opening sequence of *Los placeres ocultos* is a good example
of the way in which Eloy de la Iglesia economically establishes a
visual regime which transcends an impoverished, even banal, dialogue. Thus the gradual shift in framing (from medium long to
close-up) draws the viewer's attention to the principal character's narcissism and isolation; the cross-cutting suggests his ambivalent relation to an erotic object which fascinates him; and most
particularly, the delayed suggestion that the opening shot of the
naked youth is actually a "POV" (a shot from the older man's
point of view) implicates the spectator in a traffic of homosexual
voyeurism that is overtly commercial. The man and the audience have paid to look; the boy is paid to be looked at. According
to the script, Eduardo (Simón Andreu: "distinguished and manly,
intelligent and cultivated") watches the youth "half indifferent
and half tired, without being able to avoid a certain pleasure" (2).
The spectator, asked to identify with a gay male gaze, must also
choose to make a response.

The opening sequence thus sets up a series of binaries that the
narrative will violently disturb: subject and object, rich and poor,
private and public. It is no accident that the sequence should lead
up to a doorway, the liminal site of transition between domestic
and social space. Homosexual affect is the privileged factor that
will upset these initially static binaries. When Eduardo experiences not lust but love for a youth, then the separate and stable
territories mapped out by class and capital will be thrown into
disarray. Perhaps the most interesting point about this opening
moment, then, is that (commercial) sex between men, far from
subverting the existing social order, is shown to be safely (if dis-

creetly) submerged within it. De la Iglesia thus neatly reverses one of the traditional techniques of melodrama mentioned previously by John Hopewell: the dissolution of the family (and of narrative equilibrium) is effected not through erotic desire for an external object, but through a sublimated affect which is doomed to dissatisfaction.

As the narrative develops, the relation between homosexuality and a number of different areas is explored. Eduardo is a banker, and parallels are drawn between the different modes of exploitation effected by prostitution and capitalism. He is also a devoted son to his clinging mother: the first cutaway after the opening sequence in his flat is to the family apartment in the upmarket Barrio de Salamanca in Madrid. Here, as so often, mise en scène is wholly functional, and works solely as an index of social value: Eduardo's studio is modern and functional, his mother's home crammed with pictures and carpets. The first time we see her, a crucifix is prominently displayed on the wall behind her. At a time when the continuing modernization of Spain was much debated, homosexuality is here offered (curiously perhaps) as the essence of modern, secular society in opposition to the old Spain of family and religion: Eduardo's office with its steel table and sleek executive toys is also emphatically marked as modern.

On one of his regular cruising sessions in the university area, Eduardo meets (and fails to pick up) a youth, Miguel. The latter has a girlfriend, Carmen, and a married lover, Rosa (Charo López). Eduardo finds the impoverished Miguel a job in his office, confesses his love for him, and attempts to build a new family for himself with Miguel and Carmen. The spurned Rosa wreaks revenge on both of them: she arranges to have Eduardo beaten and robbed by male prostitutes and Miguel shamed by putting about the rumor that he too is gay. The amorous conflict (with hetero- and homosexual lovers competing for the same youth) is clearly beyond resolution; and, as we shall see, the ending of the film is left disturbingly open.

Los placeres ocultos offers a series of contradictory images of homosexuality, which are distributed schematically among the characters. Thus Eduardo is the Good Homosexual: a loving son, respected employee, and devoted (platonic) lover who gives up commercial sex for unconsummated but passionate romance. The

Bad Homosexuals are Eduardo's camp friends whom he neglects on meeting Miguel. Sipping lurid cocktails in an improbable gay club ("a luxurious and sophisticated atmosphere"), they mock him for his chaste devotion, claiming he must have become a socialist or a nun. The queens' scorn for politics is set against the political engagement of another variety of Good Homosexual: Eduardo's colleague and ex-lover Raúl, who encourages him to join in the collective struggle against homosexual oppression. The saint, the queen, and the liberationist: these, then, are the three models of male homosexual life offered by the film.

At times *Los placeres ocultos* offers explicit apologies for the characters' behavior. Thus in one scene Eduardo dutifully explains to the bemused Miguel that, no, homosexuality is not an illness and that, yes, each person has the right to be as he or she really is. But elsewhere apologetics are compromised by an awareness of the inextricability of homosexuality and capital. Thus when Miguel exclaims to Raúl that he will not allow gay men to take advantage of his poverty, the latter suggests (improbably for a banker) that he should place homosexual prostitution within the context of capitalist exploitation: "Learn how to struggle, but not just against a queer [*marica*] who offers you 500 pesetas to sleep with him... Think that you may be selling more important things than your arse and you haven't even realized that's what you're doing. That's why I say to you: learn how to struggle." In this utopian dialogue the revolutionary homosexual exposes the false consciousness of the proletarian heterosexual.

More interesting than these schematic exchanges are the curious, indeed irreconcilable, contradictions that accumulate at the level of the plot. Most of these contradictions involve women. Charo López's Rosa is a voracious man-eater. In an early sequence she devours cream cakes with Miguel as they make love, a sign of her rampant sexuality; and in the most purely melodramatic scene of the film she pleads with Eduardo to make Miguel return to her, before threatening him with blackmail. Inversely, Miguel's bland and initially virginal girlfriend, Carmen, pliantly accepts Eduardo's amorous interest in her fiancé. In a montage sequence the three thrill to the delights of the funfair before swimming together in a deserted lake: the amorous triangle can flourish only in the non-cultural spaces of play and nature. Finally, Eduardo's long-suffering mother reveals (on her deathbed) that she knew her son's secret but was compelled to remain silent: women of her class are obliged to play the fool in order to make their men feel proud of them. These three examples of womanhood (*the femme fatale*, the pliant virgin, and the bourgeois mother) are all marginalized by homosexual desire: Miguel prefers the father figure Eduardo to his female ex-lover or girlfriend (both of whom are abandoned by the narrative before the end of the film); the mother can acknowledge her son's homosexuality only as she lies dying. De la Iglesia thus both reconfirms and inverts the homosocial triangle which Eve Kosofsky Sedgwick has identified in the nineteenth-century novel.[12] Women continue to serve in traditional style as a vehicle through which two men explore the relationship between each other; but unlike in the classic texts, this relationship is desublimated, openly acknowledged to be based on erotic desire. The problem remains, however, that the woman is still effectively excluded from the baseline of the founding male relationship, and can adopt only the thankless roles of shrewish harridan (Rosa) or long-suffering victim (Carmen, the mother). As long as male homosexual desire is presented as a disturbance in existing heterosexual and familial relations, there can be no re-evaluation of female desire, whether hetero- or homosexual.

Los placeres ocultos offers no example of a reciprocal relationship between men of equal status. Even Eduardo's colleague Raúl, as cultivated and bourgeois as his ex-lover, was once, like Miguel, a poor youth illicitly introduced into the workplace by Eduardo. We have seen that this asymmetry in the homosexual relation is reinforced by class and financial inequality, but the asymmetry is bizarrely underlined here by the heterosexuality of the love object. At one point Raúl attacks Eduardo: once he merely bought boys' bodies; now he buys their lives. The latter replies that he is trying to form a kind of family with the youthful couple, to feel like a father or grandfather to their future children. By doing so he will avoid a lonely old age. Raúl, the sexual revolutionary, replies that he and his comrades will not be alone either at the time of struggle; it is useless to rely on individual efforts.

Homosexuality is here presented both as a mimicry of the heterosexual (an attempt to recreate its structures) and as a deviation from it (a perversion of the natural order). Yet, as Jonathan

Dollimore has suggested, the problem of the perverse is inextricably linked to the normal; that far from constituting the other to the "normal" same, it is already inherent in it from the very beginning. Initially negative and patronizing, Eloy de la Iglesia's idiosyncratic decision to have his gay hero love a straight man reveals the necessary coexistence of homo- and heterosexuality in the same social space, and under the same economic laws. As a narrative it may perhaps be more subversive than one set in the hermetically sealed space of an all-gay sociality. In interviews of the period, de la Iglesia claimed that what interested him in this film (and in his next, which treated bestiality)[13] is not a specific sexual practice, but the general social process by which certain groups are marginalized. Through a somewhat indirect (deviant) route he may well have achieved that result here.

But how do these ideological fissures reveal themselves at the formal level of the filmic text? The fundamental disorder of heterosexuality (and the horror of female sexuality) is vehicled by grotesque shock cuts or rhythmic crosscutting. Thus when Rose and Miguel have sex, we cut from a close-up of her breast to a religious print on the bedroom wall. Or again when Rosa seduces the hooligan who will attack Eduardo we crosscut from the sexual act to a scene in which she washes the youth's hair. Camera angle is used emphatically to reiterate class positions: Eduardo is often shot from below, as he sits in his chair or car, as he surveys the workers from his glass-walled office. The impoverished Miguel is shot from above; at one early point the camera looks down from the ceiling on the tiny bedroom that he shares with his brother in the family shack. These devices rarely draw attention to themselves. Cinematography and editing, like mise en scene, are reduced to a functional, emblematic level.

More important, however, than editing and camera angle is a more emphatic mannerism pointed out by *Contracampo* racking focus (shifting the area of sharp focus from one plane to another during a single shot). Thus when Eduardo spies on young lovers Miguel and Carmen in the park, the blurred green matter at the front of the image is revealed (with a change of focus) to be the leaves behind which Eduardo is hiding. Here, as in the opening sequence, the spectator is implicated in the homosexually motivated voyeurism of the protagonist. Or again, when Miguel and

Carmen first have sex in Eduardo's apartment, the focus shifts from a framed photograph of Eduardo in the foreground to the naked bodies of the lovers in the background. This literal change of perspective within a single shot is an emphatic means of underlining the irreconcilability of the two gazes in the film: the man's amorous regard for the youth, and the youth's erotic pleasure in his girlfriend.

By the end of the film this homosexual gaze has been (overtly at least) de-eroticized: as Eduardo looks at the naked and inviolate Miguel lying on his bed, the script tells us that this is not a "lascivious observation . . . he contemplates him . . . as if he was seeing the most beautiful landscape or the most brilliant work of art" (77). He caresses Miguel's lips with his fingers. The only scene in the script of explicit sexual activity between the two men (when Eduardo reaches orgasm as he clutches the heedless Miguel on a motorbike) was omitted from the film itself. I would suggest, however, that this improbable relationship is perhaps more revealing of the relationship between gays and Spanish society in the period than a more plausible, reciprocal love affair might have been. The exaggeration of Eduardo's predicament (which permits no resolution) is not inept but strategic. It points indirectly to the impossible position of gay Spaniards in the transition: at once intimately linked and profoundly separated from their heterosexual partners at work and in the family. *Los placeres ocultos* does not reflect the real, but it might claim to typify it (to act out its contradictions with heightened intensity). Such a reading is clearly consistent with both the Marxist sympathies of the director in the period and the Lukácscian enthusiasms of his protectors at *Contracampo*.

At the end of the film the long-suffering Eduardo has been beaten by hooligans and exposed as a homosexual by Miguel at their place of work. In a visual echo of the opening sequence he relaxes in a chair listening to music, alone with the sunlamp. The bell rings and the camera follows him to the door. As he looks through the spyhole a smile comes to his face. The frame freezes on a close-up as he opens the door.

Los placeres ocultos was initially banned *in toto* by the censor: no provision was made, as was usually the case, for editing the film into an acceptable form.[14] For the Francoist censor, then, the

very topic of homosexuality was taboo, and would inevitably con-
taminate every inch of the film. The defiantly open ending, however, broaches a final taboo which cannot be resolved by the logic
of the narrative: it is only the return of Miguel that can satisfy
Eduardo; but the latter refuses to impose his sexual demands on
the youth. A happy ending is required, but cannot be represented.
Like the formal and ideological discontinuities we have seen elsewhere in *Los placeres ocultos*, the final freezeframe points sympto-
matically to meanings which the referential level of the film dares
not acknowledge: if homosexuality is depicted (as it is in the film)
as a disturbance in existing heterosexual relations, it will necessarily be doomed to failure; but if it is also a democratic right to
be as one really is (as the film also proposes), then in the new
Spain of the transition homosexuals can no longer be punished
for their sexual-object choice. The impossible, open ending of *Los
placeres ocultos* (so inimical to its melodramatic form) is thus the
final, paradoxical result of a compromise formed between genre
and history: between the formal desire for aesthetic resolution
and the political requirement for social change.

El diputado: The Good Homosexual

Roberto ("40 years old, square glasses, intelligent, and elegant in
his sports jacket and shirt without a tie") sits in his car outside
the police station in Madrid's Puerta del Sol.[15] We hear a voice:

> I have nothing to fear, I am a legal politician, a
> democratically elected MP, a representative of the popular
> will and, even if I'm in the opposition, in some ways I'm
> also part of the power structures. But there were so many
> years of clandestinity, of persecutions. What can my police
> file be like? . . . How many times have I defended others in
> my life! And, yet, will I be able to defend myself now?

As in the opening sequence of *Los placeres ocultos*, the dialogue
at the start of *El diputado* is unremarkable. However, it sets up
the dilemma of the main character with stark clarity. An MP belonging to the recently legalized Partido Radical Socialista (a fictional amalgam of the real Socialist and Communist Parties), he
is haunted by his past experience of oppression under Franco.
Thus from the very beginning of the film there is an implicit con-

trast between the recent emergence of Marxist activists into the political arena and the continuing clandestinity of homosexuals: both kinds of people will be described in similar terms throughout the film. And as in *Los placeres ocultos*, mise en scene is strictly functional: Roberto's casual but elegant clothes epitomize his class position as a progressive intellectual (*progre*). Even more schematically, he is defined by a single object: his heavy, square glasses, icon of "straight" respectability (Plate I). In the poster used to advertise the film the glasses recur: the contrast between public rectitude and private deviance is expressed by having the husband, wife, and lover reflected in the dark lenses of Roberto's spectacles as they embrace.

As the opening sequence continues, Roberto (the mild-mannered José Sacristán) narrates in flashback the story of his continuing homosexual tendencies, to the accompaniment of *verté* images such as a press photo of the Carretas Cinema in Madrid, a famous gay rendezvous. Attempting to reason with himself "in a scientific and Marxist way" he marries, convinced that homosexuality is a "bourgeois and counter-revolutionary deviation." But erotic obsession transcends rational analysis: while imprisoned for illicit political activities in the last days of Francoism, he encounters Paco, a tattooed male prostitute, and in a voyeuristic scene typical of Eloy de la Iglesia watches as Paco's erect penis emerges from beneath a sheet. As in the opening shower sequence of *Los placeres ocultos*, this is not simply a scandalous challenge to the censor. It is also a direct assault on the mass audience, who find themselves encouraged to identify with the sympathetic Roberto's voyeuristic fascination.[16]

Homosexuality irrupts, then, as the random encounter that eludes rational analysis and disturbs correct political positions. But the irony here is that the object of sexual and political interest is identical: the exploited proletarian represented by a lumpen youth. The marginality of the Marxist before political reform and of the homosexual before sexual liberalization is thus both similar and different. In a speech to his fellow militants Roberto exclaims, "Legal or not, we're here to stay." And his words clearly apply also to the gay constituency yet to emerge into the political arena.

In interviews on the film's release de la Iglesia repeatedly claims that *El diputado* sets out to show the contradictions between ho-

mosexuality and Marxism, between the struggle for sexual freedom and the class struggle. But he also invokes individual freedom, inciting one interviewer to ask him leadingly if the film is
autobiographical.[17] Within this framework of the individual "case
history" (enhanced by the privileged access of internal monologue
or voice-over) the narrative will progress through schematic oppositions: the noble Roberto falls in love with Juanito (José Luis
Alonso), a youth in the pay of a sinister conspiracy of the ultra-
right. But this Manicheism, so scorned by critics at the time, conceals the complex relation between gay liberation and leftist politics, which was also being explored outside Spain in the same
period.

In his excellent "Gays and Marxism," Bill Marshall explores
the relationship between the two terms in Britain, France, and
the United States in the 1970s.[18] He begins by identifying certain
strands of (non-leftist) gay political activity in the seventies:

> An emphasis on the struggle for "rights" of "gays" as an
> identified sexual (analogous with racial) minority within
> the status quo of property relations; an emphasis on the
> fundamentally revolutionary/dissident position of being
> gay; an emphasis on personal liberation with wider
> political pretensions: "the personal is political." These
> positions, sometimes distinct, sometimes interlinked, are
> clearly inimical to Marxism. They lack a *global* project,
> whether political (the transformation of class society) or
> intellectual (a theory of historical development, and within
> it, the oppression of gays); and they eschew a call to arms
> against capitalism. (259)

This "personalist" tendency shares with Marxist approaches of
the same decade a lack of interest in material conditions and an
unwillingness to consider the gay community within the context
of the distinct professions and class positions it actually occupies.
In particular, it "neglects the way in which class oppression in-
tersects with the oppression of gays" (263).

If we examine *El diputado* more closely we shall see that (coming from the very different context of the Spanish transition) *El
diputado*'s account of gays and Marxism does not assume the existence of a homogeneous gay community; indeed it insists constantly on the intersection of sexual and class interests, on the

determining force of material (economic) conditions on libidinal relations. I will argue that the personal narrative of Roberto in the film is indeed political, but that politics is inseparable from the global project of the emancipation of the working class from capitalism.

Male prostitution is recurrent in the film. We first meet the angelic Juanito ("pinkish skin, blue-green eyes") at an orgy where his presence has been paid for by older men. And there is a continuing parallel between political and (homo)sexual corruption: thus when Roberto asks the *chapero* (male prostitute) Ness why he is now in the pay of the extreme right, the latter replies: "You found it easy to buy me; so did they." Roberto's leftist, internationalist culture is contrasted with Juanito's less sophisticated tastes, through schematic contrasts: Roberto recites a poem by Cernuda to his young lover, reads to him from *Capital*, or plays him a song by Georges Moustaki. Juanito initially reacts with scorn. But while such moments can be taken as stages in the progressive education of a lumpen youth, other sequences are more disturbing. Thus when the two men first make love in the secret apartment where the party faithful had met under Franco, de la Iglesia edits the scene with a series of shock cuts between the two bodies and the revolutionary posters on the wall of the flat. Or again at certain points the characters seem to parody Marxist vocabulary by repeating formulae in inappropriate contexts. Thus after considering her reaction to her husband's revelation of his gay affair, Roberto's wife (the perfectly poised María Luisa de San José) says that she has "made a concrete analysis of a concrete situation." On the film's release, critics chose not to recognize the overtly ironic tone of such comments (an irony which is confirmed by the script), reading them as unintentionally humorous.[19] But it remains the case that at key moments such as this one, political and affective discourses are imperfectly matched, and often flagrantly contradictory.

But in a Marxist reading it would be foolish to attempt to erase such inconsistencies of tone. For contradiction is of the essence. In an interview on *El diputado*'s release, the director claims that he has set out a problem, but not attempted to resolve it.[20] And at the close of the film, as we shall see, Roberto prides himself on having borne with his contradictions to the bitter end. The problem is that it is not simply the predicament of the character that is contradictory, it is also the texture of the film surface itself. Thus at times the narrative is interrupted and José Sacristán is required to deliver unashamedly expository dialogue. A good example is an exchange with Juanito as they share a tent in the countryside, the location that serves (as in *Los placeres ocultos*) as the privileged site for illicit pleasure. Juanito asks Roberto why he's a communist: surely they are all manual laborers or people without cash; and of course none of them are queer. To this Roberto gamely replies that socialists like himself are attempting to build a new country that will offer a better future for all. As a Good Homosexual Roberto is properly patient with his youthful lover's political education. To say that his character is implausible or a cardboard cutout is to miss the point. De la Iglesia claims to have chosen Sacristán for the part because he represented the "standard" Spanish man. And he contrasts the old-style depiction of the homosexual in Spanish cinema (a heterosexual who disguises himself as a *mariquita* in order to have greater success with women) with his own representation of him ("a man who sleeps with men because he likes it, and that's it").[21] The curious anemia of Sacristán's performance is thus a significant part of the film's ideological message: as a strictly representative character (the typical Spaniard, the ordinary homosexual) he cannot be allowed any particularities of character or behavior. To do so would be to put into jeopardy his value as an emblem of a particular social and political conjunction.

It is perhaps instructive to compare de la Iglesia and Sacristán's somewhat pallid creation with a literary precedent, Jordi Viladrich's *Anotaciones al diario de un homosexual comunista*, published in Madrid in 1977, the year before the release of *El diputado*. The text purports to be the diary of a gay Marxist who sends it to the (safely heterosexual) author in order to have the benefit of his sage commentary. The lurid cover, showing a hairy-chested figure whose head has been replaced by a hammer and sickle, sets the tone for the diary, which recounts "Roberto" 's flight from the monastery where he had been sheltered and his descent into the communist cells and gay bars of the big city. It is interspersed by Viladrich's ludicrous commentary (for which "Roberto" expresses great thanks) in which he "proves" that "Roberto" 's condition derives from an unresolved fixation on his mother. The end of the volume contains a joint lexicon of gay and Marxist terminology, proof (if any were needed) that homosexuality and communism are linked, alien discourses, to be deciphered only with difficulty by the common reader.[22]

Against such a background, de la Iglesia's MP seems something of a revelation: the somewhat laborious stress on his morality and normality was no doubt necessary in the period. But what is striking about El diputado is that in spite of its personalized depiction of politics and its autobiographical narrative (complete with intimate voice-over), Roberto is never set up as a (pseudo-medical) case history, and indeed never thinks to ask himself the cause of his homosexuality. Presented and experienced as a social relation that brings him into contact with men outside his own class, it is necessarily expressed through the discourses of ethics or politics, not those of psychiatry or medicine. Roberto's superficiality (Sacristán's pale, blank face is like a reflecting screen) thus has an ideological as well as a narrative value: it suggests that once their sexual-object choice is acknowledged, homosexuals carry no psychic enigma or secret within them, are just "men who like to sleep with men." The demonstrative quality of de la Iglesia's cinema (its tendency to point things out to the audience without risking superfluous "noise") would tend to vindicate just such a functional conception of characterization in film.

But such formal and conceptual clarity can be deceptive. An excellent critique in La calle (The street) — the journal that billed itself as "the first on the left" — suggests that criticism should address itself to the clear and "diaphanous" text if it is to draw out its ideological presuppositions.[23] La calle acknowledges that de la Iglesia's objective was to analyze the confrontation between leftist politics and homosexuality. However, the anonymous writer ("F.L.")[24] claims that the film ends at the very point this confrontation begins: when Roberto is about to reveal his private dilemma to the party conference. Genuine debate is avoided because the contradiction is interiorized (played out within the character's mind) or expressed only through his relationship with his wife. De la Iglesia thus fails to examine the bourgeois sexual ideology of the Left, as he does not show the party reacting to Roberto's declaration.

What is more, the film relies on three simplistic narrative devices: schematic simplification, sentimentality, and crude topicality. Thus José Sacristán's character must be adorned with positive attributes in order to make the audience "forgive" his homosexuality; and this positive pole must be opposed by the equally monolithic evil of the far Right. But this schematicism (the division into goodies and baddies) capsizes the picture: the dualistic structure does not permit the insertion of any contradictory factor (such as Roberto's wife) or any character who evolves toward a new consciousness during the course of the film (such as the youthful Juanito who discovers his own homosexuality and his commitment to his leftist lover). The audience's sentimental identification with the protagonist is thus achieved only at the cost of abandoning the political analysis, which was the initial objective of the film. Without the "spice" (*pimienta*) of the sex scenes and the obtrusive references to actuality, the melodrama would prove unpalatable.

"F.L." 's account is the most substantial of those critics of the Left who clearly felt themselves to be threatened by the film; and it should be added that *La calle* itself subsequently published a defense of *El diputado*.[25] But for "F.L." de la Iglesia's main sin is commercialism: the feature is entitled "Out for 300 million," a reference to the number of pesetas the film was aiming for at the box office. What is more, *La calle* neglects the filmic texture of the work, reducing it to manifest content. José Luis Téllez in *Contracampo*, however, offers a more adequate reading.[26] His review is the text that first proposed that de la Iglesia's cinema be read as a pamphlet. Téllez argues that, taken in this generic context, the supposed defects of *El diputado* (archetypical characters, exaggerated situations, implausible dialogues, clumsy cinematic technique) are precisely the virtues of de la Iglesia's work. The role of such "defects" is to communicate the moral of the film to the audience with the greatest efficacy: the moral being that Spain has been freed from dictatorship only to achieve a precarious and shameful parliamentarianism. Téllez draws attention to a particular technique: from time to time, one of the characters pretends to address another and, looking into the camera, expresses one of the salient points about the transition. In this coarse, Brechtian way political analysis is made to predominate over the plot, which is merely the vehicle for it. The audience is directly addressed, invoked as the countershot to the close-up. But if this cinematic pamphlet draws on melodrama, its position is not that of the bourgeois noveletta, but rather the opposite: love is not a "bridge" that permits the character to transcend class struggle, but rather a mechanism through which class struggle becomes visible and is made more conflictory. Thus Juanito's transformation from enemy and prostitute to comrade and lover leads inevitably to his death: a final emblem of the inexorable nature of (political and sexual) destiny.

At the end of the film (as so often in Eloy de la Iglesia's work) the youth is sacrificed: his former fascist paymasters murder him in revenge for his betrayal of their cause. Previously, however, he had been curiously integrated with the heterosexual couple in an ersatz family. Roberto's wife claims that she feels Juanito could be their son, and she comes to share Roberto's passion for the youth. Hence the triangle of *Los placeres ocultos* is reiterated with a twist: here the older man's passion is sexually gratified and indeed reciprocated. Juanito finally admits that he is no longer doing it for the money: the homosexual relation transcends financial motives for a moment, only to be destroyed by its implacable opponents.

In the final scene Eduardo, about to be elected leader of his party, resolves to tell his comrades the story that we have just seen narrated in the film. The script tells us that "slowly he starts to clench his fist and he raises it firmly, angrily, hopefully. But he cannot stop his eyes filling with tears" (213). The frame freezes as the *Internationale* is played. It is an implausible, even derisory moment. But it is also a defiantly utopian image of a radicalism transformed by libidinal investment, of a Marxism inflected by homosexual affect.

El pico: Reproducing the Father[27]

A medium shot of two youths (Paco and Urko) sitting on a bridge, smoking marijuana. The camera tilts up as the boys stand: the industrial landscape of the port comes into view behind them. There are distant hills beyond. The camera follows them as they move right and a political poster comes into frame: it shows the

head and shoulders of a smiling man with the words ARAMEN-
DIA PARLAMENTURAKO. The first youth holds the other next
to the poster, comparing his image to that of the man who is
his father, Basque separatist candidate in the forthcoming elections. Behind the (unremarkable) dialogue we hear the external
diegetic sound that will recur throughout the film: a distant police siren.

This early sequence of *El pico* maps out the narrative and ideological space within which the action of the film will unfold. In
the foreground are the two youths, played by Pasoliniesque José
Luis Manzano and elfin Javier García, respectively. Their relationship will be the main one in the film. In the middle ground is the
symbolic or public space of paternal authority: Paco's father is a
Civil Guard, and Urko's (as we have seen) a politician. And in
the background the city of Bilbao: a site of political conflict, industrial decline, and inclement weather (the characters always
seem to be huddled up against the cold or sheltering from the
rain). This early image, then, suggests that the film will be concerned with relations between men: both horizontal (between
friends of the same age) and vertical (between fathers and sons).
As a narrative of genealogy or filiation, it will trace both the threats
to the patriarchal order and the exclusion of women from that
order. Like *Los placeres ocultos, El pico* is the story of a dying
mother, and like *El diputado* it is the story of a female partner excluded from a relationship between men.

It was *El pico* that made *Diario 16* say that de la Iglesia's cinema had "the aesthetics of the Y-front"[28] and made *El alcázar* claim
that one of his political aims was to "praise queers."[29] However,
as we shall see, the theme of homosexuality is less prominent in
this film than in the earlier two, in which the audience is encouraged to identify with an unambiguously gay hero. I shall argue,
however, that the explicit homosexual romance of de la Iglesia's
unmade Basque melodrama *Galopa y corta el viento* recurs in sublimated form in the various relationships between men in *El pico*
and in the central theme of heroin addiction presented here as
an eroticized spectacle of the male body. On the film's release,
the still most frequently reproduced in the press was of the bare-
chested Javier García injecting himself in the arm.

Critics have noted the information overload in de la Iglesia's narratives, the desire to "tell it all" in each film.[30] This reaches a climax in *El pico,* which has at least five main themes: the Civil Guard, the family, homosexuality, drugs, and Basque politics. Newspapers at the time of its release stressed the topicality of these elements: de la Iglesia had hoped to have a real-life politician (José María Bandrés) play the part of the Basque separatist, just as he had filmmaker Juan Antonio Bardem play himself in *El diputado.*

In his excellent review article in *Contracampo* Ignasi Bosch confirms that it is not the form but the referent of de la Iglesia's cinema that has proved so controversial: during the transition he unerringly chose to address those topics (such as homosexuality) which most Spaniards chose to ignore.[31] With transition now achieved and a Socialist government in power, political change would require both thematic and formal changes in de la Iglesia's cinematic practice. Bosch claims that those insistent (even hectoring) devices of earlier films (such as the racking focus we saw in *Los placeres ocultos*) are no longer appropriate. He calls attention to a very different technique that features, in this film, the use of long takes without camera movement, more characteristic of art film than the exploitation genre. I shall return to one such sequence (Paco's birthday party) a little later.

De la Iglesia claimed that this was his most ambiguous film to date, and critics seemed uneasy as how to read it. An extreme case is the literalism of *El alcázar,* which accused the film of promoting drug abuse by citing such lines as "drugs give you peace" out of context.[32] Other critics, taking the opposite line, attacked the film for excessive moralizing.[33] Less hostile pieces vindicated fertile contradictions within the film's modes and genres. Thus Ruiz de Villalobos noted twin tendencies to auteurism (a "fabulous" *tremendismo*) and commercialism.[34] This conflict inspires an unprecedented intensification of narrative form. José Luis Guarner notes a similar conflict in the tone of the film, which switches between solemnity and irony: de la Iglesia is a "journalist with the soul of a writer of novelettas [*folletinista*]...with a particular capacity to capture what is novelettish in real life."[35] For Guarner, therefore, there is no simple opposition between melodrama and documentary, fiction and the real. Indeed, *El pico* may come closest to the real where it appears to be most fantastic.

El pico sets the central (non-sexual) relationship between the two boys in a number of different contexts: ethnicity, the family, homosexuality. We can consider each of these in turn. The youths (repeatedly described as "intimate friends") are separated by ethnic difference: Paco is the son of a Castilian newcomer, the Civil Guard father who has been posted to a combat zone; the euskera-speaking Urko is 100 percent autochthonous: the script tells us that he has "unequivocally Basque features [*rasgos euskaldunes*]." From the very beginning, then, the body is marked by the trace of cultural or ethnic difference and by its relation to a clearly defined territory. But *El pico* does not allow its audience the luxury of a belief in the untouched purity of Basque culture. When the two youths drift into heroin dealing to support their habits they are shown making a connection with a film director. He is shooting a youth in national costume dancing to the *txistu* or Basque flute. The incongruity is deliberately grotesque, demonstrating to the viewer that even the innocence of rural tradition has been corrupted by urban vice. Much later, when Paco resolves to leave Bilbao, the alien scene of his addiction, he tells his lover and protector, the gay sculptor Mikel (bug-eyed Quique Sanfrancisco), that, the Basque country is not his homeland; the latter replies, "This land belongs to all those who wish to live here." But the exchange merely shows that the relationship between the youth and sculptor (like that between the two youths) is unavoidably marked by ethnic division. Homosexual desire can cross that divide but cannot erase it.

As always in de la Iglesia, such differences are reinforced unequivocally by mise en scène: Mikel drinks *pacharán* (the Basque liqueur); Betti, the Argentine prostitute who introduces the boys to heroin, sucks on *mate*. Or again, the cluttered vulgarity of the Civil Guard's home contrasts with the white walls and more modern tastes of the Basque politician's.

But if characters are representative of ethnic (and class) positions, they are also inextricably placed within their families. One important early sequence here is Paco's eighteenth birthday. In a single long take with only slight adjustments of the camera, the family members and maid walk in and out of frame, eating and drinking, each speaking in turn on the phone to the grandmother who has called to congratulate her grandson. The soundtrack is muddy, with overlapping dialogue and background noise from the television. Film theory has often suggested that single takes such as these demand a more active response from the spectator, who is at liberty to move at will within the frame without the co-ercive direction of continuity editing. Ignasi Bosch,[36] however, suggests that this may not be the case here: the "freedom of the look" is exercised not by the audience but by the cineast who does not allow us to avert our gaze from the scene (57). Through this "violence," de la Iglesia points to a strictly political reading of an apparently banal set-up: through purely filmic means (that is, without recourse to explanatory dialogue) he suggests that in spite of the recent election of socialist government in Spain, real change must take place at the concrete level of everyday life, far from the parliamentary assembly. The space of the family is thus implicitly presented as an ideological space, the point of strug-gle between new subjectivities and old power structures.

The crowded sequence shot of the party is followed by a scene between father and son in which editing also conveys meaning. The emblematically named Commander Torrecuadrada (square tower) (played by the stolid José Manuel Cervino) paints a mus-tache like his own on Paco's face and questions him about his sex life. A police siren is heard in the distance. When Paco claims (falsely) to be a virgin, his father commiserates: Basque women are all slags and their men queers. He thus proposes to give his son the same gift his father gave him: a visit to a high class brothel where his "first time" will be a good one. Here the editing is more traditional than in the previous party sequence, moving from a medium two-shot of the men together, to reverse angle close-ups of each as they speak in turn. However, the visual rhyme (graphic match) of the shots (the new similarity of the son to the father effected by the false mustache) heightens the sense of sym-metry inherent in the shot/countershot of continuity editing: it is a moment of homosocial reproduction, in which the father at-tempts to transmit heterosexual practices to his son.

This bonding of men is over the bodies of women: the female members of the family excluded from this man-to-man conver-sation, the prostitute women whom the father regales with tales of his potency when he takes Paco to the brothel. However, the filiation process is disturbed: Paco is with Argentine prostitute Betti and is more engaged by her drugs than her sex. Naked on the bed, he passively allows himself to be caressed: the camera moves in to focus on the syringe that lies on the table beside the lovers.

This scene with *femme fatale* Betti is typical of the way in which the film graphically juxtaposes sex and drug abuse even as it acknowledges the loss of libido produced by heroin. The most fetishistic sequence of this kind occurs later in the film: Paco and Urko have weaned themselves off heroin, but return to Betti's for a sexual threesome (once more, male relations are effected quite literally over the body of the woman). As the youths horse around offscreen in the shower, a medium long shot shows Betti on the sofa in her flat (posters of David Bowie and Marilyn Monroe),[37] languidly preparing her fix. Paco enters naked and stands behind the sofa on the right; Urko does the same on the left. Medium close-ups of the two youths looking out of frame toward each other are followed by POV shots over Betti's shoulder as she syringes the solution from the spoon. The camera pulls in for extreme close-ups of the two boys and a final *primerísimo plano* of Betti's black-nailed fingers squeezing the syringe until a pearl of the liquid drips from the end. A heartbeat is heard on the soundtrack.

The eroticization of drug abuse here does not arise solely from the nakedness of the actors or the phallic angle of the syringe. It is also inscribed in the filmic grammar that imposes an increasing identification with the youths' "point of view." It is interesting to note that de la Iglesia chooses to break the 180 degree rule (to cross the line of the axis of action) precisely in order to give us the boys' POV shots. What is more, the boys look at each other, but not at the woman who has her back toward them. Just as vertical bonding between men (father and son) is achieved through the exchange of women (prostitution), so horizontal bonding is effected through the mediation of a prostitute who is excluded once more from the traffic of the male look.

It is not too far-fetched, then, to see drug abuse as a displacement of the homosexual romance in the original Basque project for which de la Iglesia failed to find funding. The ethnic conflict between the lovers of *Galopa y corta el viento* (a non-Basque Civil Guard and a member of ETA) recurs in the relationship between the two junkie sons and between the two mismatched fathers, who are forced to join forces in order to save their children. As secrets that must be confessed to the father, as creators of a clandestine community invisible to the dominant culture it inhabits, homosexuality and heroin addiction share a similar (culturally constructed) narrative space. In each, clandestinity is dangerously combined with proximity: both are found in the heart of the family, in the centers of political power. And on a graphic level the male body is offered as an object of sacrifice to a mystic jouissance: the script tells us that Paco's face takes on an "otherworldly glow" when he speaks of the peace brought by heroin (35); Urko's white arm, held out horizontally by a police officer to display its tracks and illuminated by a table lamp, is reminiscent of Christ's on the cross. When, toward the end of the film, Urko dies of an overdose, the two fathers meet over his dead body in the morgue. The Civil Guards keeping watch outside are silhouetted against the windows, their black outlines contrasting with the deathly pallor of the youth.

Homosexual desire is thus displaced or sublimated into conventional, homosocial relations. But *El pico* does indeed contain an openly gay character, Basque sculptor Mikel. Initially presented as an outcast (sitting on his own in a bar or park), Mikel later takes over the functions of the family that Paco's authoritarian father and dying mother are respectively unwilling and unable to provide. Thus, although Mikel's interest in Paco is unequivocally sexual (and we are told that Paco does not dislike his embraces), as a Good Homosexual he shelters Paco in his studio and lovingly nurses him during his attempt at withdrawal. In an ironic inversion, then, it is the (non-reproductive) gay man who takes over the nurturing, protective function of the family.

The contradictions between radical politics and homosexuality central to *El diputado* are here confined to a marginal character. Mikel (who prides himself on the fact that people such as he will never be trusted by the Civil Guard) must also confront the ambivalent reaction of *abertzale* (separatist) politicians: Urko's father is proud of Mikel as a "great national artist," but embarrassed by his declaration of homosexuality. When Paco leaves the studio intending to set out for a new life in Madrid, Mikel is left alone, in long shot, standing against a dark, rainy window: Paco tells him that he could never give him what he really wants. As in *Los placeres ocultos*, the gay man is condemned to dissatisfaction and solitude; but as in the earlier film again, the homosexual relationship is more markedly affective, even sentimental, than its heterosexual equivalents. The music swells as Paco takes his leave.[38]

In his interview with *Contracampo* some two years before *El pico* was made, Eloy de la Iglesia complained of a new economic censorship, more subtle than the Francoist political censorship, which had prevented him from making his Basque, gay melodrama (34). However, we have seen that the dispersal or displacement of homosocial desire among the varied characters of *El pico* raises, perhaps inadvertently, questions the original, inert plot of *Galopa y corta el viento* would not have addressed: the sublimated bonding of men in all-male structures (of family, friendship, profession) from which women are definitively excluded; the eroticization of the male body in the travail of heroin addiction. At the end of the film father and son confront one another on top of a cliff: before his overdose, Urko had killed a dealer with a gun that Paco had stolen from his father, Commander Torrecuadrada. The latter places the gun and stolen heroin in his three-cornered hat and throws it into the sea: the script says that it flies through the air "like a UFO," scattering a cloud of white powder. The pun in the title of the film ("pico" refers to both the fix of heroin and the corner of the Civil Guard's hat) is thus visualized in this final image. As John Hopewell comments, it is a salutary irony that the father chooses to protect the honor of his family rather than that of the Civil Guard (he has just destroyed the only evidence that could convict his son of complicity in the murder). For as father and son go off embracing, the audience is left with the feeling that, as an institution, the family may be more insidiously oppressive than the military police (238). Paco's liberation is illusory and cannot be sustained: the sea has served the symbolic function of nature and absolved him of his contradictions; but now he must return to the cultural and historical space of the city.

The Family Romance

When de la Iglesia's *La semana del asesino* (The week of the assassin) was shown at the Berlin Film Festival in 1972, the distributors handed out sick bags to the audience (*Contracampo* interview, 29). While the violence in these films no longer seems as graphic as it once did, their sexual content would make distribution difficult in Britain and the United States today. In Spain to speak of de la Iglesia is to risk ridicule or worse: there can be few filmmakers whose work seems to be so marked by the period in which it was made, in this case the transition to democracy. In terms of distribution, his cinema profited from the brief period (1977–84) between the end of censorship and the establishment of *Salas X*, cinemas licensed to show hard pornography. It was the time of the *destape* (strip) when actors (overwhelmingly female) first appeared naked in Spanish films.[39] Once the shock value attached to the disrobing of bodies or the presentation of taboo topics had died away, the market for de la Iglesia's cinema was bound to diminish. Times were changing, and on the same day that *Diario 16* slammed *El pico* (8 October 1983) it named Almodóvar's *Entre tinieblas* (Dark habits) film of the week.

De la Iglesia himself was very conscious of the problems of exhibition his films had even at their most popular, telling *Contracampo* how *Colegas* (Mates, 1982) was removed from the upmarket Cine Fuencarral (in spite of its success) by a management fearful of the suburban hooligans it had drawn into town.[40] But by 1985 he had distanced himself from his earlier sympathies: abandoning the Communist Party, berating the Basque Nationalist Party for its provincialism, and rejecting homosexuality for an erotic pluralism.[41] His most recent film, *La estanquera de Vallecas* (The Lady in the Vallecas Kiosk, 1987), contains familiar lowlife elements and stars the now adult José Luis Manzano, but is couched in an uncertain comic tone.

In the introduction to this chapter I suggested that what was interesting about the films I have discussed here is the combination of homosexuality and mass culture. And it is significant that the emergence of gay men into commercial cinema in Spain in the 1970s parallels the experience of British and East German film in the 1960s and 1980s, respectively. Thus the British *The Leather Boys* (1963) and the German *Coming Out* (1989) both confront us with Good Homosexuals whose existing relationships with women are disturbed by their attraction to men. This would suggest that plots such as that of *El diputado* are to be expected at moments of social and political transition comparable to that of Spain (the liberalization of post-war Britain, the disintegration of Communism in East Germany). In these films (as in de la Iglesia) female desire is presented as an obstacle, and lesbian desire inconceivable.

In the sequel to *El pico* (1984) Paco is sent to jail, where his beauty makes him the object of a quarrel between jealous male lovers. As John Hopewell describes, his adoptive "family" in the prison cell is finally replaced by his father's "family": on his release Paco joins the army. He ends the sequel with a son still dealing heroin from his outwardly respectable position. In the new democratic Spain, styles may change, but patriarchal structures (fatherhood, police, army) remain the same. It is de la Iglesia's achievement, however, to have desublimated these homosocial institutions, to have laid bare the libidinal investments implicit in the same-sex communities of banking, politics, the armed forces, and prison. It is a dangerous knowledge mass audiences (and most critics) would prefer to ignore.

The Spanish critics who reviled Eloy de la Iglesia (including those such as Fernando Trueba who went on to make films of their own) argued from art-house criteria. Unsympathetic to the genre theory, which had made critics in France or the United States reevaluate B-movies or exploitation pictures, they failed to acknowledge that "quality cinema" was itself a category that was historically constructed. The endemic anemia of Spanish filmmaking under the socialists (the reliance on literary adaptations and decorative mise en scène)—an anemia challenged most forcefully by Almodóvar—owes much to this middle-brow respect for "art." The time is clearly ripe for a re-evaluation of de la Iglesia's oeuvre from the twin perspective of *auteurisme* and genre theory: while the former would account for the idiosyncratic topics and filmic language of his cinema, the latter would approach its narrative structure unimpeded by bourgeois notions of good taste. The vindication of once-neglected genres such as the horror movie or the woman's picture clearly serves as a precedent for the reappraisal of de la Iglesia's *tremendista* melodramas.

At the end of *El diputado*, the José Sacristán character says, "I signed up to change history; I ended up suffering it." This line sums up de la Iglesia's career to date: his politically engaged cinema once sought to change Spain and has now been abandoned by it. But the line also points to the essence of his characters in these films, who at once act on and are acted upon by history. Stephen Heath refers to two modes of subjectivity in cinema: the subject-process, which charts the development of character through metonymic displacement; the subject-reflection, which marks the point at which the character stops to look back at him- or herself.[42] The ceaseless displacement of the process can lead to chaos, the frozen reflection of the position to stasis. In classic (Hollywood) narrative the two modes are sewn (or "sutured") together so that no join is visible. I would argue that the discontinuity of de la Iglesia's cinema derives precisely from an unwillingness or inability to stitch together the fabrics of process and reflection, which remain distinct and jarring. Thus at some points in his films the dynamic rhythm of the plot leads to chaos; and at others the totemic nature of the characters leads to stasis. A good example here is *El diputado*, in which the extravagant complexities of the plot fail to mesh with the simple schematicism of the characters: Roberto's *prise de position* is massively overdetermined. Such inconsistencies can no longer be dismissed as simple incompetence. Rather they should be interrogated for what they tell us of a cinematic practice and its relation to a historical moment.

What characterizes de la Iglesia's cinema, finally, is a nostalgia for the family and for the reproduction of the real. Both are rendered impossible by his continuing commitment to the representation of gay men. For, according to these films, homosexuality exists primarily as a disturbance in heterosexual and familial relations; it thus follows that a homosexual hero must be a special case, cannot be representative of the totality of social circumstances at any moment in a nation's history. Moreover, this disturbance at the heart of the family resists naturalistic expression, and is best served by the conventions of melodrama. For all their love of the referent and passion for topicality (*El pico* begins with

Felipe González's inauguration) these films are also small-scale romances of the private sphere. Thus the cinema of Eloy de la Iglesia is transitional in all senses: it chronicles the historical period of the shift from dictatorship to democracy; it exploits the distribution hiatus between the end of censorship and the legalization of pornography; and it depicts in the struggles of the homosexual hero the emergence of a new figure in Spanish film: the gay man who was to speak for and of himself.

Notes

1. Augusto M. Torres, *Cine español 1896–1983* (Madrid: 1983): Ministerio de Cultura 256.

2. This connection is stressed by George De Stefano in one of the very few pieces in English on de la Iglesia, "Post-Franco Frankness," *FC* 22 (June 1986): 58–60. De Stefano gives a brief account of de la Iglesia's career and an interview with him when *Los placeres ocultos* opened the 1986 New York Gay Film Festival. The only other films available with English subtitles are *El diputado* and the teenage gangster movie *Colegas* (1982).

3. "No cerrar el pico: el director Eloy de la Iglesia lleva 20 años escandalizando," interview with Miguel Bayón, *Cambio 16* (14 Nov. 1983).

4. "Ultimo veto de la censura: *Los placeres ocultos*," *Diario 16* (26 Jan. 1977). Méndez-Leite praises the cast's performances in this film. See also the anonymous review in *El pueblo* (19 Apr. 1977), which says that the film treats the "sad problem" of homosexuality, but with "little scandal." For the banning, see Angeles Maso, "La luz roja a *Los placeres ocultos*: Eloy de la Iglesia no piensa alterar la integridad de su película," *La vanguardia* (15 Feb. 1977).

5. See "Eloy de la Iglesia: el homosexualismo en el cine," interview with Monty Padura, *Catalunya Expres* (19 Oct. 1977).

6. *El pueblo* (3 Oct. 1981).

7. *El cine español después de Franco* (Madrid, El Arquero, 1989) is an expanded and substantially revised version of *Out of the Past: Spanish Cinema after Franco* (London: British Film Institute, 1986). The section I cited here ("Del sexo de los ángeles a sexos angélicos," 164–178) does not appear in the English version. Hopewell discusses de la Iglesia in "Dando en los cojones: Eloy de la Iglesia y el populismo radical," 233–242.

8. "La homosexualidad como problema socio-político en el cine español del postfranquismo," *Tiempo de Historia* 52 (Mar. 1979), 88–91. Raúl Contel's "Cine de homosexuales," *Cinema 2002* 56 (Oct. 1979), 54–56 is on 5 QK,s (sic), a Catalan collective who made "anti-machista" parodies of pop culture.

9. "Eloy de la Iglesia," *Contracampo* 25–6 (Nov.–Dec. 1981): 21–41.

10. I cite the extract published by *Contracampo*. See also the outline held in the Biblioteca Nacional, Madrid, "Galopa y corta el viento: argumento para una historia cinematográfica escrito por Eloy de la Iglesia y Gonzalo Goicoechea" (Madrid, 23 Jan. 1980). The title is taken from the campy, popular song "Mi jaca."

11. *Los placeres* is briefly referred to in Hopewell, *El cine*, 178-236, and De Stefano (see n. 2 above) where de la Iglesia presents it as the first of a projected gay trilogy (with *El diputado* and the then-unmade *Galopa y corta el viento*). In his generally hostile "Los límites de Eloy," *Destino* (3 Aug. 1978), Jorge de Cominges concedes that *Los placeres* was the first Spanish film to treat homosexuality with dignity. I have referred to the script by de la Iglesia and Goicoechea, which has the working title "La acera de enfrente" (Madrid, n.d. [1975?]).

12. *Between Men*, 21 and throughout.

13. *La criatura* (The creature/The baby") (1978), starring Ana Belén as the wife who leaves husband Juan Diego for a dog. For the supposed feminist implications of this film see the interview with L. Fernández Ventura, "Eloy de la Iglesia: lo popular y lo político," *Diario 16* (13 Dec. 1977).

14. See Méndez-Leite (n. 4 above).

15. For *El diputado* as a continuation of *Los placeres*, see the interview by Pirula Arderius, "Eloy de la Iglesia: 'Aún no hay libertad de expresión,'" *Información* (23 Feb. 1978). Richard Dyer mentions *El diputado* as one of those European films in which "positive images [are] curtailed by social repression": *Now You See It: Studies on Lesbian and Gay Film* (London: Routledge, 1990), 267. He is not quite right in saying that this film (like the others he treats) ends with the death of the gay protagonist: it is the youthful lover, not the eponymous MP, who is killed. I have consulted de la Iglesia's script: "El diputado: título provisional" (Madrid, 1978).

16. The film found a new mass audience (of some three million) when shown on national television for the first time on 15 Nov. 1985. See De Stefano (n. 2 above).

17. See n. 5 above.

18. In *Coming On Strong: Gay Politics and Culture*, ed. Simon Shepherd and Mick Wallis (London: Unwin Hyman, 1989): 258–274.

19. See the anonymous review in *Amba* (24 Jan. 1979), which gives the film a rating of zero.

20. Antonio Egido, "*El diputado*, político y homosexual; Eloy de la Iglesia 'Los partidos políticos no deben marginar la libertad sexual,'" *El periódico* (18 Jan. 1979).

21. A.M.M. (Angeles Masó), "Llegó con *El diputado*: Eloy de la Iglesia: 'La izquierda ha heredado una moral que no es la suya,'" *La Vanguardia* (24 Oct. 1979); Diego Galán, "Eloy de la Iglesia: la ambición de un cine popular," *Triunfo* (24 Oct. 1979).

22. The copy in the Biblioteca Nacional, inscribed with marginalia correcting mistakes in the supposed "gay lexicon," proves that the readership for sensationalist and homophobic works of this kind was not exclusively "general."

23. "*El diputado* de Eloy de la Iglesia: a por los 300 millones," *La calle* (30 Jan.–5 Feb. 1979).

24. Probably Francisco (Francesc) Llinás. (In Catalan, unlike in Castilian, "ll" is not a distinct letter.)

25. Encarnación Andany, "En defensa de *El diputado*," *La calle* (13–l8 Feb. 1979). No. 1 (Apr. 1979): 51–52.

26. *La calle* No. 1 (Apr. 1979): 51–52.

27. *El pico* was highly controversial on its release; see José Arenas, *"El pico, una película de Eloy de la Iglesia que se presenta polémica,"* *ABC* (7 Sept. 1983). However, six years later, when shown on television, critics decried it as "pastiche" and "melodrama": see anonymous previews in *Diario 16* (11 Aug. 1989) and *ABC* (11 Aug. 1989). I have also referred to the script "El pico: guión (título provisional)" (Madrid, Feb. 1983).

28. Manuel Hidalgo, "Arrojarse a los pies del 'caballo,'" *Diario 16* (18 Sept. 1983).

30. See Ignasi Bosch, *"El pico:* lo viejo y lo nuevo," *Contracampo* 34 (Winter 1984): 52–60, 55.

31. Ibid., 53.

32. See n. 29 above.

33. See Jorge de Cominges, "Una historia que se permite todas las osadías," *Noticiero universal* (1 Oct. 1983); Francisco Marinero, review of *El pico, Diario 16* (8 Oct. 1983).

34. *"El pico:* el fabuloso cine tremendista de Eloy de la Iglesia," *Diario de Barcelona* (25 Sept. 1983) .

35. Review of *El pico, El periódico* (4 Oct. 1983). This is one of the very few sympathetic reviews the film received.

36. See n. 30 above.

37. Such reference alludes to an international pop culture that is not presented as being at odds with the stress on regional identity also affected by de la Iglesia's young rebels.

38. Elsewhere the music is disconcertingly incongruous, as when a cheerful tune plays over the final credits.

39. On the problematic end of censorship after the death of Franco see Hopewell, *El cine,* 140–147.

40. In the special section (see n. 8 above), 30.

41. Interview with Carel Peralta, "Eloy de la Iglesia: 'El *PNV* tiene un concepto aldeano de la moral,'" *Interviú* (30 Oct.–6 Nov. 1985).

42. "Film Performance," in *Cinetracts* 1/2 (1977), 9; cited in Steve Neale, *Genre* (London, 1987): 26–27.

Works Cited

A.M.M. (Angeles Masó), "Llegó con *El diputado*: Eloy de la Iglesia: 'La izquierda ha heredado una moral que no es la suya,'" *La Vanguardia* (24 Oct. 1979).

Andany, Encarnación. "En defensa de *El diputado*" (13–18 Feb. 1979). *La calle* 1 (Apr. 1979): 51–52.

Arderius, Pirula. "Eloy de la Iglesia: 'Aún no hay libertad de expresión,'" *Información* (23 Feb 1978).

Arenas, José. *"El pico,* una película de Eloy de la Iglesia que se presenta polémica," *ABC* (7 Sept. 1983).

Bayón, Miguel. "No cerrar el pico: el director Eloy de la Iglesia lleva 20 años escandalizando." *Cambio 16* (14 Nov. 1983).

Bosch, Ignasi. *"El pico:* lo viejo y lo nuevo," *Contracampo* 34 (Winter 1984): 52–60, 55.

Cominges, Jorge de. "Los límites de Eloy," *Destino* (3 Aug. 1978).

———. "Una historia que se permite todas las osadías," *Noticiero universal* (1 Oct. 1983).

Contel, Raúl. "Cine de homosexuales." *Cinema 2002* 56 (Oct. 1979).

De Stefano, George. "Post-Franco Frankness," *FC* 22 (June 1986): 58–60.

Dyer, Richard. *Now You See It: Studies on Lesbian and Gay Film.* London: Routledge, 1990.

Egido, Antonio. "*El diputado,* político y homosexual; Eloy de la Iglesia 'Los partidos políticos no deben marginar la libertad sexual,' " *El periódico* (18 Jan. 1979).

Fernández Ventura, L. "Eloy de la Iglesia: lo popular y lo político." *Diario 16* (13 Dec. 1977).

Galán, Diego. "Eloy de la Iglesia: la ambición de un cine popular," *Triunfo* 24 (Oct. 1979).

Hidalgo, Manuel. "Arrojarse a los pies del 'caballo,' " *Diario 16* (18 Sept. 1983).

Hopewell, John. *El cine español después de Franco.* Madrid: El Arquero 1989).

Marinero, Francisco. Review of *El pico, Diario 16* (8 Oct. 1983).

Masó, Angeles. "La luz roja a *Los placeres ocultos*: Eloy de la Iglesia no piensa alterar la integridad de su película." *La vanguardia* (15 Feb. 1977).

Méndez-Leite, Fernando. "Ultimo veto de la censura: *Los placeres ocultos.*" *Diario 16* (26 Jan. 1977).

Padura, Monty. "Eloy de la Iglesia: el homosexualismo en el cine." *Catalunya Expres* (19 Oct. 1977).

Peralta, Carel. "Eloy de la Iglesia: 'El *PNV* tiene un concepto aldeano de la moral,' " *Interviú* (30 Oct.-6 Nov. 1985).

Sedguick, Eve Kosofsky. *Between Men: English Literature and Male Homosexual Desire.* New York: Columbia University Press, 1985.

Shepherd, Simon and Mick Wallis, eds. *Coming On Strong: Gay Politics and Culture.* London, 1989.

Torres, Augusto M. *Cine español 1896–1983.* Madrid: Ministerio de Cultura, 1983.

Part IV
The Socialist Decade

◆   Chapter 13

Sexual Revolution against the State?
José Luis García Sánchez's *Pasodoble*

Ricardo Roque-Baldovinos

Pasodoble (1989), a film by José Luis García Sánchez, represents an original attempt to interrogate critically the historical experience of the *transición* (transition) in the Spanish Cinematography of the eighties. The transition to democracy was an outcome, rather than a disruption, of the modernizing process undertaken during the last decades of Francisco Franco's authoritarian regime. To be sure, the most important transformation was the institutionalization of a formal democracy. Henceforth, the political apparatus was to be submitted to popular ratification through an electoral system. At the same time, the democratic forces in Spain had at their disposal new spaces for public debate. On the other hand, since then the welfare state has been considerably strengthened, but it is fair to say that it was already in place since the times of the *caudillo*. Notwithstanding these positive developments, the fundamental economic and social structures have remained basically unchallenged. The results could hardly have been different. What was truly at stake was not the revolutionary transformation of Spanish society but the necessary adjustments that made possible Spain's entrance into the European Community.

The expectations of those Spaniards who were politically active, or had a deep emotional investment, in the struggle against the dictatorship were thus unfulfilled. In the collective memory of this period, there is a sense of disappointment, a perception that the changes were superficial, and, more importantly, a feeling of betrayal to the ideals of the Republic, the Popular Front, and the decades of struggle against the *generalísimo* and his regime. The ideology of *desencanto* (disenchantment) has played a role in politically neutralizing the impulse for radical social changes. Disillusion, skepticism against all utopias, the "end of ideologies," the entrance of Spain into "postmodernity," and all sorts of explanations have been used as self-complacent alibis for those intellectuals formerly in the Left and now acquiescent to the "good new times."

Disenchantment is far from being a spontaneous reaction. Both high culture and the "cultural industry"[1] have dispensed interpretations to the real experience of frustration and disappointment. I am not implying that this has responded to a consciously preconceived plan. The explanation has more to do with the particular experiences of the intellectuals co-opted by the dominant power who, by the access they have gained to the means of symbolic production, can present their stories of self-justification as the universal experience of the collective. José Luis Garci's *Asignatura Pendiente* (1977) is the disenchantment film *par excellence*.[2] Produced just months after Franco's death, it could be seen as the starting point of post-Francoist Spanish cinema. A commercial success, it also set the tone for a generation of Spaniards. This film narrates the story of the conversion of a formerly leftist activist lawyer into the "truths" of life. José, the character played by José Sacristán, embodies the new intellectual who heretofore has to live the split between a progressive rhetoric and the pleasures of consumer society.

Asignatura Pendiente, a commercial film, was still working within the logic of the cultural industry. *Pasodoble,* conversely, is inscribed within different conditions of cinematographic production. Now filmmakers cannot rely solely on private capital, but have access to different sources of financial support like state institutions or other nonprofit organizations. This change in the financial base, which was actively supported by the state cultural policy, would supposedly enable the emergence of a film production independent from short-sighted economical constraints. This space has made possible, although not exempt from difficulties, the work of artists such as García Sánchez whose attempts to use cinema as a medium to reflect critically on the life of contemporary Spain deserve our admiration and respect.

Pasodoble premiered in 1989. Franco had been dead for fourteen years. The socialists had been in the Moncloa since 1981. *Asignatura Pendiente* was twelve years old. Diputado [representative] Topero may well be seen as the true successor of Garci's José. Now he is ten years older, he is in power and he appears to have overcome disenchantment: his contradictions are no longer a source of agony. Although this character intervenes only in one scene, his role in the narrative is crucial. Once the victim of police repression, he is now at peace with his good old cousin: Officer Topero, a dwarf in command of the Police Special Forces. The politician admits with a dose of humor that the ultra-right-wing stance of his cousin is a source of embarrassment. At the same time he shows with pride the enlargements of photos that show him as a demonstrator fighting against fascist police. Topero is proud of his radical past but he defends family, religion and private property by reasons of state: "Not even Stalin dared to attack Family." Independently of the director's intention, this scene parodically unmasks the underlying ideological mechanism of *Asignatura Pendiente* and disenchantment. In it the status quo is accepted as a result of the discovery of values that are universal and transhistorical: the cycles of life, the charms of intimacy, and the like. *Pasodoble*'s vitriolic irony leaves no space for apologies and no excuse for false reconciliation. In this genuinely carnivalesque scene the film unforgivingly turns upside down all the myths of Spanish society and ridicules the complacent attitudes of Topero's contemporaries.

The last scene of the film provides us with important clues to think about two important issues with which I will try to deal in the following lines. In the first place, what I think is the most successful part of the film: the recourse to the carnivalesque and baroque allegory, rather than mimetic-realist narrative, as a mechanism of estrangement and reflection on contemporary social life in Spain. Second, the way the film deals with more complicated issues: the implications of the politicization of private life in contemporary critical criticism.

The fragmentation of experience, the avowed difficulties to think of society as a totality, is a constitutive part of modernity. Realist aesthetics was confident that through a study in detail of the appearances of social life it was possible to unveil a sense and an order immanent to bourgeois society. The Hollywood narrative film, institutionalized as the dominant means of cinematic representation, is to a certain extent tributary to the "routinized" version of the Realist tradition. Since Modernism[3], it has become apparent that the "reality effect" is a fabricated effect, a convention by no means more legitimate than any other convention. Moreover, in the opinion of many artists, a mimetic account of social reality not only reproduced a mystified experience but was itself a means of incorporating and of conforming readers to the alienating society that produced those appearances. Negating this mystified reality was thence a precondition to an aesthetics wishing to maintain its critical autonomy vis-à-vis the dominant powers in society. Under certain conditions, irreality and the absurd can, according to this view, be truer than realism and perhaps the only means of access to reality.

Asignatura Pendiente can be located without problems within the Hollywood narrative tradition. The film owes its efficacy to the identification effect with its protagonists, José and Elena, and the recognition by the spectators of isolated details that are given documentary value vis-à-vis the historical period that is represented. All these unconnected elements are woven together by the underlying melodramatic structure that gives the narrative its consistency and closure. History always stays in the background. The effect of historical authenticity is constructed through tangential allusions to Franco's death and other historical events, such as the popular icons of that time, and the poetry of Neruda or Hernández, icons themselves of the antidictatorship subculture. In this way, when the spectator sees him- or herself through the narrative what he or she recognizes is a mystified and vicarious experience supplied by the cultural industry.

In Spain the critical antirealist aesthetics, that I have just outlined, had an important and original proponent in Ramón del Valle Inclán and his *esperpentos*. García Sánchez's *Pasodoble* justly deserves to be inscribed in this tradition. Instead of a deconstructive artistic practice that operates through the construction of highly cerebral and esoteric products, this tradition recognizes the importance of pleasure and entertainment in aesthetic experience. Through exaggeration and black humor, through the ridicule of the conventions of the prestigious groups, our sense of reality is reduced *ad absurdum*. This tradition explodes the distancing component present in the comic and carnivalesque tradition without providing shortcuts to false and sentimental reconciliations.

In *Pasodoble* the absurd situation is the occupation of the Pontirole Mansion by a family of homeless gypsies. This occupation puts face to face two sectors of Spanish society that are at opposite ends in the social pyramid but, at the same time, represent marginal lifestyles in modern times: the gypsies and the spoils of an idle and decadent Andalusian aristocracy. The gypsies, being a group that actively and, in some cases heroically, resisted their subsumption by a capitalist work ethic, have come to represent in modern European mythology the embodiment of Romantic freedom. According to this tradition, they have maintained a communal and matriarchal style of life, governed by the principle of "use value." Acacio's shout in the occupation of the mansion, "Private property is theft!" is less a revival of the popular insurrections of the thirties, as feared by the curator and don Nuño, than an assertion of this free style of life.

On the other extreme, the aristocrats no longer are in possession of the mansion. They have been relegated to being the gypsies' guardians. The mansion is no longer a palace, a site of power, but merely a museum. Don Nuño, the president of the patronage, and his son Juan Luis struggle to maintain their status and the glamor of their lifestyle without working. Don Nuño, with the complicity of the museum curator, survives by stealing works of art from the mansion. In an evident allusion to the crumbling of the conservative myth of the "eternal" Spain, supposedly immune to the degeneration of Western capitalism, in the last decades of Francoism, the Pontirole Mansion suffers the worst kind of commodification. Don Nuño's thieving is in danger of being revealed by the occupation. Consequently, the guardians of the mansion decide not to denounce it. Suddenly, Don Nuño and the gypsies become accomplices.

The situation is complicated even more when Juan Luis falls in love with his half-sister Macarène, the result of an affair that

Don Nuño had with a Swiss woman in his youth. In a curious inversion of narrative conventions, Macarène, whose name is a French version of that of the Patron Virgin of Andalusia, is a European traveller who visits Southern Spain in order to encounter her family and to come in contact with tradition. She is naive and completely unaware of the complexities of Córdoba's society. Nevertheless, she sympathizes immediately with the gypsies. Juan Luis, the perfect *señorito*, incompetent for practical life and dominated by his passions (despite his sexual impotence), switches sides without problems. Attracted by the sensuality and the openness of the gypsies, Don Nuño and the curator's wife follow the same path. Those who are true to their own desires cannot resist the magic of the gypsies.

As the narrative unfolds, the world is turned upside down. The gypsies claim their right to occupy the mansion because their matriarch used to be Prince Pontirole's mistress. They could be their descendents. Or anyone else. For the father is always incertain. This becomes even more evident when it is revealed that Juan Luis is not Don Nuño's son. He is also the child of an illegitimate affair. He can now have sex with Macarène without committing incest. He is cured from impotence by carrying out his desires in front of the Altar of the mansion's chapel. The palace becomes that night the site of a true orgy in which individuals from different social origins encounter each other by abandoning themselves to their sensuality. This ritual is culminated when Don Nuño enters the bed of the gypsies' matriarch as she utters: "Your problem, my son, is that you are too repressed." The law of the father, that is, the law of social order, the principle of all hierarchies, has ceased to function. It is no longer recognized within the walls of the mansion. It is dissolved in a feast of lust.

The bureaucratically-minded curator and the compulsively fascist Civil Guard are the only ones left outside. They contemplate the spectacle with a horror that betrays their envy. Wives betray their husbands, priests sleep with nuns, and brothers lie with sisters. These crippled defenders of the shattering order are the ones who seek the help of the Toperos. The Special Forces are ready to intervene in the culmination of the carnivalesque feast. The film ends when a burlesque wedding is taking place. Its participants are unaware that they are surrounded by Topero's Special Forces. Will they attack? García Sánchez leaves the question open when the word "End" emerges from the trumpet of officer Topero, who has sneaked into the party with the military band that plays the music for the party.

With this open ending García Sánchez distances us from the conventional comic mechanism of reconciliation of the *agape*. Comedies derive their effectiveness by ridiculing social norms, but the contradictions are imaginarily sublated when a too-rigid social order is substituted with a more open one. In other words, when everyone recognizes his or her own imperfections without questioning the fundamental mechanisms of the social order. García Sánchez's object of ridicule is the false reconciliation of the irruption of consumer society in the still not thoroughly modernized Spain. The principles of order of the authoritarian regime have been eroded by the very dynamics of the society, even with the complicity of those who supported that regime. But the State and its means of force remain in place, ready to contain all possible disruptions of the established order. The discourses of legitimation may have changed, but the function of the State and its institutions remain the same. García Sánchez points to a situation from which there is no way out. The movement that initiated in the mansion is about to be repressed while, outside its walls, life and business continue as usual.

Even though García Sánchez seems to acknowledge the positive aspects of the cultural revolution of the sixties and its belated impact in Spain during the *destape*, he also seems to regret its depoliticization, its integration into the lifestyle of conspicuous consumption. This development has therefore made the goal of a revolutionary transformation of Spanish society even more unattainable. However, I believe that García Sánchez critical stance remains within the romantic ideological frame of Modernism and the historical avant-garde, which underlies most of the countercultural movements of the second half of this century.[4] According to this view the compartmentalized, inauthentic, and repressive character of modern capitalist society is constantly challenged, and will eventually be overcome, by the liberation of a more authentic side of human experience that remains repressed but has not been completely controlled by bureaucratic rationality. In other words, to the avant-gardists the contradictions of modern society will be overcome when Art is integrated into Life.

In *Pasodoble*'s concern with the political irrelevance of naive hedonism, it is possible to discover a belief that the cultural revolution carried out to its most radical consequences will inevitably overcome social inequalities. Thence the need for its containment and, eventually, for its repression. Spanish society has changed in appearance but not in fundamentals. There is no need for the father to be alive; there is always someone to enforce his law even when its absurdity, its ultimate irrationality are unveiled. Despite the open ending of the film, the meaning it generates is very clearly articulated around two poles: the forces of order (the state) and the unleashed forces of its other that take over the mansion. When Topero invokes Stalin, it is not private property that is at stake but a social order that is still secured by the traditional values of Francoism, especially the idealization of the patriarchal family.

In its display of the most ingenuous and transgressive humor it is not easy to discern the main paradox of the film. I mean that it scandalizes less than it pretends. One has to ask seriously whether Spanish society has become more tolerant than the film is willing to acknowledge. It is here that we encounter the main limit of the avant-garde's critique of late capitalist societies. It seems to me difficult to sustain the argument that the unleashing of sexual desire will necessarily undermine the foundations of capitalism. Quite to the contrary, consumerist culture has developed a sophisticated machinery to mobilize and contain bodily pleasure that operates by the sheer repression of sensuality. I find it therefore rather anachronistic to think of late capitalist societies as still structurally dependent on a rigid bourgeois ethos, either Protestant or Catholic. In other words, it is important to reconsider to what extent the kind of revolt glorified by *Pasodoble* is essentially at odds with post-Franco Spain.

Notes

1. Though I agree that the concept of Cultural Industry proposed by the Frankfurt School needs revision, I do believe that much remains to be gained by not making a conflation between cultural industry and popular culture as is in vogue among certain cultural critics.

2. See Oscar Pereira's article in this volume.

3. I use the term Modernism as a special development in the Western institution of art, and not as an equivalent to Hispanic *Modernismo*. For some accounts of Modernism, see Berman, Russell A., *Modern Culture and Critical Theory* (Madison: University of Wisconsin Press, 1987).

4. See Bürger, Peter, *Theory of the Avant-Garde* (Minneapolis: University of Minnesota Press); and Schulte-Sasse, Jochen, "Imagination and Modernity" (Cultural Critique no. 7, Spring 1988).

Works Cited

Berman, Russell. *Modern Culture and Critical Theory*. Madison: University of Wisconsin Press, 1987.

Bürger, Peter. *Theory of the Avant-Garde*. Minneapolis: University of Minnesota Press, 1984.

Pereira, Oscar. "Pastiche and Deformation of History in José Luis Garci's *Asignatura Pendiente*." (In this volume.)

Schulte-Sasse, Jochen. "Imagination and Modernity." *Cultural Critique* 7 (Spring 1988).

Chapter 14

A Search for Identity:
Francisco Regueiro's *Padre Nuestro*

Andrés Moreno

> *Would you please tell me where the temporal begins and where the*
> *spiritual ends in a Catholic society?*[1]

The Catholic church has played an extremely important role in Spain from the times of the Cid to Philip II to Franco. But anticlerical thought has also had a firm foothold in the country, gaining in power and influence since the nineteenth century. In the Franco years, the role of the church was a changing one: unequivocal identification with the regime at the onset,[2] but gradually becoming uncoupled later, to the extent that during the last years of the regime, the Catholic church provided the only open avenue for political participation and reform.[3] Although Spain has been described as a "Catholic country," this characterization is nothing but problematic. The film *Padre Nuestro*, by Francisco Regueiro, ostensibly tries to probe into the workings of the Catholic church and its interaction with other elements of Spanish society. By so doing, it makes a commentary on Spain's current state of affairs.

In an interview that appeared in *Fotogramas*, Francisco Regueiro states that his aim in *Padre Nuestro* is " . . . not to use fantasy to refer to an external reality, but to transform the fantastic into reality."[4] The setting of the movie in a town situated nowhere in particular confirms this intention, as does the creation of a very fine-grained "reality" in the movie, in which direct references to either

Franco or the transition years are not visibly apparent. However, the movie is chronologically set in the 1980s as indicated by the presence of John Paul II as one of the characters and by the use of cordless telephones. It is virtually impossible to achieve the effect of chronological indeterminacy in the case of Spain because of the circumstances of its recent past. Nevertheless, movies are filmed and produced in a particular context, and in Spain, the need to deal with censorship has had a profound effect on movie making, especially for those directors like Regueiro whose careers began during the Franco years. For the reasons outlined by Hopewell,[5] Spanish movies often lend themselves to allegorical interpretations, an idea strengthened by Regueiro's stated purpose in making *Padre Nuestro*. By making explicit the allegorical content of the movie, I want to show that all that is left at the end of the film is a snapshot of the transfer of power from the old Francoist guard to the new "yuppies." We might even view this film as posing a natural question to those living through *el desencanto*: if, as it can be shown, this is the way things have turned out, what can be done?

Before I start detailing Regueiro's characterization of the church, it is worth noting that during the years 1974–75, a number of films dealt with love stories between priests and women. Some films are adaptations of Spanish novels, including *Pepita Jiménez, La Regenta,* or *Tormento,* while others are placed in a contemporary setting, like *Tu Dios y mi infierno, Un hombre como los demás,* or *Ya soy mujer.* Pilar Miró characterizes this theme as a fad that is taken over by films that display nudity.[6] Thus, the idea of a cardinal having a daughter out of wedlock cannot be seen as having a great deal of shock value, but rather, as an ironic comment that Regueiro makes on the earthly quality of the moral character of the high bureaucracy of the church, all the while using a language chock-full of anticlerical undertones.

At the very start of *Padre Nuestro* we see two shots, the first showing Rome, shifting into a second shot showing Vatican City. Rather than condemning the Catholic faith, he focuses on the upper echelons of the church, which command a highly efficient and organized bureaucracy that exists to serve the earthly interests of those in its highest posts. When Monsignor Fernando García suggests that he is following God's designs by going back to his home to set his affairs in order, the Pope counters, saying "God orders you through me," thereby emphasizing the strict hierarchical discipline that makes it possible for the elite to control the church. This lesson is not lost on the cardinal, who will in turn use the services of the parish priest to negotiate a meeting of *la cardinala*, and later, to arrange her wedding to his brother—and her uncle—Abel.

The hierarchy of the church is ruthless in securing its best interests, whatever they might be. The church must maneuver to its advantage, even when choosing a Pope, as is shown in the film: a man with a checkered past can become a cardinal—with the assurance of absolute dependence and obedience on his part—but it would be impossible to elect him as Pope. There is no moral judgment in the election of the Vicar of Christ on earth, just a pragmatic decision that places the institutional needs of the church above all others. Note however that the Catholic church is not monolithic, even if its hierarchy follows a strict chain of command. It is important to realize that the Spanish church underwent a process of reform during the Franco years.

One of the few things that is indisputable about the Franco years is the unqualified support that the church gave to the regime during its early years, especially if we take into account the isolation that Spain suffered from the rest of Europe and the United States, the dominant power in Western Europe. This support came at all levels of the church, from parish priests to religious orders such as the Jesuits as well as from the Vatican. It is also clear that at least from a rhetorical standpoint, Catholicism served as a beacon of unification for the regime. Francoism tried to make the perceived distance between the religious and the national all but indistinguishable,[7] equating church and state. This relationship between the regime and the church bore fruit in the concordat of 1953, a document that in effect renders unto Caesar whatever is his, and unto the Church, whatever is left.[8] For this collaboration between the Vatican and Spain, Franco was presented with the Order of Christ, the highest award that the Vatican gives to lay church members.

The cozy relationship between the state and the Catholic church started showing signs of fatigue in the 1960s, and by the early 1970s it had become severely strained. From disagreements on labor policies and unions (recall the formation of the HOAC and JOC), the progressive deterioration of the relationship reached its climax during the assembly of bishops and priests of 1971, during which a position critical of the previous stance of the church with regard to the Spanish Civil War was presented. At the same time, a motion to abolish the concordat of 1953 was passed.

In any case, it is clear that the film singles out for criticism the traditional sectors of the church, identified by Abel with Pius XII shortly after becoming reunited with his brother. Recall that it was this Pope who gave France the Order of Christ and that relations between the papacy and the Spanish government took a sharp turn after 1962. It is also worth noting that in parallel to the economic development of Spain during the 1960s, there was the emergence of a mass culture, where the use of the media for building consensus made some of the roles traditionally assigned to the church redundant. The church itself went through a crisis, both in Spain and abroad, fracturing into various camps, all the while losing a great deal of the power it had gained during the early Franco years.

As promised by Regueiro, *Padre Nuestro* does not deal with the modern church, but evokes the Church associated with Franco. That is, the organizing social force portrayed in the movie is identified with those sectors of the old regime that had the necessary power to change existing relations. The film makes a historical detour by its setting in the countryside, a clear reference to an agrarian oligarchy that had its power taken away during the construction of the modern Spanish state during Franco's administration. This power transfer is represented in the film by the toast that the cardinal offers to the portrait of his father, and his subsequent blessing and recognition of his daughter, *la cardinala*. The actual transfer of power goes on after Franco's death, with the eventual formation of a group of young capitalists who will have a hand in the running of Spain. Mario Conde is perhaps the most visible, but by no means the only one.

The first action sequence in the movie shows a cardinal holding a conversation with the Pope. The setting is one of opulence, marked by the presence of finely appointed furniture and exquisite works of art. The film shows us a church that is anything but poor, in stark contrast to the claim made by the Pope that the church is close to God precisely because it is poor. While it is hard to sidestep the biting irony, it is undeniable that the Pope's remark highlights the great gulf between what is preached by the Gospel and the policies of the Roman church. Moreover, it is clear that the Catholicism practiced in a small Spanish town has nothing to do with the Pope's practice of the Catholic faith, underscoring the distance between the common people and the institutions that control them. The temporal wealth and power of the church are based on a doctrine that predicates high moral standards, and yet, even the wine that is used by the princes of the church during their masses does not belong to the Vatican. In a profoundly ironic twist, three-fourths of this wine belongs to an atheist (Abel) and to the estate of a whore (*la cardinala*). The small portion of the wine that does belong to the Pope is characterized as bitter, of poor quality. This distance between the official stance of the bureaucracy and the people has a parallel in Spain, during both the Franco years and the transition.[9]

In the film, the popular sectors are shown as disenfranchised. They are unable to react to the menaces presented to them by those in control, as exhibited by Damián's suicide. After the Papal audience, Regueiro shows us how Monsignor García literally comes down from the sky in a helicopter, landing in a meadow used by Damián's sheep for grazing—the church and modern-day bureaucrats are not afraid to use state-of-the-art technology to impose their wills upon others. The mission of Monsignor García is not a fact-finding one, for he has an agenda: he is going to straighten his affairs, part of which entails dictating to others how to live their lives. There cannot be concern for others, affairs of state are pressing and obey their own logic. Accordingly, he has decided to marry off his daughter to his brother, securing in this way all the family property for his granddaughter. No one has been consulted and even the laws of nature must bend to the cardinal's will. All the arrangements that Abel made to hide the indiscretions of his brother are upset, leading to a tragic death.

Damián, a poor shepherd, agreed to marry María after Fernando García—Abel's brother—left for Rome in his quest to rise in the hierarchy of the church. Monsignor García's plans call for the marriage of Damián's putative daughter to Abel, and for María, the former lover of the cardinal, to move to the family house, since it would not be proper for the mother of Abel's bride to live like a servant. There is no place for Damián, but of course, that is not a concern for the cardinal, who is not even aware of his existence and the social role that the shepherd has played for the last decades. The lack of options leads Damián to commit suicide, a death that is judged "vain" by Monsignor García before he is informed by Abel that he is the real agent behind Damián's death. A question asked at the beginning of the movie by María has been answered: it is not Damián who kills the cardinal, but the other way around, for the people are no match for the elite.

After asking for forgiveness, the cardinal forges ahead with his plans all the same. A deal is struck for the wedding of Abel and *la cardinala*, although this requires that the cardinal instruct his brother on how to successfully achieve sexual intercourse with his own daughter—outside of marriage. The callousness of the cardinal makes itself manifest by the congratulations afforded to Abel by his brother on his successful sexual encounter, having overcome his problem of premature ejaculation. The cardinal cannot be moved easily, either by Damián's death or by the idea that his brother is having sex with his daughter. The figure of the cardinal embodies a complete disregard for the moral code preached by the church and the moral code of nature (incest). There is a profound contradiction between his stated mission as a member of the church and his ruthlessness. A controlling elite cannot afford to be squeamish.

A grass-roots questioning of the political elite during the transition years produced what has been called *el desencanto*, which was described by Raymond Carr as a "...feeling of disillusion with the performance of the new democracy...based on a false perception of what democracy is about and what it can achieve as a problem-solving system."[10] For all the growth of the financial markets in Spain and the economic boom of the early 1980s, the high level of unemployment and the relatively high cost of living clouded the horizons of an emerging democracy. The Left was unable to articulate a meaningful project at the onset of the transition, and even now, the current policies of the PSOE can be seen as a compromise at best. The promises made by the politicians and the contradictions between their stated intentions and their actual policies, which have demanded a measure of sacrifice, are an everyday reality for the Spanish working class. The attitude of Monsignor García toward Damián—an empty blessing—shows the high degree of cynicism that the higher-ups can exhibit toward the common people. Abel's commentary sums it up well: "executioners always forgive their victims." There is a glimmer of hope: the people can put up some resistance, as can be seen in the case of María refusing to eat at the family table.

The logical conclusion of the film is achieved by the transfer of power from the cardinal to *la cardinala,* an image for what was completed during the transition years: the effective control of the country passes from the old Francoist guard to the young neo-capitalists. The first shot we have of *la cardinala* is her visit to the graveyard. She arrives (from the outside—the city) smartly dressed, driving a white Porsche. After paying her respects to her stepfather, she goes to visit her friend at the whorehouse. She does not exhibit grief, and has no difficulty thinking about business—her inheritance. Film sequences show her snorting cocaine and listening to headphones, activities associated with the new yuppie class that she embodies. There is a new economic elite, which defines itself unambiguously in terms of money, exercising its power in a completely secular fashion since the religious institutions used by the old guard are no longer necessary. Money talks: *la cardinala* insists that both the parish priest and the cardinal pay for the time she spends with them, and in the meeting with their father, the camera shows her handling money. Such hunger for money is caricaturized by the dialogue between the wine maker and *la cardinala* as the latter tries to ascertain the worth of her father's estate by translating it in terms of how many johns she would need to service:

> "At 10,000 pesetas a wad, how many do I need?"
> "Doña Dolores, you put me on the spot! Who knows?!"[11]

She does not consider an alternative to her marriage to Abel, for the wedding is good business. There is nothing worth pursuing more than money. What role does the traditional opposition to Francoism have to play in this new order of things? Abel, who as a self-proclaimed atheist provides the initial contrast to the cardinal, is completely ineffective. His only hopes for breaking from his brother's plan are pinned on Damián, who commits suicide.

Although he has a clear vision of reality, Abel is unable to challenge his brother. He is altogether too happy to find an *acomodo*.[12] Monsignor García's instructions allow Abel to forestall his premature ejaculation, a high enough price to buy him off. His previous impotency has now become complicity: entering into an alliance with those up and coming is a very alluring prospect. The union really is a consolidation of resources, a trend that started in the early 1980s with corporate takeovers and leveraged buyouts. There is no doubt: the solution presented is not a moral but a financial one.

Padre Nuestro shows how the common people are unable to resist the demands of the power brokers and how impotent is the opposition, which unrealistically expects to be delivered from its marginal position by a pueblo without political clout. The old guard will use whatever power they have left — the meeting between Monsignor García and *la cardinala* takes place on her terms — and the baptism of *la cardinala* shows that the new elite has already taken its place. The last scene shows the inability of the most conservative sectors of the old guard to understand the change in circumstances: the Pope has been ineffective in his quest for the vineyards of Cardinal García, and his absolution of the cardinal *after* Monsignor García has died is a confirmation and symbolizes his acceptance of the new political reality. The transition has been made, but many things haven't changed. What is to be done?

Notes

1. ¿Queréis decirme dónde empieza lo temporal y dónde termina lo espiritual en una sociedad católica? Francisco Franco, from a speech given upon acceptance of a degree *honoris causa* from the Universidad Pontificia de Salamanca, 8 May 1954. Cited in Biescas and Tuñon de Lara, 484–485.

2. For instance, the Jesuit magazine *Razón y Fe* proclaimed in 1938 that "almost all of them [the politicians in the *nacionalista* front] were friends of the Society of Jesus, which in its own way, worked for the preparation of a new state too." Gómez Pérez (65).

3. For more on the political activity of the church during the Franco years, especially the HOAC and the JOC, see Gómez Pérez.

4. *Fotogramas* #1709, June 1985 (cited by Hopewell, 238).

5. Hopewell, 89. It is also worthwhile to keep in mind Carlos Saura's comment regarding movie making under censorship: "The need to avoid mentioning the facts without evading them, forces the director to explore narrative tech-

niques and stories which gradually shape his personality." Hopewell, 72. It would be interesting to see what changes, if any, are present in the cinematic techniques used by Regueiro in the films made during the Franco regime.

6. See Miró, Pilar, "El cine español bajo la dictadura y después," in Cagigao et al., 107–127.

7. Franco himself declared in a speech on 6 June 1949: "Separate the Catholic from the Spanish, and the Spanish will be left mortally wounded in its truest substance." Gómez Pérez, 51.

8. Gómez Pérez quotes from *Le Monde*: "...the regime accorded exceptional advantages to the Church, which—although neutralized to some extent—could serve as a pillar to the system" (8 June 1974).

9. Rosa Montero summarizes this feeling well: "...and in this high-flying Spain of 1980 we all are, and we all feel marginalized. We are a country of forgotten citizens. Forgotten by the laws, by the political parties, by ourselves." Cagigao, 42–43.

10. Carr, 179.

11. -A 10,000 pelas el polvo, ¿Cuántos necesito?
-Doña Dolores, ¡Qué compromiso! ¡Ni se sabe!

12. For a personal perspective on the perceived *continuismo* between the most liberal factions of the Francoist and Spanish capitalists, see Rosa Montero's article "La marginación de la mayoría" in Cagigao, 41–58.

Works Cited

Biescas, J.A., and Manuel Tuñon de Lara. *Historia de España: España bajo la dictadura franquista, Historia de España,* ed. Manuel Tuñon de Lara. Barcelona: Editorial Labor, 1985. 10:13

Cagigao, José L., John Crispin, and Enrique Pupo-Walker, eds. *España 1975–1980: Conflictos y logros de la democracia.* Madrid: J. Porrúa Turanzas, 1982.

Carr, Raymond. *Modern Spain: 1875–1980.* Oxford and New York: Oxford Univ. Press, 1980.

Gómez Pérez, Rafael. *El franquismo y la iglesia.* Madrid: Ediciones Rialp, 1986.

Hopewell, John. *Out of the Past: Spanish Cinema after Franco.* London: British Film Institute, 1986.

◆ Chapter 15

What Did I Do to Deserve This? The "Mother" in the Films of Pedro Almodóvar

Lesley Heins Walker

In 1967 the family becomes quite explicitly the minimal political unit in Spain when Franco gives the father, as head of the family, the right to elect deputies to the Cortes. As John Hopewell remarks In *Out of the Past: Spanish Cinema after Franco*, it is not surprising that a certain Spanish cinema of the period dealt frequently with themes of familial repression and incest. An example Hopewell gives is the 1975 film *The Poachers* by José Louis Borau. In this film, mother and son live alone in the middle of a forest. The incestuous desires of the mother are made explicit toward the end of the film when the mother, while undressing her son, teasingly tells him that she can see his "willy." Such a mother, Borau explains, reminds him of Saturn: "One supposes that every night this mother, like Saturn, devours her sons. [The mother symbolizes] Spain itself, who wants her children only for herself, who loves, crushes, and devours them."[1] By the end of the film the mother has killed the son's girlfriend, and the son, in turn, murders his mother. Like Borau, Hopewell understands incest in this context to be essentially a political allegory of repression. Ostensibly because of concerns about censorship, the mother, as "head" of the household, is made to "stand in" for the father/Franco. Political critique is therefore waged through cinematic allegory. In a Spain which often collapsed the interests of the state and the interests of families into one unified ideology,[2] the mother in Spanish cinema often seems to bear an extreme ideological burden: she comes to be figured as the agent *par excellence* of both political and psychic repression.

More than any other Spanish director, Pedro Almodóvar makes films about women. His protagonists are more often than not females who find themselves trapped in a murder mystery — generally as the prime suspect. Moreover, Almodóvar's heroines only murder the men closest to them: father, husband, or lover. In this manner, the murder mystery becomes a family drama, thereby exposing its fundamentally incestuous nature. Because the Spanish family is the site of tremendous political, social, and emotional investment, incest acquires a very privileged status. It is at once the most dreaded and yet desired of transgressions. Like the films of his predecessors, Almodóvar's relentless mise en scène of perverse familial relations suggest that incest as a theme should be thought of in political terms. In my analysis of the films *Dark Habits* (1984) and *High Heels* (1992), I contend that the incest fantasies of filmmakers like Borau, Buñuel, or Saura are transformed by Almodóvar as he imagines a different kind of mother. Before beginning the analysis of Almodóvar's films, however, I touch briefly on the question of Spanish modernization and its relation to representations of the mother in order to situate historically what I have termed the "devouring mother" as well as her bourgeois counterpart.

Spain did not experience industrialization on the same scale as its northern neighbors. In 1900, two-thirds of the Spanish population were actively employed in agriculture; by 1930, one-half of the population still worked the land. Not until the early 60s did this figure of about 50 percent begin to decline.[3] Furthermore, it seems that, as long as Spain remained an essentially agrarian society, the Spanish church was able to maintain its role as chief arbiter of morality, education, and culture. One of the many consequences of the Spanish church's hegemony was that the debates over women's ability to participate in civil society, which began during the mid–nineteenth century in Europe and the United States, were seriously circumscribed in Spain. As far as the church was concerned, woman's primary role was that of mother and wife, keeper of hearth and home. While this opinion may have been shared by many people in Europe and the United States, the church in Spain had such a monopoly on cultural production that opposing discourses were rarely heard. For example, whereas in Europe and the United States the first women's colleges opened in the 1880s and women gained admission to the most prestigious universities, only about 14 percent of Spain's female population could read and write. It is not until the 1930s that women begin to go to University in Spain — and even then in *extremely* small numbers. Thus, although attitudes about women and their place may have been shared across the Pyrenees, differing institutions — the Spanish Catholic church as compared to secularizing states — produced very different representations and social practices.

If it is true that Spanish modernization occurred much later than in France, England or the United States, are we likewise to assume that the "modern mother" is absent from the Spanish scene? We need only answer this question in the affirmative, if our notion of modernity is strictly tied, indeed caused, by socioeconomic modernization. To oversimplify, it is important to remember that Spain remained for a long time a two-tiered society: the more or less wealthy *nobleza*, or aristocracy, and everybody else. Yet, this is not to say that notions of motherhood or womanhood remain static. To the contrary, if we take the literature at the end of the nineteenth century as index, it is clear that there is an emerging notion of motherhood that seeks to differentiate itself from an aristocratic tradition.

In her article "La Imagen de la Mujer," Guadalupe Gómez-Ferrer Morant examines three late–nineteenth century authors, Emilia Pardo Bazan, Armando Palacio Valdes and Benito Pérez Galdos, and comes up with a composite sketch of the aristocratic woman as well as her middle-class counterpart. Not only was the aristocratic woman materially better off than her middle-class sister, but, because of her education, she was also a purveyor of culture. Not unlike the French *salonnière* of the eighteenth century, through a sharing of "common" culture, she promoted the entrance of new people into the otherwise closed world of the *nobleza*.[4] In this manner, culture, money, and noble lineage circulated, thus guaranteeing the perpetuation of this class. In contrast to the aristocratic woman, women of the middle class were expected to become good wives and mothers: "...su finalidad es casarse y creer un hogar, siendo en este contexto familiar donde tiene asignadas unas tareas muy definidas. El cuidado de los aspectos materiales de la casa—el orden, la limpieza y demás domésticas—, y la atención al marido y a los hijos son su misión específica" (Morant, 166). Women of the middle class received very little education and, if educated at all, they memorized catechisms. A religious education was, however, the one thing that the two classes of women may have shared. Indeed, the Spanish church's position on woman and her place cuts across class lines. It was believed that women were more pious than men, that it was the woman's responsibility to safeguard morality and that the family's honor depended on her virtue.

While the church may have spoken of the duty of all women, class divisions re-emerge in fictional representation. When aristocratic women were not disparaged as hypocrits and libertines, they were increasingly seen as a conservative force who masked their intolerance of progressive ideas in religious pieties:

> A veces la mujer adquiere en las obras novelescas...una
> fuerza simbólica. Se trata de mujer de práctica religiosa
> acendrada, a las que la fe sirve de elemento de seguridad
> para revestir de intolerancia e intransigencia sus esquemas
> ideológicos en virtud de unos príncipios sagrados. En
> suma, la mujer se manifiesta a través de la literatura
> anclada en el pasado y cerrada a toda postura progresiva.
> (Morant, 157)

Thus, well before Franco, powerful women were equated with conservative political agendas, while the middle-class wife and mother was idealized for living in quiet self-effacement, keeping her house clean, and spending her husband's money wisely.

It consequently comes as no surprise that when women are represented in Spanish cinema decades later they are seen either as passive victims of male violence—Buñuel's *Viridiana* is a case in point—or identified with the church/state/family, which is generally understood as conservative and hence repressive. Thus, the question of women in Spanish cinema cannot be reduced to misogyny pure and simple. Rather, any such discussion should be framed in terms of qualities historically attributed to various women. For instance, women of the nineteenth-century Spanish *nobleza* are portrayed as active, participating in politics, culture and so forth, while middle-class women are imagined as mostly passive and, significantly, silent. Furthermore, to the extent that the aristocratic woman is identified with activity, she is increasingly figured as unnatural, indeed, un-womanly. Returning to Borau's film *The Poachers,* his critique of the "devouring mother" recalls earlier novelistic depictions of aristocratic women. The mother, through her activity, represents power in its densest and most virulent form. The state, morality, and affect are all collapsed into this one, oppressive representation: the mother as the metaphor *par excellence* for National Catholicism—a metaphor that is, in fact, a good deal older than National Catholicism itself. Yet, there is something hopelessly archaic about such violence. The death of this mother can be read to prefigure the collapse of Francoism. The place of the devouring mother will, in the end, be filled by another figure which, unlike her middle-class ancestor, is no longer only passive and silent. In what follows, I describe the "self-sacrificing mother" who is neither active, nor passive, but both at once.

In *History of Sexuality: An Introduction,* Michel Foucault delineates what he calls the "two macro-strategies of modern power": "systems of alliance and sexuality." "Systems of alliance" function unidirectionally, from the top down, or from a center outward, while "sexuality" is necessarily mutual. "Sexuality" demands reciprocity—the priest, Foucault argues, *needs* the child to speak. While Foucault does not make the connection himself, reciprocity must further be understood as a central component of modern female subjectivity. For the moment, I will not go into a theoretical justification of this claim; it is enough to say that women in the West are continually defined—in relation to men—as beings given naturally to connectedness or mutuality. It is with these questions in mind that I turn first to Almodóvar's *Dark Habits* in an attempt to demonstrate that the "devouring mother" is passing out of Spanish film history, while *High Heels* signals the institution of the self-sacrificing mother.

Dark Habits follows in a long line of Spanish satiric novels and films that poke fun at the church and its less-than-perfect institutions. As the title implies, the film is set in a convent whose mission it is to save "fallen" women. Implicated in her boyfriend's death, Yolanda, fleeing the police, seeks refuge there. Housing only five sisters, the convent is dilapidated and on the verge of being closed down. Yolanda's arrival is consequently met with great enthusiasm by all the sisters. However, after a night in this very unconventional of convents, Yolanda is uncertain about staying. To convince her to remain a little longer, the Mother Superior shares her stash of heroin with her guest.

Despite the film's broad jokes and sardonic humor, the Mother Superior is a formidable character. Little by little it is revealed that she has an almost insatiable appetite for young women. When a woman seeks refuge in the convent, the Mother Superior supplies her with drugs, and she stays, at least for a while. In this manner, the Mother Superior ensures the complete and, indeed, infantile, dependence of the young woman. On the one hand, her lovely, oval-shaped face and serene demeanor inspire confidence; she very much looks the part of a solicitous, caring "mother." Yet, on the other hand, she is as domineering and intransigent as any dictator. The film is essentially about the Mother Superior's attempt to seduce Yolanda; however, Yolanda, a former botany teacher turned bolero singer, does not prove the passive victim that the Mother Superior desired. Yolanda too is a seductress.

Throughout the first half of the film, Yolanda reads aloud from her boyfriend Juan's diary, which she took from him after his death. She seems almost obsessed by the story of Juan's suffering and the role attributed to her by him as both dupe and torturer. On the one hand, Juan portrays himself as the victim, or child. Juan recounts how he experienced Yolanda's "care" as oppressive and yet necessary; he compares her to heroin, maintaining that she is even more addictive. On the other hand, despite the fact that Yolanda is actually supporting Juan and his habit, he has the fantasy—like a child—that he is in control. When Yolanda finally comes to the end of Juan's diary, rather than stopping, she begins to write in it as if it were hers. Indeed, she writes his death: "Yolanda me ha suicidado." The question arises: is she making *suicidarse* into a transitive verb, or is she confusing Juan with herself and thus retaining the reflexivity of the verb? It seems that Yolanda understands *suicidarse* as at once both transitive and reflexive. Yolanda's reading aloud of Juan's diary creates a sense of cotemporality in that two time frames are present at once. Yolanda's past with Juan—the time of the writing—and Yolanda's present with the Mother Superior—the time of the reading—are superimposed on one another. Yolanda thus both sees herself as the agent of Juan's death and identifies with him as victim. In fact, she has an exchange with the Mother Superior in which she repeats verbatim lines from Juan's diary.

In "Loving Women: Masochism, Fantasy, and the Idealization of the Mother,"[5] Rey Chow offers a very compelling reading of the function of cotemporality in relation to fantasies of the mother. To discuss this notion of cotemporality, she turns to Jean Laplanche's understanding of masochism as *not* necessarily the other side of sadism, but rather itself constitutive of sadism. Laplanche claims that a purely aggressive act is impossible; for the sadist to have any pleasure, he must know what it is to suffer pain. Translated in the terms of our present discussion, this means that there can be no pure act of domination; domination and subordination are necessarily present at one and the same time, as Yolanda's reading of Juan's diary makes clear. Thus, Laplanche concludes that the sadist is always already constituted as a masochist. Chow summarizes his conclusions in the following manner:

> Repeating after Freud but giving Freud's words an emphasis that was elided in his texts, Laplanche states that masochism is the "turning around of an instinct upon its subject." The "turning around" implies not only the internalization, or introjection, of a suffering object that used to be external, but also the existence of psychic reality that is neither active (as in seeing) nor passive (as in being seen) but reflexive (seeing oneself). (Chow 124)

In essence Chow understands the mother as that "object" which is introjected, or internalized and which is, subsequently, neither active, nor passive, but self-reflexive. What she means by this is that when we are moved to tears by a character's suffering in a novel, for example, we identify with the character as both sufferer (the child) and consoler (the mother):

> As an object, the mother is both passive and active, submitting to our infantile, anal-sadistic wishes while having the power to protect us or torment us. The introjection of the mother in our fantasy has to imply both

> of these qualities . . . This mutual shifting of positionalities
> between "maternal" and "infantile" is what accounts for
> the fantasy involved in the idealization of the "mother,"
> and for the pleasure-in-pain that is fundamental to
> masochism." (Chow 127)

An example of the operation of this structure is Yolanda reading
Juan's diary. As she reads it, we witness a kind of doubling oc-
curring; she suffers *passively* in her identification with Juan, the
child and, at the same time, is the *active* agent of his suicide.

Chow is able to link masochism and the maternal through an
understanding of self-sacrifice as an especially feminine "virtue" —
not only in the West, but in China as well. She shows how the
formal structure of sacrifice should be, like masochism, understood as reflexive. In other words, sacrificing is never a simple gesture, but contains within itself the same doubling. Whence the
following questions:

> [W]ho is sacrificing for whom? Is the one who sacrifices,
> the "subject" and the one who receives the "object" — or
> the reverse: the one who receives, the "subject" and the
> one who sacrifices, the "object"? Could sacrificer and
> receiver both be subjects? For that to happen, sacrifice
> would need to be *self*-sacrifice, which would need to be
> practiced by two parties mutually, and not only by one
> party for the other. (Chow 159)

What Chow's formulation of self-sacrifice allows us to see in
great detail is the workings of an economy of mutuality, which
demands the creation of a certain reciprocity between two individuals — particularly mother and daughter. Chow's description
of this economy is not incompatible with Foucault's notion of
sexuality. Indeed, it seems to me that Chow's account allows us
to navigate the difficult terrain of inside and out through her understanding of the mother as a "psychic fantasy of incorporation."
Chow's formulation insists that, because the mother is incorporated as both active and passive, constituted by pleasure-in-pain,
that the active quality of this "mother fantasy" should not be overlooked. To use a mercantile metaphor, in such an economy, one
both owes a debt to the mother for her "care" and is owed "care"
as the child of this mother. It is precisely this mechanism of reci-

procity or mutuality that guarantees the ideological reproduction of self-sacrificing mothers.

Returning to *Dark Habits* with the above remarks in mind, Yolanda and the Mother Superior are to a certain extent mirror images of one another. The only possible relationship that either can have is one of complete control and domination. Seduction is the means by which they obtain their power over others: the Mother Superior with her drugs, and Yolanda ostensibly through sex—it's no accident that she is a bolero singer. However, Yolanda goes through a transformation as she reads Juan's diary. To the extent that she identifies with him—in the writing of his diary—and accepts heroin from the Mother Superior, she can be said to occupy, in effect, his position as child and victim. Furthermore, it would seem to be Yolanda's capacity to occupy this space which eventually allows her to escape both the convent and the Mother Superior. Once Yolanda sees herself as both mother and child, she becomes a "new woman." She now has the strength to overcome her heroin addiction and even decides to go back to teaching. Yolanda accordingly establishes relationships of complicity and mutuality; one of the last scenes of the film is exemplary in this respect. After much cajoling by the other sisters, Yolanda agrees to sing at the Mother Superior's birthday party. Her song, *Salí por que salí* (I left because I left), is powerfully seductive—the lyrics repeat over and over "as soon as I love you, I forget you." While Yolanda dedicates the song to the Mother Superior, she sings it with the accompaniment of the other sisters. This "singing together" exemplifies the economy of mutuality.

And the Mother Superior, what kind of mother is she? Like the mother in Borau's *The Poachers,* the Mother Superior loves, crushes and eventually devours her children. For instance, one of her former charges, who is sought by the police, comes to her for protection. After a brutal exchange in which the Mother Superior tells the girl that she "has been forgotten," the Mother Superior lets her stay the night, only to hand her over to the police the next morning. Indeed, like the "devouring mother," the Mother Superior could be said to represent the conjunction of the three supreme Spanish authorities: she plays the role of father in her relationship to the other sisters, she manages the convent while the priest learns to sew, and she even stands in for the Caudillo to the extent that her "mission" is similar to his: saving Spain's children. However, what I would like to ask is, why, in 1984, almost ten years after Franco's death, does Almodóvar need to find a substitute for the father? Why is the Mother Superior made to bear such excessive historical baggage? In other words, why is this mother being beaten? And, moreover, who is beating her?

It seems to me that the Mother Superior and Yolanda represent two different affective economies. The Mother Superior could be said to represent "old Spain" in that her relationships are rigidly hierarchical; "loving" does not imply mutuality, but duty and loyalty. For instance, the Mother Superior and another of the sisters, Perdita, almost form a husband/wife couple in the film. The Mother Superior is in complete control; she supplies Perdita with LSD and Perdita spies on the other members of the community. The fact that the Mother Superior is indeed "forgotten" by the end of the film would therefore seem to signal a triumph for the economy of mutuality. Reciprocity and complicity are valorized over domination. Is this ending not a step in the right direction? Should not a feminist critique be satisfied with a solution that valorizes mutuality over domination? However true this may be, I am still bothered by the relentless dispossession of the Mother Superior.

To attempt an answer to these questions, let's turn to *High Heels* and an examination of the economy of mutuality. Similar to *Dark Habits*, *High Heels* stages a struggle for love between two women; this time, however, the struggle is between mother and daughter. While in *Dark Habits*, the transformation of Yolanda happens rather quickly through her reading/writing Juan's diary, *High Heels* is essentially about that transformation. Rebecca desires desperately to establish a relationship with her mother, Becky, who has been absent from her life for the last twenty years. The film opens with Becky's return; after years of a singing and film career in Mexico, she has decided to come back to Spain. Importantly, while *Dark Habits* gives us the perspective of the mother, *High Heels* is told from the child's point of view. In short, the film is about Rebecca's continual efforts to force her mother "to think of her." It is precisely this which Becky is incapable of doing. She repeatedly puts her desires before those of her daughter's. Ultimately, Rebecca manages to make her mother comply with her wishes. I examine, on the one hand, how Rebecca finally makes her mother "confess her guilt" — the pronoun is meant to be ambiguous, as is the mother's guilt — and on the other, the extraordinary intensity of Rebecca's desire.

While awaiting the arrival of her mother's airplane, the teary-eyed Rebecca relives two childhood memories — related to the viewer through flashbacks. The first of the memories takes place when Rebecca, her mother, and her mother's second husband, Alberto, are on vacation in the Antilles. Becky buys a pair of earrings and the seven-year-old Rebecca asks her mother to buy the same pair for her, which she does. The second memory is more disconcerting. Alberto and Becky are fighting because Becky has an offer to make a movie in Mexico and Alberto will not allow her to go. We see the little Rebecca go into Alberto's bathroom and switch pills from one container to the other. The next scene is of a television news program which announces Alberto's death in a car accident. The flashback ends and we are returned to the film's present. Rebecca's tears charge the initial scenes of the film with extreme emotivity. Rebecca's excitement and anxiety are palpable to the viewer, and yet, her mother misses them entirely. For example, she recognizes the earrings that Rebecca is wearing as the ones she used to own, but does not remember buying an identical pair for her daughter. As another example, Becky scolds her daughter for not having notified the press of her arrival, saying that she had hoped to be welcomed home with a little more enthusiasm. Rebecca is visibly crushed by this comment. Rebecca's desire to be with her mother, to be noticed by her mother at any cost, introduces the film's central theme of self-sacrifice. Indeed, Rebecca will tell her mother later that she was willing to do *anything* so that her mother could be free to pursue her career as a singer and actress. However, Becky is unable to understand the implication of her daughter's sacrifice.

In the context of Chow's discussion of self-sacrifice, what is striking about the film *High Heels* is that the self-sacrificing mother does not exist at the beginning of the film. Indeed, I want to suggest that the film is a veritable mise en scène of the institutionalization of this sacrificing mother. As noted earlier, Rebecca's life seems to be organized around an attempt to capture her mother's love. This is not an innocent gesture. It is perhaps significant that Almodóvar's film recalls Carlos Saura's "*Cría cuervos...*" (1975), which similarly stages the parricidal fantasies of a little girl. Interestingly enough, the title of Saura's film is taken from a Spanish proverb that warns against bad parenting, "Cría cuervos y te sacarán los ojos" (Raise crows and they will peck out your eyes). On their way home from the airport, mother and daughter discuss, for the first time, the fact that Rebecca has married her mother's former lover, Mickey. Reminiscent of Freud's comment about the way children, playing with dolls, imitate their parents and thus learn their social identities, Rebecca's marriage to Mickey is clearly an "imitation" of her mother. And yet, it is also too close. Not, however, because Mickey is like her father, thus recalling a classical Oedipal scene, but rather because Rebecca seeks an erotic identification with her mother. It should be recalled that Rebecca has already killed one of Becky's husbands in order "to be with" her mother. The difficulty of this erotic identification is that in occupying the identical position of her mother, she effectively supersedes her, and thereby effaces her. In fact, the crisis of the film is precipitated precisely by the "come back" of Becky—a kind of return of the repressed. In effect, because Becky refuses to relinquish her place—as Mickey's lover, or as a sexual being *tout court*—Rebecca seems unable to accede to her own identity, remaining narcissistically fixed on both identifying and desiring her mother. Similarly, Becky finds herself locked in a kind of egotism which does not allow her to be a "good mother" to Rebecca. The film makes it clear that, for Becky to be a "good mother," she needs to renounce her sexuality. At one point, Mickey, in an overture of seduction, tells Becky that she has always been a "fantastic woman." She retorts that she no longer wants to be only a fantastic woman, but would like to be a fantastic person. Despite Becky's good intentions, she becomes Mickey's lover again. And in complete desperation Rebecca murders him.

The second half of the film is a search for the murderer, a search for the guilty party. Both women are immediately questioned and both deny that they murdered Mickey. However, on the evening news, Rebecca, who is the anchorwoman, announces that she killed her husband. At this point, the viewer does not know if she is telling the truth. She is taken promptly to prison where the most moving of the film's scenes is played out. Rebecca's emotional imprisonment is literalized on the opening night of her mother's comeback. Sobbing in her tiny prison bed, Rebecca hears her mother sing "Piensa en mi" (Think of me). Becky, in a grandieloquent gesture, dedicates this first song, like any mother would, she says, to her daughter who is spending the night in prison. The refrain, which is sung over and over, is extremely moving: "Think of me when you suffer, think of me when you cry, think of me..." The camera cuts back and forth between the concert hall and the prison. It becomes painfully clear that mother and daughter have reached an impasse: Becky is only capable of "performing" motherhood for thousands of strangers, while her own daughter remains abandoned in a prison dormitory.

This impasse is, in the end, mediated by a rather peculiar figure. Early in the movie, Rebecca, Becky, and Mickey go to a drag show where a singer named Letal impersonates Becky. It turns out that Letal is also Rebecca's best friend and confidant. Not only is Letal a visual double of Becky, but he/she also fills in for Becky's absence: Rebecca tells her mother that when she was lonely, she would go to see Letal. After Letal's show, Rebecca goes backstage to assist him/her out of his/her costume. To Rebecca's surprise, he/she makes love to her. The juxtaposition of the real and unavailable mother to the loving and caring substitute yet again underlines the incommensurability of the two women's desire. To complicate matters further, Letal turns out not to be a drag queen after all, but the judge in charge of investigating the murder.

The last scenes of the film reconcile mother and daughter. On her deathbed, Becky decides to lie to the judge and admits to being the murderer although she as well as the viewer knows that her daughter did it. By confessing to Rebecca's crime, however, Becky sacrifices herself for her daughter's well-being and can, while dying, at last feel that she has become the "good mother." To the extent that Becky "gives" her "innocence" to her daughter, she "receives" her daughter's gratitude. Rebecca is similarly indebted to her mother. In accepting the gift of her mother's sacrifice, she "gives up" her mother, which will, finally, allow her to assume her social identity as both different and yet the same. Thus, the formal structure of the virtuous self-sacrificing mother is finally put in place.

In staging the drama of the mother, both *Dark Habits* and *High Heels* are articulating an extremely important fantasy of Spanish modernity. In contrast to other Spanish directors, such as Borau or Saura, Almodóvar imagines a drama of motherhood in which the mother can be seen as an active force in the life of her children. Unlike earlier representations of an active mother, however, this activity does *not* destroy or maim the child. In a sense, Almodóvar invests the late-nineteenth-century middle-class mother with agency. She is no longer passive and silent, but has an active role to play in the formation of her child as a "sexual" being. As Rey Chow's analysis allows us to see, the mother's desire and the child's desire for the mother overlap, producing a fantasy whereby the child comes to see herself, at one and the same time, as the infant-in-need-of-care and the responsive-mother. Because the child is constituted by the doubling of give and take, demand and response, her relation to others is likewise never simple. In other words, her relationships will ideally be sympathetic ones in that she is neither "mother" nor child, but both. The end of *High Heels* is exemplary in this respect: the last shot is of pregnant Rebecca lying across her mother's dead body, sobbing.

Yet, while all works out well for the daughter, what about the dead mother? Again Almodóvar ends this film with the literal dispossession of another mother: Becky dies. Who killed Becky? While it would not be inexact to say that it is Rebecca who loved her mother to death, I would add that the economy of mutuality is aggressively superseding that of "alliance," and that this re-articulation takes on a peculiar violence of its own.

Dark Habits addresses eloquently this struggle. As I have suggested, the Mother Superior is in some sense obsolete; she recalls the aristocratic woman to the extent that she is active without being the "good mother"; her world is passing away as a new type of "mother" comes into existence. This "new mother" is invested with interiority. Interiority does not imply a lack of feeling, caring, or intelligence on the part of the Mother Superior; rather, it signifies that she has not interiorized a particular narrative— the narrative of self-sacrifice—which would allow her to enter into what I have called an economy of mutuality. Indeed, there is something pathetic about the Mother Superior's loneliness and isolation. It clearly has to do with her inability to connect, to be one of the girls, as it were. In contrast, Rebecca's erotic desire for her mother is, while perverse, understandable and entirely "curable." What is being suggested is that erotic desire for the mother is a *necessary* component in the story of femininity, but that desire must eventually be given up. The end of erotic desire for the mother also signals the death—literal or symbolic—of the mother herself. It is the Mother Superior's brutish refusal to give up, her desire to persist in a state of archaic perversities that reminds us of the price exacted for the daughter's normality. The Mother Superior refuses to pay because she knows that even "good mothers" get killed off in the end.

Finally, my essay seeks to make two basic points. The first is an attempt to regard the Spanish family in its specificity through an understanding of a theme like incest as historically contingent and changing. Hence, I hope to have demonstrated that the same "act" carries entirely different valences; in other words, "incest" must be understood as performing various functions, and as such, productive of different ends. Secondly, the same forces that eagerly anticipate Spain's entry into the European Community, will, very likely, reinvent the Spanish family. Almodóvar's films can be read as important signs of this changing world. Already in *The Law of Desire* (1986), the viewer perceives a certain nostalgia for the lost mother. To the extent that nostalgia is always a desire of the present projected onto an imaginary past, we witness Almodóvar's re-making of Spanish history.

Notes

1. Quoted by John Hopewell, *Out of the Past: Spanish Cinema after Franco* (London: The British Film Institute, 1986), who quotes Borau in *Cinema 2002*, no. 9, November 1975: 36–39.

2. María E. Nicolás and B. López describe the pivotal role that women were asked to play in Franco Spain. Women, particularly mothers, became the relay which allowed state, church, and family to be articulated through a single ideology: National Catholicism: "El Estado franquista y la Iglesia materializaron sus intereses sobre la sociedad, de la trataban de obtener el consenso, a partir de su dedicación al tema familiar. Tanto para uno como para otra, la familia 'origen y prototipo de toda sociedad perfecta,' era la depositaria de la ideología patriarcal y autoritaria, centro y cuna de los valores cristianos. Dentro de ella, la mujer-esposa-madre constituía el eje de esta estructura, cuyo mantenimiento se convertía

en su papel fundamental." Nicolás and López, "La Situación de la Mujer a Traves..." in *Mujer y Sociedad en España 1700–1975*, ed. Rosa M. Capel Martínez (Madrid: Ministerio de Cultura, 1982): 372.

3. In *L'Espagne au XXe siècle*, Jacques Maurice and Carlos Serrano comment that Spanish demographics resembled more that of an "ancien régime" than that of a modern nation-state. "Sur période relativement longue, en l'occurence depuis le début du XIXe siècle, l'Espagne est demeurée isolée au reste de l'Europe occidentale plus encore, peut-etre par son régime démographique que par son régime politique. L'évolution de la population espagnole a, en effet, tardé àrejoindre celle du reste de l'Ouest européen développé, conservant pendant longtemps un modèle démographique d'Ancien Régime à fortes natalité et mortalité, notamment infantile... et une persistante vulnérabilité aux épidémies, qui l'enferme dans une sorte d'anachronisme. Ces caractéristiques, dues aux difficultés, et finalement à l'echec de ce qu'il conviendrait sans doute d'appeler la première révolution industrielle..." 113–114. Jacques Maurice and Carlos Serrano, *L'Espagne au XXe siècle* (Paris: Hachette, 1992). Hereafter all references to Maurice and Serrano will be indicated by their names in parentheses followed by a page number.

4. Morant sums up the conjunction of culture, money, and lineage in the following way: "En suma, la mujer de la alta burguesía será la encargada de romper el antiguo hermetismo de la nobleza reuniendo en un feliz maridaje blasones y talegas." 155. Guadalupe Gómez-Ferrer Morant, "La Imagen de la Mujer..." in *Mujer y Sociedad en España*, ed. Rosa M. Capel Martínez (Madrid: Ministerio de Cultura, 1982).

5. In *Woman and Chinese Modernity: The Politics of Reading between West and East* (Minneapolis: University of Minnesota Press, 1991). Hereafter references to Chow are indicated in parentheses by her last name followed by a page number.

Works Cited

Capel Martínez, Rosa M. *El trabajo y la educación de la mujer en España*. Madrid: Ministerio de Cultura, 1982.

Chow, Rey. "Loving Women: Masochism Fantasy, and the Idealization of the Mother." *Women and Chinese Modernity: The Politics of Reading between West and East*. Minneapolis: Univ. of Minnesota Press, 1991.

Foucault, Michel. *History of Sexuality: An Introduction*. Trans. Robert Hurley. New York: Vintage, 1980.

Gómez-Ferrer, Guadalupe. "La imagen de la mujer." *Mujer y sociedad en España*. Ed. Rosa Capel Martínez. Madrid: Ministerio de Cultura, 1982.

Hopewell, John. *Out of the Past: Spanish Cinema after Franco*. London: British Film Institute, 1986.

Kaplan, Ann. *Motherhood and Representation*. New York: Routledge, 1992.

Maurice, Jacques and Carlos Serrano. *L'Espagne au XXe siècle*. Paris: Hachette, 1992.

Nicolás, María E. and B. López. "La situación de la mujer a traves..." *Mujer y sociedad en España 1700–1975*. Ed. Rosa M. Capel Martínez. Madrid: Ministerio de Cultura, 1982.

Saura, Carlos. "*Cría cuervos...*," 1975.

Chapter 16

Vicente Aranda's *Amantes*: History as Cultural Style in Spanish Cinema

Marvin D'Lugo

> *Nostalgia film, consistent with postmodernist tendencies generally, seeks to generate images and simulacra of the past, thereby — in a social situation in which general historicity and class traditions have become enfeebled — producing something like a pseudo-past for consumption . . .*[1]

Nostalgia and Historical Knowledge

Like a prodigious number of Spanish films over the last decade, Vicente Aranda's *Amantes* (1991) returns to a generic moment in the Francoist past as the cultural referent through which to anchor its narrative. In doing so, the film self-consciously inserts itself into a Spanish nostalgia genre that regularly transforms the politically charged periods of the civil war and immediate postwar periods into the mise en scène of narratives that have little or nothing to do with politics or history in the conventional sense. The popular appeal of this genre according to José Enrique Monterde is to be found in the force that a certain cultural depiction of life during the early Franco years still exerts in popular memory. In part, as Monterde contends, it is the fact that for a particular sector of the Spanish public such films represent the recuperation of their childhood or youth, while, for a younger generation with only an indirect knowledge of the recent past, the lure of the period comes from the popularity of a retro style of *la moda de los 40 y los 50*.[2]

For such an audience, it may be argued, the early decades of the dictatorship constitute something of a lost object of desire, an age of innocence that, in retrospect, has been shattered by the uncertainty of the world beyond Francoism. This appeal is all the more understandable in the 1990s as the traditional concept of Spain itself is under the continual mark of erasure through the refiguration of subnational or regional cultures and realignment of Spain in Europe and the world. But while *Amantes* appears to partake of that peculiarly postmodern approach to historical representation, it also pointedly demonstrates that the price of that simulacrum of innocence is the displacement of any rigorous sense of historical consciousness by the glossy images of a generic past that effectively dissolves political difference as well as historical meaning.

Questions of history are never openly enunciated as such in *Amantes* but rather take shape in the pastiche of nostalgia conventions—objects, sounds, clothing, images—that, instead of representing the past, only provide a series of highly stylized visual tropes, all of which convey the generic sense of an indeterminate pastness. Against this commodified notion of history, *Amantes* poses through its narrative an essential questioning of the aesthetic surfaces that have displaced any questioning of the historical by mere style. The result is a film that appears to take a seemingly ambivalent approach to historical representation, adhering on the surface to the contemporary nostalgia mode, but gradually drawing its viewers' attention to the contradictory connotations of those stylistic conventions.

In part, the source of that ambivalence lies in the very problematic international context that *Amantes,* like any Spanish film, must confront. In order to be economically viable, it must simultaneously address two distinct audiences: a Spanish spectatorship shaped by a series of culturally specific determinants and, as well, a foreign audience that sees Spanish cinema within the context of an already constructed notion of Spanishness. Thus the stylistic commodification of the historical becomes doubly problematized in *Amantes* in both a national and an international context. We note this in the curious way that the film presupposes its audience's prior knowledge of its historical context and yet, at the same time, schematizes and reduces to caricature certain of its historical intertexts, obviously seeking in this latter move to produce a certain "international" legibility for foreign audiences unfamiliar with historical specifics.

Commenting on his own recent development in the historical genre with a series of at least four works over a period of five years,[3] Aranda observes the appeal that themes related to the civil war and Francoism have for foreign markets: "Apenas hay películas sobre la Guerra Civil ya que hay un deseo de olvidar este suceso histórico, y creo que como argumento se puede exportar porque en el extranjero interesa."[4] But, as Stephen Crofts reminds us, there is a necessary "bleaching-out of domestic cultural specificity"[5] in the international targeting of films, precisely the kind of schematization and reduction to aesthetic stereotypes that generally tends to weaken culturally specific historical representation.

Through the formulation of its narrative material as a tension between national and foreign notions of the historical, however, *Amantes* effectively allegorizes as plot this schism between notions of historical culture rooted in the Francoist past and a conception of contemporaneity that aligns cultural identity with the outside world. What thus emerges is a highly complex narrational structure that addresses its Spanish audience necessarily through the mediation of debased foreign simplifications of national historical experience. Such a dialogism, of Spaniards looking at themselves and the commodified simulacra of their history through the eyes of the other, underlies the film's subtle interrogation of the interpretative implications of such stylized historical representation.

Originally proposed as a one-hour episode for Spanish television, *Amantes* was to be part of a series, *La huella del crimen*, in which noted Spanish directors were invited to develop episodes based on famous crimes. Aranda had already participated successfully in an earlier cycle of this series with his film *El crimen del Capitán Sánchez* (1985). For the new series he chose the notorious "Crimen de Tetuán" of the late 1940s, a crime of passion that occurred in the working-class barrio de Tetuán in Madrid and was widely talked about at the time but which received very little press coverage. The lack of background information on any of the principal characters involved in the murder led the director and co-scriptwriters, Alvaro del Amo and Carlos Pérez Merinero, to invent a fuller narrative out of the few corroborated details available about the original murder.[6] Production of the television series was delayed and Aranda became interested in expanding the project into a more elaborate feature-length film. The decision to shift the time of action from the 1940s, when the events actually occurred, to a more generically unspecified time in the 1950s was dictated by budgetary concerns, the cost of recreating an authentic period look for the 1940s being much more expensive than the setting of the 1950s.[7]

The Aesthetics of an Already Known History

In making the shift to the cultural milieu of the fifties, the film develops a self-referential enunciative strategy that flaunts a number of cinematic genre conventions as the basis of its evocation of the historical. The prominence given to images of army officers and of religion, coupled with the sounds of radio programs of the 1950s, all seem calculated to evoke through a few broad strokes a retro style of Spanish historical genre films as described by Carlos Heredero and José Enrique Monterde.[8] Similarly, the elaborate plotting of Madrid's underworld milieu and the shaping of the murder plot of *Amantes* flaunts the recognizable genre of American neo–film noir of works such as *Chinatown* and *Body Heat*.

Such genre associations may well appear as merely additional symptomatic marks of the erasure of a sense of cultural specificity for the Spaniard as historical consciousness of a Spanish past is gradually replaced by a more generic mode of nostalgia. Yet, the extremes of stylization in the aesthetic elaboration of pastness in *Amantes* suggests a critical distance if not a mark of resistance to that blurring of the historical as the film shifts attention away from the idea of history per se to a scrutiny of what Fredric Jameson argues is "historicity." That is, " . . . neither the representation of the past nor a representation of the future; it can, first and foremost, be defined as a perception of the present as history; that is, as a relationship to the present which somehow defamiliarizes it and allows us that distance from immediacy which is at length characterized as a historical perspective. . . . what one might in the strong sense call a trope of the future anterior — the estrangement and renewal as history of our own reading present ... by way of the apprehension of that present as the past of a specific future."[9]

Thus, while the outward visual style of *Amantes* suggests precisely the imposture of the historical, certain elements of the film's visual and narrative construction postulate an equivalent to that future anterior position as they draw our attention to seeming "gaps" in the surface construction of pastness that will serve as the sites of a contemporary interrogation and reflection. In effect, two contrary forces of reading history converge in *Amantes*: the one, a series of familiar stylized tropes that inevitably guide a reading of the past as a chain of already known images and stereotypes; the other, a contemporary vantage that seeks implicitly to promote a self-consciousness of its own "reading present" in relation to those constructions of pastness. The formulation of a commodifiable cinematic narrative around the Tetuán murder, marked as it is with the recognizable tropes and stereotypes of *la moda de los 40 y los 50*, concretizes those two opposing tendencies.

Paco (Jorge Sanz), a young soldier who has just completed military service, is in search of both a steady job and lodging. His girlfriend, Trini (Maribel Verdú), employed as a maid with Paco's former military commander, gives him the address of a widow who is renting a room in her apartment. The widow turns out to be the attractive Luisa (Victoria Abril), who quickly seduces her new tenant. So intense is Paco's sexual attraction for Luisa, that he abandons Trini for long periods of time, finally showing up at the commander's house begging forgiveness.

Though the largely passive Paco is fully prepared to continue his twin relations, he is thwarted by the desires of the two women. Trini suspects something and Luisa, who knows of Trini's existence, is wildly jealous of her rival. Things become more complicated for Paco by Luisa's shady business dealings with Minuta and Gordo, members of a gang of swindlers whom she owes some fifteen thousand pesetas. They have threatened her life and Paco, attempting to aid his lover, suggests that he get the money by swindling Trini of her savings. Luisa would prefer that they simply kill Trini.

The plan is for Paco to propose marriage to Trini and bring her to the provincial city of Burgos where they have planned to purchase a bar. When Paco takes the money and disappears, Trini realizes the fraud and understands that her love for Paco is doomed. When he returns to the hotel room and confesses the plan, Trini tells him she prefers death to abandonment. Thwarted in her attempt to cut her own wrists with Paco's razor, she begs him to kill her since that is what he really wants. Later, as the two sit in the rain on a bench in front of the imposing cathedral of Burgos, Trini hands Paco the razor. The film ends as Paco comes to the train station in Burgos and signals to Luisa that the mission has been accomplished. The couple embraces passionately on the train platform as a freeze frame signifies their renewed passion.

Though there appeared to be no political subtext associated with the original murder case, the striking mise en scène of the film's opening sequence and crucial scene construct a pseudo-political matrix within which the sordid love triangle and murder is situated. Genre style here helps secure a seemingly coherent reading of the narrative as a symptomatic scenario of the individual, Trini, as the victim of her blind adherence to the tenets of a traditional society associated with the cultural ideology of Francoism.

The opening sequence begins with an intertitle, "*Madrid, Años cincuenta,*" and a slow pan of the backs of the heads of a row of soldiers as the voice of a priest officiating over a religious service is heard. Gradually the scene is revealed as a mass performed apparently in the stable of an army barracks. The panning shot is broken by a close-up of Trini looking to her side toward a row of young soldiers among whom stands Paco, who nods recognition to his fiancee. Only retrospectively do we discern the logic of this initial mise en scène as it places the couple within a symbolic space that joins the two spheres of Francoist ideology — the army and the church. Tellingly, the site of the religious ritual is a makeshift one, a barracks space temporarily converted into a chapel, suggesting the marriage of convenience of church and state in Francoist Spain. Though the importance of Francoism as a cardinal signifier of the narrative will recede from prominence in the ensuing action, this initial foregrounding seems designed to cast the plot as a symptomatic tale of the effects of the repressive and corrupt milieu on the lives of two exemplary characters.

The symbolic space of the opening is paired with the climactic scene near the film's end in which Trini is killed by Paco as the two sit on a bench facing the facade of the provincial cathedral of Burgos. As in the opening images of the film, the scene is shot from behind the bench so that we see only the backs of the two characters, the shadowy cathedral facade serving to remind the audience once again of the backdrop of moral hypocrisy of Spanish society under Francoism. The choice of this final setting, rhyming as it does with the opening scene, reinforces the notion of Trini as having been victimized not only by Paco and Luisa, but also by the duplicitous social and moral codes identified from the beginning of the film with traditionalist Spain.[10]

In the film's reliance on hoary stereotypes for its formulation of pastness, it casts the rivalry between Trini and Luisa as a reinscription of the popular motif of the two Spains, particularly as it was picked up as a Manichaean structuration of Spanish society in literature and film during the early decades of the dictatorship.[11] Trini is seen as the conservative, Catholic traditionalist identified with the pure Spanishness of the provinces. This appears to be, in part, the plot motivation for her return with Paco to her native village at one point in the film. Luisa, on the other hand, is identified exclusively with the corruption and depravity of the city.

This binary opposition is, however, not without its critical ambivalence. For imperceptibly, the valorization of Trini as martyred heroine leads to a radical transformation of the historical connotation of the plot as it moves logically to the final intertitle of *Amantes* which explains: "Esta historia estaba basada en un hecho real. Tres días después, Paco y Luisa fueron detenidos en Valladolid." The inclusion of this coda, again rhyming with the film's initial "historical" intertitle, produces the impression of a closure not unlike that formalized as a standard practice of Francoist censorship of the fifties and sixties which insisted upon retribution by all moral and social transgressors.[12] Here that device has the ironic effect of reinterpreting the symbolic *menage-à-trois* in the anachronistic terms of the moralizing cinema of the Francoist period in which Trini comes off as the embodiment of traditional Spain victimized by her perverse rival, the evil Luisa.

In effect, the pastiche of genre tropes that has secured the retro style of pastness recuperates along with its innocent nostalgia for a simpler time the reactionary position of Francoist cultural ideology. This result is not surprising, for as Judith Hess Wright and others have argued, the underlying ideological implication of the mobilization of cinematic genre is often the reaffirmation of reactionary or status quo values in culture.[13]

Resemanticizing the Historical: Luisa as "Other"

In the context of this predictable ideological slippage of the filmic narrative into a regressive political mode, the character of Luisa assumes a more critical conceptual significance. She, in effect, becomes the textual site of resistance to the ideology of traditional Spanish values and, as well, to the aesthetic mode identified with that tradition. From her first appearance in the film, Luisa is marked with a sense of foreignness. In her first scene, when Paco comes inquiring about lodgings, she appears at the door of her apartment wearing a kimono with a chain of Christmas tinsel draped around her neck. Not only is the tinsel a jarring disruption of the space of historical nostalgia thus far presented, but it also services to alight Luisa from her very first appearance with the artifacts of foreign culture.

Tellingly, when she entices Paco to her bedroom for their first lovemaking, she brings the artificial tree in from the living room and sets it on the side of the bed, providing in this way a visual bridge between her condition of otherness and her sexual power. What is significant about Luisa's sexuality, however, is not the often commented explicitness of its depiction, nor even its melodramatic juxtaposition against Trini's chastity, but its potency as a disruption of the social world defined elsewhere in the film. We discern this in the subversive effect of her sexual power over Paco who, through Luisa's presence, is transformed into the passive object of the female gaze and of female desire. In each of the couple's sexual liaisons it is Luisa who initiates the action. At one early morning encounter when Paco attempts to entice her to bed, tellingly, she resists. Yet, in a later scene, after she has met him by chance with Trini in the street, he returns to the apartment to find Luisa furious with her rival. She orders Paco to the bed and he follows submissively.

It gradually becomes clear through such scenes that what is at stake with Luisa's presence is the very conception of patriarchal culture to which not only Trini but also Paco are bound. This is the point of the much-commented handkerchief scene in which Luisa inserts a red handkerchief in Paco's anus before they make love so she can control his orgasm. The importance of such a scene obviously derives, in part, from its graphic depiction of the power Luisa exerts over Paco on the individual level. But it also contains an iconographic value, for its representation of the female as the dominant sexual figure implies from the contemporary spectatorial vantage a genealogy that connects with the logic of post-Franco sexual liberation and the demarginalization of the female. In this way the glossy historical "effect" of the nostalgia style is contested by a deeper level of discursive historicity as it displaces the history of gendered repression of liberation. In this context, it is relevant to acknowledge the unique national/international star persona of Victoria Abril identified in many of her roles as a sexual force. The contemporary audience thus comes to read her character in line with that array of sexually emancipated contemporary women she has played.

Such textual and extratextual elements contribute to an unconventional kind of allegorical reading in which the ideological binarism of the two Spains is internally weakened and gradually transformed into a tension between an authoritarian discourse associated with the aura of pastness, embodied principally in the figure of Trini, and a counter-hegemonic discourse of contemporary liberating values embodied in Luisa. It is ultimately on this level that the implications of the nostalgia mode are confronted and interrogated for the contemporary viewer.

Speaking of the distinction between authoritative and persuasive discourses, Mikhail Bakhtin observes:

> The authoritative word demands that we acknowledge it, that we make it our own; it binds us quite independent of any power it might have to persuade us internally[14] ...
> Authoritative discourse may embody various contents: authority as such, or the authoritativeness of tradition, of

generally acknowledged truth, of the official line and other similar authorities.[15]

Persuasive discourse, on the other hand, is for Bakhtin, a form of intellectual seduction in that it holds the power to entice by the self-evidence of its own force, which thereby constitutes its very power. In explaining the conceptual lure of dialogical imagination, Bakhtin speaks of the notion of "contemporaneity" as part of a persuasive discourse that is opposed to an authoritarian discourse:

> The internally persuasive word is either a contemporary word, born in a zone of contact with unresolved contemporaneity, or else it is a word that has been reclaimed for contemporaneity; such a word relates to its descendants as well as to its contemporaries as if *both* were contemporaries; what is constitutive for it is a special conception of listeners, readers, perceivers. Every discourse presupposes a special conception of the listener, of his aperceptive background and the degree of his responsiveness; it presupposes a specific distance. All this is very important for coming to grips with the historical life of discourse. Ignoring such aspects and nuances leads to a reification of the word (and to a muffling of the dialogism native to it).[16]

It is through this reinscription of the two Spains as positions in the history of cultural representation that the binarism established between Trini and Luisa leads the audience to sense Jameson's notion of the future anterior of historicism insofar as that tension makes them aware of the reification of the notion of temporality that has lured and sustained them through the film. Not only is Luisa marked in this context as a counter-hegemonic force but also as a largely anachronistic presence, enunciating through the affirmation of her body a sense of identity that seems strikingly to transcend the period ambiance in which the narrative locates her.

In the shifting cultural space of a Europe without boundaries, Spanish cinema, attempting to reflect Spanish cultural reality in some way, finds itself torn between the familiar models and figurations of the past and the uncertainty of new formulations of individual and social identity. Compounding the dilemma is the progressive impact of an international postmodern culture that weakens in individuals the awareness of the weight of their own history. Thus, in its search for a cultural identity, Spanish cinema appears to have found a convenient niche in the nostalgic valorization of its tumultuous past, particularly as embodied in the civil war and the Franco dictatorship. A film such as *Amantes* contests that deceptively facile slide into a surface style of a pseudopast by exposing the conceptual snares that belie the glossy surfaces of a hollow retro style and showing, as Jameson contends, that nostalgia cinema is not so much a reflection of national history as of the debilitated status of contemporary readings of pastness.

Notes

1. Fredric Jameson, *Signatures of the Visible* (New York and London: Routledge, 1992): 137.

2. José Enrique Monterde, "El cine histórico durante la transición política," *Escritos sobre el cine español 1973–1987*. Valencia: Ediciones Textos Filmoteca, 1989: 56–57.

3. *Tiempo de silencio* (1986); *Si te dicen que caí* (1989); *Los jinetes del alba* (1990); *Amantes* (1991).

4. Soledad Juárez, "El cine sobre la Guerra Civil interesa en el extranjero," *El Periódico* (Barcelona), 4 Apr., 1991.

5. Stephen Crofts, "Reconceptualizing National Cinema/s," *Quarterly Review of Film and Video* 14, 3 (Autumn 1993): 56.

6. Vicente Aranda as cited in Rosa Alvarez, y Belén Frías, *Vicente Aranda: El cine como pasión* (Valladolid: 36 Semana Internacional de Cine, 1991): 238.

7. Rosa Alvarez, Belén Frías, 238.

8. Heredero notes the stylistic emergence during the period of the transition of a cinema which eschewed conventional historical representation in favor of the deployment of "la historia como referente." See Carlos F. Heredero, "El reflejo de la evolución social y política en el cine español de la transición y de la democracia: Historia de un desencuentro," *Escritos sobre el cine español 1973–1987* (Valencia: Ediciones Textos Filmoteca, 1989): 22–26. Monterde views this same tendency as the development of "un confortable espacio de reconocimiento," "filmes capaces de permitir comprender de 'otra' manera la Historia (o incluso 'otra' Historia), como e utilizar el cine histórico como aparente demonstración de la entidad del cambio operado en la sociedad española; de ahí el predominio de una trayectoria de referentes ficcionales y de detalles 'significativos'; por sí mismos de cara a esa acción de reconocimiento sobre la tentativa de integrarlos en un proceso más coherente y elaborado de presentación histórica." (See Monterde, 47–48).

9. Fredric Jameson, *Postmodernism; or, The Cultural Logic of Late Capitalism* (Durham, N.C.: Duke University Press, 1991): 284–85.

10. Although the dialogue indicates that the setting of this scene is Aranda del Duero, the sequence was actually shot in Burgos. Thus the imposing cathe-

dral facade may evoke for some Spaniards the further association of this mise en scène with the Nationalist government headquarters during the civil war.

11. The most influential cinematic example of this model is to be found in Sáenz de Heredia's 1941 film *Raza* scripted by Franco under the pseudonym of Jaime de Andrade. The narrativization of this Manichaeism, however, was even more far-reaching as historians of the literature of the period attest. For a description of these tendencies in literature see Carlos Blanco Aguinaga, Julio Rodríguez Puértolas, and Iris M. Zavala, *Historia social de la literatura española III* (Madrid: Editoral Castalia, 1979): 62–64.

12. Perhaps the most notorious of these was the imposed ending of Marco Ferreri's *El cochecito* as Román Gubern notes: "En el desenlace impuesto, el anciano protagonista, después de haber intentado envenenar a su egoísta familia, se arrepentía y les llamaba por teléfono para contárselo todo; luego lo detenían como si fuese un loco. Mientras que en el final original consumaba su asesinato colectivo y era detenido por la Guardia Civil." See Román Gubern, *La censura: Función política y ordenamiento jurídico bajo el franquismo* (Barcelona: Ediciones Península, 1981): 163.

13. Judith Hess Wright, "Genre Film and the Status Quo," *Film Genre Reader*, ed. Barry Keith Grant (Austin: University of Texas Press, 1986): 41–42.

14. Mikhail M. Bakhtin, *The Dialogic Imagination*, ed. Michael Holquist (Austin: University of Texas Press, 1981): 342.

15. Bakhtin, 344.

16. Bakhtin, 346.

Works Cited

Aguinaga, Carlos Blanco, Julio Rodríguez Puértolas, and Iris M. Zavala. *Historia social de la literatura española III*. Madrid: Editoral Castalia, 1979.

Alvarez, Rosa and Belén Frías. *Vicente Aranda: El cine como pasión*. Valladolid: 36 Semana Internacional de Cine, 1991.

Aranda, Vincent. "Soledad Juárez, "El cine sobre la Guerra Civil interesa en el extranjero," *El Periódico* (Barcelona), 4 Apr. 1991.

Bakhtin, Mikhail M. *The Dialogic Imagination* . Ed. Michael Holquist. Austin: University of Texas Press, 1981.

Crofts, Stephen. "Reconceptualizing National Cinema/s," *Quarterly Review of Film and Video* 14, 3 (Autumn 1993): 56.

Gubern, Román. *La censura: Función política y ordenamiento jurídico bajo el franquismo*. Barcelona: Ediciones Península, 1981.

Heredero, Carlos F. "El reflejo de la evolución social y política en el cine español de la transición y de la democracia: Historia de un desencuentro." *Escritos sobre el cine español 1973–1987*. Valencia: Ediciones Textos Filmoteca, 1989.

Jameson, Fredric. *Signatures of the Visible*. New York and London: Routledge, 1992.

———. *Postmodernism, or, The Cultural Logic of Late Capitalism*. Durham, N.C.: Duke University Press, 1991.

Monterde, José Enrique. "El cine histórico durante la transición política," *Escritos sobre el cine español 1973–1987*. Valencia: Ediciones Textos Filmoteca, 1989.

Wright, Judith Hess. "Genre Film and the Status Quo," *Film Genre Reader*, ed. Barry Keith Grant. Austin: University of Texas Press, 1986.

Part V
Representations: Reshaping the Margins

◆ **Chapter 17**

Aimez-vous la Representation?
Notes on the Cinema of Pere Portabella
and on *Informe General*

Casimiro Torreiro

(translated by Stacy N. Beckwith)

(General Statement on some Matters of Interest for a Public Screening) — known simply as *Informe General* (General Statement) — is without doubt one of the most original films made in Spain on a concrete period of history, dissected and looked at in the present. It is an important film: at once a documentary-chronicle that brushes with fiction, as well as an indispensable, coherent link in a chain of productions by its author, filmmaker Pere Portabella. The latter has always been concerned with the limits of representation, in all facets, while over fifteen years after its release, *Informe General* has won recognition as indispensable material for the filmic (and political) analysis of Spain's transition to democracy. A period, it is worth adding, of far-reaching import in the contemporary history of the country, and a model for the transformation of an authoritarian regime into a system of freely elected government.

Informe General, then, is an important film. And this despite a certain, partly involuntary stigmatization. On the one hand lies the film's unmasked partisan nature; it is consciously removed from objective analysis. Its director, Portabella, did not hide then, (perhaps only emphasized at certain moments), nor does he dissimulate now, that the point of view taken by his investigation is unequivocally close to that of a family on the left. (Still, he has never assumed the posture of a card carrying militant. His thinking has frequently coincided with statements from the now dissolved Partic Socialista Unificat de Catalunya, PSUC, a Catalonian section of Spain's Communist party, the PCE, and Portabella was even elected senator by a coalition of variously striped political forces, through its initiative.) All of this, however, has led him to differ with, and at times to ridicule other platforms equally born of the left.

There is also a side to *Informe General* that is practically clandestine, steeped in the doings of the temporary interregnum in Spain, which was charged with liquidating Francoism and bringing about elections of the first democractic government since 1936 (the elections of 1977). At that point, all political parties were illegal, even non-existent, and some saw their militants persecuted. This with a ruthlessness little hidden by certain repressive apparatuses of the dictatorship, which were inherited by the new democratic state, as yet a babbling embryo.

The movie, in fact, was relegated to a legal life in the catacombs, as it were, never showing in commercial theaters, and only playing on the marginal or alternative circuits: parties or rallies during the early days of the democracy, stints in film clubs, and the like, all of which substantiates its secret side. Only with the full installation of the parliamentary regime did the film enjoy a single regular broadcast on Spanish Television (Televisión Española), accessing, in the end, an even wider audience through this channel. Under the name *La Clave* (The Key), the film was touched up by the director himself, who cut its nearly three hours of original showtime to a half hour.

A Filmmaker who Defies Classification

Pere Portabella i Rafols was born in Figueras (Gerona) in 1929. Son of an haut bourgeois Catalonian family, he began University studies in chemistry but soon abandoned them. An early move to Madrid for further reasons of study put him in contact with some of the most important members of the photo-journalist vanguard of the 1950s. Known as "El Paso," the group was intent on recovering the rich, cutting-edge tradition of the Republican period, broken in 1939 by the Francoist victory.[1] Also in Madrid, and before the end of the 1950s, Portabella came to know Catalonian painters Antoni Tapies and Joan Ponc, two of the most prominent members of the "Dau al Set" group.[2] The latter was an engine of the vanguard, a literal quarry in which some of the filmmaker's future collaborations were forged, such as that with Tapies himself, and that with the poet Joan Brossa, also extremely difficult to categorize. Two composers of similiar ilk should also be mentioned here; Josep Mestres Quadreny and Charles Santos, both of whom would work closely with Portabella in the future.[3]

Also in Madrid, the future director made his first contacts in the world of the cinema, most notably with young aspiring filmmakers such as Carlos Saura, Julio Diamante, Mario Camus, Manuel Revueltas, or camera projectionist José Julio Baena. All were then studying in the center for cinema set up by the state, the Institute for Research and Cinematographic Experiments (IIEC). The Catalonian's first attempt was an abortive bullfighting documentary which would have been directed in 1957 by the now distinguished photographer and publicist, Leopoldo Pomes. The movie never made it to the screen. Instead, Portabella's first real work in film media was released one year later. A medium length production, financed by Movierecords publishing house, *La Chunga* (The Merrymaker) featured a celebrated gypsy "dancer."

Then, in 1959, intending to produce Carlos Saura's first full-length work, Portabella founded his own studio, Films 59. Operating under the open hostility of the Franco administration, all of its productions rated very low on the state classification scale. While this made commercial distribution more difficult, in just two and a half years Films 59 produced three pictures notably removed from the ensemble of works then being made in Spain. *Los Golfos* by Saura, *El Cochecito* (1960) by the Italian Marco Ferreri, and *Viridiana* (1961), the latter marking a return to Spain by its major film artist in exile, Luis Buñuel, and becoming the object of a spectacular upset at the Cannes Film Festival.[4] In the words of historian Julio Pérez Perucha all of the above evince "a daring and considerable break not only with the whole of Spanish cinema at the moment, but with a meager, emaciated topos of contemporary progressive film as well."[5]

Following these productions, Portabella returned to Barcelona and to his directing projects, establishing contact with a figure who, over time, would emerge as one of the most important forces from the later-termed Barcelona School. This was filmmaker and painter Jacinto Esteva, with whom Portabella collaborated on a cinema tribute to Picasso (shot but never released), and with whom he also worked on the film short, *Autour des Salines/Alrededor de las Salinas/In and around the Saltworks* (1962). The two shared equally in the complex production stage of the full-length feature and documentary, *Lejos de los Arboles* (1965–1970), which took a harsh beating by the censors. Further, along with Esteva and other members of the future Barcelona School (Ricardo Bofill, Joaquin Jorda and Antonio de Senillosa), Portabella also devoted himself to the release of a film of sketches, from which he then pulled away in order to make his directing debut in 1967. This he did with the same script he had attempted to use in the film with Esteva. *No competu amb els dits,* as it was called, was a medium-length piece whose narrative structure, fragmented, and autonomous in each segment of the work, both copied and ridiculed that of contemporary "filmlets." The latter, then a novelty on the Spanish screen, served as publicity spots for the cinema.[6]

Earlier, in 1964, Portabella had collaborated on the script of *Il momento della verita/El momento de la verdad/The Moment of Truth,* a full-length production by the Italian Francesco Rosi, shot in Barcelona. He also wrote or collaborated on the editing of a few scripts that could never be shot for reasons including certain rejection by the censors of their thematic material. Meanwhile, Portabella's first full feature, *Nocturno 29* (Nocturne 29) (1968), made reference in its title to the number of years Franco had then been in power. The film was a lucid study of the outlook of Portabella's own social class, as well as a probe, critical and incensed, into a grim and weighty reality that is propitiated by Francoist authoritarianism and always a theme in the better part of the Catalonian filmmaker's work.[7]

Indeed, *Nocturno 29* per se was in some sense a late arrival, as its release coincided with a re-hardening of censorship after a brief period of help and protection for the young cinema industry, which had begun under the administration of Director General García Escudero.[8] Needless to say, this aided little in the consolidation of Portabella's filmmaking career. From then on he, as also were many colleagues of the same generation who did not go into exile, was forced to operate out of a creative ghetto. The situation was doubly uncomfortable: a lack of state and private subsidies given the prevailing atmosphere of draconian repression, an absence of the minimal conditions conducive to the distribution of films to a potential public, and a ban on the use of professional format. Portabella fell back on filming in sixteen millimeter, in the black and white stock, and on the production of a few works that were automatically relegated to administrative obscurity for not having scored with the censors.

Far from despairing however, the producer/director took up four different courses of work, not counting his active political militancy (he was, for example, one of the founders, in 1969, of the Asamblea de Catalunya, a united front of all Catalonian democratic parties against Francoism). In terms of film, Portabella accepted documentary projects on commission. There ensued, in 1969, some short pieces produced by Barcelona's School of Architecture, for the famous exposition dedicated to the painter Joan Miró (corroborating, again, the connection between Portabella and the historic artistic vanguard). The films included *Aidez l'Espagne* (Come to the aid of Spain [Miró 1937]) *Premios Nacionales* and *Miró-l'altre* (followed in 1973 by *Miró tapiz* and *Miró forja*, on the artistic method of their painter-namesake, and financed by a private institution, the Maeght Gallery).

Along with these projects, Portabella began teaching courses on film directing in a shcool called Aixala located in Barcelona. All this did not lead him to neglect the shooting of personal pieces, however, of both short and medium length: *Poetes catalans* (1970); *Play-back* (1970), on a recording by his regular collaborator, musician and composer Charles Santos; and *Cantants 72,* on three anti-Francoist singers. Most notably, though, Portabella broached the creation of an openly militant cinema: *Advocats laboralistes* (1973) centered on the everyday work of labor defense attorneys before the courts of the Dictatorship. *El sopar* was a lengthy roundtable-interview in which a dinner among friends serves as the occasion for convening four men and one woman of various ages and social extractions. Each takes the opportunity to examine the traumatic experience signified by jail, in which they were all confined for anti-Francoist militancy. And perhaps as a means of returning to his old tasks as a producer of foreign films, Portabella also agreed to undertake the production of *Hortensia/Beance* (1969), an extensive, four hour long, experimental full feature by the late young director Antonio Maenza. This was another picture never shown, and is virtually lost today.

At the same time, Portabella kept to the line of formal investigation to which he had dedicated himself at the start of his career, and which, in these years, would yield the most celebrated pair of works from his oeuvre. The compound of *Vampir/Cuadecuc* (1970) and *Umbracle* (1972) were justifiably so, and brought the artist recognition in certain foreign film circles of the time. The first piece uses the same shots obtained for the making of a discrete horror film directed by Jesus Franco (*El conde Dracula/ Count Dracula*, a Spanish-British co-production whose protagonist is played by Christopher Lee). *Vampir/Cuadecuc* is an unrelenting exercise in generic deconstruction carried out at the level of montage. It is engendered by emptying the narrative structures of horror cinema of their content, by distorting their stylistics (use of color to signify, use of sound, set duration of shots), and by posing in their stead a disquieting question: Is it possible to sustain a poetic treatment of the fantastic in a film through elements that have nothing to do with conventional narrative, nor with the guidelines prevailing in commercial cinema?

Umbracle is also of interest. Without abandoning the field of militant cinema, and continuing to make inroads into the revival of a certain national collective memory that had been virtually sequestered by the Francoist state, the film and its maker attempted a certain admixture. From the first they sought to blend documentary reality (personal interviews with anti-Francoist intellectuals) with a frustrating, abrupt, and unsettling fiction story (also featuring Christopher Lee and Jeanine Mestres as protagonists). The latter has recourse to a number of stylistic supports; a persistent, asynchronic sound, for example. All of these repeatedly confront the spectator with the uncomfortable sensation of contemplating not a conventional slice of life, but an episode, suffocating, frustrated, and inconclusive—just as its country of production is suffocating, frustrated, and most likely inconclusive, as well.

For in Portabella's view, engaging with history (with that re-cuperation of collective memory mentioned earlier) entails, above all, an investigation of those unwritten but burdensome norms and regulations pertaining to a narration. As in a cinematographic rendering, these subsisted (and subsist) thanks to that "neutral-ity" so well defined by André Bazin. It is the kind of narration largely brushed over by filmic enunciation, by the assigning of a story to a certain, more or less hard-core set of rules, and by the way in which filmic text and spectator interrelate. The spectator, in fact, has already been converted into the type designated by Noël Burch as being "of the Institution,"[9] as exhibiting, perforce, an admiring alienation—in short, an acquiescence, a common laziness in readership, all of which play crucially into his or her functioning.

What is more, dialoguing with history also entails working through the kind of art to which spectators often turn for a com-parison, that is, to the militant cinema. Portabella does not create films for the converted, nor is his a practice masking its deficien-cies with justifications based on the ostensible "historic impera-tives." Cinema of deconstruction, a brutal interrogation of the spectator and his or her social function vis-à-vis the milieu, a "de-spairing report on Franco's Spain," according to critic Jonathan Rosenbaum,[10] *Umbracle* is all of this. Once again, it is also an ob-sessive journey through those "years of darkness" lived out by the filmmaker, and sadly, by several similarly fated generations of Spaniards along with him. (Of note is the covering [umbráculo] in the title, a sort of winter greenhouse whose plants grow in an asphyxiating semi-darkness that serves as disquieting metaphor for the Spanish reality of the moment).

On a Country That Has Made Itself Through Its Own Dismantling

Informe General was shot in the months leading from November of 1976 (exactly one year after the death of General Franco) to February/March of 1977, a little shy of one half year before Porta-bella himself was voted in as senator in the first democratic elec-tions experienced by Spain since February of 1936. (In fact, the film director's political dedication accounts for his many years away from the cinema, a period which ended concretely in 1990, when he made *El pont de Varsovia* [The Bridge of Varsovia].) *Informe General* itself was a Spanish-Italian co-production, drawing support from a firm such as UNITELEFILM, which then maintained clear, organic ties with the Italian Communist Party. The picture's intention was clear: to depict, insofar as possible, the nation's "general state of being," and to this end, to question qualified representatives of some political parties on their projects for the future. (These parties were still illegal, though already a few months into introducing themselves to the Spanish citizenry).

In the film they are asked about their concepts for organizing the state, for transitioning from an authoritarian regime to a formal democracy with a minimum of trauma, and for concluding pacts between political and social blocks of various persuasions, as they, as parties, will have to do. Everyday practices, in short, to which any system of democratic representation is accustomed, but which had certainly been absent from the Spanish landscape in the four decades just concluded. And if the film exists it is, according to the personal testimony of its author Portabella, "because the State television" (the only one then in existence) "was still controlled by the same cadre of professionals and politicos who had created it twenty years earlier." For the filmmaker, then, the picture was primarily about giving voice and image to those whom, until then, had been banished from the principal channels of mass communication.

Further, consistent with the political positions of its author, the film leaves out those groups or organizations which advocated at that time a radical and armed rupture from the nascent democratic rules of play. This is not to say that it erodes any praise for, or recognition of, those who, like the armed Basque nationalist Euskadi to Askatuta (E.T.A.) contributed to the cracking of the dictatorship: there is a long sequence featuring the lawyers of the last two anti-fascist militants executed before the death of Franco in October of 1975. It highlights the fortitude of those facing the firing bullets and serves, in passing, to acknowledge (and only to acknowledge) the part played by this organization in the recent past. That is all: for Portabella, as for many others (though it may not have been readily apparent in those days), democratic

Spain no longer had room for revolutionary stances (let alone behavior types).

Yet neither does the film extend word to those who were not of the Marxist tradition, but nonetheless played a transcendental role on the left during the Second Republic. That is, it accords no voice to the anarchists, whose syndicate (the National Confederation of Labor, CNT) held an overwhelming majority in Catalonia dating back to the start of the century. The CNT generally figured throughout Spain with considerable influence; it should be remembered that when the center-left forces encompassed by the Frente Popular (Popular Front) triumphed in the elections of February 1936, the success was attributable to the non-beligerency of the CNT and its leadership vis-à-vis the coalition.

And the former continued to organize actively in any case, both at home and in exile. Portabella, on the other hand, was logically more concerned with questioning those whom current political observers saw as fit for some leading role in the new situation. Clearly, he reserved considerable room for personal opinion, for sanction, and for irony. Indeed, the filmmaker had chosen an ideological path from the beginning: marginalizing some (as in the two cases cited above, which were choices to do with history and not yet with the future), and questioning others. Beyond this, the work has an elaborated mise en scène (contrary, once again, to the "objectivity" traditionally ascribed to documentary cinema; the latter encompasses the most subjective of modes, having determined that these are the best suited to masking its intentions and strategies of seduction). Here, the mise en scène places the onus of signification, unobscured, into the hands of those participating in its chat-sessions and in its few direct interviews with select speakers.

For their part, militants from the traditional left (communists and socialists), consistently appear as the picture of moderation, well dressed and amicable. Their spoken language assumes a certain clarity, ever wary of projecting a revanchist image and scaring off the wide segments of non-politicized citizenry that will form an arsenal of potential votes in the future democracy. Their "normality," however, seems consciously designed to contravene, at every turn, a Francoist propaganda which, had it blundered, could not have been less omnipresent or efficient in its mission to depict the men and women of the left as demons. At the very least they were to come off as threatening, as harbingers of chaos and disorder.

Politicians from the center-right who figure in the film, meanwhile, are generally surrounded by imposing bookshelves, and wrapped in an air of patriarchal repose proper to the serenity of those who know themselves to be protagonists in a political process. Sooner or later, the latter will call them to the fore perforce: the clearest case is that of the old Democratic-Christian leader, José María Gil Robles, noted lawyer repudiated by Francoism despite his having been the main legal opponent of the center and leftist governments during the Republican period.

Returning to the left, the Marxist-Leninist extreme is also present, also questioned. So active during the final years of the Franco regime, it gleaned from electoral polls the promise of a substantial say in the future, notwithstanding its evident dissolution into small, dispersed organizations. And novel here is the film's inclusion of a mise en scène (and a performance, of course) both eminently ideological, overwritten by a visually radical epitaph and composed in conjunction with it: Portabella brings three of his political leaders[11] together on a Madrilenian terrace, with striking scenography of neoclassical inspiration. The three talk on foot, the presence of the camera is ostensible, it is cold, the wind blows: the sound is picked up with difficulty. An improvising waiter enters the scene with some coffees, the camera captures him, he is given a sign to continue with his service, the conversation is momentarily interrupted.

There is no mistaking the sanctioning intentions of the *metteur en scène*: those who speak from a lofty perch (in the clouds?) are totally removed from the real country, from ground level. In short, their discourse is unfathomable even as courteous give and take. Their "prescriptions" for the future, sooner ideological than political (more in the form of schemes than of concrete elaborations) seem as ephemeral as the wind on the set; so fragile as to shatter with any intrusion from the real world—with that of the waiter, for example. They also appear thus both on purpose and in fun, through the presence of a hand-held camera and the instability reflected in its image, reaffirming as it wavers and disturbs. These characters will have nothing to bring into the future, says the picture; nothing with which to help that country which, according to the sound definition of socialist historian José Prats, has constructed itself through a process of tearing asunder and confronting, "it has made itself through its own undoing."[12]

Aimez-vous l'Opera?

Yet in the final analysis, what is politics if not one more form of representation, a mask used to present oneself, in society, a series of people/personalities engaged in a task (the procurement of power) which, like the cinema, also has its norms, its ceremony, its mise en scène, its mechanisms of signification? As noted earlier, Portabella always left on his oeuvre the indelible mark of the study of representation, of its limits, and of the tolerance/intolerance of the public for accepting these. In this sense, *Informe General* stands out as one of the most radical experiments broached by the Catalonian producer in terms of what is referred to as the demystification of the conventional cinematographic narrative.

To wit: the film opens with documentary images shot in Barcelona during the two historic democratic demonstrations of February 1976, a milestone in the country's recent history. But surprisingly, Portabella inserts an episode of fiction, the supposed detention of a demonstrator (in reality, an actor) by a number of agents equally connected with the police. Yet there is no noticeable rupture in the thread of the documentary: integrated into the larger segment, one would take this fragment for part of the same material.

On the other hand, there is an instance when the narrative flow halts abruptly, midway into the projection. This, to make room for something apparently extraneous—the placid filming of actor Alfred Luchetti, "cicerone" lead in the picture, engaged in a series of gym exercises. (His is a continuous presence, gracing such important frames and sequences as those shot in the interior of the palace of El Pardo, official sanctuary of the deceased dictator, and seat of his legitimacy. The camera "taints" the latter in its surprise uncoverings, opening in full these hidden back rooms of power to a country that had never contemplated them, nor their total lack of books, for example. Here, however, the spectator is able to comprehend clearly that what is being shown amounts to nothing more than a representation: its documentary nature notwithstanding, in moments of fiction the film readily supplies a character as reader/spectator, but one ultimately reduceable to just that, a mere persona.

This protagonist reappears, of course, in another, now unmistakably studio-staged sequence of hair-raising brutality, that exhibits the modus operandi of Franco's repressive apparatuses. In tandem, a neutral voice from off screen intones the clauses of the Universal Declaration of Human Rights. Alternatively, the public may easily be reminded of another instance of representation involving Portabella's use of the film *Raza* (Race). Produced in 1941 by José Antonio Sáenz de Heredia,[13] the latter was based on a script by one Jaime de Andrade (actually a pseudonym providing cover for none other than Francisco Franco himself).

Portabella incorporates the film by showing it on the very screen in the private hall of the dictator's living quarters. His restaging is admirable, synthesizing those ideological operations deployed in *Raza*'s complex fictional frame: idealized countenance of the general and his tortured (*redentorista*) psychology, for example. Embedded in the core of *Informe General* itself, *Raza* becomes a synecdoche for all of Francoist cinema, for its supreme masking of a partisan (and false) reading of Spanish history, and for its related occlusion of nothing less than the reality of a country torn apart through war and omnipotent repression.

Informe General, then, is a demystification of the dictatorship, a "profanation" of the real settings of power, a rupture in the public image and the mass-scale communications favored by the regime as its cloak of choice. Portabella's camera penetrates El Pardo and the ancient seat of the Catalonian government (el Palau de la Generalitat). It enters the locus of the popular dictates, the Barcelona Parliament, relieved of its dust for the purpose of showing/ restoring to the spectator those places of long-lost ceremony, the seats of democratic representation. Yes, it is indisputable. The Catalonian director's spirit of transgression stands out in perfectly clarity, the length and breadth of the film.

What is more, so does representation itself, having come under scrutiny by the picture's own material. There is at the end of the film an interview, innocuous enough, with one of the most popular monarchist politicians of those years, Antonio de Senillosa.

After coming out with the startling and comic phrase, "Aimez-vous l'opera?" the guest himself proposes to his interlocutor that they listen to a fragment of Richard Strauss'*Salome*. The voice of soprano Montserrat Caballé sounds off screen, but is quickly superseded by the real image of her singing in the Palau de la Musica de Barcelona (Barcelona Palace of Music), an ironic ending on two scores.

When the curtain falls on her it falls on the film as well: end of story, end of representation. And the start of another story, of another round of representation, now the history of democratic Spain. Many of its actors have spent long hours expressing their points of view before the camera. Other voices, other masks, though the game be similar. This one is also equipped with its own norms, its own ceremonies (the Parliament, the debates, the more or less civilized exchange of opinions, the public appearances just beginning in the years when the film was in production). Still, one may well be compelled to agree with Portabella that this game has somewhat less to do with representation, and in the end, more with justice.

Notes

1. The group "El Paso," founded in Madrid in February of 1957, was composed of painters such as Antonio Saura, M. Millares, Juana Francés, L. Feito, A. Suárez, R. Canogar and M. Rivera, sculptor Pablo Serrano and critics J. Ayllon and M. Conde, with painters Martín Chirino and Manuel Viola added later. Short-lived (the group dissolved in May of 1960, having already succumbed to some depletion), it is credited with a wide-ranging programmatic statement and a few exhibits (including that given by its originator, Oviedo y Gijón).

2. The group "Dau al Set" was formed in 1948 by young artists and writers (Joan Brossa, Arnau Puig, Modest Cuixart, Joan Pong, Antoni Tapies and Joan Josep Tharrats), to which would later be added names such as Alexandre Cirici i Pellicer and that of critical art historian and poet Juan Eduardo Cirlot, among others. Long before "El Paso" and other similar, but dispersed groups in Spain, "Dau al Set" attempted the recuperation, via neosurrealist positions, of the vanguardist tradition lost as the civil war concluded. It was also the editor of a similarly named journal which enjoyed little circulation but great prestige in the artistic climate of the period. Prior to closing the publication in 1956, "Dau al Set" organized a number of expositions (the most important being the anthological collection of members' works, shown in Barcelona, 1951). From here, slow dissolution followed, lasting into the early 1960s. Today the former members are among the most sought-after artists in Spain's contemporary painting scene.

3. Poet enamored of wishful thinking, scriptwriter for cinema and prolific author for the theater, Joan Brossa (Barcelona, 1919) was one of the greatest cata-

lysts within "Dau al Set." He was a personal friend of the poet J.V. Foix, the in-
carnation of vanguardist literary spirit in the 1930s. He was also a close friend of
Joan Miró, Catalonia's greatest genius in painting this century. Portabella also
had inexhaustible admiration for the cinema, and especially for the masters of
silent film, primary among them, Georges Meilies. The latter worked with him
on the scripts for *No competu amb els dits, Nocturno 29, Vampir-Cuadecuc* and *Umbracle*. The musical arrangements for the first two were authored by Josep Mestres
Quadreny (1929), a musician recruited from the rich postdodecaphonic vanguard.
Charles Santos (Vinaroc, Valencia 1938) was the most faithful of Portabella's col-
laborators and created the soundtrack for all of the cinematographer's films,
from *Nocturno 29* (co-authored by Mestres Quadreny) to *El pont de Varovia* (1990).

Indeed, "Over and above the (hardly negligible) quality of the creations it
generated, the collaboration between Portabella, Brossa and Mestres Quadreny,
which later expanded to include Charles Santos, was especially significant. It sig-
nalled not only the director's desire to integrate into his films such artistic elements as he personally considered appropriate and in harmony with his formal
conception of the cinema, but it was also particularly instrumental in allowing
him to establish a true working partnership with the artistic vanguard. In Catalonia the latter had never shared in the adventure of ensconcing itself function-
ally at the core of a film, and at the same time, of redirecting attention toward a
current of thought and an artistic praxis that had made memory one of its prime
raisons d'etre. Nor had it participated in the use of language in a clear frame of
resistance to the militant — military — intransigence of Francoism." Eteve Riambau
and Casimiro Torreiro, *Temps era temps. El Cinema de L'Escola de Barcelona iel seu
entorn* (Barcelona, Ed. de la Generalitat de Catalunya). (Forthcoming).

4. Without contributing capital, Films 59 took part in the financing of *Viridiana* along with Uninci Productions, a stop-gap firm created and controlled by the
PCE, and Mexican producer Gustavo Alatriste. The harsh criticism that the film
received in the pages of the official Vatican diary, *L'Osservatore Romano*, on the
occasion of its showing at the Cannes Festival resulted in the resounding dis-
missal of then Director General of Spanish Cinema, Juan Muñoz Fontan, Vice
Count of San Javier (June 1961). It also led to the withdrawal of Spanish nationality from association with the film (from then on the picture was formally considered Mexican). Uninci was also liquidated by the Spanish authorities, and Portabella was expelled, his unionist activities among producers ended.

5. Julio Pérez Perucha, "Portabella como productor ejemplar" ("Portabella
as Exemplary Producer"), in the brief *Pere Portabella pres al camp de batalla* (Valencia, May 1981), edited by the Valencia City Council on the occasion of a retrospective dedicated to the filmmaker.

6. The administrative title of the film could not be this, however, but its Castilian translation, *No conteis con los dedos/Don't Count with your Fingers*, as the Catalan original was ruled out by the Committee on Censorship.

7. French critic and future filmmaker Luc Beraud was not mistaken when
he wrote in *Cahiers du Cinema*, "Nocturno 29 is like a diagram ... A drawing (image)
to a set scale (the cinema) representing, on one or several different levels (realist,
oneiric, surrealist), the ensemble of influences (etats d'ame, customs, aspirations)
on diverse parts of a three dimensional figure (the Spanish bourgeoisie)." (Barcelona, Cine-club, College of Engineers, May 1975), *Pere Portabella*, 144. Edited

on the occasion of the first integral retrospective dedicated to the work of the filmmaker.

8. Groping for some international outlet indispensable to buoying the Spanish economy, the Franco administration initiated in 1962 a cautious liberalization of its internal censor regulations. In the field of cinema, this relaxation took place under the brief directorship of José María García Escudero in the General Office of Cinematography and Theater (1962–1967). Prestigious military judge and ex-functionary for the state, García Escudero undertook considerable reforms (among other measures, a reduction in censorship, an automatic 15 percent subsidy on ticket prices for every Spanish film, and the promotion of a new generation of directors emerging from the Official School of Cinematography). The trend was toward bringing Spain, in the area of culture, into line with the European democracies. The policy failed as much through the brief interior and international repercussions occasioned by films of the "New Cinema" sponsored by Escudero (including those from the School of Barcelona), as through more powerful, deep-seated reasons and determinants. These included the resurgence of internal repression by which the regime intended to suffocate the increasingly keen democratic aspirations of the opposition (especially from 1967 on). They also have to do with the hostility proper coming from influential corners in the leadership of the administration, and leveled at the politics of openness in their entirety.

9. Noël Burch, *El tragaluz del infinito. Contribución a una genealogía del lenguaje cinematográfico,* (Madrid: Cátedra, Col. Signo e Imagen, 1988).

10. *The Village Voice* (London, June 1972).

11. These are Amancio Cabrero of the Revolutionary Workers' Organization (ORT), Eugenio del Río of the Communist Movement of Spain, and Nazario Aguado of the Labor Party of Spain (PTE). The three organizations of Maoist affiliation have not existed as such in the political scene in many years. Not one was able to place any of its militants in the Spanish Congress through the democratic process.

12. The presence in the film by José Prats, future senator, of José Carretero, advisor to the last president of the Spanish Republic, and of doctor Juan Negrín, is also laden with connotations. Living symbols of an endangered intelligentsia, both men stroll through the gardens in Madrid's Retiro while they speak of the past and of their painful exile in American and European parts. It is autumn and the leaves form a carpet on the ground, rustling loudly when stepped on, their noise mingling with the words of the two elderly men. The latter are irremediable witnesses to a past as worn as those dry, fallen autumn leaves.

13. Sáenz de Heredia, cousin to José Antonio Primo de Rivera, founder of the Falange (parafascist group that would be one of the political pillars of Francoism), was indisputably the official filmmaker of the regime, though his career originated (during the Second Republic) within the ken of Filmofono. This was a firm unequivocal in its Republican sympathies, with heads of production such as Luis Buñuel, the most important cinematographer in exile after 1939.

Works Cited

Beraud, Luc. As cited in *Cahiers du Cinema. Pere Portabella.* Barcelona: College of Engineering Film Club, 1975: 144.

Burch, Noël. *El tragaluz del infinito. Contribución a una genealogía del lenguaje cine-matográfico.* Madrid: Ed. Cátedra, Col. Signo e Imagen, 1988.

Perucha, Julio Pérez. "Portabella como productor ejemplar." *Pere Portabella pres al camp de batalla.* Valencia: Diputación de Valencia, 1981.

Riambau, Esteve and Casimiro Torreiro. *Temps era temps. El cinema de l'Escola de Bar-celona i el seu entorn.* Barcelona: Ed. de la Generalitat de Barcelona, forthcoming.

———. *The Village Voice.* London: June 1972.

◆ Chapter 18

Scripting a Social Imaginary:
Hollywood in/and Spanish Cinema

Kathleen M. Vernon

> *When one talks of cinema, one talks of American cinema. The influence of cinema is the influence of American cinema ... For this reason, every discussion of cinema made outside Hollywood must begin with Hollywood.*
>
> —Glauber Rocha

This essay is not a study of the influence, or rather, domination of Hollywood cinema over the Spanish film industry. The story of the U.S. film industry's virtual occupation of Spanish movie screens has been told in detailed economic and political terms in books such as Santiago Pozo's *La industria del cine en España* and Manuel Vázquez Montalbán's *La penetración americana en España*. Nor is it, strictly speaking, a study of the influence of the representational modes of Hollywood, understood somewhat monolithically as "classic narrative cinema," on both cinematic creation and reception in Spain. Rather than the "real" of American cultural hegemony, I am interested in the strategic *uses* of American film in constructing an alternative "imaginary" in opposition to dominant cultural practices, a phenomenon analogous to the role of American culture in recent postwar German cinema (Fassbinder and Wenders in particular) or in the gay subculture's appropriation of certain Hollywood actresses.[1]

I ground my study in the analysis of the intertextual presence of Hollywood cinema, in the form of "direct quotations" or film clips, in a selected number of Spanish films, where I argue that it provided a point from which to construct an oppositional "imaginary" of resistance, initially against the attempts by official Francoist cinema to impose a self-serving national imaginary modeled by the repressive religious and militaristic values of the regime, and later after Franco's death, where it speaks from the margins, questioning the dominant value system even in newly democratic Spain. The potential repertory of films for this study represents a broad range of historically and aesthetically significant films, including Lorenzo Llobet-Gracia's *Vida en sombras* (1948), Luis García Berlanga's *Bienvenido Mr. Marshall* (1952), Victor Erice's *El espíritu de la colmena* (1973) and *El sur* (1983), and Pedro Almodóvar's *¿Qué he hecho yo para merecer esto?* (1984), *Matador* (1985), and *Mujeres al borde de un ataque de nervios* (1988). And their American intertexts, *Rebecca* (Alfred Hitchcock, 1941), genre films (Western and film noir), *Frankenstein* (James Whale, 1931), *Splendor in the Grass* (Elia Kazan, 1961), *Duel in the Sun* (King Vidor, 1946), and *Johnny Guitar* (Nicholas Ray, 1954) for their part provide an uncannily representative roster of Hollywood film history. For reasons of space I will limit my analysis to two case studies, one drawn from the Francoist period and one from the post-Franco era.

My intention is to read these films in their intertextuality as instances of a process of "semiotic layering," a concept I borrow from Maureen Turim who defines it as "the accrual and transformations of meanings associated with an artifact as it passes through history, or as it is presented in different versions" (377). Thus I will analyze the meaning and function of the Hollywood intertexts in their original cultural, historical, and generic context as well as their recontextualization within certain Spanish films, each with its own specific historical and cultural circumstances.

Bienvenido Mr. Marshall

According to Peter Besa (35–6), Berlanga's brilliant 1952 comedy *Bienvenido* began as commission for an *españolada,* a folkloric comedy featuring mostly Andalusian dance and singing, typical of the government-supported products of the period. While technically fulfilling the conditions of the film's producers — a setting in Andalusia and four musical numbers for newcomer Lolita Sevilla, sister of the established *españolada* star Carmen Sevilla — Berlanga

and his co-scriptwriters Juan Bardem and Miguel Mihura con-
cocted a double-edged paean to the illusionistic power of cinema
that is at the same time a wicked critique of the Spanish film industry and the regime that supported it.

While the title makes reference to the Marshall Plan dollars
Spain never was to receive, though its pariah status among Western democracies was soon to come to end with the 1953 Conve-
nio granting the United States access to Spanish military bases, a
more central theme of the film is the reach of Hollywood into the
hearts and minds of even the most isolated inhabitants of a small
Spanish town. The plot involves the town's preparations for the
arrival of an American delegation that, according to the Delegaod
General and his band of Spanish bureaucrats who announce the
visit, are sure to reward their Spanish hosts with money and gifts.
At the urging of the government officials, the mayor don Pablo
and Manolo, the impresario and manager of the flamenco star
performing at the town's cafe, concoct a script to transform their
Castilian village into a movie set version of Andalusia, precisely
the tourist poster image of Spain promoted by the *españolada*.

As in *El espíritu de la colmena* some ten years later, the social
function of moviegoing and the preference for American genre
films over the home grown product are documented in the townspeople's attendance at the weekly movie — usually a Hollywood
Western, we are told — in the town hall. Given the shape of Spanish film production in the forties and early fifties, this rejection
was understandable. Dominated by the tendentious didacticism
of patriotic epics on one hand, and on the other by the nostalgic
evocation of a harmonious rural existence of eternal Spain in the
españolada, the regime-supported film industry left Spanish audiences easy prey for the clearly more alluring Hollywood im-
ports.[2] Indeed, this rejection of domestic cinema is thematized in
the film. Carmen Vargas (played by Lolita Sevilla), the visiting
"songbird of southern Spain" hired by the mayor and cafe owner,
is portrayed in parallel scenes that mirror the Spanish audience's
attitude toward the genre. During her first performance, the cafe's
clientele are quiet and her number's completion is met with at-
tentive applause. But by the time of the second onscreen performance, several sequences later, the cafe-goers talk through her
number and the applause is almost non-existent.

A similar representation of the spectator in the text, in Nick Browne's term, is the key to the film's most celebrated sequence, a series of four movie-like dreams within the film. For long before psychoanalytic film theory sought to analyze the relation between dreaming and film spectatorship, *Bienvenido* made that connection explicit. Moviegoing, as portrayed in the scene mentioned above, is described by the film's voice-over narrator as enabling or even authorizing wishing or dreaming. The film's narrative sequence, where a dream segment follows the townspeople's exit from the temporary movie theater, also confirms this linkage. Furthermore, at the conclusion of the last dream, the narrator comments on the dreamer's wish for a happy ending, noting that "all movies and dreams end like that." As this association makes clear, movies, like dreams, are not simply a form of escapism, but rather a means of indirect expression of thoughts censored by the conscious mind — or a repressive government. Nevertheless, these filmic intertexts do provide a form of escape for Berlanga, as they were to do for Erice in *Espíritu*, to move beyond the confines of an ahistorical formula film, the *españolada*, to project a critical vision of contemporary Spanish reality.

The first dream portrayed on screen belongs to the village priest, who as the representative of Francoist *triunfalismo* from the outset expresses his suspicion of American materialist ideology. His words offer a prime example of what Carmen Martín Gaite has called the celebration of the "bendito atraso," as he shuns the promised fruits of American beneficence: "They may have locomotives but we have peace of mind (*paz de espíritu*). That will be our gift to them." Later he interrupts the village schoolteacher's American geography lesson to the town to counter her recitation of U.S. industrial and agricultural production figures (ten thousand tons of wheat or pig iron annually and so on) with some statistics of his own, noting the presence of millions of Protestants, Jews, Blacks, Chinese among the American population. But this condemnation of American religious and racial pluralism will come back to haunt him. For despite his provincial horizons (we are told he has never traveled more than twelve miles from his home village) and rabid anti-Americanism, even his dreams reveal the colonizing influence of American cinema. Opening with a shot of Holy Week penitents marching in black-hooded robes to a solemn funeral procession, the dream scene lurches into nightmare as a blaring jazz score erupts on the sound track and the hooded figures, who turn to reveal the initials KKK on their backs, carry off the frightened priest. The next frame places the priest squarely within the classic mise en scène of an American crime drama. In a dark room lit by the harsh glare of a single, swinging light bulb, the priest, shot from a high angle, cowers under the interrogation of a man identified as a hard-boiled police detective type by the fat cigar clenched tightly in his teeth. Finally the dream cuts to a courtroom evoking the German expressionist roots of film noir, where the camera reveals the priest as an even more diminished figure, dwarfed by a white-robed judge mounted on a tall tribunal that bears the inscription (in Spanish): Committee on Un-American Activities. A tape recorder replays his earlier disparaging references to the diversity of American ethnic groups, and as each is mentioned, a white-robed figure rises from the jury box to give him the thumbs down.

This use of film noir, beyond its simple representativeness as a recognizably American film genre, seems no accident. Given the form's cultural and historical context, its development in the closing years of World War II and the decade or so after, as the satisfaction over victory turned to insecurity, suspicion and the anti-communist paranoia of the McCarthy years, it is a supreme irony that the priest's own xenophobic paranoia be expressed in such terms. Furthermore it is precisely the shared American and Spanish fear of communism that has brought the American "threat" to Spanish shores.

The last dream in the segment (for now I am skipping over the two middle dreams with their mirroring of Spanish and Soviet filmmaking, respectively) portrays not a nightmare but a wish fantasy as the mayor projects himself as the sheriff of a Hollywood Western. Once again great care is given to details of mise en scène and camera and editing codes—indeed the full sequence of movie-dreams constitutes a virtuosic anthology of film styles. The comic "dream work" is impeccable as well, as virtually the entire cast of townspeople are assigned new identities in the film within a film. The plot depicts the mayor and the impresario Manolo as rivals for control of the town and the affections of the saloon girl Carmen Vargas, who does a flamenco rendition of "Oh

Susanna" in the segment. After some card playing, a drinking contest, and a mock showdown, a fight erupts in the saloon and the mayor/sheriff is shot, only to die clutching the leg of Carmen Vargas. In the next shot, he awakes embracing the bed post. Once again the choice of genre, the Western, is overdetermined. Thematically, the roles of mayor and sheriff have clear similarities. The dream-film also functions as the expression of the mayor's not-so-unconscious desires, given what we know of his waking interest, despite his age, in pretty women. No doubt we should read the dream as a compensatory fantasy, given the age and physique of the actor playing the role (José Isbert) as well as the character's physical infirmity (he is hard of hearing and constantly holds up his apparently not very effective hearing aid, which looks like a sixties transistor radio with earphone). Or perhaps the dream reveals his suppressed resentment of Manolo, who ends up taking charge of the *recibimiento* for the Americans.

But the use of the Western has other meanings as well. As the quintessential myth-making genre of American cinema with its nostalgia for an imaginary past of macho heroics and westward expansion, seen as a simple contest between good guys and bad guys, the Western could be said to offer a national self-image no less appropriate to Cold War geopolitics. The appeal of the Western for Spanish audiences may be closer than we think, if we read the Western as merely the more recent version of the dream of imperial glory, Spanish style, projected in *Bienvenido* in the second dream, the nobleman don Luis's re-imagining of his ancestor's role in the original "discovery" and conquest of America.

¿Qué he hecho yo para merecer esto?

In contrast to the privileged intertextual role granted to Hollywood cinema in the films by Llobet-Gracia, Berlanga and Erice, the eclectic jumble of sources in Almodóvar might stand as a defining example of postmodernist pastiche. And whether one grants a subversive or regressive value to such density of intertextual allusion, that crucial enabling role, of Hollywood cinema as the conduit of fantasy and wish fulfillment inexpressible through more direct means, would appear to be superfluous as Almodóvar's films, in their celebration of a newly liberated, post-Francoist Spain, flaunt the open expression of desire in all its vectors and forms. What then is the function or functions of the direct quotations from three different Hollywood films, the clips from *Splendor in the Grass, Duel in the Sun,* and *Johnny Guitar,* in *¿Qué he hecho yo para merecer esto?, Matador,* and *Mujeres al borde de un ataque de nervios,* respectively? As I suggested at the outset, I believe that American cinema continues to play a role in the construction of resistance to dominant discursive practices, both filmic and social. Almodóvar's use of Hollywood cinema allows him to articulate a position on the margins of Spanish society, one which calls into question the naturalness of categories of class and gender, as caught within the cinematic crossfire, as it were, of differing sociohistorical contexts.

Of the three films where the director makes use of excerpts from American films, *¿Qué he hecho yo* is the most pointed in its strategic use of cinematic references. Abandoning, at least temporarily, the campy contextuality of comics and punk/pop art and music of his first three features, the director turns initially to Italian and Spanish neorealism from the primary thematic and stylistic grounding of his film. From the musical theme of the opening/credit sequence with its evocation of Nino Rota's scores for numerous Italian neorealist films to a plot and mise en scène already familiar to viewers of the often more satiric Spanish versions of the genre from the fifties and early sixties (which focused on the plight of urban dwellers struggling to survive in a city unable to provide jobs and housing to a population swollen by recent arrivees from the economically even more desperate provinces), the director situates the history of a working class family's struggle for survival in present-day Madrid within a self-conscious film tradition. The echoes of much earlier films like Marco Ferreri's 1958 film *El pisito,* José Antonio Nieves Conde's 1959 *El inquilino,* or Berlanga's *El verdugo* from 1961 (acknowledged by Almodóvar himself) lend a sharper edge to Almodóvar's social criticism, as it reveals the lack of fundamental change despite the intervening years, years of the so-called economic miracle and the end of Francoism.

And yet while this general critique is grounded in the language of neorealism, the individual characters' personal discontent with their psychosocial reality is projected through an independent and often incompatible set of cinematic references, their mutual incomprehension represented through an allusive personal imaginary. Gloria, the harried housewife and mother whose struggle to provide for her family in both material and emotional terms constitutes the affective center of the film, is trapped—at least until the end of the picture—within the stifling libidinal (and literal) economy of the "woman's picture." Her taxi driver husband Antonio, on the other hand, is still obsessed with his experiences as a "guest worker" in Germany and his love affair with Ingrid Müller, an aging *chanteuse* for whom he forged a series of Hitler letters. The husband's narrative is characterized by its own film score, Antonio's repeated playing of his cherished cassette of "their song," "Nicht nur aus Liebe Weinen," sung by Zarah Leander, as his story plots the real historical drama of economic exile against a subversive version of the retro nostalgia film, reminiscent of Fassbinder's *Lili Marleen* or *Veronika Voss*. The younger son Miguel, though not tied to any specific film or genre, is portrayed as the "artistic" child of the family. The movie posters over his bed, the zoetrope he spins before turning out the light at night, as well as his precocious homosexuality, mark him as the director's playful stand-in.

While each of these intertextual subplots merits more extended treatment, I must turn my attention to the only two characters, grandmother and grandson, who appear to share a common space of the imaginary. This alliance initially seems quite paradoxical since the two would appear to be products of diametrically opposed social milieus, the small country *pueblo* in the case of the grandmother, urban Madrid in the case of Toni, the older son. Indeed both are endowed with a series of typical attributes which mark them as representative of their origins: the grandmother with her repertory of country sayings and religious superstitions, Toni with his successful drug trade.

This antagonistic axis—country versus city—is, of course, a classic theme of both Francoist and anti-Francoist cinema as indexes to a larger value system, tradition vs. modernity, isolationist vs. cosmopolitan. But in Almodóvar's rewriting of cinema history, the opposition is only apparent. For grandmother and grandson share a dream of return to the pueblo, a longing for return to a natural paradise lost that receives ironic expression in two im-

portant moments in the film. Returning from a trip to the bank
to deposit his drug earnings, Toni and the grandmother are shot
in silhouette between a tree and telephone pole against the twilight sky, the claustrophic urban landscape, for once, absent from
view. In this unique scene of wide-open spaces the grandmother
discovers a lizard huddled beneath a rock. Toni, the naturalist,
proclaims him to be hibernating, but the grandmother takes personal pity upon another fellow creature, displaced, like her, from
nature in a hostile urban environment. Scooping him up, she
vows to take the reptile home, as the camera in a reverse angle
reframes the characters and the now almost invisible tree against
the backdrop of the family's high-rise building and a parking lot
crowded with cars. As if the visual irony were not sufficient, the
subsequent dialogue over an appropriate name for the animal
further undercuts the pastoral moment. The grandmother decides
to name him after something she likes, dubbing him *dinero* because he's green like money.

While the camera itself conspires to deny the viability of the
characters' dreams in the scene just described, a later sequence
portrays—once again—Hollywood cinema as the unlikely vehicle of a specifically Spanish social fantasy. Light streams from
an unidentified source high up in the rear of a darkened room,
evoking the dream scene that is the model for much psychoanalytic characterization of the spectator's experience of cinema, particularly of "classic, i.e., Hollywood, narrative cinema" (Baudry,
Metz).

In the absence of any distinguishable images, an exchange of
dialogue between an older and younger man expresses the latter's rejection of education as the path to success: "I'd like to work
on that ranch you own outside of town." Finally the camera low-
ers its focus to the heads of the spectators, glowing in the flicker-
ing light of the movie theater, and grandson and grandmother
come into view in the middle of the audience. Toni's identification with the rebellious son in the film is immediate: "Maybe I'll
set up a ranch in the pueblo," he exclaims as the grandmother
signals her enthusiastic assent. Their conversation continues after
a brief ellipsis as they exit the theater, passing in front of a giant
poster for the film they have just seen, Elia Kazan's 1961 film version of a William Inge play *Splendor in the Grass*, starring Warren

Beatty and Natalie Wood. The irony for the (second degree) spectator in Bud Stamper's (Beatty) desire to return to a simpler, American age of innocence in a small Kansas town on the eve of the stock market crash underscores the untimeliness and "unplacefulness" of Toni's dream as well. The small town is portrayed as a stifling, sexually repressive place in the Inge/Kazan story, just as it is in such Spanish films as *Calle mayor* (Bardem, 1955).

Finally, in an ultimate irony, the character's flight from the city at the end of *¿Qué he hecho yo,* though it marks the apparent fulfillment of their shared dream, reenacts the conclusion of the founding film of Spanish neo-realism, José Antonio Nieves Conde's *Surcos* (1950). Hailed as the "first glance at reality in a cinema of paper-maché," (José García Escudero, *La historia del cine español en cien palabras*) for its treatment of the problem of the rural exodus to the cities, in the hands of Falangist Nieves Conde, it also served as a cautionary tale regarding the moral corruption and destruction of family structures that awaited new immigrants to the city. The film's conclusion, tightened by the censor's decision to eliminate the undying lure of life in the city for the daughter Tonia, projects the family's chastened return to the fields they never should have left.

Far from an instance of the postmodern denial of history through pastiche, as in Fredric Jameson's account of the mode, through its juxtaposition of filmic intertexts, the ironic American pastoral *Splendor* with the Spanish cautionary tale *Surcos*, *¿Qué he hecho yo* casts suspicion on the workings of the cinematic imaginary. The longing for return is revealed as return to the past of Francoism, a past Almodóvar's films disavow even as they actively rewrite it.

Notes

A revised version of this essay was included in "Reading Hollywood in/and Spanish Cinema: From Trade Wars to Transculturation," in *Figuring Spain: Cinema/Media/Representation.* ed. Marsha Kinder. Durham: Duke University Press, 1997, 35–64.

1. Scholars who have analyzed this aspect of German cinema include Tony Rayns, Thomas Elsaesser and Timothy Corrigan; Richard Dyer's works on the phenomenology of stardom for both gay and straight audiences are the key studies in this area.

2. The story of the regime's tacit encouragement of this state of affairs, beginning with the 1942 law requiring obligatory dubbing of all foreign films and further promoted by the financing schemes of the forties and early fifties which granted subsidies to government-approved films in the form of import licenses, is an important factor, which unfortunately, I have no time to consider here.

Works Cited

Baudry, Jean-Louis. "Ideological Effects of the Basic Cinematic Aparatus." *Film Quarterly* 28.2 (1974): 39–47.

Besas, Peter. *Behind the Spanish Lens: Spanish Cinema under Fascism and Democracy.* Denver: Arden Press, 1985.

Brown, Nick. "The Spectator-in-the-Text: The Rhetoric of *Stagecoach.*" *Film Quarterly* 29.2 (1975–76): 26–44.

Jameson, Frederic. "Postmodernism and Consumer Society." In *The Anti-Aesthetic.* Ed. Hal Foster. Port Townsend, Wash.: Bay Press, 1983. 111–25.

Martín Gaite, Carmen. *Usos amorosos de la postguerra española.* Barcelona: Anagrama, 1987.

Metz, Christian. "The Fiction Film and its Spectator." *New Literary History* 8.1 (1975): 75–105.

Pozo, Santiago. *La industria del cine en España.* Barcelona: Publicacions i Edicions de la Universitat de Barcelona, 1984.

Turim, Maureen. "Gentlemen Consume Blondes." In *Movies and Methods.* Ed. Bill Nichols. Berkeley: Univ. of California Press, 1985: 369–38.

Vásquez Montalbán, Manual. *La penetración americana en España.* Madrid: Cuadernos para el diálogo, 1974.

Vernon, Kathleen M. "Melodrama Against Itself: Pedro Almodóvar's *¿Qué he hecho yo para merecer esto? Film Quarterly,* 46.3 (1993): 28–40.

◆ Contributors

Stacy N. Beckwith is a doctoral candidate in Cultural Studies and Comparative Literature at the University of Minnesota. She has written on the representation of national themes in literature and film and is exploring competing interpretations of Jews and Hispano-Arabs through diaspora.

Juan-Miguel Company-Ramón is associate professor of Literary Theory and Film at the Universitat de Valencia. He has published on literary history and theory, film and psychoanalysis. His more recent books are *Ingmar Bergman, El trazo de la letra en la imagen,* and *El aprendizaje del tiempo.*

Tom Conley is professor of French at Harvard University. He has written on Renaissance French literature, literary theory, and film. His most recent books are *Su realismo. Lectura de* Tierra sin pan, *The Graphic Unconscious,* and *Film Hieroglyphics.*

Marvin D'Lugo is professor of Spanish and Director of Screen Studies at Clark University in Worcester, Massachusetts. He is the author of *Carlos Saura. The Practice of Seeing.*

Jesús González-Requena is associate professor of Communication and Film Theory at the Universidad Complutense, Madrid. He has published on film theory and history, mass media and psychoanalysis, and is the author of, among other books, *La metáfora del espejo: el cine de Douglas Sirk, El discurso televisivo,* and *S. M. Eisenstein.*

Román Gubern is professor of Communications and Film history at the Universidad Autónoma of Barcelona and has been a visiting professor and lecturer at many U.S. and European Universities. He has authored more than 20 books, among them *El cine español en la 2ª República, El discurso del cómic,* and *El simio informatizado.*

Lesley Heins Walker received her Ph.D. in Cultural Studies and Comparative Literature from the University of Minnesota. She currently works at the Getty Center for the Study of the Arts and Humanities and is finishing a book about Literature, Politics and the French Revolution.

Francisco Llinás is a critic and a freelance writer. He was founding editor of *Contracampo,* one of the most influential cinema journals in Spain during the 1980s. He has authored many books, among them *El cadáver del tiempo,* and *Directores de fotografía en el cine español.*

Antonio Monegal is associate professor of Spanish at Cornell University, and of Literary theory at the Universitat Pompeu Fabra, Barcelona. He has published widely on Spanish Vanguard and Comparative Literature, and has authored a book on Buñuel.

Andrés Moreno is assistant professor of Spanish at Saint Johns University in Collegeville, Minnesota. His areas of interest are Spanish Golden Age studies, and film.

Oscar Pereira is assistant professor of Spanish at the University of Nebraska. He has written several essays dealing with the literature and culture of early modern Spain and has finished a book titled *Literatura y representación pública en la primera modernidad española.*

Ricardo Roque-Baldovinos received his Ph.D. in Cultural Studies and Comparative Literature at the University of Minnesota. He currently teaches at the University of El Salvador.

Paul Julian Smith is professor of Spanish at the University of Cambridge. He is he author of several books, among them *The Body Hispanic: Gender and Sexuality in Spanish and Spanish American Literature; Laws of Desire,* and *Vision Machines: Cinema, Literature, and Sexuality in Spain and Cuba (1983–1993).*

Ann Marie Stock is an assistant professor in the Department of Modern Languages & Literatures at the College of William & Mary in Virginia. Her work has been published in such books and journals as *Historia general del cine* (Cátedra), *Revista canadiense de estudios hispanos, Studies in Latin American Popular Culture, Marges,* and *Cine-Lit.* Her edited volume entitled *Framing Latin American Cinema* was published by the University of Minnesota Press in 1997.

Jenaro Talens is professor of Literary Theory and Film at the Universitat de Valencia, and a regular visiting professor at the University of Minnesota since 1983. He has authored twenty books of poetry, and translated many classics of German and English poetry into Spanish. His more recent books are *Through the Shattering Glass: Cervantes and the Self-Made World, The Branded Eye: Buñuel's "Un Chien andalou"* and *Historia general del cine* (general editor).

Casimiro Torreiro is assistant professor of Film History at the Universidad Autónoma, Barcelona, and film critic in *El País.* He has published on Catalan cinema, has done screenwriting, and is one of the editors of the *Historia general del cine.* He is currently finishing a monograph on Antonioni.

Kathleen M. Vernon is associate professor of Spanish at SUNY, Stony Brook. She has edited *Post-Franco, Postmodern: The Films of Pedro Almodóvar* and *The Spanish Civil War and the Visual Arts.*

Teresa Vilarós is assistant professor of Spanish at Duke University.

Santos Zunzunegui is professor of Communication and Film Theory at the Universidad del País Vasco. He has been visiting professor at the University of Paris III (Sorbonne), and has lectured in many other European universities. He has published widely on film history, semiotics, photography and mass media. His more recent books are *Pensar la imagen, Paisajes de la forma, La mirada cercana,* and *Historia general del cine* (editor).

◆ Index

Compiled by David R. Castillo